Investigative Interviewing

Ray Bull
Editor

Investigative Interviewing

 Springer

Editor
Ray Bull
University of Derby
Derby
United Kingdom

ISBN 978-1-4614-9641-0   ISBN 978-1-4614-9642-7 (eBook)
DOI 10.1007/978-1-4614-9642-7
Springer New York Heidelberg Dordrecht London

Library of Congress Control Number: 2014931575

Printed on acid-free paper

Springer is part of Springer Science+Business Media (www.springer.com)

Preface

In January 1998 in the High Court in London, England a man was awarded £ 200,000 compensation relating to his arrest and police interviews in 1987, and his subsequent years in prison. *The Daily Telegraph* (20 January 1998, p. 9) reported that "An innocent man ... spent 'five hellish years' in jail after being beaten by a detective and forced to sign a confession...The court heard how (he) ...was butted and punched by a detective and threatened with injection by a syringe."

One of the major assumptions underlying justification for the use of coercive interrogation techniques are the pervasive beliefs (as noted by Leo 2008) that

"...suspects almost never confess spontaneously but virtually always in response to police pressure" (p. 162) and that

> Confessions, especially to serious crimes, are rarely made spontaneously.Rather they are actively elicited...typically after sustained psychological pressure. (p. 119)

Indeed, in 2002 Holmes (formerly of the Miami Police Department) stated in the preface of his book entitled '*Criminal interrogation: A modern format for interrogating criminal suspects based on the intellectual approach*' that "When you finish reading this book, I hope you have one predominate thought, 'You don't obtain confessions by asking the suspect questions. You have to convince a suspect to confess by the use of persuasive interrogational arguments'" (p. x).

In contrast, in England in 1993 Williamson (a senior police officer, who subsequently was in charge of the 'murder squad' in London) stated that "Unethical behaviour by interrogators has undermined public confidence and left the police service with a serious skills deficit in its ability to obtain evidence through questioning" and that "it does not take much skill to beat a confession out of a suspect detained in police custody" (p. 107).

In England in the mid-1980s in light of

1. various decisions by the (national) Court of Appeal to quash previous convictions based on confessions that were 'unreliable' (e.g. because of police interviewing behaviour)
2. media and public concern about police interviewing

the Government brought in the *Police and Criminal Evidence Act* which mandated that from 1986 all interviews with suspects be recorded (e.g. on audio-tape).

Studies in several countries have found that some police officers believe that the main aim of the interview is to gain a confession. For example, several years ago in England Stephenson and Moston (1994) found that 80 % of officers said that getting a confession was the main purpose of their interviews with suspects. Prior to the start of their actual interviews with each suspect a large sample of police officers were asked if they were already sure that the suspect was guilty—70 % said 'yes'.

This emphasis on trying to obtain confessions could probably explain why Moston, Stephenson, and Williamson (1992) found that in the majority of several hundred (taped) interviews the police spent little time, if any, trying to obtain the suspects' accounts of events. Instead they soon (after their interviews/interrogations commenced) revealed all the 'incriminating' information they had and then accused the suspects of the offence. More recently in Taiwan in their survey of several hundred detectives/interviewers Tsan-Chang Lin and Chih-Hung Shih (2013) found that a substantial proportion (especially of those who had not received training) indicated that they usually commenced their interrogations/interviews by revealing "evidence of guilt".

It is noteworthy that the belief that perpetrators will usually deny being involved in serious wrong-doing and will not willingly admit/confess has not benefitted from research on the views of offenders themselves. Relatively recent, innovative research involving offenders has found that only a minority enter the police interview/interrogation with their mind set on denial (see Des Lauriers-Varin and St-Yves 2006). For example, in Australia Kebbell et al. (2006) found that only a half of the convicted sex offenders with whom they held a research interview said that they had entered the police interview having already decided whether to deny or confess— 20 % had planned to deny and 30 % had planned to confess. Of utmost importance was the additional finding that the other 50 % had entered the police interview not yet having decided whether to deny or confess.

Kebbell et al. (2006) noted that some guilty suspects who (prior to and/or at the beginning of the interview) may be considering whether to confess could subsequently decide not to simply because of the way they are being interviewed. This 'psychological reactance' has also been mentioned by Gudjonsson (2003) and by Holmberg and Christianson (2002) among others, but the frequency with which it occurs in the interviewing of suspects is deserving of much greater research attention.

Whether denial or admittance occurred was related by Holmberg and Christianson (2002) to the reported style of interviewing. They found a relationship between the interviewees' reactions and denial/admittance, in that those who reported being frightened, stressed, insulted were less likely to have admitted. These researchers concluded that a "dominant interviewing style is associated with suspects denying crime" (p. 42). The 'accusatory' style found in interviews conducted in England the late 1980s by Moston et al. (1992) has some similarities with the 'dominant' style.

In 1992 the Home Office (part of the Government in England and Wales) published the pioneering research by Baldwin that it had commissioned. Prior to this very little research had been published on what goes on in police interviews. Baldwin (1992, 1993) found of the 600 audio or video recorded interviews conducted in the late 1980s that he analysed, "most were short and surprisingly amiable discussions in which it often seemed that officers were rather tentative in putting allegations to a suspect. . . . Indeed in almost two-thirds of all cases. . . no serious challenge was made by the interviewers to what the suspect was saying" (p. 331). In only 20 of the 600 interviews Baldwin examined did suspects "change their story in the course of an interview. In only nine of these cases was the change of heart attributable to the persuasive skills of the interviewer, and even here only three involved offences of any seriousness . . . .The great majority of suspects stick to their starting position—whether admission, denial, or somewhere in between" (p. 333).

In the light of such pioneering research by Baldwin and others (see Milne and Bull, 1999) a major change in police interviewer training occurred in England and Wales. This change was based on the new **PEACE** approach (and its underlying philosophy) that came into being in 1992. **PEACE** contains much psychology (Milne and Bull 1999) and formally introduced the 'investigative interviewing' approach. The committee of police officers that drafted the new **PEACE** training courses had access to an unpublished overview of relevant psychological research. In 1990 the senior police officer Tom Williamson (who then had a Bachelor's degree in psychology) had convened a 'working group' to discuss and then compile a substantial (unpublished) document on aspects of psychology that could be relevant to the interrogation/interviewing of suspects, witnesses and victims. This working group included a small number of psychologists including myself, Eric Shepherd, and Stephen Moston (who had the important role of compiling the document).

The **PEACE** approach is based on a number of basic principles which were chosen by the police. These include:

1. the purpose of investigative interviewing is to obtain accurate and reliable information from suspects, witnesses or victims in order to discover the truth about matters under investigation;
2. interviews should be approached with an open mind. Information obtained from the person who is being interviewed should always be tested against what the investigator already knows or what can reasonably be established.

PEACE is an acronym for the five phases that all interviews/interrogations must go through, these being
Firstly, P = planning and preparation
Secondly, E = engage and explain
Thirdly, A = account
Fourthly, C = closure
Finally, E = evaluation.

Over the last 20 years a number of countries and organisations have formally adopted the **PEACE** approach and others are considering doing so.

The first chapter within this book offers research based guidance for interviewing in connection with sex offences and it adopts an investigative interviewing perspective rather than an interrogational, confession-driven approach. True versus false confessions are the main focus of the second chapter. The third chapter presents a substantial analysis of how police (in the United States of America) actually do question juvenile suspects. The following chapter focuses on the importance of there being a 'working alliance' between interviewer and suspect. The next chapter reviews the interview techniques used in investigations conducted by international criminal courts and tribunals, whereas the sixth provides a comprehensive review of developments (in Japan) regarding the interviewing of children. The seventh chapter presents new research on the extent to which communication skills are essential for effective criminal investigations. The next examines methods of training interview competencies. The ninth focuses on when in interviews to reveal information to suspects and the tenth contains a review of the different types of consistency demonstrated by liars and by truth tellers. The penultimate chapter focuses on the evolving topic of 'human intelligence' interviewing and on the challenges of developing an ethical, evidence-based approach similar to that underlying investigative interviewing. The final chapter innovatively reports on prosecutors' recommendations for improving the interviewing of children in abuse investigations.

The chapter authors purposely were chosen to be from several different countries and at various stages of their careers. Importantly, the chapters all present important, new findings and contain a variety of innovative research methods.

October 2013   Ray Bull

References

Baldwin, J. (1992). *Video-taping of police interviews with suspects—An evaluation.* Police Research Series Paper No. 1. London: Home Office.

Baldwin, J. (1993). Police interview techniques. Establishing truth or proof? *British Journal of Criminology, 33,* 325–352.

Deslauriers-Varin, N. & St-Yves, M. (2006). *An empirical investigation of offenders' decision to confess their crime during police interrogation.* Paper presented at the Second International Investigative Interviewing Conference, Portsmouth, July.

Gudjonsson, G. (2003). The psychology of interrogations and confessions: A handbook. Chichester: Wiley.

Holmberg, U., & Christianson, S-A. (2002). Murderers' and sexual offenders' experiences of police interviews and their inclination to admit or deny crimes. *Behavioral Sciences and the Law, 20,* 31–45.

Holmes, W. (2002). *Criminal interrogation: A modern format for interrogating criminal suspects based on the intellectual approach.* Springfield, Ill.: C.C. Thomas.

Kebbell, M., Hurren, E., & Mazerolle, P. (2006). *An investigation into the effective and ethical interviewing of suspected sex offenders.* Final report to the Australian Criminology Research Council.

Leo, R. (2008). *Police interrogation and American justice.* Boston: Harvard University Press.

Milne R., & Bull, R. (1999). *Investigative interviewing:* Psychology and practice. Chichester: Wiley.

Stephenson, G., & Moston, S. (1994). Police interrogation. *Psychology, Crime and Law, 1,* 151–157.

Tsan-Chang Lin & Chih-Hung Shih. (2013). *A study of police interrogation practice in Taiwan.* Paper presented at the Asian Conference of Criminal and Police Psychology, Singapore.

Williamson, T. (1993). From interrogation to investigative interviewing: strategic trends in police questioning. *Journal of Community and Applied Social Psychology, 3,* 89–99.

Contents

Contributors

Ray Bull University of Derby, Derby, UK

Kimberlee S. Burrows Deakin University, Melbourne, Australia

Jacqueline R. Evans Florida International University, Miami, Florida, USA

Barry C. Feld University of Minnesota Law School, Minneapolis, Minnesota, USA

Pär Anders Granhag University of Gothenburg, Göteborg, Sweden

Maria Hartwig John Jay College of Criminal Justice, New York, USA

Kate A. Houston University of Texas at El Paso, El Paso, Texas, USA

Mark Kebbell Griffith University, Queensland, Australia

Christian A. Meissner Iowa State University, Ames, Iowa, USA

Becky Milne University of Portsmouth, Portsmouth, United Kingdom

Makiko Naka Hokkaido University, Hokkaido, Japan

Melanie O'Brien Griffith University, Queensland, Australia

Martin O'Neill University of Portsmouth, Portsmouth, United Kingdom

Martine B. Powell Deakin University, Melbourne, Australia

Imke Rispens School of Detectives, Graduate School for Investigation, Police Academy, Apeldoorn, The Netherlands

Lotte Smets Training, Coaching en Counselling, Lanista Antwerp, Belgium

Peter J. van Koppen VU University Amsterdam, Amsterdam, The Netherlands
Maastricht University, Maastricht, The Netherlands

Miet Vanderhallen Antwerp University, Antwerp, Belgium

Maastricht University, Maastricht, The Netherlands

University of Leuven, Leuven, Belgium

Geert Vervaeke University of Leuven—Leuven, Flanders, Belgium

Annelies Vredeveldt VU University Amsterdam, Amsterdam, The Netherlands

Nina J. Westera Griffith University, Queensland, Australia

About the Authors

Ray Bull is Professor of Criminal Investigation (part-time) at The University of Derby. He is also Emeritus Professor of Forensic Psychology at the University of Leicester, Visiting Professor at the Universities of Portsmouth and of London South Bank. His major research topic is investigative interviewing. In 2012 he was elected *'President-Elect'* of the European Association of Psychology and Law. In 2012 he was made the first *Honorary Life Member of the International Investigative Interviewing Research Group*. In 2010 he was "Elected by acclaim" an Honorary Fellow of the British Psychological Society *"for the contribution made to the discipline of psychology"* (this honour is restricted to a maximum of 40 living psychologists). In 2010 he received from the Scientific Committee of the Fourth International Conference on Investigative Interviewing a *"Special Prize" for his "extensive contributions to investigative interviewing"*. In 2009 he was elected a Fellow by the Board of Directors of the Association of Psychological Sciences (formerly the American Psychological Society) for "sustained and outstanding distinguished contribution to psychological science" (FAPS). In 2009 Ray received from the 'International Investigative Interviewing Research Group' the *'Senior Academic Award' for his 'significant lifetime contribution to the field of investigative interviewing'*. In 2008 Ray received from the European Association of Psychology and Law the *'Award for Life-time Contribution to Psychology and Law'*. In 2005 he received a Commendation from the London Metropolitan Police for *"Innovation and professionalism whilst assisting a complex rape investigation"*. He has advised a large number of police forces in several countries on the interviewing of persons of interest, suspects, witnesses and victims, and he has testified as an expert witness in a considerable number of trials. He has authored and co-authored a large number of papers in quality research journals and has co-authored and co-edited many books including *Investigative Interviewing: Psychology and Practice (1999—a second edition is now being written)* and *Witness Identification in Criminal Cases (2008)*. He has been an invited speaker at a variety of meetings around the world. In recognition of the quality and extent of his research publications he was in 1995 awarded a higher doctorate (Doctor of Science).

Kimberlee Burrows is a PhD candidate at Deakin University, Melbourne, with a background in law and psychology. Her thesis (currently in its final revisions) focuses on prosecutors' perceptions of child witness interviews and is entitled

'The admissibility and sufficiency of child witness interviews in child abuse prosecutions'. Miss Burrows works closely with Crown prosecutors throughout Australia to elucidate and articulate the evidential needs of child witness interviews.

Jacqueline R. Evans is a psychologist whose research focuses on how social and cognitive psychology affect investigative interviewing contexts. She completed her PhD in 2008 and then spent several years as an Intelligence Community Post-doctoral Research Fellow at the University of Texas at El Paso. She spent 2 years in the Department of Psychology and Counselling at the University of Texas at Tyler, and is now faculty at Florida International University in their Legal Psychology program. Her research interests include deception detection, interrogation, and investigative interviewing.

Barry C. Feld is Centennial Professor of Law at the University of Minnesota Law School. His research and scholarship focus on serious young offenders and youth sentencing policy, the impact of race and gender on juvenile justice administration, procedural justice and delivery of legal services, and police interrogation of juveniles. He has written ten books and more than eighty law review and peer-reviewed criminology articles and book chapters on juvenile justice administration. His scholarship has been cited by more than eighty state and federal appellate courts including the United States Supreme Court. His most recent books include: *Kids, Cops, and Confessions: Inside the Interrogation Room* (NYU Press 2013); *Oxford Handbook of Juvenile Crime and Juvenile Justice* (OUP 2012); *Cases and Materials on Juvenile Justice Administration* (Thomson West 4th Ed., 2013); and *Bad Kids: Race and the Transformation of the Juvenile Court* (Oxford University Press 1999), which was the first book in criminology to receive the outstanding book awards from both the American Society of Criminology (2002) and the Academy of Criminal Justice Sciences (2001). He is a Fellow of the American Society of Criminology, a member of the American Law Institute, and a recipient of American Bar Association's Livingston Hall Award for juvenile justice advocacy.

Pär Anders Granhag is Professor of Psychology at the University of Gothenburg (Sweden) and visiting Professor at the Police University College in Oslo (Norway). He has for 20 years conducted research on deception detection, eyewitness testimony and investigative psychology. He has published more than 200 articles and book chapters on these and related topics. He is the author or editor of five books, among them *The Detection of Deception in Forensic Contexts* (Cambridge University Press 2004), and Forensic Psychology in Context: Nordic and International Approaches (Willan Publishing 2010). He has for 15 years trained legal practitioners in interviewing, interrogation and lie detection. He is the funding director of the research unit for *Criminal, Legal and Investigative Psychology* (CLIP, www.psy.gu.se/clip). He is the funding coordinator of the *Nordic Network for research on Psychology and Law*, which was established in 2004 (NNPL, www.nnpl.net). He is the current President of the *European Association of Psychology and Law* (EAPL).

Maria Hartwig completed her graduate training in her native Sweden. where she conducted empirical research on social perception and judgment in legal settings. In 2006, she joined the faculty of John Jay College of Criminal Justice, where she is an

Associate Professor of Psychology. She has published research on the psychology of deception and on interview and interrogation techniques using a broad sample of lay people, legal professionals and prison inmates. She has also carried out extensive training of a variety of legal professionals, including prosecutors, judges, and police detectives. She is an editorial board member of Law and Human Behavior and Legal and Criminological Psychology, and an associate editor of the official newsletter of the American Psychology-Law Society. In 2008, she received an Early Career Award by the European Association for Psychology and Law, and in 2012, she received the Saleem Shah Award for Early Career Excellence in Psychology and Law, awarded by the American Psychology-Law Society and the American Academy of Forensic Psychology.

Kate A. Houston is an experimental psychologist conducting research on social-cognitive principles which are then applied to field contexts. Having received a PhD from the University of Aberdeen, UK (2011) she is now a Research Assistant Professor at the University of Texas at El Paso in the USA. Her research primarily focuses on investigating factors which may affect the cognitive processes of encoding and retrieval of memory, such as emotional arousal and familiarity, as well as the psychological mechanisms of interpersonal communication and social influence as they can be applied in criminal and intelligence interviewing contexts.

Mark Kebbell is Professor in the School of Applied Psychology at Griffith University and a Registered Psychologist with the Psychology Board of Australia. His expertise/research is in the area of Forensic Psychology particularly with regards the investigation and prosecution of serious crime. His research has included writing the guidelines for police officers in England and Wales (with Wagstaff) for the assessment of eyewitness evidence and developing a variety of applied risk assessment protocols for high risk offenders. His research has three overlapping themes: (1) identifying high-risk offenders; (2) the investigation and prosecution of high-risk offenders; and (3) investigative psychology.

Peter J. van Koppen is professor of Law and Psychology at the Departments of Law of both the Free University Amsterdam and Maastricht University. He is a psychologist. He studied psychology at Groningen University (graduation 1978) and law at Groningen University and Amsterdam University. He received a J.D. in 1984 from Erasmus University Rotterdam. He was President of the European Association for Psychology and Law. He is co-editor of *Psychology, Crime, and Law.* He is fellow of the Netherlands Institute for Advanced Study in the Humanities and Social Sciences (NIAS) in Wassenaar. He served as expert witness in some 400 civil and criminal cases. He published a large number of books and articles on evidence, psychology and law, and police and criminal behaviour. His research encompasses the broad area of social science research in law. He has written on negotiation behavior of attorneys in civil cases, on recovered memories, on geographic profiling of criminal behaviour, execution of court decisions, on lie detection, on judicial decision-making and sentencing, on scent line-ups with dogs and visual identification by witnesses, on the history of appointments to the Dutch Supreme Court, on justice decision, on police behavior in major cases, on police interrogations and false confessions, and on phone tapping and the value of forensic evidence.

Christian A. Meissner is Professor of Psychology at Iowa State University. He holds a Ph.D. in Cognitive and Behavioral Sciences from Florida State University (2001) and conducts empirical studies on the psychological processes underlying investigative interviews, including issues surrounding eyewitness recall and identification, deception detection, and interrogation. His research has been funded by the National Science Foundation, the U.S. Department of Defense, the U.S. Department of Justice, and the U.S. Department of Homeland Security. He has participated on advisory panels for the National Science Foundation, the National Academy of Sciences, the U.S. Department of Defense, and the U.S. Department of Homeland Security. From 2010 to 2012, he served as Program Director of Law and Social Sciences at the National Science Foundation. In 2008 he received the Early Career Award ("Saleem Shah") from the American Psychology-Law Society, in 2011 the Book Award from the same society, and in 2013 the Academic Excellence Award from the International Investigative Interviewing Research Group.

Becky Milne is Reader in Forensic Psychology at the Institute of Criminal Justice Studies at the University of Portsmouth. She is the course leader of the FdA Investigation and Evidence and the FdA in Police Studies, distance learning degree programmes specifically for investigators. A chartered forensic psychologist and scientist and Associate Fellow of the British Psychological Society, she is an Associate Editor of the International Journal of Police Science and Management and is a member of the ACPO Investigative Interviewing Strategic Steering Group. She has worked closely with the police and other criminal justice organisations (in the UK and abroad) through training of the Enhanced Cognitive Interview, Witness Interview Advising and also in the interviewing of vulnerable groups (Tier 3 and 5) and providing case advice as an expert advisor. Becky was part of a writing team who developed the National guidance document Achieving Best Evidence that outlines the best ways to interview witnesses and victims for legal purposes (Home Office, 2007). Becky was given the Tom Williamson award for her outstanding achievements in the field of investigative interviewing by ACPO in April 2009.

Makiko Naka is Professor of Psychology at Hokkaido University in Japan. She has conducted research on developmental and cognitive psychology, including indirect speech acts, memory for conversation, leaning through conversation (e.g., numerical classifiers), daily memory activities (e.g., repeated-writing mnemonics), autobiographical memory, and eyewitness testimony. In 1990's, she was asked to evaluate the credibility of a child witness testimony, which brought her to realize not only to point out the problems in interviews but also to improve interviewing methods are important to protect both children and alleged offenders from legal misjudgement. For this reason, besides her academic research and writing of more than 160 articles/book chapters, she started to give training to professionals on child investigative interviews. She is now a head of 'Psychology and Human Science', a project run by Grant-in-Aid for Scientific Research on Innovative Areas by Japanese Ministry of Education, Culture, Sports, Science and Technology. Under this umbrella, 18 research groups are conducting research in the four fields of 'Basis of the Criminal

System and Legal Education', 'Investigative Processes', 'Saibanin-saiban (lay judge court)', and 'Criminal Procedures and Social Welfare.'

Melanie O'Brien is a Research Fellow in the ARC Centre of Excellence in Policing and Security at Griffith University in Brisbane, Australia. Her research and supervision areas include peacekeeping, international criminal law, international humanitarian law (IHL), human rights, feminist legal theory, public international law, comparative criminal law, and military law. Melanie has been a Visiting Fellow at Peking University and a delegate observer for the American Society of International Law at the 52nd Session of the Committee on the Elimination of Discrimination Against Women at UN Headquarters in New York. Melanie is a member of the Editorial Board of *Human Rights Review*, and the Interim Editorial Board of *Genocide Studies and Prevention*. She is a member of the Australian Committee of the Armed Forces Law Association of New Zealand, the Advisory Board of the International Association of Genocide Scholars, and also of the QLD IHL Committee of the Australian Red Cross. From July 2013, Melanie will take 12mths leave to undertake the role of Human Rights Legal Officer at the Office of the Ombudsman in Samoa, through Australian Volunteers for International Development. She will be working with the new National Human Rights Institute of Samoa.

Martin O'Neill is currently a serving police officer with Kent Police with over 29 years' experience. He has extensive training experience, having dedicated many years to the training of detectives of all ranks. He has taught all of the current national detective courses, including Initial Crime Investigator Development Programme (ICIDP), Initial Management of Serious Crime (IMSC) and the Detective Inspector Development Programme (DIDP). Additionally, he has taught programmes relating to the investigation of rape and serious sexual assault, and developed training in relation to domestic abuse. He provides advice and guidance to officers undertaking current criminal investigations, including serious and major crime investigations. His specialisms include sexual offences, fraud, evidence, and homicide investigations. Whilst a serving officer he has successfully completed a law degree, a Master's degree in law, a Master's degree in research and a PhD. His research, entitled "what makes a successful volume crime investigator", encompassed interviews and tests of detectives from different police forces throughout the country. He has taught as an external lecturer at Canterbury ChristChurch University, Kent for nearly 15 years, in both law degree and policing degree modules. Martin is keen to engage in further research into detective practice and hopes to do so when he retires from the police service in April 2014.

Martine Powell is Professor of Forensic Psychology at Deakin University, Melbourne, with 20 years' experience as a researcher in child witness testimony and investigative interviewing. Her early career training was in child development, human memory and human learning processes. She currently has over 160 publications addressing four themes: analyses of child memory and language and the effectiveness of various interview techniques; development of strategies to promote transfer of learning from investigative interviewer training programs to the field; evaluations of criminal justice reforms related to child abuse investigation and methods of minimising the mental health impact of working in the area of child exploitation. Professor Powell has played a major role in the design and implementation of forensic interview training programs for police, lawyers, judges, psychologists and social workers throughout Australia.

Imke Rispens is a psychologist who works as a behavioural scientist and investigative psychologist at the Police Academy, School of Detectives (Graduate School for Investigation) in The Netherlands. She studied clinical psychology and neuropsychology then graduated on the topic of the reliability of eyewitness statements and person recognition. She also participated in research on missing persons at the University of Utrecht. At the Police Academy she teaches on a variety of topics and also coordinates training courses on the interviewing of vulnerable persons.

Matthew D. Semel is a lawyer by training from New York Law School in 1987. He also holds an M.S. in Journalism from Northwestern University. After 13 years as a public defender in the South Bronx, he became the staff attorney for the Civil Rights Clinic at Touro Law School. He has represented capital offenders on appeal. His research interests include capital punishment, terrorism, culture and crime, and criminal law. He received his PhD from John Jay College of Criminal Justice, his dissertation being on military and counter-terrorism interrogation techniques.

Lotte Smets is a Clinical Psychologist with specialty in Psychology and Law. She achieved her PhD at the Criminology Department of the University of Ghent. Based on the principles of coaching she studied the effect of two newly developed training methods and how these can be used to optimise daily police interview practices. Nowadays she organises various training events aiming to optimize interview techniques of police officers, lawyers, probation officers and others. Her current major project is the integration of interview coaches in the Belgian police landscape. Therefore she educates experienced police interviewers to interview coaches during the 'Interviewing coach' training. This one-year training is the valorisation of her doctoral research.

Miet Vanderhallen in 2007 completed her PhD on 'The working alliance in police interviewing'. Currently, she works as an assistant professor psychology and law at Antwerp University and as an assistant professor criminology at Maastricht University. Besides, she is an affiliated senior researcher at KULeuven. She teaches psychology and law, criminology, and methods of empirical research at the faculty of law. Her main research interest concerns investigative interviewing. She is particularly interested in research regarding building rapport and research on the (evidential) value of suspects' statements. In the aftermath of the Salduz case law, she is currently involved in various (international) studies on legal advice at the police station. In addition to her research activities, she takes part in many (advanced) investigative interview training programs at the national police academy on criminal investigation and regional police academies. Her latest projects addresses supervision of interviewers at police stations as well as joint training for interviewers and lawyers. She has published several (inter)national articles and book chapters on investigative interviewing.

Geert Vervaeke is doctor in psychology and full professor in psychology and law at the Faculty of Law of the KULeuven and the Faculty's project officer 'management of justice'. He is the former president of the High Council of Justice of Belgium and was Executive board Member of the European Network of Councils for the Judiciary and the European Association on Psychology and Law. He is conducting research in the field of the explanation of crime (sexual crime, stalking and partner violence) and in the field of the justice system (public trust, police interviewing, selection of judges and prosecutors).

Annelies Vredeveldt is a Postdoctoral Research Fellow at the University of Cape Town. She graduated from University College Utrecht with a BA degree in the social sciences in 2007, and from Maastricht University with a M.Sc. degree in Psychology and Law in 2008. She obtained her Ph.D. degree from the University of York in 2011, where she worked with Alan Baddeley and Graham Hitch. Her area of expertise is legal psychology, with a specific focus on cognitive processes that play a role in the legal arena. Her research interests include eyewitness memory, social cognition, deception detection, face recognition and facial composites. She has published various peer-reviewed articles on these topics. She has been awarded a number of prizes, including awards from the American Psychology-Law Society and the British Psychological Society. The Society in Science in Zürich has recently awarded her a prestigious Branco Weiss Fellowship to support a 5-year research programme on the potential memorial benefits of discussion between witnesses, to be taken up in October 2013.

Nina Westera is Research Fellow at the Centre of Excellence in Policing and Security at Griffith University in Queensland. Nina specialises in the application of psychology to law. Her research interests include investigative interviewing (witnesses, suspects, vulnerable interviewees); eyewitness testimony; investigating and prosecuting alleged sexual and violent offences; evidence; juror decision-making; the criminal justice process; and investigative training and development. Nina began her career as an officer in the New Zealand Police, where she worked in a variety of roles that included the investigation of serious crime and the implementation of evidence-based policy and practice for interviewing witnesses and suspects. Nina has educated and advised police officers, lawyers, judges and other criminal justice sector professionals in Australia, New Zealand and around the world about best practice in investigative interviewing.

Chapter 1
Investigative Interviewing in Suspected Sex Offences

Nina J. Westera and Mark R. Kebbell

Suspected sex offences are difficult to investigate and prosecute. In many instances, the only evidence that exists is an account from a complainant and one from a suspect. This means that the way that these accounts are elicited with an investigative interview are critical. In this chapter, we will outline what we know about effective strategies for interviewing both complainants and suspects. Effective interviewing of complainants can dramatically increase the volume of information a complainant provides and has the potential to increase the credibility of this evidence. This is especially relevant now that recorded police interviews can be provided as evidence-in-chief in some jurisdictions. Suspect interviewing can be enhanced by using nonjudgmental approaches, allowing suspects to give their own account, and by other methods. We will draw together complainant and suspect interviewing to show how effective investigative interviewing can enhance the investigation and prosecution of sex crimes.

Changing attitudes and legal reforms in Western countries over the last 30 years have led to an increase in the reporting of rape, especially adult acquaintance and inter-partner sex offences (Daly and Bouhours 2010). However, this increased reporting has not been matched by increased conviction rates (Daly and Bouhours 2010). A difficulty for these cases lies in establishing the issue of consent. Here, often the only evidence available to determine the facts in issue are the complainant's and suspect's accounts. Ambiguity is rife and the high standard of proof requiring a jury or judge to be satisfied 'beyond a reasonable doubt' means convictions are relatively rare. In rape cases, it is therefore imperative that effective interviewing methods are used to optimise the information available from these two main sources, the complainant and the suspect.

Promisingly, a move towards video and audio recording these interviews allows psychological researchers to now examine this previously hidden world

N. J. Westera (✉)
Griffith University, Queensland, Australia
e-mail: n.westera@griffith.edu.au

M. R. Kebbell
e-mail: m.kebbell@griffith.edu.au

R. Bull (ed.), *Investigative Interviewing*, DOI 10.1007/978-1-4614-9642-7_1,
© Springer Science+Business Media New York 2014

(Baldwin 1993). Coupled with methodological advances, this access has resulted in an increasingly sophisticated understanding about how to effectively interview suspects and complainants. In this chapter, we examine how this growing body of research might help improve the *completeness and accuracy* of information available for investigations into sex offending against adults.[1] We also add to the body of literature by exploring the less researched area of how to optimize the *relevance* of information to help an investigation and any subsequent prosecution establish criminal culpability. We suggest that applying these understandings provides a pathway to increase the likelihood that not only are the guilty convicted, but also the falsely accused are exonerated. We start by providing context about how rape investigations are often conducted and hence what type of information is likely to influence the outcome of cases. We then turn our attention to how to elicit this information from the complainant and the suspect(s).

Sexual Offence Investigations

In several countries, the offence of rape has changed. Prior to the 1970s the legal definition for rape in Western countries was far narrower than it is today (Estrich 1987; Lees 2002). Such changes in legislation reflect a change in social consciousness as a result of the women's rights revolution challenging the social construction of rape. Estrich (1987) described the prevailing social construction of rape as 'real rape', which involved either a stranger attacker, use of a weapon, or high levels of force against the complainant. However, more typically cases fall outside of this 'real rape' construct, but these cases were seldom reported and, when they were, the justice system struggled to respond effectively (Estrich 1987; Kalven and Zeisel 1966; Lees 2002). Legal reforms in several countries have now extended the definition to include rape within marriage and different types of bodily penetration, and to remove the need for corroboration and evidence of physical resistance as required in many traditional definitions. These reforms were adopted as part of a broader approach that aimed to reduce the under-reporting of cases that do not fit the 'real rape' construct.

Research suggests that since these legal reforms were introduced reporting has increased, but convictions rates have decreased. Daly and Bouhours' (2010) comprehensive comparison of attrition studies over time in Australia, Canada, England and Wales, Scotland, and the USA offers some insight into how rape and sexual assault reporting has changed. The picture is complex and not entirely consistent across countries and so we only present the main trends. Reported sexual assault cases per member of the population increased after legal reforms were introduced in different countries, suggesting that increased reporting has resulted from these reforms

---

[1] In this chapter, we specifically examine the less researched topic of alleged sex offences against adult victims rather than child victims, and on female victims of male offenders to reflect the gendered nature typical to this type of the violence (see Estrich 1987). This is not meant to undermine the traumatic effect of sexual violence when the victim is a male or child and many of the approaches described in this chapter may also apply to these groups.

(Daly and Bouhours 2010). Not so promising have been the effects of legal reform on the proportionate outcome of cases. Between the 1970–1989 period and the 1990–2005 period conviction rates for all reported sexual assault cases decreased significantly from 18 to 12.5 %. By country, rates decreased in England, Wales, Canada, and Australia whilst remaining stable in the USA and Scotland. Daly and Bouhours suggest one explanation for this decline is an increased reporting of acquaintance and inter-partner rapes that do not result in conviction. To explore this possibility they conducted a 'mini-study' within their review, which identified 13 studies (mainly from the USA and England and Wales) that reported the relationship between the victim and the offender. In these cases, the total proportion of reported cases that were stranger rapes dropped from 48 % in the 1970s and 1980s to 26 % in the 1990s onwards. These findings suggest that the decrease in conviction rates over time may be due to an increased proportion of rapes that do not fit the 'real rape' construct being reported but not resulting in conviction. This is supported by a substantial body of research suggesting that in these types of cases, despite legislative reform, social attitudes have been slow to change. The police may be reticent to charge the alleged offender, prosecutors reticent to continue with the prosecution, and juries reticent to convict (Daly and Bouhours 2010; Lees 2002; Tempkin and Krahé 2008).

The need to effectively investigate and prosecute reported rape cases requires an increasingly sophisticated understanding about what is relevant to these types of cases. With stranger rapes, the ability to identify the alleged offender is often central to the investigation. In contrast, many cases nowadays involve a complainant and an alleged offender who are known to each other. The issue is not identity, but whether the complainant consented to sex or the accused had reasonable grounds to believe the complainant consented. Physical evidence, such as DNA and bodily fluids, confirming the sex took place typically adds little value. More relevant usually is what happened leading up to and during the commission of the alleged offence that might help to establish if consent was given. The objective of most complainant and suspect interviews is therefore to optimise accurate detail about the behaviour of the suspect and how the complainant responded to that behaviour. This is likely to include details at the time of the event such as conversations between complainant and suspect, the possible use of force by the suspect, any physical resistance offered by the complainant, the nature of any threats or perceived threats to the complainant, and the displayed emotion of the suspect and the complainant. Gaining as much information as possible about these details should help to establish the state of mind of the complainant (whether or not she did consent) and the suspect (whether he perceived that she was consenting). This approach is also likely to assist with the detection of false complainants. For example, Hunt and Bull (2012) compared 80 allegations of rape that were classified as false with 160 allegations of rape that were classified as genuine. Many of the factors that were found to discriminate between 'false' and 'genuine' allegations related to behaviours at the time of the event (e.g. genuine complaints were associated with behaviours such as the offender conning the complainant, more sexual acts and verbal resistance from the complainant).

Prevailing 'rape myths' that bias decision-making towards blaming the complainant (Ellison and Munro 2009b; Schuller et al. 2010; Tempkin and Krahé 2008) can mean that just exploring what happened during the commission of the offence is unlikely to be enough. Rape myths include stereotypes that justify sexual violence against women (Costin 1985). Some of these myths relate to the attributes or purported character of the woman. For example, 'She led him on because she was wearing a short skirt.' Other myths that relate to the complainant's behaviour are typical in cases where the suspect knows the complainant because what happened may appear more similar to a consensual sexual encounter than to 'real rape' (Ellison and Munro 2009a). Social expectations that 'normal sex' involves the woman playing a coy and passive role, and wants to be dominated by a male, feed into rape myths that place blame on the victim (Ellison and Munro 2009a; Frohmann and Mertz 1994). For example, the myth that if the complainant went to the suspect's apartment voluntarily he should justifiably expect sex and hence she is blameworthy. Other myths are that a 'real' complainant will fight back or high levels of force from the offender are required, when in reality 'freezing' is a common response and physical injury is often not present (see Lees 2002).

There are two promising approaches that can be applied at interview that may assist with countering the biases of these myths. When describing a case construction approach to prosecuting sex offences, Ellison (2007) suggests maximising the completeness of the information from the complainant, especially cognitions and emotions, may help make her counterintuitive behaviour more understandable to jurors/judges. For example, the complainant explaining that she did not fight back due to fear that the violence would escalate. Encouraging the complainant to disclose information she may otherwise choose to withhold due to embarrassment or concern that it would diminish her credibility is also recommended. For example, that the complainant consensually kissed the accused earlier the evening prior to the rape event. Having this type of information upfront can assist with case preparation rather than being exposed in a credibility-damaging way later during the judicial process. In a previous paper, we suggested that instead of the prosecutor eliciting these types of detail pre-trial as recommended by Ellison, the complainant interview provides an earlier opportunity to do so (Kebbell and Westera 2011). Capturing this information earlier provides the opportunity to influence the decision-making of investigators and lawyers. Empirical research is needed to test what difference this added detail can make to key decision-makers, however, we suggested that eliciting a full account that optimises cognition and emotion details is relevant in rape investigations.

In addition to exploring what happened during the event, the relationship between the complainant and the suspect may also help decision-makers to understand the complainant's behavioural response. Emerging work by Tidmarsh, Powell, and Darwinkel (2012) describes a 'whole story' framework, which is underpinned by the assumption that sexual offending is perceived by the offender within the context of a relationship where the offender attempts to gain compliance from the complainant through manipulation. Understanding the offending thereby requires an understanding of this relationship. In adult sex cases, this type of approach is likely to be particularly relevant to inter-partner rape where a history of gradually escalating violence or other intimidation may induce compliance from the complainant and blur the issue of consent. For example, if violence had previously been used when sex was refused may lead to the complainant complying without resistance for fear of another violent reprisal. Again, research is required to empirically test this approach, but exploring the relationship history during both the complainant's and suspect's interviews may provide relevant information that could help to explain what may otherwise appear to be counterintuitive behaviour by the complainant.

In sum, relevant to rape cases is obtaining a complete account about what happened leading up to and during the commission of the alleged offence as it relates to consent and understanding why the complainant behaved in the way that she did. Next, we examine how our understanding of interviewing complainants and suspects can help to gain a more complete account about these relevant matters.

Interviewing Complainants

Information from the complainant is central to most rape investigations. When consent is the defence, if the suspect invokes his right to silence, then the sole source of information is typically the complainant. In current times, there are three potential objectives for the complainant interview. First, to obtain complete, accurate, and relevant information for the investigation. Second, to ensure the justice system responds to rape complainant ethically and with respect for her welfare (Frohmann and Mertz 1994). Third, in some countries, to use the video-recorded investigative interview of the complainant as the basis for her evidence at trial. We will now review the research that explores how to meet these three, sometimes competing, objectives.

Objective 1: The Investigation

Recommended police practice in countries such as England and Wales, and New Zealand is to use the cognitive interview (CI) when interviewing rape complainants (Criminal Justice System 2007; New Zealand Police 2009). As the most successful and empirically tested method for interviewing adult eyewitnesses, the CI has been shown to increase the amount of information obtained without reducing overall rates of accuracy (Köhnken et al. 1999; Memon et al. 2010). Originally developed by psychologists Ron Fisher and Ed Geiselman in the 1980s (Geiselman et al. 1984), the CI is based on encoding specificity theory (Tulving 1974; Tulving and Thomson 1973). This theory proposes that memory for an event is made up both of the memory trace laid down from the original encoding of the memory and the retrieval cues present in the person's cognitive environment at the time of memory recall. The original CI used four mnemonics in an attempt to increase the feature overlap between the memory trace and retrieval cues, and hence increase the likelihood of information is recalled (Geiselman et al. 1984; Tulving and Thomson 1973). The 'context reinstatement' mnemonic encourages the witness to reconstruct the physiological and psychological context of the event at the time of encoding. 'Report everything' encourages the witness to recall in detail even partial and incomplete memories. 'Change of order' encourages multiple retrieval attempts, for example, by asking the witness to now recall events in a reverse temporal order. 'Change of perspective' requires the witness to try to recall extra information from a perspective different from what she has used so far. Other mnemonics such as reporting from different sensory modalities were later added to the CI (see Fisher and Geiselman 1992). No research that we are aware of specially examines use of the CI with rape complainants. Ethical issues that impede this type of research also limit studies that seek to simulate features common in rape cases such as the reporting of stressful and emotionally arousing events, leaving these areas also unexplored (see Memon et al. 2010).

When the CI is used, there are good reasons why it may increase the amount of relevant details about events in rape investigations. A meta-analysis suggests that the CI produces on average 40 % more details about the event without comprising accuracy (Köhnken et al. 1999). Relevant information is likely to increase with this general increase, particularly when the interviewer explores aspects of the account relating to consent and other relevant issues. The CI mnemonic of reporting events from different sensory modalities may be particularly helpful (Fisher and Geiselman 1992). For example, asking the complainant to report what she heard may generate more details about conversations around consent. Asking the complainant to report what she physically felt may lead to information about the degree of force used and any resistance offered. Furthermore, witnesses have been found to report more potentially important emotions and cognitions when interviewed using the CI compared to a 'structured' comparison interview (Bembibre and Higueras 2012).

Adopting a witness-controlled approach to the interview as advocated by the CI may be particularly helpful (Fisher and Geiselman 1992). In addition to explicitly stating to the witness that it is her interview and she should guide the process, the CI also involves using open questions, silences and pauses, and not interrupting the witness. The overall purpose is to encourage the witness to control her own memory retrieval and report in narrative responses. By doing so the complainant is more likely to engage in elaborate memory retrieval, and hence recall and report more detailed information (Powell et al. 2005). A narrative approach also reduces the risk of leading the complainant. As questions become more closed and specific answers tend to become less accurate, due to a tendency of a witness to comply with the social demands of the interviewer (Kebbell and Wagstaff 1999). This is because with closed questions, the interviewer asks the witness for information the interviewer wants them to remember ('What colour was his shirt?') rather than just asking the witness what it is she remembers ('Describe his clothing'). Leading or suggestive questions that imply the desired answer and that have been found to reduce response accuracy are discouraged in the CI (Fisher and Geiselman 1992; Loftus and Palmer 1974; Loftus and Zanni 1975), as they are in the 'PEACE' approach to interviewing (Milne and Bull 1999).

Also helpful in rape cases, is the emphasis on the social environment incorporated in the CI and other interview protocols (Criminal Justice System 2007; Fisher and Geiselman 1992). For example, building rapport to put the witness at ease may make rape complainants feel more comfortable disclosing personal information such as the nature of the sexual acts and other aspects of the suspect's behaviour at the time of the sexual acts that may be relevant to consent. This environment may also encourage the complainant to disclose information they perceive as potentially credibility damaging that, as previously discussed, is better known early in the investigation to assist the investigation and case preparation (Ellison 2007).

Another important feature is how the interview is recorded. Video recording is likely to result in a more complete and accurate record than the traditional method of an officer preparing a written statement based on what was said at interview. This is because the cognitively and linguistically demanding process of preparing a written statement is prone to bias and will at best result in a semi-accurate summary of the complainant's account (Köhnken 1995; Köhnken et al. 1994; Lamb et al. 2000; Rock 2001). Video recording the interview also improves transparency allowing the types of questions asked and interview methods used to be reviewed to help determine the reliability of the responses provided. This may be helpful to key decision-makers. For example, both lawyers and police investigators have been found to rate a mock rape complainant's account as less accurate when closed and leading questions were used to elicit the account rather than open questions (Westera et al. 2011, 2013a). Finally, video recording enables the same interview to be used later as evidence in court and, as we will discuss next, may help to improve the investigation and prosecution process for complainants.

Objective 2: The Complainant

Adhering to evidence-based interview practice as just described may well also improve the experience of rape complainants. The police have previously been criticised for not allowing complainants to be able to give their story, feel listened to, or believed (Jordan 2001; McMillan and Thomas 2009; Patterson 2011). Adopting a witness-controlled narrative approach to the interview is one means of meeting these needs. Troublingly, police struggle to use a witness-controlled approach with research suggesting both the CI and open questions are seldom used (Clarke and Milne 2001; Clifford and George 1996; Dando et al. 2009; Griffiths et al. 2011). Interestingly, a questionnaire on the perceptions of 136 police investigators in New Zealand suggests that complainant dissatisfaction with the police response may in part be due to the written statement method of recording (Westera et al. 2011). Many investigators perceived that video recording the interview reduces the need for them to interrupt the complainant and use repetitive questioning because the interviewer is no longer required to remember everything that was said to produce a written statement.

Adopting a nonjudgemental approach is likely to improve the experience for complainants and assist the investigation (Jordon 2001; McMillan and Thomas 2009; Patterson 2011). For example, in the USA, Patterson (2011) interviewed 20 rape victims about their experiences with the police. In cases that did not result in prosecution (in these cases the offender was usually known to the complainant), complainants reported that they were not able to give their story about events, questioning was repetitive and direct, and they felt they were disbelieved from the onset. In contrast, in cases that proceeded to prosecution, complainants felt that they could tell their story in their own pace and time, and were listened to. They reported feeling more at ease and supported, and thereby more likely to disclose additional information about events. An open-minded approach and using the CI is also likely to assist when false complaints do occur, by encouraging a detailed account that can be verified or disproved through further lines of enquiry.

Another means of improving the experience of complainants is what we will examine next, the ability in some countries to use the video recording as evidence. Many vulnerable witnesses may indeed want the option of video-recorded evidence (Hamlyn et al. 2004; Kebbell et al. 2007). Further, police and lawyers also perceive that video-recorded evidence is likely to improve the court process for complainants by reducing the stress of having to again recall events in the courtroom (Westera et al. 2011, 2013a).

Objective 3: Video-Recorded Evidence

Video-recorded evidence involves playing the investigative interview as the basis for the complainant's evidence-in-chief. After the interview is played, the prosecutor asks supplementary questions and defence counsel cross-examines the complainant live in the courtroom or via other special measures such as closed-circuit television (Mahoney et al. 2007). This facility has recently been extended from children to adults in some countries (e.g. England, Wales, Northern Ireland, Norway, New Zealand, and the Northern Territory of Australia; Australian Law Reform Commission 2010; Criminal Justice System 2007; Mahoney et al. 2007; personal communication with Superintendent Rygh of the Norway Police Service).

There are three main reasons why video-recorded evidence may enhance the completeness, accuracy, and relevance of complainant testimony. First, the smaller time delay between the event and interview when compared to trial means that the account is less likely to suffer from the effects of forgetting and memory distortions that can occur over time (Ebbinghaus 1913; Gabbert et al. 2003; Loftus et al. 1975; Read and Connolly 2007; Rubin and Wenzel 1996). Secondly, the courtroom environment is likely to be less conducive to memory recall when compared to the interview room. Recalling what happened on the stand in the presence of the accused is likely to be stressful for the complainant and stress has been found to negatively affect cognitive performance (Deffenbacher et al. 2004). In addition, expectations of giving testimony in a formal environment may temper what the complainant says (Konradi 1999). These environmental features may be particularly detrimental to recalling highly personal but relevant information such as the sexual acts and how the complainant was feeling. Thirdly, in contrast to interview methods that encourage free narrative responses, for presentation reasons advocacy guidance suggests the use of questions that encourage short answers (Evans 1995; Hutcheson et al. 1995; Milne and Bull 1999; Poole and White 1991; Powell et al. 2005). Controlling the witness to elicit 'sound-bite' responses in this way is also likely to detract from the completeness and accuracy of recall.

Westera, Kebbell, and Milne (2013) explored what difference it would make to the content of a rape complainant's testimony if the video interview was used as evidence. They compared the same complainant's police interview (that could have been but was not used as evidence) with their live courtroom evidence-in-chief in ten actual rape cases in New Zealand. Details that went towards establishing consent (e.g. 'I told him I didn't want him near me') and what happened during the commission of the alleged offence (e.g. 'From the moment he pushed me onto to the bed until he rolled over and fell asleep') were examined because these details are what jurors should be using to make decisions about guilt. Details in evidence-in-chief were coded against details the video interview as 'consistent' (the same in both the interview and evidence); 'omitted' (in the interview but not in evidence); 'distorted' or 'contradictory' (inconsistent between the interview and live evidence); or 'new' (in live evidence but not the interview). The analysis found that details in the interview were significantly more likely to be omitted from live evidence than repeated consistently. Indeed the loss was marked, on average two-thirds of these central details in the interview were lost in evidence-in-chief. Only a small number of distortions and contradictions were found between live evidence and the interview, suggesting that video evidence is more likely to affect the completeness than the accuracy of evidence. A limitation to this study is that only ten cases were examined, but the findings are consistent with more general understanding about the effects of delay, questioning, and the recall environment on memory (Read and Connelly 2007; Milne and Bull 1999; Powell et al. 2005). In other words, video-recorded evidence is likely to provide jurors/judges with more complete information from the complainant about the facts in issue.

Another notable finding in the Westera et al. study was the type of detail omitted. Each detail was also coded as a 'physical action', 'cognition', 'verbalization', 'emotion', or 'person/surround description'. 'Cognition' details about what the complainant was thinking suffered the greatest loss to the extent that they were virtually nonexistent in live evidence. As mentioned above, these cognition details could help to explain the complainant's behaviour that might otherwise appear counterintuitive (Ellison 2007; Kebbell and Westera 2011). For example, 'I didn't cry out because my daughter was asleep next door and I didn't want her to know what her father was doing to me.'

For evidence purposes, it is not just the content of the account that matters, but also how the account is perceived by jurors/judges. Legal professionals have expressed concern that video-recorded evidence is less coherent than live testimony and this has a negative effect on evidence presentation (Criminal Justice Joint Inspection 2009; Powell and Wright 2009; Stern 2010; Westera et al. 2013a). These concerns may actually be due to the narrative nature of the interview (Westera et al. 2013a; Read and Powell 2011). Indeed, Westera et al. (2013b) found that police elicited five times the length of response to open questions than lawyers did, suggesting that police interviews are in more of a narrative format. A conflict thereby exists between (a) providing the court with the highest quality information as is likely from a narrative account and (b) current beliefs about how evidence is presented effectively.

How this format of evidence affects perceptions of testimony needs further research. To date, the few studies examining this issue have found very little difference between the narrative and short answer format (Fisher et al. 1999; Lind et al. 1978). The long narratives in the interview may make the testimony more complex and cognitively demanding to process. If this is the case, jurors may more readily rely on heuristic rather than systematic processing to the detriment of effective decision-making (Chaiken and Eagly 1976, 1983). On the other hand, the complainant spontaneously giving information in free narrative format may be more convincing if it more closely resembles a story narrative (Snow et al. 2009). Detail may in itself enhance credibility (Bell and Loftus 1988, 1989). Indeed, suspects may find this enhances the weight of the evidence against them. We now turn our attention to suspects.

Interviewing Suspects

When interviewing a suspect two broad possibilities exist. First, that the suspect is guilty of an offence. A guilty suspect who admits to the offending during a police interview is more likely to later plead guilty and save the complainant the distress of, and the justice system the cost of a lengthy trial (Gudjonsson 2003). The second possibility is that the suspect is innocent. Not gaining an appropriate account from an innocent suspect puts the suspect at risk of the stigma associated with being charged with sex crime, facing a lengthy justice process, and possible wrongful conviction (Gudjonsson 2003). Of course, there are nuances to these two possibilities such as offenders who have not done all that the complainant claims or who are not guilty because of mental illness. However, whether guilty or innocent, making the most of the opportunity to gather complete, accurate and relevant information from the suspect during the investigative interview is crucial for a police investigation. Some clear patterns have emerged about how to effectively interview a suspected sex offender. Now we will examine each of the three main steps to a suspect interview: encouraging the suspect to talk, obtaining relevant information from the suspect, and giving the suspect an opportunity to respond to the available evidence.

Encouraging the Suspect Talk

When discussing the sensitive topic of the alleged sexual offending with a suspect many of the same principles to interviewing the complainant apply. Interviews with suspects differ, however, because there are two main disincentives for a suspect to talk to an investigator. The information given by the suspect can be used against him in a court of law; hence, the suspect has and may exercise his legal right to silence.

In rape cases, the frequent scarcity of available evidence and risk of long sentences of imprisonment may further discourage the suspect from talking or lead defence lawyers to advise against the suspect providing an account that may potentially incriminate him (McDonald and Tinsely 2012). Further, shame may drive a desire to deny the offence and hide from the associated stigma (Ward et al. 1997; Quinn et al. 2004). It may be embarrassing to talk about what happened. As Read, Powell, Kebbell, and Milne (2009) point out, in many cases where persons suspected of committing sexual abuse are truly guilty, shame and fear of exposure are likely to be driving factors underlying possible nondisclosure.

The first step for the interviewer to attempt is to overcome these barriers by creating an environment where the suspect wants to give his account. The sensitive nature of the allegations means that building rapport, which is common to most interviewing protocols, is likely to be especially important (Milne and Bull 1999; Powell et al. 2005; Read et al. 2009; Shepherd 2007). Despite the emphasis on the importance of rapport, how it is to be established is not well researched due to ethical constraints about making an interviewee feel at ease versus uncomfortable (Powell et al. 2005). Academics generally agree that the key elements include features such as expressing empathy, adopting a nonjudgemental attitude, and using appropriate questioning and active listening (Kebbell et al. 2006; Oxburgh and Ost 2011; Read et al. 2009; Shepherd 2007). To encourage an honest and detailed account it is important that the interviewee perceives that his account will be heard, understood, and not unduly judged. Convicted sex offenders strongly endorse interviewing strategies that they believe to be fair and not aggressive (Holmberg and Christianson 2002; Kebbell et al. 2010). This endorsement is consistent with a non-leading, open-ended approach adopted nowadays by most modern interviewing protocols and with the approach adopted by many clinicians to encourage disclosure of sensitive information in therapeutic settings (Kebbell and Wagstaff 1998).

By law, most countries require the interviewer to fairly explain to the suspect the nature of the allegations or the interview may be rendered inadmissible as evidence. Explaining the allegations, the purpose of the interview and the interview process may also form an important part of establishing a working relationship with the suspect (Shepherd 2007). The interviewer establishing a common purpose with the suspect and adopting a fair and transparent approach may motivate the suspect to participate in the interview. Explaining the process may also reduce anxiety the suspect has about what is happening and hence place them more at ease about providing an account.

Obtaining an Account

As discussed above, obtaining a detailed account of what happened during the alleged offending is likely to provide the most relevant information for the investigation. Specifically, establishing the suspect's perceptions about the complainant's consent is likely to be pivotal to decisions about prosecution. The suspect's behaviour, cognitions, and emotions during the alleged offending may help to determine these issues.

Also, the reaction of the suspect immediately after the sexual acts may provide valuable circumstantial evidence. For example, a suspect who feels guilty about what he has done may cry or apologise after the sex act. Exploring the relationship between the suspect and the complainant may also help to provide a context for what happened (Read and Powell 2011). Planning for the interview lays a foundation that will help ensure that these and other relevant investigative and evidential details are covered (Shepherd 2007). In addition to reviewing the complainant's interview to obtain this information, the growth of technology means important investigative information is potentially available from a wide variety of sources. Text messaging, emails, and social media, such as Facebook, are all potential sources of information about prior and subsequent communications between the suspect and the complainant or other people, and may help to corroborate or refute the allegations and can be explored at interview.

Maintaining a nonjudgmental and fair approach as at the beginning of the interview is also likely to encourage the suspect to talk. The CI may also be useful when the suspect is co-operative and forthcoming with information. Using broad invitations when initially raising the topic of concern also provides benefits. Open-ended invitations are perceived as nonthreatening and less interrogative compared to a series of specific questions (i.e. those that dictate what specific information is required and offer the interviewee little time to collect his or her thoughts). This is because open-ended questions portray a relationship where interviewee's perspectives are valued and heard and because open-ended questions allow suspects to portray themselves in a positive light if they want to (Kebbell et al. 2008). For example, child sex offenders may wish to emphasize their personal bonds and relationships (Benneworth 2007), whilst rapists may focus on criticising the alleged victim's character and credibility. Both may wish to emphasise reasons why they are not fully culpable, for instance, that they are stressed or were under the influence of alcohol, and so open-ended questions also minimise the risk that interviewers will raise specific case-related information (when discussing the allegation) in an attempt to confirm their own preconceptions or prior knowledge (Meissner and Kassin 2002).

However, not all suspects are prepared to answer open questions. A study by Kebbell, Porter, and Milne (2012) sheds light on how suspected sex offenders respond during police interviews. Eighty-five police interviews with suspected sex offenders were analysed and smallest space analysis (SSA) was used to explore the thematic structure of suspects' interview behaviour using the presence or absence of these behaviours. The SSA uses the correlates between these behaviours to represent how they are associated to each other in geometric space. Three broad themes emerged, each characterized by different behaviours: hostile, evasive, and sympathy.

Behaviours within the 'hostile' theme included aggressive and defiant responses from the suspect. However, the most frequent behaviour clustered within this theme was the suspect stating that he had poor memory for the event. This is unsurprising as many sex offenders are drunk when they commit offences and they may be faking memory loss to avoid discussing unpleasant events. Further behaviours in the hostile theme included suspects claiming not to understand the question, repeating questions back, responding to questions with questions, and failing to acknowledge questions. Again, encouraging an uninterrupted account may be of assistance here.

The 'controlling' theme was characterized by failing to answer questions and evasiveness, blaming the complainant, controlling the interview, and trying to change the subject. Whilst the ultimate way in which a suspect can avoid answering a question is to decline to be interviewed, in this study, all participants had consented to be interviewed. Thus, their avoidance of answering questions was much more subtle. To overcome these challenges interviewers must pay careful attention to how they ask questions and ask them as simply as possible. Suspects in the controlling theme also blamed the complainant during the interview. Again, it is relatively common for sex offenders to blame their victims (Beech et al. 2003) because it makes the offender feel less culpable. However, in this context it may be a necessary step for suspects to make before giving a full account as it means they can present themselves in a more positive light.

The 'sympathy' theme was characterised by minimization of *actus reus* (acts done) and *mens rea* (mental state) often in the context of confessions. Offenders may confess for a variety of reasons, including feelings of guilt and a desire to get things 'off their chest' (Gudjonsson 2003). However, another reason is to give their account of what happened and this seems to sit well with this theme. Making admissions allows the suspect to minimize their actions and their mental culpability. For instance, they might say that they did not do everything the victim said, or that they were drunk or mentally unwell in order to make their actions seem less bad. A strategy to encourage admissions might therefore be to allow the suspect to talk, give their side no matter how self-serving and not to interrupt them until later on. Further aspects of this theme include appeals for sympathy, showing remorse, and emotional responses.

The implication of these findings is that interviewers should be trained to expect and respond to these behaviours. Providing an empirically based typology of suspects' behaviour could be used to enhance the formulation of expertise to identify what types of behaviour should be expected and responded to.

Presenting the Evidence

The next step is to allow the suspect an opportunity to respond to the evidence. This step is important for both psychological and legal reasons. From a psychological perspective, a growing body of literature indicates that the strength of evidence is highly influential on suspects' decisions to confess or deny. For example, Gudjonsson and Petursson (1991) surveyed 74 Icelandic prisoners concerning their reasons for confessing. Offenders were required to respond to questions using a Likert scale ranging from 'not at all' (1 or 2) to 'very much so' (6 or 7). The majority (55 %) of offenders gave scores of 6 or 7 to the question, 'Did you think the police would eventually prove you did it?' This was the most frequently given reason for confessing. Similarly, Moston, Stephenson, and Williamson (1992) investigated confessions for 1,067 suspects who had been interviewed by detectives for a range of crimes. The results showed that when the evidence was rated weak by researchers then confessions occurred in less than 10 % of cases. However, when evidence was rated as strong by the researchers, confessions occurred in 67 % of cases.

Specifically related to sex offenders, Kebbell et al. (2010) surveyed 43 convicted sex offenders concerning how they were interviewed and looked at how this related to their decisions to confess or deny. Evidence presenting strategies not only influenced offenders' decisions to confess to their own crimes, but were also suggested by respondents as being strategies that investigating officers should use to increase the likelihood of a suspect responding honestly. The implication of this is that officers should ensure they have the most evidence possible and the previous section concerning the complainant gives some guidance as to how this can be achieved.

Indeed, providing the enhanced account from the complainant on video to the suspect and/or his lawyer has the potential to demonstrate the strength of the evidence. If it is strong, it may facilitate guilty suspects' truth telling however, to date, research has not explored this. Further, the previously mentioned research by Gudjonsson and Petursson (1991) found that 40 % of respondents gave a 'very much so' rating to the question, 'Did you confess because you felt guilty about the offence.' If the complainant video interview provides a comprehensive and valid account, viewing it may also enhance the suspect's feelings of guilt and therefore increase the likelihood of a confession and a subsequent guilty plea. Feelings of guilt may be further heightened if police and prosecutors perceptions, that the recency of the offending means the video often captures a highly emotional complainant, are correct (Westera et al. 2011, 2013a).

Finally, from a legal perspective the suspect has a right to respond to the allegations. Read and Powell (2011) interviewed 16 sex offender interviewing experts (who were a mixture of legal professionals, police officers, and academics) about what constitutes effective suspect interviewing practices. 'Letting the suspects answer the allegations put to them', was one of four themes that emerged. This included allowing the suspect to respond to allegations that were put fairly to them in an open manner. The experts perceived that integral to this was planning for the interviews, so the interviewer was aware of the exact nature of the available evidence and any potential defence so they could present all relevant evidence to the suspect in a fair way.

Conclusion

Interviewing complainants and suspects in sex cases is one of the most challenging but important tasks for investigators. Fortunately, a growing body of research identifies how to do so effectively. Integral to these types of interviews is the interviewer adopting a nonjudgemental and fair approach, building rapport, and encouraging the interviewees to give a narrative account. These features will help to ensure that the account given is as complete and accurate as possible. Using these methods will maximise the evidence available for investigators, legal professionals, and jurors/judges to enable more informed decisions. Thus, the understanding of how to interview complainants and suspects will increase just outcomes and fairness of alleged sex offence investigations.

References

Australian Law Reform Commission. (2010). Family violence—a national legal response. Retrieved on 1 April 2013 from http://www.alrc.gov.au/26.%20Reporting,20%Prosecutionand%20Pretrialprocesses.

Baldwin, J. (1993). Police interviewing techniques: Establishing truth or proof? *British Journal of Criminology, 33*, 325–351.

Beech, A. R., Fisher, D. D., & Thornton, D. (2003). Risk assessment of sex offenders. *Professional Psychology: Research and Practice, 34*, 339–352.

Bell, B. E., & Loftus, E. F. (1988). Degree of detail of eyewitness testimony and mock juror judgments. *Journal of Applied Social Psychology, 18*, 1171–1192.

Bell, B. E., & Loftus, E. F. (1989). Trivial persuasion in the courtroom: The power of (a few) minor details. *Journal of Personality and Psychology, 56*, 669–679.

Bembibre, J., & Higueras, L. (2012). Comparative analysis of true or false statements with the source monitoring model and the cognitive interview: Special features of the false accusation of innocent people. *Psychology, Crime & Law, 18*, 913–928.

Benneworth, K. (2007). Just good friends: Managing the clash of discourses in police interviews with paedophiles. In J. Cotterill (Ed.), *The language of sexual crime* (pp. 42–62). Hampshire: Palgrave Macmillan.

Chaiken, S., & Eagly, A. H. (1976). Communication modality as a determinant of message persuasiveness and message comprehensibility. *Journal of Personality and Social Psychology, 34*, 605–614.

Chaiken, S., & Eagly, A. H. (1983). Communication modality as a determinant of persuasion: the role of communicator salience. *Journal of Personality and Social Psychology, 45*, 241–256.

Clarke, C., & Milne, R. (2001). *National evaluation of the PEACE investigative interviewing course.* Police Research Award Scheme: Report No. PRAS/149. Institute of Criminal Justice Studies, University of Portsmouth.

Clifford, B. R., & George, R. (1996). A field evaluation of training in three methods of witness/victim investigative interviewing. *Psychology, Crime & Law, 2*, 231–248.

Costin, F. (1985). Beliefs about rape and women's social roles. *Archives of Sexual Behavior, 14*, 319–325.

Criminal Justice Joint Inspection. (2009). *Report of a joint thematic review of victim and witness experiences in the criminal justice system.* London: Home Office.

Criminal Justice System. (2007). *Achieving best evidence in criminal proceedings: Guidance in interviewing victims and witnesses, and using special measures.* London: Home Office.

Daly, K., & Bouhours, B. (2010). Rape and attrition in the legal process: A comparative analysis of five countries. *Crime and Justice: An Annual Review of Research, 39*, 565–650.

Dando, C., Wilcock, R., & Milne, R. (2009). The cognitive interview: Novice police officers' witness/victim interviewing practices. *Psychology, Crime & Law, 15*, 679–696.

Deffenbacher, K. A., Bornstein, B. H., Penrod, S. D., & McGorty, E. K. (2004). A meta-analytic review of the effects of high stress on eyewitness memory. *Law and Human Behavior, 28*, 687–706.

Ebbinghaus, H. (1913). *Memory: A contribution to experimental psychology* (Trans: H. A. Ruger & C. E. Bussenius). New York: US Teachers College Press.

Ellison, L. (2007). Promoting effective case-building in rape cases: A comparative perspective. *Criminal Law Review, 9*, 691–708.

Ellison, L., & Munro, V. E. (2009a). Of 'normal sex' and 'real rape': Exploring the use of socio-sexual scripts in (mock) jury deliberation. *Social & Legal Studies, 18*, 291–312.

Ellison, L., & Munro, V. E. (2009b). Reacting to rape: Exploring jurors' assessments of complainant credibility. *British Journal of Criminology, 49*, 202–219.

Estrich, S. (1987). *Real rape.* Cambridge: Harvard University Press.

Evans, K. (1995). *Advocacy in court: A beginner's guide* (2nd ed.). London: Blackstone.

Fisher, R. P., & Geiselman, R. E. (1992). *Memory enhancing techniques for investigative interviewing: the cognitive interview.* Springfield: Thomas.

Fisher, R. P., Mello, E. W., & McCauley, M. R. (1999). Are jurors' perceptions of eyewitness credibility affected by the cognitive interview? *Psychology, Crime & Law, 5,* 167–176.

Frohmann, L., & Mertz, E. (1994). Legal reform and social construction: Violence, gender and law. *Law and Social Inquiry, 19,* 829–851.

Gabbert, F., Memon, A., & Allen, K. (2003). Memory conformity: Disentangling the steps toward influence during a discussion. *Applied Cognitive Psychology, 17,* 533–543.

Geiselman, R. E., Fisher, R. P., Firstenberg, I., Hutton, L. A., Sullivan, S. J., Avetissian, I. V., & Prosk, A. L. (1984). Enhancement of eyewitness memory: An empirical evaluation of the cognitive interview. *Journal of Police Science & Administration, 12,* 74–80.

Griffiths, A., Milne, B., & Cherryman, J. (2011). A question of control? The formulation of suspect and witness interview question strategies by advanced interviewers. *International Journal of Police Science & Management, 13,* 255–267.

Gudjonsson, G. H. (2003). *The psychology of interrogations and confessions: A handbook.* Chichester: Wiley.

Gudjonsson, G. H., & Petursson, H. (1991). Custodial interrogation: Why do suspects confess and how does it relate to their crime, attitude and personality? *Personality and Individual Differences, 12,* 295–306.

Hamlyn, B., Phelps, A., Turtle, J., & Sattar, G. (2004). *Are special measures working? Evidence from surveys of vulnerable and intimidated witnesses.* London: Home Office.

Holmberg, U., & Christianson, S. (2002). Murderers' and sexual offenders' experiences of police interviews and their inclination to admit or deny crimes. *Behavioral Sciences and the Law, 20,* 31–45.

Hunt, L., & Bull, R. (2012). Differentiating genuine and false rape allegations: A model to aid rape investigations. *Psychiatry, Psychology and Law, 19,* 682–691.

Hutcheson, G. D., Baxter, J. S., Telfer, K., & Warden, D. (1995). Child witness statement quality: Question type and errors of omission. *Law and Human Behavior, 19,* 631–648.

Jordan, J. (2001). Worlds apart? Women, rape and the police reporting process. *British Journal of Criminology, 41,* 679–706.

Kalven, H., & Zeisel, H. (1966). *The American Jury.* Boston: Little, Brown and Company.

Kebbell, M. R., & Wagstaff, G. F. (1998). Hypnotic interviewing: The best way to interview eyewitnesses? *Behavioral Sciences and the Law, 16,* 115–129.

Kebbell, M. R., & Wagstaff, G. F. (1999). *Face value? Evaluating the accuracy of eyewitness information.* London, Home Office.

Kebbell, M. R., & Westera, N. J. (2011). Promoting pre-recorded complainant evidence in rape trials: Psychological and practice perspectives. *Criminal Law Journal, 35,* 376–385.

Kebbell, M. R., Hurren, E., & Mazerolle, P. (2006). Sex offenders' perceptions of police interviewing: Implications for improving the interviewing effectiveness. *The Canadian Journal of Police and Security Services, 4,* 67–75.

Kebbell, M. R., O'Kelly, C. M. E., & Gilchrist, E. L. (2007). Rape victims' experiences of giving evidence in English Courts: A survey. *Psychiatry, Psychology and Law, 14,* 111–119.

Kebbell, M. R., Allison, L. J., Hurren, E. J., & Mazerolle, P. (2010). How do sex offenders think police should interview to elicit confessions from sex offenders? *Psychology, Crime & Law, 16,* 567–584.

Kebbell, M., Porter, L., & Milne, R. (2012). Interviewing suspected sex offenders: Confession, denial and behavioural themes. Unpublished Manuscript, Griffith University, Australia.

Köhnken, G. (1995). Interviewing adults. In R. Bull & D. Carson (Eds.), *Handbook of psychology in legal contexts* (pp. 215–233). New York: Wiley.

Köhnken, G., Thurer, C., & Zoberbier, D. (1994). The cognitive interview: Are interviewers' memories enhanced, too? *Applied Cognitive Psychology, 8,* 13–24.

Köhnken, G., Milne, R., Memon, A., & Bull, R. (1999). The cognitive interview: A meta-analysis. *Psychology, Crime & Law, 5,* 3–27.

Konradi, A. (1999). I don't have to be afraid of you: Rape survivors' emotion management in court. *Symbolic Interaction, 22,* 45–77.

Lamb, M. E., Orbach, Y., Sternberg, K. J., Hershkowitz, I., & Horowitz, D. (2000). Accuracy of investigators' verbatim notes of their forensic interviews with alleged child abuse victims. *Law and Human Behavior, 24,* 699–708.

Lees, S. (2002). *Carnal knowledge: Rape on trial* (2nd ed.). London: The Women's Press.

Lind, E. A., Erickson, B. E., Conley, J., & O'Barr, W. M. (1978). Social attributions and conversation style in trial testimony. *Journal of Personality and Social Psychology, 36,* 1558–1567.

Loftus, E. F., & Palmer, J. C. (1974). Reconstruction of automobile destruction: An example of the interaction between language and memory. *Journal of Verbal Learning and Verbal Behavior, 13,* 585–589.

Loftus, E. F., & Zanni, G. (1975). Eyewitness testimony: The influence of the wording of a question. *Bulletin of the Psychonomic Society, 5,* 86–88.

Loftus, E. F., Altman, D., & Gebelle, R. (1975). Effects of questioning upon a witness' later recollections. *Journal of Police Science & Administration, 3,* 162–165.

Mahoney, R., McDonald, E., Optican, S., & Tinsley, Y. (2007). *The Evidence Act 2006: Act and analysis.* Wellington: Brookers.

McDonald, E., & Tinsley, Y. (2012). *From "real rape" to real justice: Prosecuting rape in New Zealand.* Wellington: Victoria University Press.

McMillan, L., & Thomas, M. (2009). Police interviews of rape victims: Tensions and contradictions. In M. Horvath & J. Brown (Eds.), *Rape: Challenging contemporary thinking* (pp. 255–280). Devon: Willan.

Meissner, C. A., & Kassin, S. M. (2002). "He's guilty!": Investigator bias in judgments of truth and deception. *Law and Human Behavior, 26,* 469–480.

Memon, A., Meissner, C. A., & Fraser, J. (2010). The cognitive interview: A meta-analytic review and study space analysis of the past 25 years. *Psychology, Public Policy and Law, 16,* 340–372.

Milne, R., & Bull, R. (1999). *Investigative interviewing: psychology and practice.* Chichester: Wiley.

Moston, S., Stephenson, G. M., & Williamson, T. (1992). The effects of case charateristics on suspect behaviour during police questioning. *British Journal of Criminology, 32,* 23–40.

New Zealand Police. (2009). *Witness Guide.* Wellington.

Oxburgh, G. E., & Ost, J. (2011). The use and efficacy of empathy in police interviews with suspects of sexual offences. *Journal of Investigative Psychology and Offender Profiling, 8,* 178–188.

Patterson, D. (2011). The impact of detectives' manner of questioning on rape victims' disclosure. *Violence Against Women, 17,* 1349–1373.

Poole, D. A., & White, L. T. (1991). Effects of question repetition on the eyewitness testimony of children and adults. *Developmental Psychology, 27,* 975–986.

Powell, M. B., & Wright, R. (2009). Professionals' perceptions of electronically recorded interviews with vulnerable witnesses. *Journal of the Institute of Criminology, 21,* 205–218.

Powell, M. B., Fisher, R. P., & Wright, R. (2005). Investigative interviewing. In N. Brewer & K. Williams (Eds.), *Psychology and law: An empirical perspective* (pp. 11–42). New York: Guilford.

Quinn, J. F., Forsyth, C. J., & Mullen-Quinn, C. (2004). Societal reaction to sex offenders: A review of the origins and results of the myths surrounding their crimes and treatment amenability. *Deviant Behavior, 25,* 215–232.

Read, J. D., & Connolly, A. (2007). The effects of delay on long-term memory for witnessed events. In M. P. Toglia, J. D. Read, D. R Ross, & R. C. L. Lindsay (Eds.), *Handbook of eyewitness psychology: Volume I Memory for events* (pp. 117–155). New York: Lawrence Erlbaum Associates.

Read, J. M., & Powell, M. B. (2011). Investigative interviewing of child sex offender suspects: Strategies to assist the application of a narrative framework. *Journal of Investigative Psychology and Offender Profiling, 8,* 163–177.

Read, J. M., Powell, M. B., Kebbell, M. R., & Milne, R. (2009). Investigative interviewing of suspected sex offenders: A review of what constitues best practice. *International Journal of Police Science & Management, 11,* 442–459.

Rock, F. (2001). The genesis of a witness statement. *Forensic Linguistics, 8,* 44–72.

Rubin, D. C., & Wenzel, A. E. (1996). One hundred years of forgetting: A quantitative description of retention. *Psychological Review, 103,* 734–760.

Schuller, R. A., McKimmie, B. M., Masser, B. M., & Klippenstine, M. A. (2010). Judgments of sexual assault: the impact of complainant emotional demeanor, gender, and victim stereotypes. *New Criminal Law Review, 13,* 759–780.

Shepherd, E. (2007). *Investigative interviewing: The conversation management approach.* Oxford: Oxford University Press.

Snow, P. C., Powell, M. B., & Murfett, R. (2009). Getting the story from child witnesses: Exploring the application of a story grammar framework. *Psychology, Crime & Law, 15,* 555–568.

Stern, V. (2010). *The Stern review.* London: Home Office.

Tempkin, J., & Krahé, B. (2008). *Sexual assault and the justice gap: A question of attitude.* Portland: Hart.

Tidmarsh, P., Powell, M., & Darwinkel, E. (2012). 'Whole story'; a new framework for conducting investigative interviews about sexual assault. *Investigative Interviewing: Research & Practice, 4,* 33–44.

Tulving, E. (1974). Cue-dependent forgetting. *American Scientist, 62,* 74–78.

Tulving, E., & Thomson, D. M. (1973). Encoding specificity and retrieval processes in episodic memory. *Psychological Review, 80,* 352–373.

Ward, T., Hudson, S. M., Johnston, L, & Marshall, W. L. (1997). Cognitive distortions in sex offenders: An integrative review. *Clinical Psychology Review, 17,* 479–507.

Westera, N., Kebbell, M. R., & Milne, R. (2011). Interviewing rape complainants: Police officers' perceptions of interview format and quality of evidence. *Applied Cognitive Psychology, 25,* 917–926.

Westera, N., Kebbell, M., & Milne, B. (2013a). It is better, but does it look better? Prosecutor perceptions of using rape complainant investigative interviews as evidence. *Psychology, Crime & Law, 19,* 595–610.

Westera, N., Kebbell, M., & Milne, B. (2013b). Losing two thirds of the story: A comparison of the video recorded police interview and live evidence of rape complainants. *Criminal Law Review, 4,* 290–308.

Chapter 2
Psychological Processes Underlying True and False Confessions

Kate A. Houston, Christian A. Meissner and Jacqueline R. Evans

Overview

Chris Ochoa was told he would receive the death penalty for the crimes of which he was accused, but that if he confessed he would live. Eleven and a half years later, DNA testing exonerated Ochoa of any connection to the crimes for which he was imprisoned. Keith Brown was charged with the sexual assault of a woman and her 9-year-old daughter after falsely confessing due to high levels of pressure exerted by investigators. Brown served 4 years of a 35 -year sentence before he was exonerated via DNA testing. Finally, Nathaniel Hatchett falsely confessed to rape and robbery, serving 10 years in prison before he was exonerated due to DNA testing. Nathaniel was told that if he cooperated (and confessed) he would be allowed to go home. Chris Ochoa, Keith Brown, Nathaniel Hatchett; these three men are but a sample of the growing problem of false confessions within the legal system and together they served 25.5 years in prison as innocent men (The Innocence Project 2010).

There is a substantial need to determine the mechanisms under which an individual may be enticed to falsely confess to a crime that he or she did not commit. In an effort to address these questions, previous research has investigated a variety of situational and dispositional factors under which a false confession may occur. For example, research has demonstrated that certain police interrogation techniques have the potential to elicit false confessions (Meissner et al. 2012), and that being innocent can actually place interviewees at risk in interrogation settings (Kassin 2005). Furthermore, it has been shown that certain individual difference factors

K. A. Houston (✉)
University of Texas at El Paso, El Paso, Texas, USA
e-mail: khouston@utep.edu

C. A. Meissner
Iowa State University, Ames, Iowa, USA
e-mail: cmeissner@iastate.edu

J. R. Evans
Florida International University, Miami, Florida, USA
e-mail: jacevans@fiu.edu

R. Bull (ed.), *Investigative Interviewing,* DOI 10.1007/978-1-4614-9642-7_2,
© Springer Science+Business Media New York 2014

such as adolescence or mental retardation may place interviewees at risk for false confessions (Drizin and Leo 2004; Owen-Kostelnik et al. 2006). There are many excellent reviews of the false confession literature (e.g., Drizen and Leo 2004; Kassin et al. 2010; Lassiter and Meissner 2010; Leo 2008), and we encourage interested readers to access these for further details. To date, many of the recommendations for preventing false confessions in the USA have focused on identifying and discouraging interrogation approaches that may lead to false confessions, and advocate for the requirement of videotaping interrogations to provide courts with an objective record of the approaches used.

Over the past few years, researchers have also called for a more positive approach where the aim is to offer scientifically based techniques that might improve the diagnostic value of confessions (e.g., Evans et al. 2012; Meissner et al. 2010a). To this end, our laboratory has conducted a number of studies designed to assess the effectiveness of various interrogative approaches on confession likelihood (Horgan et al. 2012; Narchet et al. 2011; Russano et al. 2005a). These experimental studies used a paradigm designed to model the psychological processes experienced by a suspect (Russano et al. 2005a), and aimed to identify interrogative approaches that would elicit the greatest likelihood of true confessions from guilty individuals while limiting the likelihood of false confessions from innocent individuals. Further, our research has sought to better understand the psychological processes that might distinguish true and false confessions. Various psychological or decision-making models have been proposed to account for the role of social, cognitive, and affective factors in confession provision; however, little empirical data have been generated to assess the validity of the proposed theories or their relation to current interrogative practices (cf. Madon et al. 2013; Narchet et al. 2011).

The current chapter will provide a brief review of the relevant theoretical approaches to understanding confessions and describe the variety of internal and external pressures that individuals may experience in the interrogation process. We consider decision-making approaches that focus on the consequences of confession as a key motivator (Hilgendorf and Irving 1981), as well as the role of emotional or affective responses resulting from the interrogative process (Jayne 1986; Madon et al. 2013). We also assess the potential influence of internal experiences of guilt, remorse, and accountability, which may lead a suspect towards a "need to confess" (Berggren 1975; Reik 1959), and the influence of external social pressures to comply with the demands of an interrogator (Davis and O'Donohue 2004). Finally, we discuss the framework offered by Gudjonsson (2003) that brings together these and other motivational factors.

After considering the various theoretical accounts of confession, we discuss field studies that have begun to assess key psychological motivators for providing true versus false confessions (Sigursdon and Gudjonsson 1996; Redlich et al. 2011). We then present a meta-analysis of the various social, cognitive, and affective factors leading to confession across six experimental laboratory studies we have conducted using the Russano et al. (2005a) paradigm, contrasting our laboratory findings with those of prior studies. We synthesize this research by proposing a process model, highlighting key differences in the psychological states that may lead to true and false confessions. Our thesis is that true and false confessions may be distinguished by several key psychological factors, and that an understanding of such factors can lead to the development of diagnostic interrogative approaches. Specifically, we propose that guilty individuals can be driven to confess based upon their perceptions of the evidence against them and certain internalized feelings of guilt, accountability, and responsibility for their actions. In contrast, we propose that false confessions are driven by innocent suspects' perceptions of the potential consequences of confessing and the social pressures placed upon them to comply with an interrogator's request for a confession.

Research on True and False Confessions

The false confession phenomenon has generally been studied in two domains: in the field via either observations of law enforcement interrogations or surveys of convicted felons, or in the laboratory. Both field and laboratory work have advantages and drawbacks (Meissner et al. 2010b). Field research, while high in external validity (the degree to which the parameters of a study correspond to the relevant context) has a weakness in the lack of ground truth that would support internal validity of the findings. Without knowledge of whether a suspect is factually innocent or guilty, or whether the prisoner who claims to have made a false confession actually did so (see Gudjonsson 2010), findings from the field will always require some form of validation in alternative contexts. The advantage of conducting experimental research in the laboratory, in contrast, is principally high internal validity resulting from control over the study context and knowledge of ground truth (Meissner et al. 2010b). Experimental laboratory research, however, generally lacks external validity, and researchers must seek to induce some degree of psychological realism in the laboratory if they wish to generalize their findings. Ultimately, the absence of a perfect scientific methodology leads researchers to seek convergent validity from findings across multiple contexts and approaches.

The classic experimental paradigm used to study false confessions was pioneered by Kassin and Keichel (1996) in their well-known "ALT-key paradigm". In this novel experiment, Kassin and Keichel asked college students to complete a typing task in pairs. Unbeknownst to the participant who was given the role of the typist, the other participant, whose role it was to read out a list of letters, was a confederate to the experiment. The researchers explained that due to a glitch in the computer program participants should refrain from pressing the ALT key during the task, as doing so would crash the computer and could lead to the loss of all data. Although none of the students hit the ALT key, the computer would always crash during the experimental session and the typist would subsequently be accused of pressing the ALT key. For half of the participants in this study, the confederate would claim to have seen the typist press the ALT key just before the computer crashed, while for the remaining half the confederate would claim not to have seen anything relevant. Following several direct accusations made by the researcher, participants were asked to sign a piece of paper stating that they were responsible for pressing the ALT key and causing the computer to crash. An overwhelming 69 % of participants signed this "false confession" statement. Furthermore, participants were significantly more likely to provide a false confession when the interrogation technique of the other participant presenting false incriminating evidence was used.

Within the experimental literature, there have been numerous replications of the Kassin and Keichel (1996) paradigm and findings. For example, researchers have demonstrated that when confronted with false evidence of the misdeed, by way of a "witness", participants will sign a false confession even when doing so results in a financial penalty or having to return to the laboratory for 10 hours (Horselenberg et al. 2006; Redlich and Goodman 2003). Redlich and Goodman (2003) also found that younger participants were more likely to sign a false confession for pressing the ALT key. Klaver et al. (2008), on the other hand, investigated whether cultural and personality differences may influence the likelihood of a false confession. They found that having a compliant personality significantly increased the risk of false confession, as did the use of minimization interrogation techniques. Although Kassin and Keichel's ALT-key paradigm has been highly successful at allowing researchers to understand the false confession phenomenon, it also has certain limitations. For example, all of the participants are factually innocent—that is, none have pressed the ALT key, accidently or otherwise. Thus, the paradigm can only provide an assessment of factors that lead innocent (but not guilty) participants to provide a confession (e.g., Schacter 2003). Further, while the "crime" in the Kassin and Keichel paradigm is highly plausible—it is easy to imagine that one may accidentally have pressed the ALT key—it lacks ecological validity in that crimes are generally committed with both volition and a memory trace for the act (with the possible exception of cases involving psychological illness and/or pathology).

To address these shortcomings, Russano et al. (2005a) created a new experimental procedure for studying interrogations. They attempted to navigate the ethical challenges involved in studying confessions in the laboratory while preserving high psychological realism and successfully transposing key psychological processes believed to operate in the decision to confess. In their "cheating paradigm", they had participants enter the laboratory believing they were taking part in a study assessing the problem solving performance of individuals and teams. To that end, they and a partner would each complete a series of problems: for some of these problems, they would work together to reach an answer, while for the remaining problems, they would work individually and not seek assistance from their partner. The second participant in this paradigm, however, was a confederate who would either ask the (real) participant for the answer to one of the individual questions (guilty condition) or simply complete the problems on their own without asking for help (innocent condition). Upon completing the problem-solving tasks, the experimenter would reenter the room to collect and evaluate their responses. In each case, however, when the experimenter reentered the room he/she would claim that a problem occurred such that he/she needed to speak with each of the participants separately. Following a brief delay, in which the participant is isolated, the experimenter rejoins the participant and begins an interrogative process that accuses the participant of sharing answers and breaking the rules of the experiment. In their initial study, Russano et al. assessed the influence of direct offers of leniency (a "deal") and implications of leniency (minimization).

It is important to note that half of the participants were factually guilty of sharing answers and half were not, therefore, the Russano et al. paradigm afforded the first opportunity to assess the underlying mechanisms of true and false confessions from the same sample. In this way, this paradigm investigated the diagnosticity of confession evidence gained under different interrogation techniques. When participants were offered both the deal and the minimization tactics, 87 % of those who were guilty truthfully confessed and 43 % of those who were innocent falsely confessed (Russano et al. 2005a). When comparing these findings to the condition where no deal and no minimization techniques were used, truthful confessions drop from 87 to 46 % and only 6 % of innocent participants falsely confessed (Russano et al. 2005a).

Further iterations of the Russano et al. paradigm within our laboratory have evaluated a number of other aspects relating to the interrogative context. For example, Narchet et al. (2011) examined the influence of investigator biases on the likelihood of false-confession provision, finding that investigators who believed the participant to be guilty, employed more aggressive and manipulative tactics than the interviewers who believed the participant to be innocent, which was associated with a higher likelihood of false confessions from innocent participants. Horgan et al. (2012) investigated perceptions of the influence that certain interrogation techniques have on confession likelihood, finding that while participants were able to recognize that certain interrogation techniques were designed to manipulate individuals into confessing, they were not able to recognize that the techniques would increase their own false confession likelihood. Horgan et al. (2012) also found that manipulating the consequences of confessing significantly increased the likelihood of an innocent participant falsely confessing and significantly reduced the likelihood of a guilty participant confessing. Finally, Meissner, Russano, Rigoni, and Horgan (2011) conducted two experiments to compare the diagnosticity of confession evidence gained either via accusatorial interrogation techniques (which involve a combination of minimization and maximization approaches to interrogation), or information-gathering approaches (which involve a rapport-based approach to interrogation utilizing positive confrontation and elicitation strategies). Meissner et al. (2011) found that the diagnosticity of confession evidence was highest in the information-gathering conditions—in other words, false confessions were the lowest and true confessions were the highest when participants were interviewed with information-gathering approaches (see Meissner et al. 2012). The Russano et al. paradigm has proved useful for simulating the interrogative context and the generation of true and false confessions in a controlled laboratory setting. As will be discussed below, the paradigm also affords an opportunity to understand the psychological processes that underlie decisions to (truthfully or falsely) confess.

Theories of Confession

A variety of theories have been proposed to account for why an individual may confess (see Gudjonsson 2003). Some theories are based upon internal accountability models (e.g., Reik 1959) while others take into consideration external situational factors that may influence the decision process of the interviewee (e.g., Gudjonsson 2003; Hilgendorf and Irving 1981). Unfortunately, existing theories generally fail to distinguish between processes that may lead to true versus false confessions, and little empirical data have been collected to offer validation or refinement of these accounts.

Internal Accountability Models of Confession

Perhaps the first and most controversial model of confession, proposed by Reik (1959), suggests that when one has transgressed against a societal or moral norm, a deep-seated internal feeling of guilt is experienced. This guilt is believed to lead to high levels of anxiety and discomfort in transgressors, resulting in their seeking an authority figure to whom they can confess, thereby alleviating the guilt (Gudjonsson 2003). This theory is based in part on the work of Freud (1916), and suggests a nonconscious motivation may be responsible for seeking resolution of the guilt and anxiety that is experienced. Although the model has been viewed as controversial, there is good reason to believe that internal accountability mechanisms may underlie truthful confessions from guilty individuals. For example, Horgan et al. (2012), Narchet et al. (2011), Redlich et al. (2011), and Sigurdsson and Gudjonsson (1996), have all found evidence, either in the laboratory or in the field, for the role of guilt or remorse in the provision of a true confession.

Decision-Making Models of Confession

Decision-making models, such as that proposed by Hilgendorf and Irving (1981), argue that interviewees calculate a cost-benefit ratio when determining whether or not to confess. In an interrogation context, suspects are believed to consider the possible courses of action currently available to them, the proximate and distal benefits and costs associated with such actions, and the probabilities associated with such benefits and costs. With this information, suspects could determine the utility of each action and generate a confession decision based upon this information, selecting the action that leads to highest levels of gains or utility value (Gudjonsson 2003). It is important to note here, however, that the weights assigned to this assessment involve the suspect's subjective perception of the situation—a perception that can be manipulated by an interrogator to increase the likelihood of a decision to confess. For instance, if the interviewee determines that confessing may increase the likelihood that he/she will not be prosecuted for the act, while not confessing would result in further investigation and prosecution, then a decision to confess may be more likely. Psychological manipulation of a suspect's perception of the evidence or the consequences associated with confession has been shown to influence the decision to confess in both guilty and innocent suspects (e.g., Horgan et al. 2012; Horselenberg et al. 2006; Russano et al. 2005a).

The Use of Anxiety and Social Pressure to Elicit a Confession

The desire to escape and/or terminate an uncomfortable situation is one that is played upon by some interrogation models (see Ofshe and Leo 1997 for a categorization of false confessions obtained via social pressure as stress compliant; see also Davis and O'Donohue 2004; Jayne 1986). One of the first to argue that stress and anxiety play a role in interrogation was Jayne (1986), who noted that anxiety and negative emotional states during interrogation are experienced by suspects when they are deceptive about their guilt. To that end, Jayne (1986) argued that any anxiety a suspect experiences should be increased by the interrogation tactics in order to increase the discomfort of being deceptive. A suspect's decision to confess is then associated with a reduction in the experience of negative emotions, such as anxiety and fear. Accusatorial approaches to interrogation rely upon this theory, often seeking to induce social pressure (and therein perceived anxiety) through repeated accusations of guilt and maximization of the perceived evidence against the suspect. While such approaches may lead to the elicitation of true confessions from some guilty individuals, a growing body of research suggests that such tactics may also induce false confessions from the innocent (see Meissner et al. 2012).

It may be useful to pause here and note an important distinction between models of anxiety and social pressure and models of internal accountability. While they may appear similar, a distinguishing characteristic involves the source of the psychological experience. Internal accountability models posit that guilty individuals will naturally experience feelings of remorse, guilt, and accountability for the misdeed; in contrast, anxiety and social pressure models suggest that interrogation tactics must be applied to induce stress and anxiety on the part of the suspect. In this way, the role of internal versus external motivations to confess may offer the potential to distinguish between the mechanisms leading to true versus false confessions, respectively (see Horgan et al. 2012; Narchet et al. 2011; Redlich et al. 2011; Sigurdsson and Gudjonsson 1996).

Cognitive Behavioral Model

A cognitive behavioral model was proposed by Gudjonsson (2003), which incorporates many of the theoretical perspectives discussed above. This model argues that the likelihood of confession is best understood as a relationship between the antecedents and consequences of providing a confession. For example, an antecedent to confession could involve social isolation due to confinement, emotional distress, and/or situational factors such as the presence or absence of a lawyer. Gudjonsson proposes that suspects will consider both the short-term and long-term consequences of such antecedents to inform their decision to confess. Consistent with other decision-making accounts (e.g., Hilgendorf and Irving 1981), a suspect's perceptions of these factors can be manipulated by the interrogator. The model includes a variety of psychological, criminological, and situational factors that may lead to confession, and affords certain predictions regarding factors that increase the likelihood of false confession.

Theory Testing: Empirical Assessments of True and False Confessions

Although psychological theories of confession, as described above, have been proposed over the years, little empirical data have been used to validate the psychological processes suggested as leading to confession. Two surveys of convicted felons, however, begin to distinguish between the motivations leading to true and false confessions. In the first study, Sigurdsson and Gudjonsson (1996) surveyed prisoners in Iceland using the Gudjonsson Confession Questionnaire (the GCQ) regarding self-reported motivations for any false confessions they admitted to giving, and compared these to their current offense, which they reported truthfully confessing to. These authors found that external mechanisms of perceived pressure to confess, intimidation by the interviewing officers, and fear of the consequences of not confessing were significantly higher for interrogations leading to false confessions. Alternatively, true confessions were more likely to result from internal pressures, such as confessing to relieve the distress and guilt feelings caused by the crime committed. Redlich et al. (2011) conducted a similar survey with American prisoners regarding the factors leading to true and false confessions using a revised form of the GCQ. Consistent with prior work, Redlich et al. found that when prisoners spoke of their false confessions they cited factors related to external pressures, such as social pressure by the interrogator to confess, as well as perceived short-term gains in confession (such as terminating the interrogation), and perceived leniency if they confessed. However, when these prisoners described interrogations leading to true confessions they were more likely to cite internal pressures, such as feelings of guilt, as well as perceptions of the evidence held against them and feelings that their involvement in the crime would inevitably be revealed.

As mentioned above, the drawback to field surveys such as those of Sigurdsson and Gudjonsson (1996) and Redlich et al. (2011), is that it is impossible to determine whether the false confessions reported actually occurred (Gudjonsson 2010). Thus, it is important to seek convergent validity for such findings by relying upon alternative methodologies, such as experimental laboratory studies. Over the past decade, our laboratory has engaged in studies seeking to understand the psychological mechanisms leading to true and false confessions. Since the introduction of the Russano et al. (2005a) paradigm, we have conducted five empirical studies assessing factors that may influence confessions (Horgan et al. 2012; Meissner et al. 2011; Narchet et al. 2011; Russano et al. 2005a, b). In addition to manipulating key facets of the interrogation context, we have also asked participants to complete a questionnaire that evaluates the psychological basis for their decision to confess (or not). Five key areas, relating to the theories described previously, have been explored in these studies, including participants' perceptions of: affective or anxiety-based responses to interrogation; the consequences associated with confessing (or not); the strength of the evidence (or proof) against them; feelings of guilt, shame, responsibility, or accountability; and the external, social pressures being placed upon them to provide a confession. Independently, data from these studies appear to support a pattern of findings similar to that of Sigurdsson and Gudjonsson (1996) and Redlich et al. (2011). For example, both Narchet et al. (2011) and Horgan et al. (2012) found evidence suggesting that true confessions were associated with internal motivations to resolve feelings of guilt, shame, or accountability, while false confessions were motivated by external, social pressures being placed upon the participants in the interrogative context.

In the next section, we present a meta-analysis assessing the associations between these five factors and the likelihood of true and false confessions across all six studies. Our interest is to determine whether these laboratory studies might replicate the findings of prior field surveys, involving prisoner samples and whether unique patterns might emerge that distinguish the motivations associated with true versus false confessions. Our hypothesis is that, consistent with prior research, external social pressures will be associated with false confessions while internal motivations to resolve feelings of guilt, shame, or responsibility will be associated with true confessions. In contrast, we also expect that both true and false confessors will be influenced by their perceptions of the consequences associated with the decision to confess (or not). Finally, perceptions regarding the strength of evidence or proof against the participant (suspect) are expected to influence true confessions. To the extent that presentation of evidence is manipulated by the interrogator, it is also possible that innocent participants may rely upon their perceptions of proof in determining whether or not to provide a false confession.

Meta-Analysis of Psychological Factors Leading to True and False Confessions

Given the limited empirical data assessing current theories of confession and the need to evaluate psychological factors that might distinguish true and false confessions, the current meta-analysis sought to assess the association between key psychological factors self-reported by participants in our experimental laboratory studies and the likelihood of confession by innocent and guilty participants.

Method

Sample of Studies. Six experiments from five empirical studies conducted in our laboratory were included in this analysis (Horgan et al. 2012; Meissner et al. 2011; Narchet et al. 2011; Russano et al. 2005a, b). All studies employed the Russano et al. (2005a) paradigm in which participants were randomly assigned to a guilt or innocence condition—a total of 555 guilty participants and 519 innocent participants were included for this analysis. Each of the studies manipulated certain factors relevant to an interrogation, such as the interrogation approaches that were employed or the knowledge of the experimenter prior to interrogating the participant about the alleged act of cheating. In each study, participants were provided with a debriefing questionnaire assessing various factors that might influence their decision to confess (truthfully or falsely). Below we provide a brief description of each study.

Horgan et al. (2012): In this study, the authors explored the use of interrogation tactics that manipulate a suspect's perception of the consequences associated with confessing. Using the Russano et al. (2005a) paradigm, the study found techniques that psychologically manipulate the perception of consequences were significantly less diagnostic of guilt when compared with approaches that retain an accusatorial approach but do not influence participants' perception of consequences.

Meissner et al. (2011; unpublished manuscript): Across two experiments, the authors examined the use of information gathering and accusatorial methods using the Russano et al. (2005a) paradigm. Both experiments observed a consistent advantage for information-gathering approaches in yielding more diagnostic outcomes.

Narchet et al. (2011): This study assessed the influence of interrogators' perceptions of the guilt or innocence of the suspect on the likelihood of eliciting true versus false confessions. Using the Russano et al. (2005a) paradigm, the authors found that a belief in guilt led interrogators (experimenters) to elicit more false confessions and to engage in a process of behavioral confirmation. The study also demonstrated that information-gathering approaches significantly reduced the likelihood of false confessions.

Russano et al. (2005a): In the first study of its kind, the authors engaged participants in a problem-solving task and manipulated whether participants were induced to cheat on the task (or not) with a confederate. As mentioned above, participants were later confronted with the accusation of cheating and were interrogated using minimization techniques, an explicit deal of leniency, both minimization and a deal, or neither (the control condition). The ratio of true to false confessions decreased with the use of accusatorial methods.

Russano et al. (2005b; unpublished manuscript): Using the Russano et al. (2005a) paradigm, this study assessed the influence of presenting false evidence to guilty and innocent participants on the likelihood of eliciting true versus false confessions, respectively. Participants in the false evidence condition were shown a written confession statement that appeared to have been signed by a second participant (a confederate to the experiment) prior to being asked to sign their own confession statement. There was no significant effect of the presentation of this false evidence.

Psychological Predictor Variables. Five psychological factors were assessed across the studies. First, a combination of items relating to the degree of stress, worry, and anxiety experienced by participants were combined to yield a factor referred to as *affect*, reflecting participants' emotional reaction to the interrogation. Four items related to participants' perceptions of the consequences of confessing and not confessing were combined to yield a factor referred to as *consequences*. Two items relating to participants' perceptions regarding the strength of any evidence against them and proof of their guilt were combined to produce a factor referred to as *evidence*. Three items probed participants' feelings of guilt, remorse, and responsibility for the alleged act as a product of the interrogation—these items were combined to yield a factor referred to as *guilt*. Finally, participants were asked to

Table 2.1 Mean weighted effects sizes and 95 % confidence intervals for the association between psychological factors and the likelihood of false and true confessions

	False Confessions-Innocent				False Confessions-Innocent			
	N	K	r	95 % CI	N	k	r	95 % CI
Affect	371	5	0.046	(−0.058, 0.150)	407	5	0.115[a]	(0.016, 0.214)
Consequences	371	5	0.139[a]	(0.035, 0.243)	407	5	0.162[a]	(0.063, 0.261)
Evidence	371	5	0.071	(−0.033, 0.175)	407	5	0.140[a]	(0.041, 0.239)
Guilt	371	5	0.028	(−0.076, 0.132)	407	5	0.203[a]	(0.104, 0.302)
Pressure	371	5	0.295[a]	(0.207, 0.382)	555	6	0.064	(−0.021, 0.148)

[a] denotes a significant effect

rate the degree of pressure placed upon them by the interrogator and interrogation context to provide a confession, producing a factor referred to as *pressure*. Items varied slightly across studies, though all five factors were present in five of the six experiments assessed here. The original Russano et al. (2005a) study included only the items relating to *pressure*.

Estimate of Effect Size and Meta-Analytic Approach. Our primary measure of effect size was Fisher's Z_r, calculated as a measure of association between each of the key psychological factors (described above) and the likelihood of true and false confession, respectively. This effect size was calculated by creating a path model in each study that controlled the direct and indirect effects of the study manipulations while also estimating the correlations among the psychological process predictors. Fisher's Z_r was then calculated based upon the critical ratio test for the direct effect of each psychological process predictor on true and false confession samples independently. Our meta-analysis involved estimating the mean weighted effect size for each psychological predictor across the sample of experimental laboratory studies using a fixed effects model (Hedges and Olkin 1985; Johnson et al. 1995). Mean weighted effects sizes were then back transformed into r coefficients to facilitate interpretation.

Results

Table 2.1 provides the mean weighted effect sizes and 95 % confidence intervals calculated for the association between each of the psychological process factors and the likelihood of true and false confessions, respectively. Positive values indicate an increased likelihood of confession being associated with an increase in the psychological response. Below we discuss the pattern of findings for true and false confessions, and we describe the robustness of the findings by presenting a fail-safe N calculation for all significant effects.

False Confessions. Across our sample of experimental laboratory studies, false confessions were associated with participants' considerations of the consequences associated with confessing and with their perceptions of the external social pressures being placed upon them by the interrogator and the interrogative context. The influence of *consequences* was small, accounting for only 2 % of the variance in false confessions, and appeared potentially unstable with a $N_{FS} = 4$. In contrast, the influence of perceived *pressure* was rather robust ($N_{FS} = 60$) and accounted for nearly 9 % of the variance in false confessions. The role of external social pressure and perceptions of the consequences associated with confession are rather consistent with the literature on false confessions in general (cf. Gudjonsson and Kassin 2004; Kassin et al. 2010; Lassiter and Meissner 2010) and with prior surveys regarding psychological factors associated with false confessions (Redlich et al. 2011; Sigurdsson and Gudjonsson 1996). The psychological factors of *affect*, *evidence*, and *guilt* proved nonsignificant predictors of false confessions across studies.

True Confessions. Much like their innocent counterparts, guilty participants also showed a significant association between consideration of the *consequences* associated with confession and the likelihood of providing a true confession. This effect accounted for nearly 3 % of the variance and appeared somewhat robust ($N_{FS} = 8$) given the small sample of studies here. Beyond this effect, however, a distinct pattern emerged for true confessions suggesting that different psychological mechanisms may be associated with decisions by guilty compared to innocent participants. Participants' emotional responses to the interrogation (*affect*) were significantly associated with true confessions, though this small effect accounted for only 1 % of the variance and was quite unstable ($N_{FS} = 1$). Although we note that self-report assessments of affective responses can be problematic, recent research by Guyll et al. (in press) using physiological data is rather consistent with the role of affect in guilty participants. True confessions were also associated with perceptions of the *evidence* that may be available to investigators, a small effect accounting for 2 % of the variance with $N_{FS} = 7$. Finally, and most importantly, true confessions were significantly associated with participants' perceptions of responsibility, remorse, and *guilt*. This effect accounted for 4 % of the variance and appeared rather robust ($N_{FS} = 17$). Consideration of these factors, particularly the role of evidence and internal psychological motivations, is rather consistent with prior research (Redlich et al. 2011; Sigurdsson and Gudjonsson 1996) and suggests that certain factors may be useful for distinguishing true and false confessions.

Discussion: Theory and Application

The present meta-analysis sought to further clarify the underlying psychological processes that may increase the likelihood of true and false confessions elicited under the Russano et al. (2005a) paradigm. Using data collected in our laboratory over the last decade, we aimed to test predictions of the relevant theoretical models and, more specifically, the potential role of internal versus external motivations found in prior field surveys by Gudjonsson and Sigurdsson (1996) and Redlich et al. (2011). Consistent with the prior literature, our meta-analysis suggested that some of the factors to which guilty and innocent persons attend during interrogation overlap, such as a perception of the consequences of providing a confession. However, consistent with the surveys of Gudjonsson and Sigurdsson (1996) and Redlich et al. (2011) we also found that true and false confessions may be distinguished by the influence of internal versus external psychological motivations, respectively.

As discussed above, a variety of theories propose to account for the underlying psychological processes involved in decisions to confess (see Gudjonsson 2003). Although these theories are not mutually exclusive, little empirical data have sought to assess or validate the various accounts and few studies have proposed an explanatory framework for distinguishing between true and false confessions. Notwithstanding the limitations of our experimental laboratory approach, our meta-analytic findings provide convergent validity to prior field surveys and suggest that different psychological processes may mediate the decision to provide a true or false confession. As such, it will be important that theoretical frameworks seeking to explain confessions generated through an interrogative process consider the mechanisms that may influence the guilty and innocent, respectively.

Taken together, true confessions appear to be the product of individuals' feelings of guilt, remorse, and accountability for the misdeed, providing support to internal accountability models (Reik 1959). Guilty individuals also appear to consider the strength of the evidence against them and the potential consequences associated with confessing (or not)—providing support for decision-making models such as that proposed by Hilgendorf and Irving (1981) and Gudjonsson (2003). To a lesser extent, our data suggest that affective processes may also play a role in true confessions. Though we note that self-report data on emotional states can be unreliable, physiological approaches taken by Guyll et al. (in press) may provide a more fruitful line of inquiry for further validating such processes in guilty versus innocent individuals.

False confessions from the innocent appear to be principally based upon perceived external social pressures to confess that stem from the interrogation approaches employed, the persistent accusations, disbelief, and requests for compliance from the interrogator, or the interrogation context itself. Such findings provide further support to our understanding of the factors leading to false confessions (see Kassin et al. 2010; Lassiter and Meissner 2010; Ofshe and Leo 1997), and to the potentially detrimental effects of accusatorial approaches to interrogation (Meissner et al. 2012). Our data also suggest that innocent participants engage in a cost-benefit analysis when considering the potential consequences associated with providing a confession (or not). As discussed below, this suggests that interrogators may need to exercise caution when psychologically manipulating the consequences associated with confession (see also Horgan et al. 2012).

Overall, our findings lend support to the Cognitive Behavioral theory posited by Gudjonsson (2003), suggesting that the likelihood of confession is motivated by a relationship between factors, rather than any one factor in isolation. At the same time, the available empirical data also suggest that Gudjonsson's model could be updated to reflect further distinctions in the internal and external psychological factors that may influence the guilty and innocent, respectively. Further theoretical and empirical research appears warranted to afford a fuller understanding of the psychological and criminological mechanisms associated with confession (see also St-Yves and Deslauriers-Varin 2009).

While there exists some research on the correlates and causal factors of false confessions (see Kassin et al. 2010), less is known regarding the psychological mechanisms by which various interrogation practices exert their influence on suspect decisions to confess. In the USA, accusatorial interrogation techniques (broadly construed) seek to directly manipulate the external pressures placed upon the suspect as well as an individuals' perceptions of the consequences of complying (confessing) versus resisting the interrogation (Davis and O'Donohue 2004; Lassiter and Meissner 2010). In general, interrogators assume that by increasing the anxiety and social pressure placed upon a suspect and manipulating their perceptions of the likely consequences, individuals will more often comply with a request for confession/information, than resist (Jayne 1986). Research assessing the efficacy of these accusatorial techniques, however, suggests that they increase the likelihood of false confessions (Kassin et al. 2010; Lassiter and Meissner 2010; Meissner et al. 2012; Ofshe and Leo 1997), a pattern of data consistent with the role of external social pressure being associated with false confessions in the current meta-analysis. Alternative methods of interviewing, for example information-gathering approaches popular in countries such as the UK, Norway, Australia, and New Zealand, have proven effective at gaining truthful and complete accounts from suspects (and witnesses) when compared to standard US interview protocols (Evans et al. 2013; Meissner et al. 2012). While it is beyond the scope of this chapter to provide a comparative review of such methods (see Bull and Soukara 2010; Meissner et al. 2012), research in our laboratory suggests that information-gathering approaches may be effective principally because they highlight internal psychological mechanisms that promote true confessions while simultaneously reducing external social pressures associated with false confessions.

In closing, we propose that a strong theoretical understanding of the psychological mechanisms leading to true versus false confessions may offer insights into the development of interrogative approaches that prove useful for eliciting diagnostic confession evidence. We believe that such a process of "reverse engineering" could promote a positive perspective in the development of alternative approaches to interrogation that might replace methods which are detrimental to the collection of evidence despite their frequent use in certain countries (cf. Meissner et al. 2010a). Ultimately, we hope that the current discussion will encourage other social and behavioral scientists to join us in developing an ethical, evidence-based perspective on interrogation that ultimately replaces "art" with "science".

References

Berggren, E. (1975). *The psychology of confessions*. Leiden: E. J. Brill.

Bull, R. H., & Soukara, S. (2010). Four studies of what really happens in police interviews. In G. D. Lassiter & C. A. Meissner (Eds.), *Police interrogations and false confessions: Current research, practice, and policy recommendations*. (pp. 81–95). Washington, D.C.: American Psychological Association. doi: 10.1037/12085-000.

Davis, D., & O'Donohue, W. T. (2004). The road to perdition: "Extreme influence" tactics in the interrogation room. In W. T. O'Donohue & E. Levensky (Eds.), *Handbook of forensic psychology* (pp. 897–996). New York: Elsevier Academic Press.

Drizin, S. A., & Leo, R. A. (2004). The problem with false confessions in the post-DNA world. *North Carolina Law Review, 82,* 894–1007.

Evans, J. R., Houston, K. A., & Meissner, C. A. (2012). A positive, collaborative and theoretically-based approach to improving deception detection. *Journal of Applied Research in Memory and Cognition, 1,* 122–123. doi: 10.1016/j.jarmac.2012.02.004.

Evans, J. R., Meissner, C. A., Ross, A. B., Houston, K. A., Russano, M. B., & Horgan, A. J. (2013). The elicitation of guilty knowledge in human intelligence interrogations: A novel experimental paradigm. *Journal of Applied Research in Memory and Cognition, 2,* 83–88. doi: 10.10.16/j.jarmac.2013.03.002.

Freud, S. (1916). *Vorlesungen zur einführung in die psychoanalyse,* [Introductory lectures on psycho-analysis]. Leipzig/Vienna. Retrieved 14th May, 2013 from http://www.scribd.com/doc/31127286/Freud-Introductory-Lectures-on-Psycho-Analysis-1916–1917. Accessed 14th May 2013.

Gudjonsson, G. H. (2003). *The psychology of interrogations and confessions: A handbook.* Chichester: John Wiley & Sons Ltd.

Gudjonsson, G. H. (2010). The psychology of false confessions: A review of the current evidence. In G. D. Lassiter & C. A. Meissner (Eds.), *Police interrogations and false confessions: Current research, practice, and policy recommendations.* (pp. 31–47). Washington, D.C., USA: American Psychological Association. doi: 10.1037/12085-000.

Guyll, M., Madon, S., Yang, Y., Lannin, D., & Scherr, K., Greathouse, S. (in press). Innocence and resisting confession during interrogation: Effects of physiologic activity. *Law and Human Behavior.* doi: 10.1037/lhb0000044.

Hedges, L. V., & Olkin, I. (1985). *Statistical methods for meta-analysis.* San Diego: Academic Press.

Hilgendorf, E. L., & Irving, M. (1981). A decision-making model of confessions. In M. Lloyd-Bostock (Ed.), *Psychology in legal contexts: Applications and limitations* (pp. 67–84). London: MacMillan.

Horgan, A. J., Russano, M. B., Meissner, C. A., & Evans, J. R. (2012). Minimization and maximization techniques: Assessing the perceived consequences of confessing and confession diagnosticity. *Psychology, Crime & Law, 18,* 65–78. doi: 10.1080/1068316X.2011.561801.

Horselenberg, R., Merckelbach, H., Smeets, T., Franssens, D., Peters, G. Y., & Zeles, G. (2006). False confessions in the lab: Do plausibility and consequences matter? *Psychology, Crime and Law, 12,* 61–75. doi: 10.1080/10683410042000303076.

Jayne, B. C. (1986). The psychological principles of criminal interrogation. In F. E. Inbau, J. E. Reid, & J. P. Buckley (Eds.), *Criminal interrogation and confessions* (3rd ed., pp 327–347). Baltimore, MD: Williams & Wilkins.

Johnson, B. T., Mullen, B., & Salas, E. (1995). Comparison of three major meta-analytic approaches. *Journal of Applied Psychology, 80,* 94–106. doi: 10.1037/0021.9010.80.1.94.

Kassin, S. M. (2005). On the psychology of confessions: Does innocence put innocents at risk? *American Psychologist, 60,* 215–228. doi: 10.1037/0003-066X.60.3.215.

Kassin, S. M., & Kiechel, K. L. (1996). The social psychology of false confessions: Compliance, internalization and confabulation. *Psychological Science, 7,* 125–128. doi: 10.1111/j.1467-9280.1996.tb00344.x.

Kassin, S. M., & Gudjonsson, G. H. (2004). The psychology of confession evidence: A review of the literature and issues. *Psychological Science in the Public Interest, 5,* 35–69.

Kassin, S. M., Drizin, S., Grisso, T., Gudjonsson, G. H., Leo, R. A., & Redlich, A. D. (2010). Police-induced confessions: Risk factors and recommendations. *Law and Human Behavior, 34,* 3–38. doi: 10.1007/s10979-009-9188-6.

Klaver, J. R., Lee, Z., & Rose, V. G. (2008). Effects of personality, interrogation techniques and plausibility in an experimental false confession paradigm. *Legal and Criminological Psychology, 13,* 71–88.

Lassiter, G., & Meissner, C. A. (2010). *Police interrogations and false confessions: Current research, practice, and policy recommendations*. Washington, DC: American Psychological Association. doi: 10.1037/12085-000.

Leo, R. A. (2008). *Police interrogation and American justice*. Cambridge: Harvard University Press.

Madon, S., Yang, Y., Smalarz, L., Guyll, M., & Scherr, K. C. (2013). How factors present during the immediate interrogation situation produce short-sighted confession decisions. *Law and Human Behavior, 37*, 60–74. doi: 10.1037/lhb0000011.

Meissner, C. A., Hartwig, M., & Russano, M. B. (2010a). The need for a positive psychological approach and collaborative effort in improving practice in the interrogation room. *Law and Human Behavior, 34*, 43–45. doi: 10.1007/s10979-009-9205-9.

Meissner, C. A., Russano, M. B., & Narchet, F. M. (2010b). The importance of a laboratory science for improving the diagnostic value of confession evidence. In G. D. Lassiter & C. A. Meissner (Eds.), *Police interrogations and false confessions: Current research, practice and policy recommendations*. Washington, DC: American Psychological Association.

Meissner, C. A., Russano, M. B., Rigoni, M. E., & Horgan, A. J. (2011). Is it time for a revolution in the interrogation room? Empirically validating inquisitorial methods. Unpublished manuscript.

Meissner, C. A., Redlich, A. D., Bhatt. S., & Brandon, S. (2012). Interview and interrogation methods and their effects on true and false confessions. *Campbell Systematic Review, 2012:2013*, 4–52. doi: 10.4073/csr.2012.13.

Narchet, F. M., Meissner, C. A., & Russano, M. B. (2011). Modeling the influence of investigator bias on the elicitation of true and false confessions. *Law and Human Behavior, 35*, 452–465. doi: 10.1007/s10979-010-9257-x.

Ofshe, R. J., & Leo, R. A. (1997). The social psychology of police interrogation: The theory and classification of true and false confessions. *Studies in Law, Politics & Society, 16*, 189–251.

Owen-Kostelnik, J., Reppucci, N., & Meyer, J. R. (2006). Testimony and interrogation of minors: Assumptions about maturity and morality. *American Psychologist, 61*, 286–304. doi: 10.1037/0003-066X.61.4.286.

Redlich, A. D., & Goodman, G. S. (2003). Taking responsibility for an act not committed: The influence of age and suggestibility. *Law and Human Behavior, 27*, 141–156. doi: 10.1023/A:1022543012851.

Redlich, A. D., Kulish, R., & Steadman, H. J. (2011). Comparing true and false confessions among persons with serious mental illness. *Psychology, Public Policy, and Law, 17*, 394–418. doi: 10.1037/a0022918.

Reik, T. (1959). *The compulsion to confess: On the psychoanalysis of crime and punishment*. New York: Farrar, Straus and Cudahy.

Russano, M. B., Meissner, C. M., Narchet, F. M., & Kassin, S. M. (2005a). True and false confessions to an intentional act: A novel paradigm. *Psychological Science, 16*, 481–486. doi: 10.1007/BF01061711.

Russano, M. B., Narchet, F., & Meissner, C. A. (2005b). Investigating the effects of presenting false evidence on true and false confessions. Poster presented at the 2005 American Psychology-Law Society Conference, La Jolla, CA, USA.

Schacter, D. L. (2003). *How the mind forgets and remembers: The seven sins of memory*. London, UK: Souvenir Press LTD.

Sigurdsson, J. F., & Gudjonsson, G. H. (1996). The relationship between types of claimed false confession made and the reasons why suspects confess to the police according to the Gudjonsson Confession Questionnaire (GCQ). *Legal and Criminological Psychology, 1*, 259–269. doi: 10.1111/j.2044-8333.1996.tb00324.x.

St-Yves, M., & Deslauriers-Varin, N. (2009). The psychology of suspects' decision making during interrogation. In R. Bull, T. Valentine, & T. Williamson (Eds.), *Handbook of psychology of investigative interviewing: Current developments and future directions* (pp. 1–15). Chichester, UK: John Wiley.

The Innocence Project. (2010). *250 exonerated, too many wrongfully convicted: An innocence project report on the first 250 DNA exonerations in the U.S.* New York: Benjamin N. Cardozo School of Law, Yeshiva University.

Chapter 3
Cops and Kids in the Interrogation Room

Barry C. Feld

The US Supreme Court repeatedly has cautioned that juveniles may lack the ability to exercise *Miranda* rights or make voluntary statements, but it has not required special procedures to protect them (Haley v. Ohio 1948; Gallegos v. Colorado 1962; In re Gault 1967; Fare v. Michael C. 1979; Yarborough v. Alvarado 2004; J.D.B. v. N. Carolina 2011). Instead, it uses the adult legal standard—knowing, intelligent, and voluntary—to gauge juveniles' *Miranda* waivers (Fare v. Michael C. 1979). On the other hand, developmental psychologists question whether juveniles understand *Miranda* or are competent to exercise the rights. Younger adolescents may not understand *Miranda*'s words or the rights it conveys and may not be as able as adults to exercise the rights (Grisso 1980; Grisso et al. 2003). Most youths, 16 years of age and older, appear to understand *Miranda* on par with adults, although they lack mature judgment and may be more susceptible to adult authority influence (Grisso 1980, 1981; Feld 2013).

This chapter examines what happens when police interrogate older youths charged with felony offenses. Part I analyzes the law governing interrogation of juveniles and research on their competence to exercise the rights. Part II examines how police interrogate suspects and research on interrogation practices. Part III describes the study's data and methodology. Part IV reports how police questioned 307 delinquents 16 years of age or older whom prosecutors charged with felonies. It describes how police secure *Miranda* waivers, how they interrogated youths, and how juveniles responded.

Interrogating Juveniles: Legal Expectations and Developmental Psychology

The Supreme Court recognized that youthfulness, lengthy questioning, and absence of counsel or parents could render juveniles' statements involuntary (Haley v. Ohio 1948; Gallegos v. Colorado 1962). The Court in In re *Gault* (1967) granted

B. C. Feld (✉)
University of Minnesota Law School, Minneapolis, Minnesota, USA
e-mail: feldx001@umn.edu

R. Bull (ed.), *Investigative Interviewing,* DOI 10.1007/978-1-4614-9642-7_3,
© Springer Science+Business Media New York 2014

delinquents the privilege against self-incrimination, and reiterated concern about youths' vulnerability during questioning. Fare v. Michael C. (1979) used the adult "totality of the circumstances" test to evaluate juveniles' *Miranda* waivers. *Fare* denied that youths' developmental differences required additional procedural safeguards and demanded children to assert the rights clearly. J.D.B. v. N. Carolina (2011) ruled that age was an objective factor to consider in *Miranda*'s custody framework and concluded that police could gauge how a youth's age would affect feelings of liberty restraint.

Most states use the same *Miranda* framework for juveniles and adults and require only an understanding of the rights and not collateral consequences (Feld 2006a, b, 2013). Trial judges consider how offenders' age, education, I.Q., and prior police contacts, and the location, methods, and length of interrogation affected their *Miranda* waivers. About ten states require a parent to assist juveniles to invoke or waive *Miranda* (Larson 2003; Farber 2004; Drizin and Colgan 2004; Woolard et al. 2008).

Developmental psychologists distinguish between youths' cognitive ability and maturity of judgment. By mid-adolescence, most youths can distinguish right from wrong and possess cognitive abilities comparable with adults (Steinberg and Cauffman 1999; Scott and Steinberg 2008; Steinberg et al. 2009). However, the ability to make good choices under laboratory conditions differs from the ability to make adult-like decisions under stress and with incomplete information (Steinberg and Cauffman 1996; Spear 2000).

Since the mid-1990s, the MacArthur Network on Adolescent Development and Juvenile Justice has studied decision-making and adjudicative competence (Scott and Steinberg 2008). The research distinguishes between cognitive ability and mature judgment, self-control and ability to resist external influences (Scott and Steinberg 2008). Although most youths 16 years of age or older exhibit cognitive abilities comparable with adults, they do not develop adult-like self-control and mature judgment for several more years.

Differences in knowledge, attitude toward risk, impulse control, and appreciation of consequences contribute to youths' poorer decisions (Scott and Grisso 1997; Steinberg 2005; Scott and Steinberg 2008). Adolescents tend to underestimate risks, use a shorter frame, and focus on gains rather than losses (Furby and Beyth-Marom 1992; Grisso 2000). The widest divergence between juveniles' and adults' perceptions of and preference for risk occurs during mid-teens (Scott and Steinberg 2008). Neuroscientists attribute these differences to brain maturation and the increased ability of the prefrontal cortex (PFC) to perform executive functions and control impulses (Baird et al. 1999; Spear 2000; Dahl 2001; Gruber and Yurgelun-Todd 2006; Maroney 2009).

Despite these developmental differences, most states do not provide additional procedural safeguards, but use adult standards to gauge juveniles' *Miranda* waivers. Some youths may not understand the words of the *Miranda* warning (Rogers et al. 2007; Rogers et al. 2008a, b). Some concepts—the meaning of a *right*, the term *appointed* to obtain counsel, and *waive*—render *Miranda* incomprehensible to many juveniles (Goldstein and Goldstein 2010).

Grisso (1980, 1981; Grisso et al. 2003) reported that many youths do not adequately understand and cannot exercise *Miranda* rights. Although juveniles 16 years or older understood *Miranda* about as well as did adults, substantial minorities of both groups misunderstood some components (Grisso 1980). Other studies report similar age-related improvements in cognitive ability and *Miranda* comprehension (Viljoen and Roesch 2005; Viljoen et al. 2007; Kassin et al. 2010). Even youths who understand *Miranda* may not be able, as adults to exercise their rights. Juveniles do not fully appreciate the function or importance of their rights (Grisso 1980, 1981), and perceive them as a privilege that authorities allow, but may unilaterally withdraw (Grisso 2002).

To be competent to stand trial, a person must understand proceedings, make rational decisions, and assist counsel (Dusky v. United States 1960; Drope v. Missouri 1975). Development limitations impair youths in the same ways that mental illness leaves adults incompetent (Grisso et al. 2003; Scott and Grisso 2005; Redlich 2004). Many juveniles 14 years of age and younger may be as severely impaired as adults found incompetent to stand trial (Bonnie and Grisso 2000). Differences in maturity and judgment cause even nominally competent adolescents to make poorer decisions than young adults (Grisso et al. 2003; Scott and Grisso 2005). Compromised competence affects youths' ability to exercise *Miranda* rights.

Miranda characterized custodial interrogation as inherently compelling because a police-dominated environment created psychological pressures to comply. Children questioned by authority figures yield more easily to negative pressure (Gudjonsson 2003; Billings et al. 2007), and acquiesce more readily to suggestions during questioning than do adults (Ainsworth 1993; Bull and Corran 2003; Drizin and Leo 2004). Even older youths who understand *Miranda* may be more susceptible to power differentials and more prone to relinquish their rights.

Interrogation Practices and Empirical Assessments

Most police interrogators in the USA are trained in the Reid Method (Leo 2008). It teaches isolation and psychological manipulations—maximization and minimization techniques—to elicit confessions (Inbau et al. 2004). Police use negative incentives—confrontational tactics to scare or intimidate a suspect—and positive incentives—themes, scenarios, or sympathetic alternatives—to make it easier to confess (Kassin and McNall 1991; Ofshe and Leo 1997; Leo 2008). Maximization tactics "convey the interrogator's rock-solid belief that the suspect is guilty and that all denials will fail. Such tactics include making an accusation, overriding objections, and citing evidence, real or manufactured, to shift the suspect's mental statement from confident to hopeless" (Kassin et al. 2010, p. 12). Minimization techniques "provide the suspect with moral justification and face-saving excuses for having committed the crime in question. Using this approach, the interrogator offers sympathy and understanding; normalizes and minimizes the crime" (Kassin et al. 2010, p. 12). Reid training does not distinguish between youths and adults (Owen-Kostelnik et al.

2006; Meyer and Reppucci 2007), and teaches police to interrogate both similarly—
"principles discussed with respect to adult suspects are just as applicable for use with
younger ones" (Inbau et al. 2004, p. 298).

Interrogation in the UK is less confrontational and designed to elicit information
rather than to secure a confession (Milne and Bull 1999; Bull and Milne 2004; Pearse
and Gudjonsson 2003). In England and Wales, the Police and Criminal Evidence
Act (PACE 1984) has required police to record interrogations for nearly two decades
(Milne and Bull 1999; Bull and Soukara 2010). Police, psychologists, and lawyers developed an information-gathering method of interviewing that is less confrontational
than the Reid approach (Gudjonsson 2003; Milne and Bull 1999). The mnemonic
PEACE describes the five components of this interview approach—"Planning and
Preparation," "Engage and Explain," "Account," "Closure," and "Evaluate" (Milne
and Bull 1999). Minnesota interrogation practices reflect both Reid and PEACE
elements (Nelson 2006).

In the decades since *Miranda*, we have remarkably few studies of how police question people (Leo 2008). Post-*Miranda* research in the late-1960s evaluated whether
police warned suspects and how warnings affected rates of confessions (Wald et al.
1967; Neubauer 1974; Leo 1996a, c; Feld 2006a). In the mid-1990s, Richard Leo
(1996b, c) conducted the only field study of interrogation in the USA. Legal scholars
and criminologists have used indirect methods and studied tapes and transcripts of
interrogations (Feld 2006a, b, 2013; King and Snook 2009), or attended prosecutors'
charging sessions and interviewed police about interrogations (Cassell and Hayman
1996). In England and Wales, analyses of PACE recordings have generated a substantial body of empirical research (Gudjonsson 2003; Milne and Bull 1999; Bull
and Soukara 2010; Pearse and Gudjonsson 2003). Psychologist Saul Kassin and
associates have conducted laboratory research on interrogation for decades (Kassin
and Gudjonsson 2004; Kassin 2005; Kassin et al. 2010). Studies of false confessions provide another glimpse into how police interrogate suspects and highlight the
vulnerability of youths (Drizin and Leo 2004; Garrett 2011).

Methodology and Data

The Minnesota Supreme Court in State v. Scales (1994) required police to record
custodial interrogations of criminal suspects, including juveniles. County attorneys
in Minnesota's four largest counties—Anoka (suburban), Dakota (suburban), Hen-
nepin (Minneapolis), and Ramsey (St. Paul)—allowed me to search closed files of
16- and 17-year-old youths charged with a felony and to copy those in which police
interrogated or juveniles invoked *Miranda*. Delinquency trials of 16- and 17-year-old
youths charged with felony offenses are public proceedings (Minn. Stat. Ann. 2005).
Police conducted these interviews between 2003 and 2006. The four most populous
counties account for almost half (47.6 %) of the state's population and nearly half
(45.6 %) of the delinquency petitions filed. The two urban counties accounted for
somewhat more than half (53.4 %) the files. These files contained *Scales* interrogation tapes—i.e., recorded interrogation required by the Court in *State v. Scales*—or

transcripts, police reports, juvenile court records, and sentences. Court Orders authorized access to juvenile courts files, but included confidentiality stipulations to protect juveniles' identity and imposed methodological limitations.[1]

I adapted and expanded codebooks used in prior interrogation research (Wald et al. 1967; Leo 1996b; Pearse and Gudjonsson 2003).[2] I reviewed police reports to learn about the crime, the context of interrogation, and evidence police possessed prior to questioning. I coded each file to analyze where, when, and who was present at an interrogation, how police administered the *Miranda* warning, whether juveniles invoked or waived, whether officers used Reid Method maximization and minimization techniques, and how juveniles responded. There may be some sample selection bias because these are cases in which prosecutors charged serious delinquents and perhaps include a larger proportion of juveniles who waived *Miranda*.[3] Despite these caveats, the data comprise the largest number of felony interrogations in the USA. More than 150 police officers from more than 50 agencies conducted these interrogations. I did saturation interviews with police, prosecutors, defense lawyers, and juvenile court judges to elicit their views, learn from their experience, and buttress my findings.[4]

---

[1] I personally transcribed interrogation tapes and coded all of the files to address county attorneys and juvenile court judges' concerns about data confidentiality. Court-ordered confidentiality restrictions precluded use of multiple coders, so I could not obtain inter-rater reliability scores. Earlier studies of interrogation in the USA did not use multiple-coders or provide inter-rater reliability scores (Wald et al. 1967; Leo 1996b).

[2] Copies of the 180 variable codebook are available upon request.

[3] The sample includes only juveniles whom prosecutors charged with a felony and for whom an interrogation or invocation record exists. The four counties identified almost 1,400 youths 16 and 17 and charged with a felony, but only 307 that reported youths invoked or waived *Miranda*. Other evidence being equal, prosecutors are more likely to charge suspects who waive than those who invoke *Miranda* because they have plea bargain advantage. Police made these *Scales* recordings during custodial interrogation and the files do not include unrecorded, noncustodial interviews. I do not know how the felony cases that prosecutors charged and that contained transcripts differ from those in which juveniles invoked *Miranda* and police did not forward the cases, cases that prosecutors did not charge, or those that they charged, but which did not contain tapes or transcripts.

[4] I conducted structured, open-ended interviews with nineteen police officers, six juvenile prosecutors, nine juvenile defense lawyers, and five juvenile court judges from both urban and suburban counties. The police officers averaged 18.4 years of professional experience; the prosecutors averaged 14.5 years; the public defenders averaged 13.3 years; and the juvenile court judges, 16 years. Four of the five judges presided in urban county juvenile courts. Half of the prosecutors worked in the urban counties and the other half in the suburban counties. Two-thirds of the defense lawyers worked in the urban counties and one-third in the suburban counties. Seven police officers worked in suburban counties and twelve in urban counties. I interviewed sergeants, detectives or investigators, and school resource officers (SROs)—the ranks and specialties that conduct most custodial interrogations of juveniles. These recorded interviews lasted between 30 and 80 minutes, and averaged about 45 minutes. The interviews provide thick descriptions of the process. I purposively recruited justice system professionals to interview. I called juvenile court judges directly. I recruited prosecutors and defense attorneys through their juvenile division administrators who solicited volunteers. I recruited police in several ways. I contacted police juvenile division administrators who recruited juvenile officer volunteers to interview. In several departments, I used a snowball sampling technique—initial interviewees recruited other officers with relevant background and experience

Police Interrogation

This section examines what happens in the interrogation room. It examines characteristics of youths who waived or invoked *Miranda*. It analyzes how police secured *Miranda* waivers and questioned those youths who waived. It focuses on the length and outcomes of interrogations.

Sample Characteristics

Table 3.1 reports that males comprised the vast majority (89.3 %) of youths whom police questioned. Prosecutors charged about half (55.0 %) with property offenses—burglary, larceny, and auto-theft—and nearly one-third (31.6 %) with crimes against person—murder, armed robbery, aggravated assault, and criminal sexual conduct. They charged the remaining youths with drug crimes (6.2 %), firearm offenses (5.5 %), and other felonies (1.6 %). They charged about half (56.4 %) with one felony, an additional quarter (25.1 %) with two crimes, and the remainder with three or more. Prosecutors filed certification motions and juvenile court judges transferred some of the most serious offenders to criminal court.

Nearly one-third (30.6 %) of juveniles had no prior arrests. Police previously had taken more than one-third of these youths into custody for noncriminal status offenses (15.3 %) or misdemeanors (22.8 %). About one-third of these youths (35.1 %) had one or more prior felony arrests and more than half (57 %) had prior juvenile court referrals. Nearly one-third (29.9 %) were under court supervision—probation, placement, or parole status—when police interrogated them. About half of the youths were white (52.1 %) and the others (47.9 %) members of ethnic and racial minority groups—Black, Hispanic, Native American, and Asian. Black juveniles accounted for more than one-third (34.9 %) of the sample. The youths whom police interrogated included a larger proportion of males, more youths charged with property and violent crimes and with prior court referrals, and fewer charged with drug offenses than these counties' 16- and 17-year-old felony dockets (Feld and Schaefer 2010a, b).

Securing Miranda Waivers

Miranda requires officers to warn suspects whom they take into custody and interrogate to dispel the inherent coercion of isolation and questioning. Police had formally arrested the vast majority (86.6 %) of these juveniles prior to questioning, and made

---

from their own and other departments. In those instances, officers acted as referrals and intermediaries to other officers. I conducted saturation interviews until I reached a point of diminishing returns—no new data, themes, or conceptual relationships emerged.

Table 3.1 Characteristics of juveniles interrogated

Characteristics of juveniles interrogated	N	Percentage (%)
Gender		
Male	274	89.3
Female	33	10.7
Age		
16	171	55.7
17	132	43.0
18	4	1.3
Race		
White	160	52.1
Black	107	34.9
Asian	17	5.5
Hispanic	15	4.9
Native American	5	1.6
Offense		
Property[a]	169	55.0
Person[b]	97	31.6
Drugs[c]	19	6.2
Firearms[d]	17	5.5
Other[e]	5	1.6
Prior arrests		
None	94	30.6
Status	47	15.3
Misdemeanor	70	22.8
One felony	43	14.0
Two or more felonies	37	21.1
Prior juvenile court referrals		
None	126	43.0
One or more	167	57.0
Court status at time of interrogation		
None	142	46.3
Prior supervision	61	19.9
Current probation/parole	75	24.4
Current placement	17	5.5

[a] Crimes against property include: burglary, theft of a motor vehicle, arson, receiving stolen property, possession of stolen property, possession of burglary tools, criminal damage to property, theft, forgery, theft by swindle, and credit card fraud

[b] Crimes against the person include: aggravated and simple robbery, aggravated assault, murder and attempted murder, criminal vehicular homicide, criminal sexual conduct, and terroristic threats

[c] Drug crimes include: sale or possession of a controlled substance—crack, methamphetamine, marijuana, codeine, ecstasy, heroin—possession of a forged prescription, and tampering with anhydrous ammonia equipment (methamphetamine)

[d] Firearm crimes include: possession of a firearm, discharge of a firearm, theft of a firearm, possession of an explosive device, and drive-by shooting

[e] Other offenses are fleeing a police officer

a *Scales* recording whether they initially arrested or later released a youth. Police detained nearly two-thirds (61.7 %) of those whom they questioned and released the others to parents. About half (55.7 %) of interrogations took place in police stations and another quarter (23.1 %) in juvenile detention centers. Thus, police questioned more than three-quarters (78.8 %) of youths in interrogation rooms. Nearly one-tenth (8.1 %) of interrogations took place in a police car at the place of arrest. Police also interrogations juveniles at their homes (6.2 %) or at schools (6.2 %). Every juvenile in the sample received a proper *Miranda* warning.

When police give suspects their *Miranda* warnings, they have no incentive to encourage them to invoke their rights. Police used several tactics to predispose suspects to waive *Miranda* without alerting them to its significance—admonishing them to tell the truth, minimizing the warning, or advising that it is the only opportunity to tell their story (Leo 1996b; Leo and White 1999). They may use routine booking questions to establish rapport and predispose youths to waive before they give a warning, (Weisselberg 2008; Rhode Island v. Innis 1980; Pennsylvania v. Muniz 1990). In about half of cases (52.8 %), police gave the *Miranda* warning immediately after identifying the suspect. In the remaining cases (47.2 %), police asked juveniles booking questions—name, age and date of birth, address and telephone number, grade in school, and the like—and sometimes used juveniles' responses to engage in casual conversations and to accustom them to answering questions.

Police sometimes framed a *Miranda* waiver as a prerequisite to a juvenile's opportunity to tell his side of the story and emphasized the importance of telling the truth before they gave a *Miranda* warning. Officers characterized warnings as an administrative formality to complete before the suspect can talk. They sometimes referred to it as "paper work" to emphasize its bureaucratic or ritual quality. Officers regularly referred to youths' familiarity with *Miranda* from television and movies. *Miranda*'s cultural ubiquity may detract from youths' understanding, as the warning becomes background noise at an interrogation.

Suspects must either waive or clearly invoke their *Miranda* rights to silence and to counsel (Fare v. Michael C. 1979; Davis v. United States 1994; Berghuis v. Thompkins 2010). Police established that a juvenile understands her rights by reading the warning and then eliciting an affirmative response. In this study, officers read each right to the youth followed by the question "Do you understand that?" Juveniles acknowledged receiving each warning on the record—the *Scales* tape—and in about one-fifth (19.5 %) of cases initialed and signed a *Miranda* form. Police in this study consistently obtained express waivers. After they asked juveniles if they understood the warning, they concluded the waiver process, "Bearing in mind that I'm a police officer and I've just read your rights, are you willing to talk to me about this matter?" Another waiver formula ended, "Having these rights in mind, do you wish to talk to us now?"

Miranda reasoned that police must warn a suspect to dispel the compulsive pressures of custodial interrogation. A dissent in *Miranda* asked why those pressures do not coerce a waiver as readily as an unwarned statement (*Miranda* v. Arizona 1966). Legal analysts and criminologists concur that after police isolate suspects in

Table 3.2 Juveniles who waive or invoke *Miranda* rights by offense and prior record

	Total		Waive		Invoke	
	N	Percentage (%)	N	Percentage (%)	N	Percentage (%)
Offense (juveniles who waive or invoke by offense)						
Person	97	31.6	92	94.8	5	5.2
Property	169	55.0	157	92.9	12	7.1
Drugs	19	6.2	16	84.2	3	15.8
Firearm	17	5.5	15	88.2	2	11.8
Other	5	1.6	5	100	0	0
Total	307	100	285	92.8	22	7.2
Prior arrests (juveniles who waive or invoke by prior record*)						
Non-felony	216	72	205	94.9	11	5.1
One or more felony	84	28	73	86.9	11	13.1
Total	300[a]	100	278	92.7	22	7.3

* Statistically significant at: χ^2 (1, $N = 300$) = 5.7, $p < 0.05$
[a] Seven juveniles (2.3 %) initially waived their *Miranda* rights and subsequently invoked them during interrogation, at which point interrogation ceased. Because they were truncated interrogation, I exclude them from analyses of police interrogation tactics

a police-dominated environment, a warning cannot adequately empower them to invoke their rights (White 1997; Weisselberg 2008). Post-*Miranda* studies consistently report about 80 % or more of adults waive *Miranda* (Wald et al. 1967; Leo 1996b, 2008; Cassell and Hayman 1996; Kassin et al. 2007).

Three decades of research report that juveniles waive *Miranda* rights at somewhat higher rates than do adults—typically 90 % or more (Grisso 1980; Grisso and Pomiciter 1977; Feld 2006a; Goldstein and Goldstein 2010). Juveniles' higher waiver rates may reflect their lack of understanding or inability to invoke *Miranda* effectively. Equally plausible, waivers may reflect prior justice system involvement and juveniles will have had less experience than adults will (Viljoen and Roesch 2005). Table 3.2 reports that the vast majority of youths (92.8 %) waived *Miranda*— a rate consistent with other juvenile studies and 10 % higher than that reported for adults. Justice system personnel confirmed the accuracy of these findings—almost all delinquents waived *Miranda*.[5]

Analysts report a relationship between prior police experience and *Miranda* invocations (Leo 1996b; Kassin 2005). Post-*Miranda* research reported that defendants with prior arrests and felony convictions gave fewer confessions than did those with less experience. Older youths and those with prior felony referrals invoked more frequently than did younger juveniles and those without prior contacts (Grisso 1980; Grisso and Pomiciter 1977).

---

[5] When asked how many juveniles waived *Miranda*, one officer said, "almost all of them. I couldn't even tell you the last time a kid told me he didn't want to talk." Another estimated, "Ninety percent, not very many kids that don't talk to you." Other police said, "I haven't had very many not speak to me. I would have to say 95 % of them or more talk," a second confirmed, "I'd say better than 95 %," and a third said, "Vast majority, I'd say high-90s." Almost all personnel thought that 90 % or more of youths waived *Miranda* and none estimated that fewer than 80 % waived.

About one-third (35.1 %) of these youths had one or more felony arrests prior to the offense for which police questioned them. Juveniles with one or more prior felony arrests waived their rights at significantly lower rates (86.9 %) than did those with fewer or less serious police contacts (94.9 %). Youths who waived at prior interrogations may have learned that they derive no benefit from confessing. Youths with prior arrests would have spent more time with lawyers and learned from those experiences. They also may have learned to cope with and resist the pressures of interrogation.

Police Interrogation Tactics

In the UK, Norway, New Zealand, and Australia investigative interviews tend to be less confrontational, designed to obtain a free-narrative account, and aimed to elicit facts rather than to secure a confessions (Milne and Bull 1999; Bull and Milne 2004). By contrast, police in the USA traditionally use more accusatorial tactics to obtain incriminating admissions or leads to other evidence—physical evidence, co-offenders, witnesses, or stolen property—to strengthen prosecutors' cases, and to produce guilty pleas. Police seek suspects' statements—true or false—to control changes the accused may make in their stories and to impeach their credibility. Minnesota training advises officers to portray themselves as report writers who want to learn what happened to put in a statement for prosecutors and judges to evaluate (Nelson 2006). Police often described their roles as natural fact finders. They frequently advise suspects that the interview provides their opportunity to "tell their story." Depending on how forthcoming a youth is initially, they may use maximization and minimization tactics to elicit a statement.

Police reported that they used maximization techniques regularly. They initially encouraged juveniles to commit to a story—true or false—and then used more confrontational tactics to challenge their version thereafter. Table 3.3 summarizes maximization strategies police used: confronted juveniles with evidence (54.4 %); accused them of lying (32.6 %); exhorted them to tell the truth (29.5 %); asked BAI questions (28.8 %); challenged inconsistencies (20.0 %); emphasized the seriousness of the offense (14.4 %); and accused them of other crimes (8.4 %).

In about one-third (30.9 %) of cases, police did not use any maximization techniques and in another quarter (23.1 %), they used only one. The paucity of maximization tactics suggests that most juveniles did not require a lot of prompting or intimidation to cooperate. Police used three or more maximization tactics in fewer than one-third (31.6 %) of cases.

In about half (54.4 %) the interrogations, police confronted juveniles with statements from witnesses or co-offenders, or referred to physical evidence. In most cases, police will not have analyzed DNA or fingerprint evidence in the short time between a suspect's arrest and interrogation. Sometimes, police described an investigation as if they already had obtained the evidence. In other instances, they questioned youths about potential evidence that later investigation would reveal. They asked how a

Table 3.3 Maximization and minimization questions: Type and frequency

Interrogation strategy	N	Percentage of cases (%)
Maximization tactics		
Confront with evidence	155	54.4
Accuse of lying	93	32.6
Tell the truth	84	29.5
BAI questions	82	28.8
Confront	57	20.0
Trouble	41	14.4
Accuse other crimes	24	8.4
Frequency of maximization tactics per interrogation		
None	95	30.9
One	71	23.1
Two	44	14.3
Three	38	12.4
Four	24	7.8
Five	24	7.8
Six	9	2.9
Seven	2	0.7
Minimization tactics		
Neutralization	44	15.4
Appeal to self interest	34	11.9
Empathy	30	10.5
Appeal to honor	25	8.8
Minimize seriousness	15	5.3
Third parties	10	3.5
Frequency of minimization tactics per interrogation		
None	254	82.7
One	33	10.7
Two	14	4.6
Three	5	1.6
Four	1	0.3

juvenile would respond to hypothetical evidence—"what if I told you" that someone had identified him or police found his fingerprints? Officers might ask a juvenile "is there any reason why" his DNA might be on a gun or he would appear on surveillance video?

In about one-third (32.6 %) of cases, officers accused juveniles of lying. Police typically allowed juveniles to commit to a story and then confronted them. In nearly one-third of cases (29.5 %), officers urged juveniles to be honest and tell the truth. Police intimated that their recommendations could affect prosecutors' charges and judges' decisions. They cautioned that prosecutors and judges reacted negatively to an implausible story and responded more favorably to truthful defendants.

Inbau et al. (2004) posit that innocent and guilty people respond differently to emotionally provocative questions and their reactions enable investigators accurately to classify them. Leo (1996b) reported that officers asked such Behavioral Analysis Interview (BAI) questions in about 40 % of interrogations. Police in this study used BAI questions in more than one-quarter (28.8 %) of interviews, most commonly "Do you know why I have asked to talk to you here today?" However, few of these files indicated that police had any conversations prior to *Scales* recordings and none in which they interrogated these youths.

Police began many interviews with an invitation to a youth to tell his story, but they warned that it was a time-limited opportunity. They cautioned that if youth did not take advantage of the chance to explain their involvement, then they might regret it later. Police sometimes withheld information from juveniles about the investigation to increase uncertainty and anxiety and cautioned a reluctant youth that without his version, other co-offenders might shift responsibility to him or make a deal at his expense.

Minimization tactics offer face-saving excuses or moral justifications that reduce a crime's seriousness, provide a less odious motivation, or shift blame to a victim or accomplice (Kassin et al. 2010). The Reid Method teaches police to develop a theme or scenario to neutralize guilt, minimize responsibility, and make it easier to confess (Inbau et al. 2004; Leo 2008). Criminologists have used techniques of neutralization to understand how youths rationalize delinquent behavior (Sykes and Matza 1957). Many themes are extensions of criminal law defenses—provocation, intoxication, or insanity—that provide rationales to reduce moral constraints (Matza 1964). While delinquents may reject mental illness—insanity—as an excuse, they readily embrace "going crazy" or "being mad" to rationalize criminal conduct. Police sometimes suggested that getting mad, losing control, or excitement accounted for youths' criminal misconduct. Intoxication provides an explanation for bad behavior, and juveniles readily invoked drinking alcohol or using drugs to excuse criminal conduct. Similarly, police diffused juveniles' responsibility by suggesting that they succumbed to negative peer influences. Juveniles often commit their crimes in groups (Snyder and Sickmund 2006), and police can blame others and allow juveniles to shift blame as well. Parents regularly refer to errant children's behavior as a mistake and youths learn that mistakes can mitigate responsibility. In the present study, police regularly encouraged juveniles to attribute their delinquency to a mistake.

Police used minimization tactics in about one-fifth (17.3 %) of these interrogations, far less often than they used maximization tactics (69.1 %). Although prosecutors charged all these youths with felonies, one officer explained that "most of these are fairly minor, so you don't have to do a whole lot of minimizing." Officers used scenarios or themes to reduce suspects' guilt or culpability in 15.4 % of cases. Police described benefits juveniles might derive and appealed to self-interest in one-tenth (11.9 %) of cases. They expressed empathy in one-tenth of cases (10.5 %), and in fewer offered to investigate further or assist juveniles to receive help. Officers minimized a crime's seriousness by describing its triviality in comparison with other delinquents' offenses. Even a serious crime—a drive-by shooting—could have been worse if the shooter had hit the intended target. The rationale of juvenile courts—treatment rather than punishment—provided officers with another theme with which to offer help and to minimize seriousness. The infrequency of minimization tactics is consistent with research in the UK, and Minnesota training protocols that discourages their use (Nelson 2006; Soukura et al. 2009).

Table 3.4 Outcome of interrogation and youths' attitudes

Outcome of interrogation			Youths' attitudes*			
			Cooperative		Resistant	
	N	Percentage (%)	N	Percentage (%)	N	Percentage (%)
Confession	167	58.6	162	71.4	5	8.6
Admission	85	29.8	57	25.1	28	48.3
Denial	33	11.6	8	3.5	25	43.1
Corroborating evidence	52	18.2	227	79.6	58	20.4

* Statistically significant at: χ^2 (1, $N = 285$) = 7.84, $p < 0.001$

Juveniles' Responses

How did the 285 youths who waived *Miranda* respond to police and how did their attitudes affect the information they provided? I coded the outcome of interrogations into three categories—confess, admit, or deny.[6] (Cassell and Hayman 1996; Wald et al. 1967). Table 3.4 reports that a majority (58.6 %) of juveniles confessed within a few minutes of waiving *Miranda* and did not require prompting by police. British research confirms that the majority of suspects confessed and "almost all did so near the beginning of the interviews" (Soukara et al. 2009, p. 495). The UK analysts concluded that "suspects enter a police interview having already decided whether to admit or deny the allegations against them" and interrogation tactics had little impact on whether they admit (Milne and Bull 1999, p. 81). (But see, Bull and Soukara (2010) for analyses of 40 interviews in which suspects "shifted from denying to admitting.") An additional one-third (29.8 %) of juveniles provided statements of some evidentiary value, for example, admitting that they served as a lookout during a robbery or participated in a burglary even if they did not personally steal property. Justice personnel agreed that most juveniles made some incrimination admissions.

Other studies corroborate similar high rates of admissions and confessions. Leo (1996b) found such outcomes in three-quarters (76 %) of cases in which adults waived *Miranda*. About two-thirds (64 %) of interrogations in the Yale-New Haven study yielded incriminating evidence (Wald et al. 1967). A survey of police estimated that two-thirds (68 %) of suspects incriminated themselves (Kassin et al. 2007). Other UK research reports a rate of 77 %, ranging from 64 to 97 % among various police stations (Evans 1993; Bull and Milne 2004). More than half (55 %) of delinquents held in detention reported they had confessed (Viljoen et al. 2005).

---

[6] Police elicited a confession when a juvenile admitted that he committed the crime with supporting details or when his cumulative responses satisfied all of the elements of an offense, i.e., act and intent. Questioners received an admission when it linked a youth to a crime or provided direct or circumstantial evidence of one or more elements of the offense. Admissions often occurred when a getaway driver, lookout, or co-defendant admitted participating, but minimized her role or responsibility. Police heard denials when a juvenile disavowed knowledge or responsibility or gave an explanation that did not include any incriminating admissions.

Only a small proportion (11.6%) of juveniles made no incriminating admissions. Forms of resistance included noncooperation, denial of knowledge and culpability, lying, evasion, silence, or blame shifting. When confronted with resistance, police used more maximization techniques than they did with cooperative youths, but did not question them for longer periods. Once they recognized a youth was resistant, they concluded the interrogation with the comment that prosecutors and judges would not view them favorably.

Criminologists have studied the interplay between police discretion and juveniles' attitudes (Black and Reiss 1970; Clark and Sykes 1974), and reported that for less serious crimes, deferential youths reduce likelihood of arrest and contumacious ones increase it (Piliavin and Briar 1964; LaFave 1965; Skolnick 1967; Bittner 1976). Studies of police and probation officers report that a youth's attitude affected how officials perceived, imputed moral character, and responded to him or her (Emerson 1974; Cicourel 1995).

Police reported that juveniles' attitudes ranged the gamut—"some are scared to death, and others, it's almost a joke." Many officers described youths as scared, especially "the kids that are new to the process." Although police described some youths as confrontational, justice system personnel viewed most youths as cooperative or submissive. "I would say that 90% or more would probably be cooperative and the other percentage would be the frequent-fliers so to speak." Several officers used the expression "deer in the headlights" to describe youths' demeanors in the interrogation room. Public defenders described juveniles as humbled or defeated when they confessed.

Ethnographers emphasize the variability of attitudes—"rude or impolite, aggressive or passive, laughter or tears, and the like"—and their impact on justice system processing (Cicourel 1995, p. xv). Juveniles exhibited many attitudes during interrogation—polite, cooperative, distressed, remorseful, frightened, cocky, resistant, aggressive, and confrontational—which could fluctuate from one minute to the next. Police reports frequently described juveniles' demeanors, emotional responses, and behavior during interrogation. They documented whether they believed suspects told the truth or lied and indicated whether they cooperated or resisted. Based on the characterizations in officers' reports and my impressions, I dichomized juveniles' attitudes as cooperative or resistant. Other research used similar categories and described 80% of suspects as cooperative (Baldwin 1993). Juveniles cooperate for many reasons—human decency in social interactions, fear and anxiety, dependency on authority figures, or the coercive pressures of isolation—but most exhibited positive attitudes.

As Table 3.4 indicates, the vast majority of juveniles (79.6%) exhibited a cooperative demeanor and only one-fifth (20.4%) appeared resistant. Not surprisingly, the vast majority (96.5%) of cooperative juveniles confessed or made incriminating admissions. By contrast, fewer than one in ten (8.5%) resistant juveniles confessed and almost half (43.1%) provided no useful admissions (8.6%). Only one-tenth (11.6%) of youths denied involvement, but those who exhibited resistant attitudes accounted for more than three-quarters of them (75.8%).

Table 3.5 Length of interrogation by type of offense* and weapon**

Time (minutes)	Overall N	Overall %	Person N	Person %	Property N	Property %	Drug N	Drug %	Firearms N	Firearms %	Other N	Other %
1 - 15	220	77.2	62	67.4	131	83.4	15	93.8	9	60	3	60
16 - 30	38	13.3	20	21.7	13	8.3	1	6.3	3	20	1	20
31+	27	9.5	10	10.9	13	8.3	0	0	3	20	1	20
Total	285		92		157		16		15		5	

	Cases Involving Firearms					
	Overall		No Gun		Gun	
Time (minutes)	N	%	N	%	N	%
1 - 15	220	77.2	192	80.3	28	60.9
16 - 30	38	13.3	29	12.1	9	19.6
31+	27	9.5	18	7.5	9	19.6
Total	285		239		46	

* Statistically Significant at: $\chi^2(1, N = 285) = 32.3$, $p < .05$
** Statistically Significant at: $\chi^2(1, N = 285) = 9.4$, $p < .01$

Police in the USA typically question suspects to elicit admissions or obtain statements that prosecutors can use to impeach testimony. Suspects' answers may lead to other evidence—witnesses, co-offenders, or property. Table 3.4 reports how often interrogations yielded corroborating evidence. I defined corroborating evidence as evidence which police did not possess prior to questioning—leads to physical evidence, a crime scene diagram, identity of a co-offender, or unknown witness. By this conservative standard, about one-fifth (18.2 %) of interviews yielded information that police did not already have. Thus, interrogation did not produce much collateral evidence and gathering it appears to be a secondary goal.

Some police attributed the low-yield of corroborating evidence to time pressures produced by the volume of cases they investigated. Once police obtained an admission—which they did quickly—they did not press youths for additional evidence. Prosecutors confirmed that interrogations did not often lead to corroborating evidence, but attributed it to good preliminary investigations. Police questioned more than two-thirds (69.7 %) of juveniles within less than 24 hours of their crimes—i.e., police either caught them committing the crime or very shortly thereafter. As a result, police and prosecutors had strong enough evidence with which to obtain a conviction in about two-thirds (63.2 %) of cases even without conducting an interview. Prosecutors said that juveniles' statements sometimes provided bases to obtain search warrants which produced additional evidence not disclosed directly in the interview.

Length of Interrogation

Table 3.5 reports the length of interrogations by type of offense and by whether the offense involved a firearm.[7] Police completed three-quarters (77.2 %) of interviews

---

[7] To measure the length of interrogation, in some cases, I directly timed the tape. In most transcripts, officers stated the start and stop times at the beginning and ending of an interrogation. In other cases, I

in less than 15 minutes and concluded nine in ten (90.5 %) in less than 30 minutes. In the longest interviews, police questioned three youths (1.1 %) for 1.5 hours. Although prosecutors charged youths with one or more felonies, brief interrogations are unlikely to cause false confessions (White 2001).

Although these short interviews initially seemed surprising, other research confirms that interrogations of even 2 or 3 hours are exceptional and frequently problematic (Drizin and Leo 2004; Kassin et al. 2007). Police questioned suspects for more than an hour in only 15 % of cases in the Yale-New Haven study (Wald et al. 1967). Leo (c) reported that police questioned only one-quarter (28.7 %) of suspects for more than 1 hour. Cassell and Hayman (1996) reported that only 13 % of interrogations took more than 30 minutes and only one lasted longer than an hour. Research on British interrogations of juveniles reported that "[i]nterviews tended to be very brief with the majority taking less than fifteen minutes (71.4 %). Although the average length of interviews was around 14 min, the most frequent length was around 7 minutes" (Evans 1993, p. 26). Analyses of taped UK interrogations reported that "most were short and surprisingly amiable discussions" in which more than one-third of suspects confessed at the outset (Baldwin 1993, p. 331). Kassin and Gudjonsson (2004) reported that most interviews were short—80 % lasted less than 30 minutes; 95 % were completed within 1 hour—suspects confessed in 58 % of cases, police applied little interrogative pressure, and very few suspects who initially denied guilt subsequently confessed. Inbau et al. (2004) warn against interrogations longer than 4 hours—a length of time not observed in any published research. (But see Bull and Leahy–Harland (2012) for analyses of 56 interviews with an average duration of several hours).

I asked justice professionals to estimate the lengths of interviews and they universally agreed, "They're actually very short."[8] When asked why police concluded felony interrogations so quickly, justice system personnel attributed brevity to several factors. Many professionals referred to police workload pressures. Police conducted a form of triage, questioned suspects longer in more serious cases, but did not regard most juvenile felonies as serious crimes. Several officers attributed brief interrogations to the relative simplicity of most juveniles' crimes and their ability to elicit admissions quickly.

A statistically significant relationship appeared between length of interrogation and type of offense. Police questioned a larger proportion of youths charged with property and drug crimes for 15 minutes or less than they did youths charged with other types of offenses. Crimes that involved some physical evidence—drugs, stolen

---

estimated the duration of interrogation from the length of the transcript. I cross tabulated the number of transcript pages and length of interrogation in cases in which I had both to approximate the length of interrogations for which I had only transcripts. I always rounded estimates to the longer interval.

[8] They estimated the average length of interviews which mirrored my findings: "fifteen minutes," "twenty or twenty-five minutes," "ten to twenty minutes," "maybe thirty minutes," "less than fifteen minutes," "ten to fifteen minutes." A veteran officer with 15 years of experience reported that "My longest has maybe been an hour." One judge opined, "fifteen or twenty minutes," a second judge confirmed, "usually ten to twenty minutes," and a third judge agreed, "It doesn't take very long to get them to 'fess up. Twenty minutes." A prosecutor said interrogations are "Very short, usually. I would say under 10 min, the vast majority, under ten minutes." Public defenders thought that typical interrogations took "not more than twenty minutes."

property or automobiles—may have provided police with more evidence with which to confront these juveniles, resulting in shorter interviews.

Cases involving firearms resulted in longer interrogations. Although police questioned only 9.5 % of delinquents for longer than 30 minutes, they interrogated twice as many (20 %) juveniles charged with firearms offenses for longer than 30 minutes. I compared the lengths of interrogation in *all* cases that involved guns—armed robbery, assault with a gun, firearms possession, or burglary in which youths stole guns—with cases in which juveniles used other weapons—knives, blunt instruments, or automobiles—or did not use a weapon.

Guns provide an indicator of offense seriousness (Podkopacz and Feld 1996), and police questioned these juveniles longer and more aggressively. Police wanted to recover guns used or stolen by youths, and they used more maximization and minimization tactics to retrieve them. Officers referred to the benefits that would accrue to a youth who helped them to recover a gun and described the dangers guns posed to people who held them and those around them. Only two interrogations raised constitutional issues of voluntariness and both involved questioning to recover guns. In each case, police questioned juveniles for the longest time (1 and 1.5 hours), used the most maximization techniques, and made explicit quid-pro-quo promises of leniency to recover guns used or stolen by juveniles.

Police and justice system personnel confirmed the relationship between guns and length of interrogation and suggested that guns provide a reasonable proxy for crime seriousness. Police associated guns with youths' involvement with gangs—another indicator of seriousness. Police also questioned youths to learn about other youths who had contact with the weapon. Juveniles knew that gun crimes garnered serious consequences for them, which gave them greater incentive to resist interrogators. Serious crimes are more likely to go to trial and police invested more energy to strengthen prosecutors' cases.

Policy Implications

Although *Miranda* purported to bolster the adversary system and protect citizens, warnings failed to achieve those goals. In the decades since *Miranda*, the Court's decisions have limited its scope, applicability, and the adverse consequences when police fail to comply (Slobogin 2007; Weisselberg 2008). *Miranda*'s assumption that a warning would empower suspects to resist the compulsive pressures of interrogation is demonstrably wrong. Post-*Miranda* research reports that 80 %of adults and 90 % of juveniles waive their sole protection in the interrogation room and only some sophisticated suspects invoke their rights. Although *Miranda* recognized that interrogation threatened the adversarial balance between the individual and the state, waivers provide police with a window of opportunity to conduct an inquisitorial examination. Perversely, *Miranda* allows judges to focus on ritualistic compliance with a procedural formality rather than to assess the voluntariness or reliability of a statement (Weisselberg 2008; Godsey 2005; Leo 2008). Judicial review of a *Miranda* waiver is the beginning *and* end of regulating interrogation (Missouri v. Seibert 2004).

Protecting Young Offenders in the Interrogation Room

Miranda is especially problematic for younger juveniles who may not under-stand its words or concepts. The Court has recognized youths' vulnerabilities and distinguished between younger and older youths. Developmental psychologists corroborate their differing abilities. Younger juveniles' incomplete understanding, impaired judgment, and heightened vulnerability warrant greater assistance—a non-waivable right to counsel—to assure voluntariness of a *Miranda* waiver and statement. Psychologists distinguish between youths' cognitive abilities—their ca-pacity to understand—and ability to make mature decisions and exercise self-control. *Miranda* requires only the ability to understand words, which developmental psychologists conclude that most 16 and 17-year-old youths can do.

The present study corroborates that 16 and 17-year-old juveniles appear to un-derstand and exercise *Miranda* similarly to adults. This consistency inferentially bolsters research that younger juveniles lack understanding and competence to exer-cise the rights. Many, if not most, children 15 or younger do not understand *Miranda* or possess competence to make legal decisions (Grisso 1980; Grisso et al. 2003). Research on false confessions underscores the unique vulnerability of younger ju-veniles (Drizin and Leo 2004; Gross et al. 2005; Garrett 2011). In a prior study, police obtained more than one-third (35 %) of proven false confessions from sus-pects younger than 18 (Drizin and Leo 2004), and younger adolescents are at greater risk to confess falsely than older ones (Tepfer et al. 2010).

Developmental psychologists attribute their over-representation among false confessors to reduced cognitive ability, developmental immaturity, and increased susceptibility to manipulation (Bonnie and Grisso 2000; Tobey et al. 2000; Redlich et al. 2004). They have fewer life experiences or psychological resources with which to resist the pressures of interrogation (Drizin and Luloff 2007; Redlich et al. 2004). Juveniles' lower social status and societal expectations of obedience to authority create pressures to waive (Gudjonsson 2003; Leo 2009). Juveniles are more likely than are adults to comply with authority figures, tell police what they think they want to hear, and respond to negative feedback (Gudjonsson 2003; Lyon 1999). The stress of interrogation intensifies their desire to escape in the short run by waiving and confessing (Owen-Kostelnik et al. 2006; Goldstein and Goldstein 2010). Lim-ited ability to consider long-term consequences heightens their risk (Redlich 2010). The immature adolescent brain contributes to impulsive behavior and heightened vulnerability (Birckhead 2008; Maroney 2009).

Despite youths' heightened susceptibility, police do not seem to incorporate de-velopmental differences into the tactics they employ (Owen-Kostelnik et al. 2006). Techniques designed to manipulate adults—aggressive questioning, presenting false evidence, and leading questions—may create unique dangers when employed with youths (Kaban and Tobey 1999; Tanenhaus and Drizin 2002; Redlich and Drizin 2007). Police in this study did not report receiving special training to question juveniles and used the same tactics employed with adults.

The Supreme Court excluded statements taken from youths 15 years of age or younger—*Haley, Gallegos, Gault,* and J. D. B.—and admitted those obtained from 16- and 17-year-olds—*Fare* and *Alvarado*. The Court's de facto line—15 and younger versus 16 and older—closely tracks what psychologists have found about youths' ability to understand the warning and concepts. State courts and legislatures should formally adopt the functional line that the Court and psychologists discern between youths 16 and older and those 15 and younger.

Analysts advocate that juveniles younger than 16 years of age "should be accompanied and advised by a professional advocate, preferably an attorney, trained to serve in this role" (Kassin et al. 2010, p. 28). Juveniles should consult with an attorney, rather than rely on parents, before they exercise or waive their constitutional rights (Farber 2004; Bishop and Farber 2007). More than three decades ago, the American Bar Association endorsed mandatory, non-waivable counsel because it recognized that "Few juveniles have the experience and understanding to decide meaningfully that the assistance of counsel would not be helpful" (American Bar Association 1980, p. 92).

Requiring a child to consult an attorney assures an informed and voluntary waiver (Farber 2004; Drizin and Luloff 2007). If youths 15 years of age or younger consult with counsel prior to waiver, this may limit somewhat police's ability to secure confessions. However, if younger juveniles cannot understand or exercise the rights without legal assistance, then to treat them as if they do denies fundamental fairness and enables the state to exploit their vulnerability. *Fare* emphasized lawyers' unique roles in the justice system, and *Haley*, *Gallegos*, and *Gault* recognized younger juveniles' exceptional needs for assistance.

Limiting the Length of Interrogations

Most false confessions emerge only after lengthy interrogations and youthfulness exacerbates those dangers (Drizin and Leo 2004; Kassin and Gudjonsson 2004; Gross et al. 2005). The Court recognizes that lengthy interrogations can produce involuntary confessions (Ashcraft v. Tennessee 1944), and found that questioning juveniles for 5 or 6 hours could produce an involuntary statement (Haley v. Ohio 1948; Gallegos v. Colorado 1962). Policy-makers should create a sliding-scale presumption of involuntariness based on length of interrogation and examine a confession's reliability more closely as length of questioning increases (Leo et al. 2006).

The vast majority of the interrogations analyzed were very brief. Police concluded 90 % of these felony interrogations in less than 30 minutes. Every study reviewed reports that police completed nearly all interrogations in less than an hour and few take as long as 2 hours. By contrast, interrogations that elicit false confessions are usually long inquiries that wear down an innocent person's resistance—85 %took at least 6 hours (Drizin and Leo 2004).

I cannot prescribe outer time limits because I did not encounter either lengthy or factually problematic interrogations. However, states should create a sliding-scale presumption that police elicited involuntary confession as the length of questioning increases. Police complete nearly all felony interrogations in less than 1 hour, but extract most false confessions only after grilling suspects for 6 hours or longer. These times provide a framework to limit interrogations and strengthen the presumption of coercion (White 2001; Kassin et al. 2010). Four hours would provide ample opportunity for police to obtain true confessions from guilty suspects willing to talk without increasing the risk of eliciting false confessions from innocent people.

On the Record

Within the past decade, legal scholars, psychologists, law enforcement, and justice system personnel have reached consensus that recording interrogations reduces coercion, diminishes dangers of false confessions, and increases reliability (Cassell 1998; Milne and Bull 1999; Gudjonsson 2003; Drizin and Reich 2004; Sullivan 2004, 2006, 2010; Garrett 2010, 2011). About a dozen states require police to record interrogations, albeit some under limited circumstances—homicide or young suspects (Leo 2008; Sullivan 2010; Garrett 2011). Many police departments have policies to record interrogations for some crimes (Sullivan 2006, 2010).

Recording creates an objective record and an independent basis to resolve disputes between police and defendants about *Miranda* warnings, waivers, or statements (Slobogin 2003). A complete record enables fact finders to decide whether a statement contains facts known to a guilty perpetrator or police supplied them to an innocent suspect during questioning (White 1997; Garrett 2010, 2011). Recording protects police from false claims of abuse (Cassell 1998; White 1997). It enables police to focus on suspects' responses, to review details of an interview not captured in written notes, and to test them against subsequently discovered facts (Drizin and Reich 2004). It reduces the need for an officer to take notes or a second person to witness a statement, which may chill a suspect's willingness to talk. Recording avoids distortions that occur when interviewers rely on memory or notes to summarize a statement (Milne and Bull 1999).

A recorded confession greatly strengthens prosecutors' plea bargain advantage. It enables them to avoid suppression hearings, negotiate better pleas, and obtain convictions (White 1997; Sullivan 2006). Defense lawyers can review recordings rather than rely on clients' imperfect recollections of a stressful event. *Scales* recordings have virtually eliminated motions to suppress confessions because tapes provide unimpeachable evidence. This generates substantial savings because police, prosecutors, and defense counsel do not have to prepare for and judges do not have to conduct suppression hearings about *Miranda* warnings, coercive tactics, or the accuracy of a statement. Interviews with prosecutors, defense lawyers, and judges confirmed that defenders filed few motions to suppress evidence for *Miranda* violations.

Justice system personnel attributed *Scales'* reduction of suppression motions to several factors. First, police acted professionally and complied with *Miranda's* protocol—there is no ambiguity about warnings and waivers. In addition, most juveniles confess and tapes provide unimpeachable evidence of their statements. Juveniles' statements limited defense attorneys' options and reinforce a system of plea bargains, rather than trials. *Scales* enhanced police professionalism, documented

Miranda compliance, obviated suppression hearings, led quickly to guilty pleas, and focused lawyers' attention on appropriate sentences rather than guilt or innocence. *Scales* enables professionals to administer an inquisitorial model of justice "on the record," expedites processing of routine cases, and reserves court resources for complex cases.

For recording to be an effective safeguard, police must record all conversations—preliminary interviews and interrogations—rather than just a final statement—a "post-admission narrative" (Gudjonsson 2003; Garrett 2011). Otherwise, police may conduct a pre-interrogation interview, elicit incriminating information, and then record only a final confession after the "cat is out of the bag"—a variation of the two-step practice condemned in *Missouri* v. Siebert. Only a complete record of every interaction can protect against a final statement that ratifies an earlier coerced one or against a false confession contaminated by nonpublic facts that police supplied a suspect (Kassin 1997; Garrett 2011).

The Court repeatedly insists that American criminal and juvenile justice is an adversary system. Repeated assertions do not alter the reality that states establish most defendants' guilt through an inquisitorial system in which suspects seal their fate in the interrogation room and render trial procedures a nullity—interrogation elicits confessions and confessions produce guilty pleas (Packer 1968). Because states do not and need not provide full adversarial testing in every case, we need stronger mechanisms to assure factual reliability of inquisitorial justice. Recording imposes no great burden on police, illuminates the inner-workings of the interrogation room, and provides an objective record on which a defendant may appeal to a judge. Because the vast majority of defendants do not receive a trial, judicial review of the record provides an alternative check to assure the reliability of routine felony justice.

This study is only the second naturalistic empirical study of police interrogation in the USA in the past three decades (Leo 1996b), and the first involving juveniles. We need far more empirical research on interrogations practices in general, in a number of different settings, and with more knowledge about characteristics of suspects. As more jurisdictions adopt taping and recording requirements, we will have further opportunity to conduct this type of constructive research. Recordings provide opportunities for psychologists, criminologists, police, and others to study systematically what actually occurs in the interrogation room. This will increase our fund of knowledge, enable us to develop more effective techniques to elicit true confessions from guilty defendants, reduce the likelihood of extracting false confessions from innocent suspects, and provide a stronger basis for systemic policy prescriptions.

References

Ainsworth, J. E. (1993). In a different register: The pragmatics of powerlessness in police interrogation. *Yale Law Journal, 103*, 259–322. http://yalelawjournal.org/.

American Bar Association, Institute of Judicial Administration. (1980). *Juvenile justice standards relating to pretrial court proceedings*. Cambridge: Ballinger.

Ashcraft v. Tennessee, 322 U.S. 143 (1944).

Baird, A. A., Gruber, S. A., Fein, D. A., Maas, L. C., Steingard, R. J., Renshaw, P. F., Cohen, B. M., & Yurgelun-Todd, D. A. (1999). Functional magnetic resonance imaging of facial affect recognition in children and adolescents. *Journal of the American Academy of Child & Adolescent Psychiatry, 38*, 195–199. doi:10.1097/00004583-199902000-00019.

Baldwin, J. (1993). Police interview techniques: Establishing truth or proof? *British Journal of Criminology, 33*, 325–352. http://bjc.oxfordjournals.org/content/33/3/325.full.pdf.

Berghuis v. Thompkins, 130S.Ct. 2250 (2010).

Billings, F. J., Taylor, T., Burns, J., Corey, D. L., Garven, S., & Wood, J. M. (2007). Can reinforcement induce children to falsely incriminate themselves? *Law and Human Behavior, 31*, 125–139. doi:10.1007/s10979-006-9049-5.

Birckhead, T. R. (2008). The age of the child: Interrogating juveniles after Roper v. Simmons. *Washington and Lee Law Review, 65*, 385–450. http://law.wlu.edu/deptimages/Law%20Review/65 2Birckhead.pdf.

Bishop, D. M., & Farber, H. B. (2007). Joining the legal significance of adolescent developmental capacities with the legal rights provided by *In re Gault. Rutgers Law Review, 60*, 125–173. http://pegasus.rutgers.edu/~review/vol60n1/Bishop-Farber_v60n1.pdf.

Bittner, E. (1976). Policing juveniles: The social context of common practice. In M. K. Rosenheim (Ed.), *Pursuing justice for the child* (pp. 69–93). Chicago: University of Chicago Press.

Black, D. J., & Reiss Jr., A. J. (1970). Police control of juveniles. *American Sociological Review, 35*, 63–77. http://www.jstor.org/stable/2093853.

Bonnie, R. J., & Grisso, T. (2000). Adjudicative competence and youthful offenders. In T. Grisso & R. G. Schwartz (Eds.), *Youth on trial: A developmental perspective on juvenile justice* (pp. 73–104). Chicago: University of Chicago Press.

Bull, R., & Corran, E. (2003). Interviewing child witnesses: Past and future. *International Journal of Police Science and Management, 4*, 315–322.

Bull, R., & Leahy-Harland, S. (2012). *Analyses of real-life police interviews with suspects: Strategies used and suspect responses.* Paper presented at the Annual Conference of the American Psychology-Law Society, San Juan Puerto Rico, March.

Bull, R., & Milne, R. (2004). Attempts to improve the police interviewing of suspects. In G. D. Lassiter (Ed.), *Interrogations, confessions, and entrapment* (pp. 181–196). New York: Kluwer Academic.

Bull, R., & Soukara, S. (2010). Four studies of what really happens in police interviews. In G. D. Lassiter & C. A. Meissner (Eds.), *Police interrogations and false confessions: Current research, practice, and policy recommendations* (pp. 81–96). Washington, D.C.: American Psychological Association.

Cassell, P. G. (1998). Protecting the innocent from false confessions and lost confessions—and from *Miranda. Journal of Criminal Law and Criminology, 88*, 497–556. http://www.jstor.org/stable/1144289.

Cassell, P. G., & Hayman, B. S. (1996). Police interrogation in the 1990s: An empirical study of the effects of *Miranda. UCLA Law Review, 43*, 839–932. http://www.uclalawreview.org/.

Cicourel, A. V. (1995). *The social organization of juvenile justice.* New Brunswick: Transaction.

Clarke, J. P., & Sykes, R. E. (1974). Some determinants of police organization and practice in a modern industrial democracy. In D. Glaser (Ed.), *Handbook of criminology* (pp. 455–494). Chicago: Rand-McNally.

Dahl, R. E. (2001). Affect regulation, brain development, and behavioral/emotional health in adolescence. *CNS Spectrums, 6*, 60–72. http://www.cnsspectrums.com/.

Davis v. United States, 512 U.S. 452 (1994).

Drizin, S. A., & Colgan, B. A. (2004). Tales from the juvenile confession front: A guide to how standard police interrogation tactics can produce coerced and false confessions from juvenile suspects. In G. D. Lassiter (Ed.), *Interrogations, confessions, and entrapment* (pp. 127–162). New York: Kluwer Academic.

Drizin, S. A., & Leo, R. A. (2004). The problem of false confessions in the post-DNA world. *North Carolina Law Review, 82*, 891–1008. http://nclawreview.net/.

Drizin, S. A., & Luloff, G. (2007). Are juvenile courts a breeding ground for wrongful convictions? *Northern Kentucky Law Review, 34*, 257–322. http://chaselaw.nku.edu/law_review/.

Drizin, S. A., & Reich, M. J. (2004). Heeding the lessons of history: The need for mandatory recording of police interrogations to accurately assess the reliability and voluntariness of confessions. *Drake Law Review, 52,* 619–646. http://students.law.drake.edu/lawReview/.

Drope v. Missouri, 420 U.S. 162 (1975).

Dusky v. United States, 362 U.S. 402 (1960).

Emerson, R. M. (1974). Role determinants in juvenile court. *Handbook of criminology* (pp. 621–650). Chicago: Rand-McNally.

Evans, Roger. (1993). The conduct of police interviews with juveniles, Royal Commission on Criminal Justice report. London: HMSO.

Farber, H. B. (2004). The role of the parent/guardian in juvenile custodial interrogations: Friend or foe? *American Criminal Law Review, 41,* 1277–1312. http://www.americancriminallawreview.com/Drupal/.

Fare v. Michael C., 442 U.S. 707 (1979).

Feld, B. C. (2006a). Juveniles' competence to exercise Miranda rights: An empirical study of policy and practice. *Minnesota Law Review, 91,* 26–100. http://www.minnesotalawreview.org/.

Feld, B. C. (2006b). Police interrogation of juveniles: An empirical study of policy and practice. *Journal of Criminal Law and Criminology, 97,* 219–316. doi:0091–4169/06/9701-0219.

Feld, B.C. (2013). *Kids, cops, and confessions: Inside the interrogation room.* New York: NYU Press.

Feld, B. C., & Schaefer, S. (2010a). The right to counsel in juvenile court: The conundrum of attorneys as an aggravating factor at disposition. *Justice Quarterly, 27,* 713–741. http://www.tandf.co.uk/journals/titles/07418825.asp.

Feld, B. C., & Schaefer, S. (2010b). The right to counsel in juvenile court: Law reform to deliver legal services and reduce justice by geography. *Criminology & Public Policy, 9,* 327–356. http://www.wiley.com/bw/journal.asp?ref=1538–6473.

Furby, L., & Beyth-Marom, R. (1992). Risk taking in adolescence: A decision-making perspective. *Developmental Review, 12,* 1–44. doi:10.1016/0273-2297(92)90002-J.

Gallegos v. Colorado, 370 U.S. 49 (1962).

Garrett, B. L. (2010). The substance of false confessions. *Stanford Law Review, 62,* 1051–1118. http://www.stanfordlawreview.org/.

Garrett, B. L. (2011). *Convicting the innocent: Where criminal prosecutions go wrong.* Cambridge: Harvard University Press.

Godsey, M. A. (2005). Rethinking the involuntary confession rule: Toward a workable test for identifying compelled self-incrimination. *California Law Review, 93,* 465–540. http://scholarship.law.uc.edu/fac_pubs/92.

Goldstein, A., & Goldstein, N. E. S. (2010). *Evaluating capacity to waive* Miranda. New York: Oxford University Press.

Grisso, T. (1980). Juveniles' capacities to waive *Miranda* rights: An empirical analysis. *California Law Review, 68,* 1134–1166. http://www.californialawreview.org/.

Grisso, T. (1981). Juveniles' waivers of rights: Legal and psychological competence. *Perspectives in law & psychology, 3.* New York: Plenum.

Grisso, T. (2000). What we know about youth's capacities as trial defendants. In T. Grisso & R. G. Schwartz (Eds.), *Youth on trial: A developmental perspective on juvenile justice* (pp. 139–172). Chicago: University of Chicago Press.

Grisso, T. (2002). Juveniles' competence to stand trial: New questions for an era of punitive juvenile justice reform. In P. Puritz, A. Capozello, & W. Shang (Eds.), *More than meets the eye: Rethinking, assessment, competency and sentencing for a harsher era of juvenile justice* (pp. 23–38). Washington, DC: American Bar Association Juvenile Justice Center.

Grisso, T., & Pomiciter, C. (1977). Interrogation of juveniles: An empirical study of procedures, safeguards and rights waiver. *Law and Human Behavior, 1,* 321–342. http://www.springerlink.com/content/104390/.

Grisso, T., Steinberg, L., Woolard, J., Cauffman, E., Scott, E., Graham, S., Lexcen, F., Reppucci, N. D., & Schwartz R. (2003). Juveniles' competence to stand trial: A comparison of adolescents' and adults' capacities as trial defendants. *Law and Human Behavior, 27,* 333–363. doi:0147-7307/03/0800-0333/1.

Gross, S. R., Jacoby, K., Matheson, D. J., Montgomery, N., & Patil, S. (2005). Exonerations in the United States: 1989 through 2003. *Journal of Criminal Law and Criminology, 95,* 523–560. doi:0091-4169/05/95/02-0523.

Gruber, S. A., & Yurgelun-Todd, D. A. (2006). Neurobiology and the law: A role in juvenile justice. *Ohio State Journal of Criminal Law, 3,* 321–340. http://moritzlaw.osu.edu/osjcl/.

Gudjonsson, G. H. (2003). *The psychology of interrogations and confessions: A handbook.* West Sussex: Wiley.

Haley v. Ohio, 332 U.S. 596 (1948).

In re Gault, 387 U.S. 1 (1967).

Inbau, F. E., Reid, J. E., Buckley, J. P., & Jayne, B. C. (2004). *Criminal interrogation and confessions* (pp. 377–389). Sudbury, MA: Jones and Bartlett.

J.D.B. v. N. Carolina, 131 S. Ct. 2394 (2011).

Kaban, B., & Tobey, A. E. (1999). When police question children, are protections adequate? *Journal of the Center for Children and the Courts, 1,* 151–160. http://courts.ca.gov/documents/jourvol1.pdf.

Kassin, S. M. (1997). The psychology of confession evidence. *American Psychologist, 52,* 221–233. doi:10.1037/0003-066X.52.3.221.

Kassin, S. M. (2005). On the psychology of confessions: Does *innocence* put *innocents* at risk? *American Psychologist, 60,* 215–228. doi:10.1037/0003-066X.60.3.215.

Kassin, S. M., & Gudjonsson, G. H. (2004). The psychology of confession evidence: A review of the literature and issues. *Psychological Science in the Public Interest, 5,* 33–67. http://www.jstor.org/stable/40062301.

Kassin, S. M., & McNall, K. (1991). Police interrogation and confessions: Communicating promises and threats by pragmatic implication. *Law and Human Behavior, 15,* 233–251. doi:10.1007/bf01061711.

Kassin, S. M., Leo, R. A., Meissner, C. A., Richman, K. D., Colwell, L. H., Leach, A., & La Fon, D. (2007). Police interviewing and interrogation: A self-report survey of police practices and beliefs. *Law and Human Behavior, 31,* 381–400. doi:10.1007/s10979-00609073-5.

Kassin, S. M., Drizin, S. A., Grisso, T., Gudjonsson, G. H., Leo, R. A., & Redlich, A. (2010). Police-induced confessions: Risk factors and recommendations. *Law and Human Behavior, 34,* 3–38. doi:10.1007/s10979-010-9217-5.

King, L., & Snook, B. (2009). Peering inside the Canadian interrogation room: An examination of the Reid model of interrogation, influence tactics, and coercive strategies. *Criminal Justice and Behavior, 36,* 674–694. doi:10.1177/0093854809335514.

LaFave, W. R. (1965). *Arrest.* Boston: Little Brown.

Larson, K. (2003). Improving the "kangaroo courts": A proposal for reform in evaluating juveniles' waiver of *Miranda. Villanova Law Review, 48,* 629–668. http://www.law.villanova.edu/academics/journals/law%20review.aspx.

Leo, R. A. (1996a). The impact of *Miranda* revisited. *Journal of Criminal Law and Criminology, 86,* 621–692. http://www.jstor.org/stable/1143934.

Leo, R. A. (1996b). Inside the interrogation room. *Journal of Criminal Law and Criminology, 86,* 266–303. doi:0091-4169/96/8602-0266.

Leo, R. A. (1996c). *Miranda*'s revenge: Police interrogation as a confidence game. *Law & Society Review, 30,* 259–288. http://www.jstor.org/stable/3053960.

Leo, R. A. (2008). *Police interrogation and American justice.* Cambridge: Harvard University Press.

Leo, R. A. (2009). False confessions: Causes, consequences and implications. *Journal of American Academy of Psychiatry and the Law, 37,* 332–343. http://www.jaapl.org/content/37/3/332.full.pdf+html.

Leo, R. A., & White, W. S. (1999). Adapting to *Miranda*: Modern interrogators' strategies for dealing with the obstacles posed by *Miranda. Minnesota Law Review, 84,* 397–472.

Leo, R. A., Drizin, S. A., Neufeld, P. J., Hall, B. R., & Vatner, A. (2006). Bringing reliability back in: False confessions and legal safeguards in the twenty-first century. *Wisconsin Law Review, 479,* 479–539. http://hosted.law.wisc.edu/lawreview/issues/2006-2/leo-drizin.pdf.

Lyon, T. D. (1999). The new wave in children's suggestibility research: A critique. *Cornell Law Review, 84,* 1004–1087. http://www.lawschool.cornell.edu/research/cornell-law-review/.

Maroney, T. A. (2009). The false promise of adolescent brain science in juvenile justice. *Notre Dame Law Review, 85,* 89–176. http://nd.edu/~ndlrev/.

Matza, D. (1964). *Delinquency and drift.* New York: Wiley.

Meyer, J. R., & Reppucci, D. N. (2007). Police practices and perceptions regarding juvenile interrogation and interrogative suggestibility. *Behavioral Sciences & the Law, 25,* 757–780. doi:10.1002/bsl.774.

Milne, R., & Bull, R. (1999). *Investigative interviewing: Psychology and practice.* West Sussex: Wiley.

Minn. Stat. Ann. § 260B.163 (1)(c)(2) (West 2005).

Miranda v. Arizona, 384 U.S. 436 (1966).

Missouri v. Seibert, 542 U.S. 600 (2004).

Nelson, N. (2006). *Strategies for the recorded interview.* St. Paul: St. Paul Police Department.

Neubauer, D. W. (1974). Confessions in Prairie city: Some causes and effects. *Journal of Criminal Law and Criminology, 65,* 103–112. http://www.law.northwestern.edu/jclc/.

Ofshe, R. J., & Leo, R. A. (1997). The decision to confess falsely: Rational choice and irrational action. *Denver University Law Review, 74,* 979–1122. http://law.du.edu/index.php/denver-university-law-review.

Owen-Kostelnik, J., Reppucci, N. D., & Meyer, J. R. (2006). Testimony and interrogation of minors: Assumptions about maturity and morality. *American Psychologist, 61,* 286–304. doi:10.1037/0003-066X.61.4.286.

Packer, H. L. (1968). *The limits of the criminal sanction.* Stanford: Stanford University Press.

Pearse, J., & Gudjonsson, G. H. (2003). The identification and measurement of 'oppressive' police interviewing tactics in Britain. *The psychology of interrogations and confessions: A handbook* (pp. 75–114). West Sussex: Wiley.

Pennsylvania v. Muniz, 496 U.S. 582 (1990).

Piliavin, I., & Briar, S. (1964). Police encounters with juveniles. *American Journal of Sociology, 2,* 206–214. http://www.jstor.org/pss/2775210.

Podkopacz, M. R., & Feld, B. C. (1996). The end of the line: An empirical study of judicial waiver. *Journal of Criminal Law and Criminology, 86,* 449–492. http://www.law.northwestern.edu/jclc/.

Police and Criminal Evidence Act (PACE). (1984). c. 60, pt. V (Eng.) (revised 1991).

Redlich, A. D. (2004). Law & psychiatry: Mental illness, police interrogations, and the potential for false confessions. *Psychiatric Services, 55,* 19–21. doi:10.1176/appi.ps.55.1.19.

Redlich, A. D. (2010). False confessions, false guilty pleas: Similarities and differences. In G. D. Lassiter & C. A. Meissner (Eds.), *Police interrogations and false confessions: Current research, practice, and police recommendations* (pp. 49–66). Washington, D.C.: American Psychological Association.

Redlich, A. D., Silverman, M., Chen, J., & Steiner H. (2004). The Police Interrogation of Children and Adolescents. In G. D. Lassiter (Ed.), *Interrogations, Confessions, and Entrapment* (pp. 107–26). New York: Kluwer Academic.

Redlich, A. D., & Drizin, S. (2007). Police interrogation of youth. In C. L. Kessler & L. J. Kraus (Eds.), *The mental health needs of young offenders: Forging paths toward reintegration and rehabilitation* (pp. 61–78). Cambridge: Cambridge University Press.

Rhode Island v. Innis, 446 U.S. 291 (1980).

Rogers, R., Harrison, K. S., Schuman, D. W., Sewell, K. W., & Hazelwood, L. L. (2007). An analysis of *Miranda* warnings and waivers: Comprehension and coverage. *Law and Human Behavior, 31,* 177–192. doi:10.1007/s10979-006-9054-9.

Rogers, R., Hazelwood, L. L., Sewell, K. W., Harrison, K. S., & Schuman, D. W. (2008a). The language of *Miranda* warnings in American jurisdictions: A replication and vocabulary analysis. *Law and Human Behavior, 32,* 124–136. doi:10.1007/s10979-007-9091-y.

Rogers, R., Hazelwood, L. L., Sewell, K. W., Schuman, D. W., & Blackwood, H. L. (2008b). The comprehensibility and content of juvenile *Miranda* warnings. *Psychology, Public Policy and Law, 14,* 63–87. doi:10.1037/a0013102.

Scott, E. S., & Grisso, T. (2005). Developmental incompetence, due process, and juvenile justice policy. *North Carolina Law Review, 83,* 793–846.

Scott, E. S., & Grisso, T. (1997). The Evolution of Adolescence: A Developmental Perspective on Juvenile Justice Reform. *Journal of Criminal Law and Criminology, 88,* 137–89.

Scott, E. S., & Steinberg, L. (2008). *Rethinking juvenile justice.* Cambridge: Harvard University Press.

Skolnick, J. H. (1967). *Justice without trial: Law enforcement in democratic society.* New York: Wiley.

Slobogin, C. (2003). Toward taping. *Ohio State Journal of Criminal Law, 1,* 309–322. http://moritzlaw.osu.edu/osjcl/.

Slobogin, C. (2007). Lying and confessing. *Texas Tech Law Review, 39,* 1275–1292. http://www.texaslrev.com/.

Snyder, H., & Sickmund, M. (2006). *Juvenile offenders and victims: 2006 national report.* Washington, D.C.: Office of Juvenile Justice and Delinquency Prevention.

Soukara, S., Bull, R., Vrij, A., Turner, M., & Cherryman, J. (2009). What really happens in police interviews of suspects? Tactics and confessions. *Psychology, Crime & Law, 15,* 493–506. doi:10.1080/10683160802201827.

Spear, L. P. (2000). The adolescent brain and age-related behavioral manifestations. *Neuroscience & Biobehavioral Reviews, 24,* 417–463. doi:10.1016/S0149-7634(00)00014-2.

State v. Scales, 518 N.W.2d 587 (Minn. 1994).

Steinberg, L. (2005). Cognitive and affective development in adolescence. *Trends in Cognitive Science, 9,* 69–74. doi:10.1016/j.tics.2004.12.005.

Steinberg, L., & Cauffman, E. (1996). Maturity of judgment in adolescence: Psychosocial factors in adolescent decision-making. *Law and Human Behavior, 20,* 249–272. http://www.springerlink.com/content/104390/.

Steinberg, L., & Cauffman, E. (1999). The elephant in the courtroom: A developmental perspective on the adjudication of youthful offenders. *Virginia Journal of Social Policy & the Law, 6,* 389–418. http://www.virginiasocialpolicy.org/.

Steinberg, L., Graham, S., O'Brien, L., Woolard, J., Cauffman, E., & Banich, M. (2009). Age differences in future orientation and delay discounting. *Child Development, 80,* 28–44. doi:10.1111/j.1467-8624.2008.01244.x.

Sullivan, T. P. (2004). *Police experiences with recording custodial interrogations.* Chicago: Northwestern University School of Law.

Sullivan, T. P. (2006). The time has come for law enforcement recordings of custodial interviews, start to finish. *Golden Gate University Law Review, 37,* 175–190. http://www.ggu.edu/lawlibrary/ggulawreview.

Sullivan, T. P. (2010). The wisdom of custodial recording. In G. D. Lassiter & C. A. Meissner (Eds.), *Police interrogations and false confessions: Current research, practice, and policy recommendations* (pp. 127–142). Washington, D.C.: American Psychological Association.

Sykes, G. M., & Matza, D. (1957). Techniques of neutralization: A theory of delinquency. *American Sociological Review, 22,* 664–670. doi:10.2307/2089195.

Tanenhaus, D. S., & Drizin, S. A. (2002). 'Owing to the extreme youth of the accused': The changing legal response to juvenile homicide. *Journal of Criminal Law and Criminology, 92,* 641–706. http://www.law.northwestern.edu/jclc/.

Tepfer, J. A., Nirider, L. H., & Tricarico, L. M. (2010). Arresting development: Convictions of innocent youth. *Rutgers Law Review, 62,* 887–941. http://pegasus.rutgers.edu/~review/.

Tobey, A., Grisso, T., & Schwartz, R. (2000). Youths' trial participation as seen by youths and their attorneys: An exploration of competence-based issues. In T. Grisso & R. G. Schwartz (Eds.), *Youth on trial: A developmental perspective on juvenile justice* (pp. 225–242). Chicago: University of Chicago Press.

Viljoen, J., & Roesch, R. (2005). Competence to waive interrogation rights and adjudicative competence in adolescent defendants: Cognitive development, attorney contact, and psychological symptoms. *Law and Human Behavior, 29,* 723–742. doi:10.1007/s 10979-005-7978-y.

Viljoen, J., Klaver, J., & Roesch, R. (2005). Legal decisions of preadolescent and adolescent defendants: Predictors of confessions, pleas, communication with attorneys, and appeals. *Law and Human Behavior, 29,* 253–278. doi:10.1007/s10979-005-3613-2.

Viljoen, J., Zapf, P., & Roesch, R. (2007). Adjudicative competence and comprehension of *Miranda* rights in adolescent defendants: A comparison of legal standards. *Behavioral Sciences & the Law, 25,* 1–19. doi:10.1002/bsl.714.

Wald, M., Ayres, R., Hess, D. W., Schantz, M., & Whitebread II, C. H. (1967). Interrogations in New Haven: The impact of *Miranda*. *Yale Law Journal, 76,* 1519–1648. http://yalelawjournal.org/.

Weisselberg, C. D. (2008). Mourning *Miranda*. *California Law Review, 96,* 1519–1601. http://www.californialawreview.org.

White, W. S. (1997). False confessions and the constitution: Safeguards against unworthy confessions. *Harvard Civil Rights-Civil Liberties Law Review, 17,* 105–158. http://www.cwsl.edu/.

White, W. S. (2001). *Miranda*'s failure to restrain pernicious interrogation practices. *Michigan Law Review, 99,* 1211–1247. http://www.michiganlawreview.org/.

Woolard, J. L., Harvell, S., & Graham, S. (2008). Anticipatory injustice among adolescents: Age and racial/ethnic differences in perceived unfairness of the justice system. *Behavioral Sciences and the Law, 26,* 207–226. doi:10.1002/bsl.805.

Yarborough v. Alvarado, 541 U.S. 652 (2004).

Chapter 4
Between Investigator and Suspect: The Role of the Working Alliance in Investigative Interviewing

Miet Vanderhallen and Geert Vervaeke

Interviewees often experience being questioned by the police as an uncomfortable and stressful event (Baldwin 1993; Fisher and Perez 2010; Ord et al. 2011; Vanderhallen 2007). These feelings become even stronger for those being questioned as suspects, as the police typically focus on stringent accounts of the interviewees' behaviour in order to find out whether they were involved in the crime. For many suspects, this does not create a good foundation for an open and detailed conversation.

The importance of rapport within the context of investigative interviewing has been acknowledged in the scientific literature and in interview manuals (e.g. Bull and Milne 2004; Clarke and Milne 2001; Collins and Frank 2002, 2005; Fisher and Geiselman 2006; Gudjonsson 2003; Holmberg 2004; Milne and Bull 1999; Powell et al. 2005; Shepherd 2007; St-Yves and Deslauriers-Varin 2009). The word 'rapport' originates from the Latin word *portare,* which literally means 'to carry' (Milne and Bull 1999). It is commonly agreed that building rapport is an essential ingredient for successful interviews, in that it helps conversations to flow more freely. Police officers should 'control' their interviews and not 'dominate' them, as domination is counterproductive (Green 2012). Similarly, confrontations should be avoided early in the interview, as they could hamper the process of building rapport, thereby causing the suspect to distrust the interviewer and withdraw all cooperation (Sellers and Kebbell 2009).

The ability to build rapport is considered one of the principles of successful interviewing and one of the core skills that interviewers need (Shawyer et al. 2009). St-Yves (2009) argues that the effectiveness of interview techniques depends upon good rapport, thus identifying rapport as a necessary condition for effective suspect

M. Vanderhallen (✉)
Antwerp University, Antwerp, Belgium
e-mail: miet.vanderhallen@ua.ac.be

Maastricht University, Maastricht, The Netherlands

University of Leuven, Leuven, Belgium

G. Vervaeke
University of Leuven—Leuven, Flanders, Belgium
e-mail: geert.vervaeke@law.kuleuven.be

R. Bull (ed.), *Investigative Interviewing*, DOI 10.1007/978-1-4614-9642-7_4,
© Springer Science+Business Media New York 2014

interviews. While good rapport can make it easier for an innocent suspect to provide an elaborate account, respectful treatment can also encourage a guilty suspect to provide a fuller account (Milne and Bull 1999).

Towards a Rapport-Based Approach

In recent decades, the importance of rapport in interrogations has become a focus of attention that transcends individual cases and geographical boundaries. Rapport building has thus become common property in suspect interviews. In some European countries, the Salduz case law has led to the preparation and implementation of national judicial reforms that allow lawyers to be present during interviews with suspects. This has raised questions about rapport building with suspects and also with their legal advisors.

From Sexual Crimes to Terrorism: A Case-Oriented Shift

Research in England and Wales has shown that building rapport is often limited to certain criminal cases. Interviewers often attempt to establish rapport only in cases involving crimes with an (inter)personal and emotional character, as with rape (Moston and Engelberg 1993). Similar results are reported in a study about empathic behaviour shown by police officers to arrested suspects (Poole and Pogrebin 1989). Thus, police officers may be empathic only with suspects who are able to present themselves as unfortunate and in need of help. An explanation concerning the affinity of police officers for this 'directional' rapport-building strategy is that interviewers tend to prefer a formal atmosphere instead of creating a false cordiality (Baldwin 1993).

Nevertheless, interviewers have apparently come to accept the importance of rapport when asked for their opinions—or they have at least become more compliant in their interview methods. From studies in the early 1980s–1990s, it can be derived that interviewers have begun to identify rapport as one of the most important skills in interviewing. In a self-report study by Bull and Cherryman (1996), 93 % of the participating police officers recognised the crucial role of establishing rapport. A recent study confirms these findings. In this study, questionnaires were completed by 79 experienced police officers prior to an advanced training session in investigative interviewing. The officers were asked to indicate their opinions regarding the relative importance of building rapport with suspects, in addition to providing information about their primary reasons for building rapport and the ways in which they build rapport with suspects. Similar questions were asked with regard to establishing rapport with legal advisors attending interviews. Most (97.5 %) of the police officers surveyed agreed that building rapport with suspects is important.

Moreover, interviewers report that establishing rapport is crucial for good interviews in general (Bull and Soukara 2010). The importance attributed to rapport is reflected in other studies as well. For example, Kassin and colleagues (2007) report that 31 % of the interviewers surveyed stated that they always build rapport during interviews with suspects.

Gudjonsson (2006) explicitly emphasises the need for rapport with sex offenders, as these offenders can have a strong internal need to confess, although they are reluctant to do so, due to feelings of shame. Such feelings could be overcome by establishing rapport in order to facilitate the suspect's willingness and ability to talk about the offence.

Building rapport is emphasised even more strongly with regard to interviewing psychologically vulnerable suspects. Gudjonsson (2003) states that, in addition to reducing stress, good rapport can support psychologically vulnerable suspects, given their limited capacity for coping with stress. Similar results are presented in a self-report study, in which police officers address the importance of rapport to persuading sex offenders to confess (Kebbell et al. 2006).

Despite such common acceptance of rapport in conventional law enforcement, building rapport with suspects has been questioned in interviews within the context of war or armed conflicts, as well as in extraordinary criminal cases (Pearse 2006). However, within the context of terrorism, it has been argued that aggressive strategies are ineffective, as they produce unreliable information (Borum et al. 2009; Gelles et al. 2006). The effectiveness of human intelligence (HUMINT) has come under great scrutiny due to the past use of 'enhanced' interview techniques in Iraq and other settings. The use and efficacy of torture for eliciting reliable and relevant information (i.e. the effectiveness of torture for 'educing intelligence' which refers to drawing out information that might be hidden, unexpressed or latent; Borum et al. 2009) has become a highly debatable issue (Evans et al. 2010).

For this reason, Gelles and colleagues (2006) recommend investing in establishing rapport while interviewing terrorism suspects as well. A non-accusatory rapport-based approach is required in order to elicit reliable and non-coerced information. The ultimate case for using torture or near torture is the hypothetical *ticking time bomb* scenario (Morgan and Williamson 2009). In contradiction with such traditional lines of reasoning that allow increased pressure, experts in the field nowadays recommend a rapport-based approach in order to elicit reliable information (Dixon 2009; Gelles et al. 2006; Pearse 2006; Roberts 2011). It is nevertheless argued that psychologists should invest in understanding the circumstances of terrorism cases (which can in some countries be characterised by coercive pressure) in addition to becoming familiar with non-coercive techniques that might be effective in this complex practice (Hubbard 2007).

Although building rapport is generally considered necessary in the initial stages of interviews, regardless of the type of cases or suspect (Kebbell et al. 2006), one exception has been identified. As observed by Quale (2008), one of the strategies for countering psychopathic interview behaviour is for the interviewer to be unconcerned with building rapport. Despite its value in most police interviews, rapport could be counterproductive with psychopathic suspects, as they are not concerned with such matters as trust, empathy or closeness. Such cases therefore probably call for a more formal conversational atmosphere.

From England to East and West: A Geographical Shift

In addition to its importance across a wide variety of cases, rapport is currently recommended by many interview methods that are used in a wide range of geographic locations (Bull and Soukara 2010; Fisher and Geiselman 2006; Milne and Bull 1999; Shepherd 2007; van Amelsvoort et al. 2010; Van De Plas 2007).

In general, interview methods can be divided into two categories: the information-gathering and the accusatorial (Hartwig 2005). These interview methods can be differentiated along four dimensions (Meissner et al. 2012). Information-gathering methods are directed towards finding the truth, while accusatorial methods attempt to elicit confessions (Dimension 1: Objective). In order to find the truth, information-gathering methods focus on establishing rapport (Dimension 2: Focus), use direct, positive confrontation (Dimension 3: Techniques) and employ open-ended, exploratory questions (Dimension 4: Question format). In contrast, accusatorial methods emphasise establishing control, using psychological manipulation, and employing closed-ended and confirmatory questions in trying to obtain confessions. Meissner and colleagues (2012) do identify a fifth dimension, 'detecting deception', which is less relevant for this contribution. Moreover, in Belgium, where an information-gathering method was adopted, lie detection cues referring to anxiety are still in use. According to the classification, information-gathering methods use cognitive cues for detecting deception, instead of the anxiety cues associated with accusatorial methods (Meissner et al. 2012).

The information-gathering method originated in the UK, with the introduction of the PEACE model in 1992 (the acronym PEACE stands for 'Planning and Preparation, Engage and Explain, obtain an Account, Closure and Evaluation', Bull and Milne 2004; Bull and Soukara 2010; Milne and Bull 1999). Influenced by the European Convention of Human Rights (ECTR, Art. 6), European countries have begun to pursue a more ethical way of questioning suspects without the use of such deceptive techniques as presenting false evidence (Meissner et al. 2012). In addition to the UK, Norway, New Zealand and Australia have adopted information-gathering methods throughout their national systems (Bull and Soukara 2010). Other European countries (e.g. Belgium) have also adopted information-gathering methods fashioned after the PEACE model, being characterised as having inquisitorial judicial systems or a hybrid system based on an inquisitorial legal system (De Smet 1999). In inquisitorial justice systems, the search for the truth is formally identified as the goal of interviews with suspects, although practice often reveals a somewhat contrasting picture. A self-report study conducted in Belgium reveals that police officers also consider the objectives of suspect interviews to include obtaining confessions and gathering information on the modus operandi (Ponsaers et al. 2001). This suggests that the information-gathering approach is in some countries being adopted in order to place more emphasis on the search for the truth (rapport building is necessary). Another study reports that police academies differ in the integration of the information-gathering interview method that was approved nationally in 1998 (Basic Interview Technique, covering similar phases and practices as the

PEACE model) into their training whereby the implementation of the technique was sometimes insufficient (Volckaert 2005). Despite differences in the legal systems, therefore, European countries with inquisitorial systems also need to strengthen their information-gathering approaches in order to find the truth.

The accusatorial approach, as typified in the USA, has commonly been used in Canada and many Asian countries (Davies and Shen 2010; Meissner et al. 2012; St-Yves and Deslauriers-Varin 2009). It is important to note that accusatorial methods do not incorporate rapport building as a core element in interrogation, nor do they refer to it in relation to the search for the truth. Nevertheless, these methods do recognise the importance of rapport when questioning suspects, particularly in the pre-interrogation phase, in which the suspect's guilt is yet to be determined (Buckley 2006; St-Yves and Deslauriers-Varin 2009).

In the UK, information-gathering methods were developed as an alternative to the traditional confession-oriented methods, in response to increasing criticism in the 1980s concerning the use of accusatorial methods. Miscarriages of justice due to false confessions elicited through accusatorial interview methods led to legislative changes, including the introduction of the Police and Criminal Evidence Act (PACE) in 1994 (Shawyer et al. 2009). Research findings from analysis of interviews conducted in the late 1980s highlighted the need to improve the quality of interviews with suspects, ultimately resulting in the 1992 development of the PEACE model. Both PACE and PEACE brought about a shift from a confession-oriented approach to one focused much more on gathering information. This shift was even reflected in changes in terminology (e.g. from 'interrogation' to 'investigative interviewing').

The shift from an accusatorial, confession-seeking approach to a more information-gathering approach in the search for truth is a persistent issue, which has arisen in other common law countries as well. In response to several miscarriages of justice due to poor interviewing in Canada, researchers highlighted the necessity of substantial reforms with regard to interviewing suspects (Snook et al. 2010). The recent Dixon case brought the Reid technique under scrutiny (Brean 2011). In this case, Michael Dixon was charged with burglary, a crime he did not commit. He was confronted with the accusatory tactics of the Reid technique during interrogation. After he was ultimately proved innocent, Dixon received nearly US $ 50,000 for false imprisonment, false arrest and negligent investigation.

The scientifically grounded PEACE model has been advanced as a foundation for a standardised national model to replace the current accusatorial approach (Snook et al. 2010). In the USA, the revelation of several miscarriages of justice and false confessions encouraged researchers to question the accusatorial approach. As a more effective alternative, Meissner and colleagues (2010) advocate a diagnostic interview method, which is non-accusatorial and which nevertheless supports the criminal investigation, thus referring to a scientifically supported interview method that has proved effective in identifying innocence without demonstrating any increase in true confessions. In this regard as well, the PEACE model is presented as a potentially effective alternative to the classic American method of interrogation (Kassin et al. 2010; Gudjonsson and Pearse 2011).

Australian experts are also encouraging the widespread adoption of a more ethical and information-gathering approach in suspect interviewing (Green 2012; Nolan 2009). The People's Republic of China (PRC) was recently confronted with a legislative reform as well. By allowing high-profile cases to come into the public domain, the government of the People's Republic of China indicated its intent to change the practice in which the rights of suspects were not always respected (Davies and Shen 2010). The new Criminal Procedure Law (CPL) specifies exclusionary rules for evidence (Weidong et al. 2012). Its provisions include a statement that interviews with suspects must be audio- and videotaped, that confessions must be voluntary, and that forced self-incrimination is forbidden. The prohibition against forced self-incrimination requires improvements in the interrogation techniques currently employed. Such improvements serve to facilitate the transition to a new model of investigation. In addition to these judicial reforms, the 'Prevention of torture in the PRC' project, which is funded by the European Union, aimed to develop a European-based training programme for China incorporating an information-gathering method. The method is intended to introduce Chinese police officers to current European practices (Vanderhallen and Lei 2012). It was also aimed at integrating several techniques and didactic practices into current Chinese training. The training programme has been delivered in two police academies and attended by 58 police officers from 23 Chinese provinces. The majority of the participants considered the information-gathering method quite helpful.

Evidence of the shift from an accusatorial approach to an information-gathering approach is clearly available in the practices of countries from the East to the West, with traditionally inquisitorial countries reinforcing their use of this approach as well. Thus, the adoption of the information-gathering approach is emphasising the importance of rapport building in a rapidly growing number of countries around the world.

From Suspects to Legal Advisors: A Person-Oriented Shift

Research following the introduction of the PEACE model has shown a decrease in the use of coercive techniques. These results support the model as an approach that can help to maximise the likelihood of a fair trial (Shawyer et al. 2009). In order to ensure a fair trial (Art. 6 ECHR), the European Court of Human Rights recently determined that suspects are entitled to have access to legal advice before and during the interview. This ruling, which is often referred to as the Salduz case law (the first case was *Salduz v. Turkey*, ECtHR 27 November 2008, no. 36391/02) has led to legal reforms in various European countries (e.g. Belgium and France), which allow lawyers to provide legal advice prior to the suspect interview and/or to be present during the interview.

The introduction of the lawyer into the interview room raises questions related to the need to build rapport not only with suspects (in presence of their lawyers), but with the lawyers as well. In England and Wales, legal advice during interviews has been common practice since the implementation of PACE in 1986.

A large-scale evaluation study by Clarke and Milne (2001) considered the impact of the presence of legal advisors on the performance of police officers when interviewing suspects. An analysis of 174 real-life interviews found no differences in performance between interviews in which a legal advisor was present and interviews without a legal advisor (Clarke et al. 2011). This suggests that the presence of legal advisors has no effect on police officers' rapport building with suspects (one of the activities examined in the study).

At least to some extent, this finding is supported by the self-report study (mentioned above) in Belgium in which 79 police officers filled in a questionnaire prior to an advanced interview training. In that study, 71 % of the police officers surveyed did not consider it more important to establish rapport with a suspect if a legal advisor is present. Police officers attributing more importance to building rapport in the presence of a lawyer noted that advisors tend to interrupt interviews if rapport is inadequate (perhaps because of a more confrontational style). They also noted that suspects may feel supported by their legal advisors, police officers, therefore, should invest more in rapport building with suspects since the relationship between the suspect and his legal advisor could hamper the collaboration of suspects in terms of providing information to the police.

The majority (67 %) of the police officers in this study also indicated that it is important to build rapport with legal advisors, primarily in order to find the truth and therefore to encourage the lawyers to advise their clients to cooperate.

Such findings suggest that building rapport with the suspect is important regardless of whether a legal advisor is present during the interview. Moreover, most police officers believe that building rapport with legal advisors is important as well. In contrast to the literature on the role of building rapport with suspects in relation to the interview outcome, the function of rapport building with legal advisors in suspect interviewing is under researched.

The Role of Rapport

According to Ord and colleagues (2011), police interviews can take place within a tense and unnatural setting. The experience of being questioned by the police can therefore cause feelings of stress and anxiety. Good rapport is hypothesised to help interviewees overcome these feelings and talk more freely.

Building Rapport with Witnesses

Holmberg (2009) argues that rapport can make it easier for victims to provide information during police interviewing. Studies have confirmed the facilitating role of rapport, indicating that witnesses provide information that is more accurate when good rapport has been established (Collins et al. 2002, 2005; Vallano et al. 2008). Collins and colleagues (2005) compared three rapport conditions (i.e. the abrupt mode, the neutral mode, and the rapport mode). In the rapport mode, respondents were more cooperative and provided more accurate information than they did in either the neutral or the abrupt mode. These results indicate that rapport is positively related to both quantity and quality of the information provided by witnesses. This finding was particularly strong in response to open-ended questions in interviews in which good rapport had been established (Vallano and Schreiber Compo 2011). Another study (Holmberg 2004) examined the relationship between interviewing style and the amount and accuracy of information provided by witnesses. The humanitarian interviewing style—which is characterised by friendliness, empathy and engagement—was significantly related to the provision of more accurate information by witnesses. In the absence of good rapport, both police officers and witnesses tend to react with dislike, and they are reluctant to engage in social bonding (Holmberg 2009). The results further revealed that when investigators failed to establish rapport, witnesses report a greater amount of misinformation (Vallano et al. 2008).

Building Rapport with Suspects

Suspects are likely to experience the above-mentioned feelings of stress and anxiety even more strongly than witnesses do (Ord et al. 2011; Walsh and Bull 2012a). Indeed, in a recent study by Vanderhallen et al. (2011), 39 suspects and 61 witnesses completed questionnaires immediately after being questioned by the police. The suspects experienced significantly more anxiety and felt less respected by the interviewers than did the witnesses.

In a study by Vrij and colleagues (2006), accusatory interviews generated stronger feelings of inconvenience than did interviews conducted in an information-gathering style. Besides, interviewees report a similar level of cognitive load which indicates that suspects are cognitively challenged when being invited to talk freely without feeling less comfortable. One explanation is that the cognitive load may originate from reluctance to provide information, as this may lead to their incrimination in wrongdoing (Walsh and Bull 2012a). Nevertheless, it is often argued that good rapport may encourage suspects to talk more freely about their whereabouts (Ord et al. 2011; Shawyer et al. 2009; St-Yves 2006).

Two assumptions underlie the important role of rapport in interviews with suspects. Good rapport is (1) assumed to enhance the cooperation of suspects during interviews and (2) thus result in the provision of more accurate information. With regard to the assumption of enhanced cooperation, an observational study by Bull and Soukara (2010) reports that the cooperation of suspects is positively related to the extent to which interviewers build rapport. The second assumption also stands firm. Various studies have revealed a positive relationship between good rapport and the outcome of interviews (while the dominant approach is negatively related to rapport and a successful outcome). For example, in Finland, the dominant approach (as operationalised by striving for confrontation) was not effective in establishing rapport and encouraging suspects to talk (Häkkänen et al. 2009). In interviews with prisoners, good rapport has been shown to yield information that is more detailed (Pinizzotto and Davis 1996). It is important to note, however, that prisoners have less to lose by providing information in interviews than suspects do.

Holmberg and Christianson (2002) report that convicted offenders who were interviewed in a more humanitarian manner confessed more frequently. In a recent experimental study with 146 subjects, Holmberg and Madsen (2010) also reveal that the humanitarian interview style helps interviewees to remember and provide significantly more information than the dominant style does. With regard to rapport, Holmberg states that the humanitarian interview style promotes rapport through the underlying notions of showing empathy and personalising the interview (Holmberg 2009). In this manner, the interview style may increase the likelihood that suspects will provide a full account. Such notions are supported by another study, which involved self-reports by prisoners who referred to the importance of rapport and characteristics consistent with humanity to facilitate confessions and avoid denials (Kebbell et al. 2006).

The use of self-report questionnaires may undermine the validity of the findings of studies such as those mentioned above. For this reason, Walsh and Bull (2010a, 2012a, b) conducted a series of studies based on the analysis of audiotapes of interviews with people suspected of benefit fraud. The interviewers were non-police officers (although they were governmental officials). In the initial study, 142 suspect interviews (115 audiotapes and 27 transcripts) were examined in detail (Walsh and Bull 2010a). The overall finding was that skilled PEACE interviewing was related to full accounts, including confessions. The competency that yielded by far the largest effects in both the quality and outcomes of interviews was rapport building. This competency was also the best predictor for the overall quality of the 'engage-and-explain' phase. In a second study, Walsh and Bull (2012b) analysed 85 such interviews in order to gain insight into the relationship of the skill level, tactics and attitudes of interviewers with the movement of suspects towards confession. Confessions were positively associated with the display of certain tactics and attitudes (many of which are recommended in the PEACE model), including building rapport. The effect size of this relationship, however, indicates that the contribution of rapport building was smaller than could be expected, given the prominent role attributed to rapport in literature. A third study, in which the original 142 suspect interviews were examined, reveals that interviews characterised by higher overall skill ratings and preferred outcomes were those characterised by relatively good rapport building (Walsh and Bull 2012a). These authors distinguish between rapport building at the beginning of the interview (i.e. the engage-and-explain phase) and the maintenance of rapport throughout the interview. More specifically, preferred outcomes were achieved in interviews in which rapport building was classified as 'satisfactory' and rapport maintenance was classified as 'skilled'.

Support for an information-gathering style emphasising rapport building, in order to obtain true confessions, is also provided in a recent metaanalysis conducted by Meissner and colleagues (2012). While the information-gathering and accusatory methods were similarly associated with the production of confessions in field studies, experimental data indicated that the information-gathering method increased the likelihood of true confessions, while reducing the likelihood of false confessions. As stated by these authors, however, their findings should be treated as tentative, given the small number of independent samples available at that time.

Building Rapport in Police Practice

Despite the consensus of academics and interview practitioners concerning the important role of rapport, interviewing practice unfortunately reveals disturbing shortfalls with regard to its development and maintenance. Observational studies have consistently shown that many interviewers do not invest properly in building good rapport. Increased efforts in recent years with regard to further development of training do not seem to have had a strong impact. This finding does not apply exclusively to interviews with suspects. Insufficient rapport building was identified in 40 % of the witness interviews examined in a large-scale evaluation study in the UK (Clarke and Milne 2001). A recent study conducted in the USA confirms these findings: Only 65 % of the interviews from 26 South Florida investigators included some level of rapport building (Schreiber Compo et al. 2012). In addition to long pauses, the development of rapport was one of the few frequently used positive (i.e. ethically recommended) interview techniques that these investigators employed with witnesses.

The shortcomings of rapport building in interviews have been addressed since at least the early 1990s. Despite the fact that some officers have been more successful than others in establishing rapport, most of them made no serious effort (Baldwin 1993). While only a minority of the interviewers seemed able to build a relationship with a suspect, most attempts were artificial in nature. Similar findings are reported in a study conducted shortly thereafter, with rapport having been established in only 3 % (Pearse and Gudjonsson 1996).

About 10 years after the above-mentioned studies, following the national implementation of the PEACE model, a large-scale evaluation study once again revealed little evidence of rapport building in interviews with suspects (Clarke and Milne 2001). Rapport was conducted professionally in only 7 % of the interviews, while no attempts to build rapport could be identified in 47 % of the interviews. Recent studies of benefit-fraud interviewing conducted by non-police officials have also revealed weaknesses in rapport building (Walsh and Bull 2010b). In a study by Walsh and Milne (2008) involving interviews with benefit-fraud suspects, both trained and untrained investigators received ratings of merely 'satisfactory' for rapport building. A more recent analysis of 142 interviews with benefit-fraud suspects showed that while only 20 % of the interviews failed to provide any evidence of rapport building (Walsh and Bull 2010b), interviewers who did invest in rapport building spent very little time on this task before posing a series of questions to the suspect. Even when good rapport was established in the early stages of the interview, these interviewers failed to invest in rapport maintenance throughout the interview. In addition to insight into the prevalence of rapport, another important contribution of this study is the distinction that it makes between the development of rapport at the beginning of an interview and the maintenance of rapport during the interview. Because interview manuals often focus on 'building' rapport at the beginning of the interview, interviewers may incorrectly think that rapport building is an activity to be completed only during the first part of the interview. On the contrary, once rapport has been established, good maintenance requires similar efforts up to and including the closure phase of the interview (Walsh and Bull 2012a).

Inadequacies in the development of rapport have been identified in other countries. Observation of video-recorded interviews with suspects in Australia revealed that the power relation between interviewer and interviewee is still strongly weighted in favour of the interviewer (Dixon 2007). In Belgium, self-reports by interviewers and interviewees show that witnesses experience better working alliances than suspects do (Vanderhallen et al. 2011). Similarly, the interviewers reported having better alliances with witnesses than they did with suspects. In a self-report study, police officers from India report that nonintimidating interview techniques (e.g. building rapport) are more useful than intimidating techniques are, although they did not report using these techniques in interviews any more frequently than did police officers who believed in the use of intimidating techniques (Alison et al. 2008b). Such results indicate that belief in the importance of rapport development is not associated with the actual usage of these techniques. This self-report study was also conducted in Hong Kong and found that only 19 % of police officers identify the creation of a positive atmosphere as indicative of successful interviewing (Alison et al. 2008a). About half (55 %) of these police officers reported using rapport-building strategies.

These findings suggest that interviewers all over the world have trouble establishing rapport. They are in need of good building blocks with which to improve their ability to develop rapport with suspects.

How Can Rapport Be Built?

One of the explanations for the poor and mediocre levels of rapport building in interview practice may be found in the conceptual and theoretical definition of the construct of rapport, as reflected in the suggestions on how rapport should be established. Despite consensus that developing rapport involves more than simply being nice to or sympathising with suspects (Gelles et al. 2006), the literature refers to a variety of procedures that (1) sometimes overlap or that are classified distinctively and that (2) often do not explain the extent to which these recommendations are scientifically grounded, particularly in the context of investigative interviewing. Unfortunately, these weaknesses impede the general understanding of what interviewers should do to establish rapport. The following paragraphs list attitudes and skills that are frequently identified as beneficial to the rapport-building process, structured into seven categories of building blocks suggested in the literature.

First, interviewers must be empathic (Fisher and Geiselman 1992; St-Yves 2006; Yeschke 2003). Barrett-Lennard (1962) defines this as follows:

> an active process of desiring to know the full, present and changing awareness of another person, of reaching out to receive his communication and meaning, and of translating his words and signs into experienced meaning and matches at least those aspects of his awareness that are most important to him at the moment. It is an experiencing of the consciousness 'behind' another's outward communication, but with continuous awareness that this consciousness is originating and proceeding in the other.

Within the context of investigative interviewing, according to Davies (1983) police officers should show empathy, understand their interviewees, appreciate their emotions and distress, and communicate this to interviewees both directly and indirectly. To date, empirical research about the role of empathy in establishing rapport during investigative interviewing is scarce. According to one recent study that investigates the use of empathy in obtaining Investigation Relevant Information (IRI), the interview style is more beneficial for this purpose, while empathy has no impact (Oxburgh and Ost 2011). Bull and Cherryman (1996) distinguish competent from incompetent interviews, finding that one of the greatest differences between competence and incompetence involves the extent to which interviewers demonstrate empathy, thus confirming the important role that empathy can play in the overall quality of the interview.

A second building block for establishing rapport with suspects is active listening (Fisher and Geiselman 1992; Milne and Bull 1999; Yeschke 2003). According to some authors, active listening concerns both nonverbal and verbal behaviour (St-Yves 2006), while other authors address only verbal behaviours (Milne and Bull 1999).

Consensus exists with regard to the role of active listening, which aims at encouraging the suspect to talk. This type of encouragement can increase the amount of speech by up to three or four times (Wainwright 2003 in St-Yves 2006), and it has been found helpful in building rapport between therapists and clients (Bedi et al. 2005). Examples of encouragement include nodding, facial expressions (nonverbal, St-Yves 2006) and the use of such utterances as 'hum', 'OK' and 'I see' (verbal, Milne and Bull 1999). Within the verbal component, various additional strategies for demonstrating active listening can be identified (Milne and Bull 1999; St-Yves 2006). First, interviewers should use summaries. This technique also allows interviewers to check their understanding of what suspects have said, and it facilitates the storage of the information in the interviewer's memory. In addition to summarising, interviewers should engage in echo probing, which means the interviewer repeats the exact last words uttered by the suspect. By doing so, the interviewer can also urge the suspect to elaborate. St-Yves (2006) adds four additional activities to the verbal component of active listening: paraphrasing, open questions, the use of 'I' and the identification of emotions. According to St-Yves (2006), interviewers may also demonstrate the depth of their empathy by putting the emotions expressed by the suspect into words. This technique has also been shown to contribute to rapport building between therapists and their clients (Bedi et al. 2005).

Additional nonverbal activities for engaging in active listening include eye contact (St-Yves 2006) and the use of silence to provide the suspect (as well as the interviewer) with time to think. Several studies have provided evidence that eye contact helps to establish rapport between therapists and their clients (Bedi et al. 2005).

Although it is not always mentioned as a component of active listening, the nonverbal behaviour of mirroring has been identified as helping to build rapport (Frank et al. 2006; Milne and Bull 1999). Mirroring is often used to infer rapport in social interactions (Tickle-Degnen and Rosenthal 1987). Research in therapeutic settings confirms this role, showing that postural mirroring occurs significantly more in conversations, in which good rapport has been established (Sharpley et al. 2001). A certain level of caution is advised, however, as it is important to execute and interpret nonverbal signs correctly (Sanchez-Burks 2002).

A third building block for interviewers involves adopting an informal, friendly style of conversation (Moston and Engelberg 1993; Vallano and Schreiber Compo 2011). This is supported by a study conducted by Collins and colleagues (2002), who observe that interviewees report higher levels of rapport when they are approached in a friendly, gentle and relaxed manner. This style of conversation is reflected in paralanguage (e.g. timbre, loudness, utterance), which allows suspects to read more than the words alone (Milne and Bull 1999). For example, the way in which a question is posed can affect the message that is conveyed.

A fourth contributor concerns the personalisation of the interview (Schreiber Compo et al. 2012; Fisher and Geiselman 1992; Milne and Bull 1999), including the use of self-disclosure (Fisher and Geiselman 1992; Milne and Bull 1999). Personalisation means that interviewers and suspects treat each other as individuals (Milne and Bull 1999). Rapport is even more important when highly personal information is needed from the suspects. In such cases, it may be helpful for interviewers to disclose information about themselves. By doing so, interviewers can also demonstrate what is expected from the suspects. Self-disclosure can also help to personalise the interview, as it can make it easier for the suspect to identify with the interviewer. Research has confirmed that some interviewers use self-disclosure with the goal of affiliating with suspects (Stokoe 2009). In the therapist-client relationship, self-disclosure can be successful in establishing rapport, although not in all situations (Bedi et al. 2005). In the context of witness interviews, however, self-disclosure by interviewers does not facilitate a more comfortable atmosphere, nor does it result in additional witness-recall benefits (Vallano and Schreiber Compo 2011). Nevertheless, self-disclosure by the interviewer may personalise the interview, as subjects interviewed in a no-rapport mode have been observed to perceive such interviews as too professional. Alternative approaches to self-disclosure in the context of investigative interviewing should also be examined.

A fifth building block states that interviewers should consider their own positions in terms of proximity, posture and orientation (Milne and Bull 1999). Proximity refers to the distance between the interviewer and the suspect. Research has shown that the invasion of personal space can increase the stress experienced (and expressed) by the interviewee (Baxter and Roselle 1975 in Milne and Bull 1999). Posture and orientation refer to the angle at which the interviewer is sitting/standing in relation to the suspect. Research has shown that different orientations relate to different relationships, with a 120-degree angle increasing the comfort of the conversation (Cook 1970).

Genuineness also plays an important role in developing rapport (Inbau et al. 2004; St-Yves 2006). According to St-Yves (2006), this is a significant factor in the establishment of rapport, given that genuine relationships are more likely to generate trust and confidence, thereby encouraging interviewees to provide truthful accounts. In therapeutic settings, authenticity (as one part of congruency) is considered as contributing to the therapeutic relationship, together with empathy and unconditional positive regard (Gelso and Carter 1985).

St-Yves (2006) addresses the importance of good initial contact (e.g. a warm welcome followed by an explanation of the goals of the interview). A warm and personalised greeting has been shown to contribute to the development of rapport between therapists and their clients (Bedi et al. 2005). Moreover, several of the prescribed tasks could be expected to contribute to the development of rapport in the initial phase of the interview (Walsh and Bull 2012a). Examples include the presentation of all parties involved and the official notifications, including the caution. In this regard, Shepherd and Milne (2006) emphasise that the clear explanation of the reason, goal, proceedings and instructions for the interview enhances the development of rapport.

In addition to these relatively general notions concerning how to build rapport, several other recommendations have been made. For example, St-Yves (2006) addresses the impact of transference and counter-transference. It has also been suggested that concern for the suspect's welfare can be helpful in building rapport (Kalbfleisch 1994; Moston and Fisher 2007), as can demonstrations of fairness and maybe compassion (Yeschke 2003). With regard to the disclosure of incriminating evidence, late evidence disclosure is preferable to early evidence disclosure for enhancing rapport (Sellers and Kebbell 2009).

Finally, the use of 'tandem interviewers' could jeopardise the development of rapport with a suspect. In some countries, interviews are conducted by two interviewers rather than one. In a self-report study, 34 % of the 126 interviews were found to be conducted by two interviewers (Vanderhallen 2007). However, exploratory research on the impact of a third party (i.e. a second interviewer) on rapport in investigative interviewing reveals no significant difference in the suspect's perception of rapport, suggesting that the impact of two interviewers in the initial phase of the interview is relatively small or even nonexistent (Driskell et al. 2012).

The observations and arguments found throughout the literature on investigative interviewing clearly suggest that further research on the role and construct of rapport is needed if the level of rapport in suspect interviews is to be improved.

A Step Towards Unravelling the Construct of Rapport

Research has shown that rapport plays a significant role in achieving successful interview outcomes. The construct of rapport has traditionally been referenced in clinical settings, with therapists often referring to the importance of a 'therapeutic alliance' to the success of various therapies (Bedi et al. 2005). Nevertheless, the construct suffers from a conceptual weakness, which generates methodological restrictions that hamper research in the field (Collins et al. 2002). Various authors have proposed a multitude of conceptual definitions. Sandoval and Adams define rapport as 'a relationship or communication characterized by harmony' (2001, p. 2). Harmony is also a core element of the definition applied by Newbury and Strubbs, who define rapport as 'a harmonious, empathetic or sympathetic relation or connection to another self' (1990, in Collins et al. 2002, p. 71). Clarke and Milne describe rapport as 'a professional relationship' (2001, p. 36). In contrast, Coleman refers to an emotional aspect by defining rapport as 'the good feeling or warmth that exists between people, an interpersonal relationship characterized by a spirit of cooperation, confidence and harmony' (in Yeschke 2003, p. 72).

This conceptual confusion is often exacerbated by the lack of a thorough theoretical framework. Probably, the most comprehensive framework of rapport was developed by Tickle-Degnen and Rosenthal (1990), who define rapport as comprising three components: (1) mutual attentiveness, (2) positivity, and (3) coordination. Mutual attentiveness refers to the cohesiveness generated by shared interest and focus. Positivity refers to feelings of mutual friendliness and caring, while coordination reflects the balance and harmony between the parties.

In research on interviewing styles, Holmberg (2009) uses the humanitarian interviewing style to operationalise rapport from an insider perspective. Rapport is treated as a phenomenon involving mutual feelings, again following the theoretical framework developed by Tickle-Degnen and Rosenthal. According to these authors, this framework makes it totally possible to distinguish the construct of rapport from other constructs (e.g. empathy). Nevertheless, a valid measurement of rapport remains absent.

Given the conceptual complexity and theoretical weakness of the concept, the measurement of rapport is challenging. Most studies use observers or interviewees to code the degree of rapport. In general, two measurements can be identified. The first type of measurement involves post-session measurement, which captures rapport using a single question on 'the presence of rapport' (Clarke and Milne 2001; Collins et al. 2002, 2005). This post-session measurement is sometimes more elaborate, as in operationalisations of the three-component model developed by Tickle-Degnen and Rosenthal. The 'bond' scale from the Working Alliance Inventory is sometimes used in this regard as well (Sharpley and Ridgway 1992; Sharpley et al. 2001). The second measurement type involves in-session measurement (Sharpley and Ridgway 1992). During the interview, the interviewee or observer codes the degree of perceived rapport (every minute), ranging from very low, low, moderate, high to very high. In a few studies, a combination of these two measures is used.

Working Alliance and Police Interrogation

Despite the consensus concerning the importance of the relationship between police officers and interviewees, the conceptualisation and operationalisation of the relationship differ considerably throughout the literature. This poses a problem for both research and training. In order to develop more clarity, it could be helpful to consider the rich theoretical and research history existing within another professional area in which conversation is a key to goal attainment, i.e. psychotherapy (Fisher and Geiselman 1992). An interesting differentiation encountered when exploring the literature is the dichotomy between the specific and nonspecific factors of the intervention (Butler and Strupp 1986). Specific factors are the theoretical orientations (e.g. humanistic, cognitive-behavioural, psychodynamic) behind an intervention. They also include the techniques for facilitating behavioural change (e.g. focusing, exposure, response prevention, challenging dysfunctional cognitions), which are also derived from theory. Transferred to the context of police interviews, specific factors that can be identified include the legal demands and the objectives of the interview, the procedure for conducting interviews (including the various phases, with special attention to free recall and the use of open-ended questions and retrieval cues), the manner of handling evidence during the interview, the level of knowledge about the case and the level of knowledge about the offence at hand. Nonspecific factors are related to the relationship between the interviewer and interviewee (e.g. the degree of warmth, empathy, acceptance, the perceived prestige of the interviewer and the expectations of the interviewee).

Within the field of psychotherapy, the professional relationship is defined as the feelings and attitudes that the participants have towards each other and the ways in which these feelings and attitudes are expressed (Gelso and Carter 1994). The relationship is further subdivided into three components: the transference relationship, the real relationship and the working alliance (Bordin 1976; Gelso and Carter 1985, 1994). The transference relationship can be defined as part of the relationship that is determined by previous experiences, feelings and behaviour on the part of both the participants in comparable or other interpersonal contexts. The real relationship is determined along the continuum from liking to disliking. In other words, it is determined by the general attractiveness of the other person, as well as by the formal characteristics of the relationship. Examples include the location of the conversation, the duration of the encounter, the fact that one of the participants (the professional) is an expert in the process while the other (the suspect) may be an expert in the relevant content, coercion in the context of police interviews (at least for suspects), and the legal rights of the suspect. The third component, the working alliance, is further subdivided into three subcomponents: an *agreement* on the goal, an *agreement* on the tasks of both participants, and an emotional bond of mutual trust and acceptance. The working alliance has been operationalised according to a psychometrically sound instrument: the Working Alliance Inventory (Horvath and Greenberg 1989). The working alliance is fostered and fed by an attitude of empathy, unconditional positive regard and authenticity. Empathy refers to the interviewer's genuine interest in the world of the other, efforts to experience and view the world from the perspective of the interviewee, and the associated communication. Unconditional positive regard involves respecting the person regardless of any actions that could generate disapproval and believing that the individual can continue to grow.

Finally, authenticity refers to the openness of individuals towards their own experiences and their awareness about their own strengths and weaknesses, avoiding the urge to present themselves in a better light (Watson and Geller 2005).

Research in psychotherapy has indicated that nonspecific factors are just as important as specific factors to the realisation of behavioural change, with the working alliance as the nonspecific factor that contributes the most (Beutler et al. 2004; Hentschel 2005; Horvath 2005; Horvath and Bedi 2002; Horvath and Symonds 1991; Luborsky et al. 1997; Martin et al. 2000; Orlinsky and Howard 1986; Orlinsky et al. 1994; Orlinsky et al. 2004). The effect sizes of the predictive value of the working alliance for therapy outcomes range from .22 to .29 (Horvath 2005). A variety of client, therapist, technical and therapist-client interaction variables are related to the quality of the working alliance, thus implying the necessity of differential attention to the development of the working alliance depending upon the case at hand (Vanderhallen 2007).

An in-depth conceptual analysis of the various definitions of rapport in police interviewing and the working alliance in therapeutic contexts (Vanderhallen 2007) leads to the conclusion that rapport is defined as a factor that cultivates the working alliance and, more specifically, agreement regarding the objective of the intervention (Tickle-Degnen 2002). Rapport can also be seen as the equivalent of the emotional bond component of the working alliance (Sharpley et al. 1994; Sharpley and Guidara 1993). In some studies, rapport is even measured according to the bond scale of the Working Alliance Inventory (WAI-B, Sharpley and Ridgway 1992; Sharpley and Guidara 1993; Sharpley et al. 2001).

Based on the comprehensive and clear definition of the relationship components in conversation-based interventions, the vast and consistent amount of research confirming the important role of the working alliance and the indications that the working alliance is also applicable within the context of police interviews (Fisher and Geiselman 1992; Tickle-Degnen 2002), Vanderhallen (2007) explores the role of the working alliance in concrete police cases. More specifically, the study examined relevant characteristics identified in previous research of both the interviewer (e.g. hostility, empathy, interview style) and the interview (e.g. level of clarity) in relation to the working alliance, as well as to the level of satisfaction about the interview. A possible mediating role of the working alliance was also explored.

Participants

The empirical analysis drew upon data regarding 126 interviews conducted by 59 police investigators (all but one male) from five different police departments in Belgium, from real cases. Before the interview started, each interviewee signed a letter of informed consent. The interviewees completed self-report questionnaires as soon as possible after being interviewed. Interviewees had two options for returning their questionnaires: they could submit them in a locked clearance box in a public part of the police department (e.g. entrance hall) or return them by post (postage paid)

Table 4.1 Type of interviewee (%)

	Victim	Witness	Suspect	Other	Do not know
According to investigator	18.3	28.6	46.8	4.8	1.6
According to interviewee	15.9	32.2	31.7	8.8	9.6

to the university. The latter option was expected to enhance participation, especially amongst suspects.

Of the 126 interviewees, 77.8 % were male ($N = 98$) and 22.2 % were female ($N = 28$). The average age was 41 years (min $= 18$, max $= 80$). The interviewees were interviewed in relation to various offences, including financial crimes, theft without violence, drugs, sex offences, manslaughter, murder and trafficking.

In at least some cases, there was a discrepancy between the perceptions of investigators regarding the role of interviewees (i.e. victim or witness or suspect) and the perceptions of interviewees regarding their role at the time of the interview.

As shown in Table 4.1, the discrepancy between the interviewer and interviewee was the largest regarding the role of the suspect. It may be difficult to build a working alliance when there is not an agreement concerning the role of the interviewee.

Instruments

Based on previous research, the following predictors of the working alliance were used: self-reported hostility (subscale of the Symptom Checklist; Arrindell and Ettema 1989), the investigator's perceived empathy (the Dutch revision of Barrett-Lennard Relationship Inventory; Lietaer 1976), perceived interview style (humanitarian and dominant interview-style questionnaire developed by Christianson and Holmberg (2002), and interview clarity. Interview clarity was measured along a nine-item, five-point Likert scale probing various aspects of the police interview: reason for the interview, relevance of the interview to the case, interview questions, rights of the interviewee, objective of the interview, procedure, the investigator-interviewee relationship and the importance of their contributions to the case and criminal investigation (Vanderhallen 2007; Vanderhallen et al. 2011). Finally, participants were asked about their feelings of anxiety and perception of being respected, as measured along a ten-item, seven-point Likert scale, using a questionnaire developed by Christianson and Holmberg (2002).

The working alliance was measured according to a short adjusted version of the Working Alliance Inventory (Horvath and Greenberg 1989): the WAI-SR (Hatcher and Gillaspy 2006). It is interesting to note that principal component analysis failed to identify the three-factor structure (task, goal, bond) or two-factor structure (contract and bond) predicted by the theoretical framework. Only one underlying factor could be determined. This is not necessarily problematic, however, as the single-factor structure is supported in the literature as well (Kokotovic and Tracey 1990; Seps 1997).

Table 4.2 Regression analysis of the independent variables on working alliance

		Beta	Sig.	R^2 change
Model ($N = 82$)	Humanitarian style	.302	.000	.516
	Dominant style	− .371	.000	.119
	Clarity	.257	.000	.058
	Empathy	.190	.007	.028
F	$F_{(4,77)} = 49.838, p < .001$			
R^2	.721			
ΔR^2	.707			

Interview satisfaction was measured according to a 12-item, ten-point Likert scale questionnaire probing various elements of an interview: procedure, person and result. Principal components analysis yielded two factors: procedure/person (8 items, explaining 65.5 % of the variance, Cronbach's alpha score: .95) and result factor (4 items, explaining 7.7 % of the variance, Cronbach's alpha score: .85).

The psychometric characteristics of all the measures were acceptable to optimal (Vanderhallen 2007; Vanderhallen et al. 2011).

Results

Stepwise multiple regression analysis[1] revealed that clarity, empathy and a humanitarian interview style made significant positive contributions to the prediction of the working alliance (see Table 4.2). A significant negative contribution was found for the dominant interview style. Contrary to expectations, hostility did not contribute separately to the prediction of the working alliance.

Results of the regression analysis of working alliance and satisfaction with procedure and person indicate that the working alliance has a potentially mediating role between the clarity of the interview, a humanitarian interview style, and satisfaction with procedure and person. Further, regression analysis revealed that the working alliance is a significant predictor ($b = .466$, beta $= .539$, $p < .001$) of satisfaction regarding person and procedure ($R^2 = .747$, $\Delta R^2 = .739$, $F(3, 88) = 86.692$, $p < .001$).[2] In this analysis, the clarity of the interview ($b = .219$, beta $= .113$, NS, $p = .091$) is no longer significant, and b decreases (from .552 to .219), thus suggesting a mediating role between clarity and satisfaction with procedure and person. The humanitarian interview style ($b = .400$, beta $= .318$, $p < .001$) remains significant when adding the working alliance, although the predictive value decreases (b from .511 to .400).

These results thus provide evidence of a partial mediating role of the working alliance between clarity and humanitarian interview style, as well as between the interviewee's satisfaction about person and the procedure of the interview.

---

[1] No evidence of multicollinearity was found (VIF $= 1.868$, tolerance $= .535$).

[2] Two potential outliers were identified (two cases with a standardised residual > 3), which yielded no difference when deleted: $R^2 = .784$, $\Delta R^2 = .777$, $F_{(3,88)} = 104.30$, $p < 001$.

With regard to the possible mediating role of the working alliance regarding satisfaction with the interview result, regression analysis shows that the working alliance ($b = .288$, beta $= .549$, $p < .001$) significantly predicts satisfaction with the result ($R^2 = .520$, $\Delta R^2 = .503$, $F_{(3,85)} = 30.666$, $p < .001$).[3] The perceived empathy ($b = .127$, beta $= 110$, NS, $p = .223$) and clarity of the interview ($b = .200$, beta $= .156$, NS, $p = .100$) are no longer significant, and b decreases (empathy: from .492 to .110; clarity: from .415 to .156). These results indicate that the working alliance has a mediating role between the perceived empathy and clarity of the interview and satisfaction with the result of the interview. Due to the proportion of the mediating effect (0.76 clarity of the interview, 0.57 perceived empathy), a partial mediating role can be identified.[4]

Discussion

Although this 2007 study provides evidence for only one general working-alliance factor, using a shortened version of the original instrument, the results suggest that the development of the working alliance can be facilitated by paying explicit attention to three components of the interview. The first facilitator for the working alliance is an empathic attitude. Although theoretically expected and previously found, the results show that empathy also fosters the working alliance in police interviewing. It is interesting to note that the operationalisation of empathy used in this study was originally constructed for psychotherapeutic contexts, consistent with the Rogerian conceptualisation. This suggests that it could be interesting to deepen the knowledge that interviewers have with regard to this rich construct from the field of psychotherapy in order to explore further its potential for the police context.

The second facilitator for the working alliance in police interviewing involves the use of an information-gathering, humanitarian interview style and the avoidance of a dominant style (characterised by unfriendliness, impatience, and a condemning attitude). These findings on empathy and interview style support the findings of Oxburgh and Ost (2011) regarding interviews with sex offenders, in which both components were found to facilitate the elicitation of IRI.

Finally, clear-cut communication about the reason for and objective of the interview, the procedure and the expectations with regard to the interviewee is favourable for the development of the working alliance. This finding is also in line with previous research (Shepherd and Milne 2006).

These findings provide support for some of the previously identified building blocks for enhancing the professional relationship with the interviewee: these being empathy and the information-gathering interview style. They also support the suggestion to utilise some administrative task (e.g. official notifications) since they clarify the interview framework to the suspect, as emphasised by Walsh and Bull

---

[3] No outliers were identified.

[4] The mediation is partial, as the regression coefficients differ from 0 (www.davidakenny.net; Baron and Kenny 1986).

(2012a). In addition to being important at the beginning of the interview, clarification (including asking clear and straightforward questions to the interviewee) proved important throughout the entire interview as well, thus highlighting the need for rapport maintenance.

Although police interviews are not necessarily intended to generate satisfied clients, the fact that the working alliance plays a role in satisfaction with procedure/person and result is worthwhile, given that a positive attitude towards the police can facilitate further positive collaboration during the investigation, and it can contribute indirectly to the improvement of opinions about the police. This can help the interviewer to close the interview in a positive atmosphere, as often suggested in the literature on investigative interviewing (Fisher and Geiselman 1992; Milne and Bull 1999).

The Future of Rapport

Rapport has often been emphasised as a necessary condition for successful interviewing. Research within the context of investigative interviewing with suspects supports the role of rapport in improving the accuracy of the information provided, including confessions. Although research has clearly established the benefits of good rapport, and although practitioners systematically refer to the importance of rapport, experience shows that rapport is usually poorly put into practice. This may be due to a lack of clear understanding of how to establish rapport. The literature is vague with regard to factors that contribute to rapport building. Aside from the fact that too little attention has been paid to the distinction between building rapport and maintaining rapport, many of the recommended actions are still in need of empirical testing in interviews in general and, more specifically, in interviews with suspects. Research on the working alliance in investigative interviewing now highlights the need for empathy, an information-gathering style, and clarity in order to facilitate the working relationship between interviewers and suspects. This also explains the underlying relationships between these essential components in investigative interviewing. The working alliance was found to contribute to satisfaction concerning the interview, which could help to close the interview in a positive atmosphere, thereby stimulating future cooperation.

An alternative explanation for the disappointing level of rapport in real-life suspect interviews is insufficient training. A study by Walsh and Milne (2008) in the context of interviews with benefit-fraud suspects revealed no significant improvement after training with regard to rapport building. Other studies, however, report conflicting results. For example, in a study on the effectiveness of advanced training on investigative interviewing, Griffiths and Milne (2006) report that general quality (i.e. the usage of the overall principles of investigative interviewing) improved after training. This effect applied at least during the initial period following the training, but this initial improvement diminished over time with regard to both building and maintaining rapport. This suggests that training in the development of rapport can be effective, although the deterioration of the acquired skills over time is consistent with the finding that training alone is not sufficient to generate success. Based on research findings, intensive training accompanied by follow-up (including monitoring and refresher training) has been recommended as a solution for improving individual performance (e.g. Clarke et al. 2011; Crawshaw et al. 1998; Powell et al. 2005). With regard to rapport building, a recent supervision project conducted in Belgium has revealed several practical experiences (Vanderhallen et al. 2013). As rapport developed, participants in the project became less challenging towards suspects' accounts. This experience is supported by research, in which challenging the account of the suspect became less prevalent during interviews in which more rapport had been established (Walsh and Bull 2012a).

In addition to the necessity of future empirical research, training and follow-up, a final recommendation concerning rapport in suspect interviews is in order. Fisher (2010) appropriately raises questions regarding how rapport can be developed with people from different cultures, given that the previously mentioned building blocks are vulnerable to possible differences due to the cultural backgrounds of both the interviewer and interviewee. Similar obstacles can be formulated with regard to interviews using video conferencing and interviews in the presence of interpreters, lawyers or other third parties. Finally, with regard to the personality of the suspect, it is easier to build rapport with some suspects than it is with others. Building rapport with suspects thus obviously poses an ongoing challenge.

References

Alison, L., Sarangi, S., & Wright, A. L. (2008a). Human rights is not enough: The need for demonstrating efficacy of an ethical approach to interviewing in India. *Legal and Criminological Psychology, 13,* 89–106.

Alison, L., Kebbell, M., & Leung, J. (2008b). A facet analysis of police officers' self-reported use of suspect-interviewing strategies and their discomfort with ambiguity. *Applied Cognitive Psychology, 22,* 1072–1087.

Arrindell, W. A., & Ettema, J. H. M. (1989). *SCL-90. Handleiding bij een multidimensionele psychopathologie-indicator.* [Manual for a multidimensional psychopathology-indicator] Groningen: Vakgroep Klinische Psychologie.

Baldwin, J. (1993). Police interview techniques: Establishing the truth or proof? *The British Journal of Criminology, 33*(3), 325–352.

Baron, R. M., & Kenny, D. A. (1986). The moderator-mediator variable distinction in social psychological research: Conceptual, strategic and statistical considerations. *Journal of Personality and Social Psychology, 51*(6), 1173–1182.

Barrett-Lennard, G. T. (1962). Dimensions of therapist response as causal factors in therapeutic change. *Psychological Monographs, 76,* 1–36.

Bedi, R. P., Davis, M. D., & Williams, M. (2005). Critical incidents in the formation of the therapeutic alliance from the client's perspective. *Psychotherapy: Theory, Research, Practice, Training, 42,* 311–323.

Beutler, L. E., Malik, M., Alimohamed, S., Harwood, M. T., Talebi, H., Noble, S., & Wong, E. (2004). Therapist Variables. In M. J. Lambert (Ed.), *Bergin and Garfield's handbook of psychotherapy and behavior change* (pp. 227–306). New York: Wiley.

Bordin, E. S. (1976). The generalizability of the psychoanalytic concept of the working alliance. *Psychotherapy: Theory, research and practice, 16*(3), 252–260.

Borum, R., Gelles, M. G., & Kleinman, S. M. (2009). Interview and interrogation: a perspective and update from the USA. In T. Williamson, B. Milne, & S. P. Savage (Eds.), *International developments in investigative interviewing* (pp. 111–125). Cullompton: Willan Publishing.

Brean, J. (2011). Police interrogation techniques under scrutiny due to false confessions, *National Post*, 25 November 2011.

Buckley, J. P. (2006). The Reid technique of interviewing and interrogation. In T. Williamson (Ed.), *Investigative interviewing. Rights, research, regulation* (pp. 190–206). Cullompton: Willan Publishing.

Bull, R., & Cherryman, J. (1996). *Helping to identify skills gaps in specialist investigative interviewing: Enhancement of professional skills.* London: Home Office, Police Department.

Bull, R., & Milne, R. (2004). Attempts to improve the police interviewing of suspects. In D. G. Lassiter (Ed.), *Interrogation, confessions and entrapment* (pp. 181-196). New York: Kluwer Academic/Plenum Publishers.

Bull, R., & Soukara, S. (2010). Four studies of what really happens in police interviews. In G. D. Lassiter & C. A. Meissner (Eds.), *Police interrogation and false confessions. Current research, practice and policy recommendations* (pp. 81–96). Washington: American Psychological Association.

Butler, S. F., & Strupp, H. H. (1986). Specific and nonspecific factors in psychotherapy: A problematic paradigm for psychotherapy research. *Psychotherapy, 23,* 30–40.

Clarke, C., & Milne, R. (2001). *National evaluation of the PEACE investigative interviewing course. Report n°: PRAS/149.* London: The Home Office.

Clarke, C., Milne, R., & Bull, R. (2011). Interviewing suspects of crime: The impact of PEACE training, supervision and the presence of a legal advisor. *Journal of Investigative Psychology and Offender Profiling, 8*(2), 149–162.

Collins, R., Lincoln, R., & Frank, M. G. (2002). The effect of rapport in forensic interviewing. *Psychiatry, Psychology and Law, 9*(1), 69–78.

Collins, R., Lincoln, R., & Frank, M. G. (2005). *The need for rapport in police interviews. Humanities & Social Sciences papers.* Robina: Bond University.

Cook, M. (1970). Experiments on orientation and proxemics. *Human Relations, 23*(1), 61–76.

Crawshaw, R., Devlin, B., & Williamson, T. (1998). *Human rights and policing: Standards for good behaviour and a strategy for change.* Den Haag: Kluwer International.

Davies, M. H. (1983). Measuring individual differences in empathy: Evidence for a multidimensional approach. *Journal of Personality and Social Psychology, 44*(1), 113–126.

Davies, M., & Shen, A. (2010). Questioning suspected offenders: The investigative interviewing process in the People's Republic of China. *Criminology and Criminal Justice, 10*(3), 243–259.

De Smet, B. (1999). *Internationale samenwerking tussen Angelsaksische en continentale landen: Een studie over breuken tussen accusatoire en inquisitoire processtelsels bij de uitlevering, kleine rechtshulp en overdracht van strafvervolging* [International collaboration between Common law and continental countries: a study on flaws between accusatorial and inquisitorial legal systems]. Antwerp: Intersentia.

Dixon, D. (2007). *Interrogating images audio-visually recorded police questioning of suspects.* Sydney: Sydney Institute of Criminology.

Dixon, D. (2009). From criminal justice to control process: Interrogation in a changing context. In R. Bull, T. Valentine, & T. Williamson (Eds.), *Handbook of Psychology of investigative interviewing. Current developments and future directions* (pp. 91–108). Chichester: Wiley-Blackwell.

Driskell, T., Blickensderfer, E. L., & Salas, E. (2012). Is three a crowd? Examining rapport in investigative interviews. *Group Dynamics: Theory, Research, and Practice,* 1–13.

Evans, J. R., Meissner, C. A., Brandon, S. E., Russano, M. B., & Kleinman, S. M. (2010). Criminal versus HUMINT interrogations: The importance of psychological science to improving interrogative practice. *Journal of Psychiatry & Law, 38*(1 & 2), 215–249.

Fisher, R. P. (2010). Interviewing cooperative witnesses. *Legal and Criminological Psychology, 15,* 25–38.

Fisher, R. P., & Geiselman, R. E. (1992). *Memory-enhancing techniques for investigative interviewing: The cognitive interview.* Springfield: Charles C. Thomas Publisher.

Fisher, R. P., & Perez, V. (2007). Memory-enhancing techniques for interviewing crime suspects. In S. A. Christianson (Ed.), *Offenders' memories of violent crimes* (pp. 329–354). Chichester: Wiley.

Frank, M. G., Yarbrough, J. D., & Ekman, P. (2006). Investigative interviewing and the detection of deception. In T. Williamson (Ed.), *Investigative interviewing. Rights, research, regulation* (pp. 229–255). Cullompton: Willan Publishing.

Gelles, M. G., McFadden, R., Borum, R., & Vossekuil, B. (2006). Al-Qaeda-related subjets: A law enforcement perspective. In T. Williamson (Ed.), *Investigative interviewing. Rights, research, regulation* (pp. 23–41). Cullompton: Willan Publishing.

Gelso, C. J., & Carter, J. A. (1985). The relationship in counseling and psychotherapy: Components, consequences and theroretical antecedents. *The Counseling Psychologist, 13,* 155–243.

Gelso, C. J., & Carter, J. A. (1994). Components of psychotherapy relationship: Their interaction and unfolding during treatment. *Journal of Counseling Psychology, 41,* 296–306.

Green, T. (2012). The future of investigative interviewing: Lessons for Australia. *Australian Journal of Forensic Sciences, 44*(1), 31–43.

Griffiths, A., & Milne, R. (2006). Will it all end in tiers? Police interviews with suspects in Britain. In T. Williamson (Ed.), *Investigative interviewing: rights, research and regulation* (pp. 167–189). Cullompton: Willan Publishing.

Gudjonsson, G. H. (2003). *The psychology of interrogations and confessions: A handbook.* Chichster: Wiley.

Gudjonsson, G. H. (2006). Sex offenders and confessions: How to overcome their resistance during questioning. *Journal of Clinical Forensic Medicine, 13,* 203–207.

Gudjonsson, G. H., & Pearse, J. (2011). Suspect interviews and false confessions. *Current Directions in Psychological Science, 20*(1), 33–37.

Häkkänen, H., Ask, K., Kebbell, M., Alison, L., & Granhag, P. A. (2009). Police officers' views of effective interview tactics with suspects: The effects of weight of case evidence and discomfort with ambiguity. *Applied Cognitive Psychology, 23,* 468–481.

Hartwig, M. (2005). *Interrogation to detect deception and truth: Effects of strategic use of evidence.* Sweden: Göteborg University.

Hatcher, R. L., & Gillaspy, A. J. (2006). Development and validation of a revised short version of the working alliance inventory. *Psychotherapy Research, 16*(1), 12–25.

Hentschel, U. (2005). Therapeutic alliance: The best synthesizer of social influences on the therapeutic situation? On links to other constructs, determinants of its effectiveness, and its role for research in psychotherapy in general. *Psychotherapy Research, 15,* 9–23.

Holmberg, U. (2004). *Police interviews with victims and suspects of violent sexual crimes: Interviewee's experiences and outcomes.* Stockholm: Stockholm University, Department of Psychology.

Holmberg, U. (2009). Investigative interviewing as a therapeutic jurisprudential approach. In T. Williamson, B. Milne, & S. P. Savage (Eds.), *International developments in investigative interviewing* (pp. 149–175).

Holmberg, U., & Christianson, S.-A. (2002). Murderers' and sexual offenders' experiences of police interviews and their inclination to admit or deny crimes. *Behavioral Sciences and the Law, 20,* 31–45.

Holmberg, U., & Madsen, K. (2010, June). Humanity and dominance in police interviews; causes and effects. Paper presented at the 4th International Investigative Conference, Brussels.

Horvath, A. O. (2005). The therapeutic relationship: Research and theory. An introduction to the special issue. *Psychotherapy Research, 15,* 3–7.

Horvath, A. O., & Bedi, R. P. (2002). The alliance. In J. C. Norcross (Ed.), *Psychotherapy relationships that work: Therapist contributions and responsiveness to patients* (pp. 37–70). Oxford: University Press.

Horvath, A. O., & Symonds, D. B. (1991). Relation between working alliance and outcome in psychotherapy: A meta-analysis. *Journal of Counseling Psychology, 38*(2), 139–149.

Horvath, A. O., & Greenberg, L. S. (1989). Development and validation of the Working Alliance Inventory. *Journal of Counseling Psychology, 36*(2), 223–232.

Hubbard, K. M. (2007). Psychologists and interrogations: What's torture got to do with it? *Analyses of Social Issues and Public Policy, 7*(1), 29–33.

Inbau, F. E., Reid, J. E., Buckley, J. P., & Jayne, B. C. (2004). *Criminal interrogation and confession.* Sudbury: Jones and Bartlett Publishers.

Kalbfleisch, P. J. (1994). The language of detecting deceit. *Journal of Language and Social Psychology, 13,* 469–496.

Kassin, S. M., Appleby, S. C., & Torkildson Perillo, J. (2010). Interviewing suspects: Practice, science, and future directions. *Legal and Criminological Psychology, 15,* 39–55.

Kassin, S. M., Leo, R. A., Meissner, C. A., Richman, K. D., Colwell, L. H., Leach, A.-M., & La Fon, D. (2007). Police interviewing and interrogation: A self-report survey of police practices and beliefs. *Law and Human Behavior, 31,* 381–400.

Kebbell, M., Hurren, E., & Mazerolle, P. (2006). *An investigation into the effective and ethical interviewing of suspected sex offenders* (Final Report, Criminology Research Council 12/03–04). Canberra: Criminology Research Council.

Kokotovic, A. M., & Tracey, T. J. (1990). Working alliance in the early phase of counseling. *Journal of Counseling Psychology, 37*(1), 16–21.

Lietaer, G. (1976). Nederlandstalige revisie van Barrett-Lennard's Relationship Inventory voor individueel-tehrapeutische relaties. *Psychologica Belgica, 16,* 73–94.

Luborsky, L., McLellan, A. T., Diguer, L., Woody, G., & Seligman, D. A. (1997). The psychotherapist matters: Comparison of outcome across twenty-two therapists and seven patient-samples. *Clinical Psychology: Science and Practice, 4,* 53–65.

Martin, D. J., Garske, J. P., & Davis, K. M. (2000). Relation of therapeutic alliance with outcome and other variables: A meta-analytic review. *Journal of Consulting and Clinical Psychology, 68*(3), 438–450.

Meissner, C. A., Redlich, A., Bhatt, S., & Brandon, S. (2012). *Interview and interrogation methods and their effects on true and false confessions. Campbell Systematic Reviews 2012:13.* Oslo: The Campbell Collaboration.

Meissner, C. A., Russano, M. B., & Narchet, F. M. (2010). The importance of a laboratory science for improving the diagnostic value of confession evidence. In G. D. Lassiter & C. Meissner's (Eds.), *Police Interrogations and false confessions: Current research, practice, and policy recommendations* (pp. 111–126). Washington, DC: American Psychological Association.

Milne, R., & Bull, R. (1999). *Investigative interviewing: Psychology and practice.* Chichester: Wiley.

Morgan, R., & Williamson, T. (2009). A critical analysis of the utilitarian case for torture and the situational factors that lead some people to become torturers. In T. Williamson, B. Milne, & S. P. Savage (Eds.), *International developments in investigative interviewing* (pp. 129–148). Cullompton: Willan Publishing.

Moston, S., & Engelberg, T. (1993). Police questioning techniques in tape recorded interviews with criminal suspects. *Policing and Society, 3,* 223–237.

Moston, S., & Fisher, M. (2007). Perceptions of coercion in the questioning of criminal suspects. *Journal of Investigative Psychology and Offender Profiling, 4*(2), 85–95.

Nolan, M. (2009). Case Commentary. Counter-terrorism interviewing and investigative interoperability: R v ul-Haque [2007] NSWSC 1251. *Psychiatry, Psychology and Law, 16*(2), 175–190.

Ord, B., Shaw, G., & Green, T. (2011). *Investigative interviewing explained.* Chatswood: Lexis Nexis.

Orlinsky, D. E., Grawe, K., & Parks, B. K. (1994). Process and outcome in psychotherapy—noch einmal. In A. Bergin & S. L. Garfield (Eds.), *Handbook of psychotherapy and behavior change* (pp. 270–378). New York: Wiley.

Orlinsky, D. E., & Howard, K. I. (1986). Process and outcome in psychotherapy. In S. L. Garfield & A. E. Bergin (Eds.), *Handbook of psychotherapy and behavior change* (pp. 311–384). New York: Wiley.

Orlinsky, D. E., Rønnestad, M. H., & Willutzki, U. (2004). Fifty years of psychotherapy process-outcome research: Continuity and change. In M. J. Lambert (Ed.), *Bergin and Garfield's handbook of psychotherapy and behavior change* (pp. 307–390). New York: Wiley.

Oxburgh, G., & Ost, J. (2011). The use and efficacy of empathy in police interviews with suspects of sexual offences. *Journal of Investigative Psychology and Offender Profiling, 8*(2), 178–188.

Pearse, J. J. (2006). The interrogation of terrorist suspects: The banality of torture. In T. Williamson (Ed.). *Investigative interviewing. Rights, research, regulation* (pp. 64–83). Cullompton: Willan Publishing.

Pearse, J., & Gudjonsson, G. H. (1996). Police interviewing techniques at two South London police stations. *Psychology, Crime and Law, 3,* 63–74.

Pinizzotto, A. J., & Davis, E. F. (1996). Interviewing methods. A specialized approach is needed when investigating police deaths. *Law and Order, november,* 68–72.

Ponsaers, P., Mulkers, J., & Stoop, R. (2001). *De ondervraging: Analyse van een politietechniek.* Antwerpen: Maklu.

Poole, E. D., & Pogrebin, M. R. (1989). Attribution and empathy: Detectives and subjects under arrest. *Police Studies, 12*(3), 132–139.

Powell, M. B., Fisher, R. P., & Wright, R. (2005). Investigative Interviewing. In N. Brewer & K. Williams (Eds.), *Psychology and law: An empirical perspective* (pp. 11-42). New York: The Guilford Press.

Quale, J. (2008). Interviewing a psychopathic suspect. *Journal of Investigative Psychology and Offender Profiling, 5*(1–2), 79–91.

Roberts, K. A. (2011). Police interviews with terrorist suspects: Risks, ethical interviewing and procedural justice. *The British Journal of Forensic Practice, 13*(2), 124–134.

Sanchez-Burks, J. (2002). Protestant relational ideology and (in)attention to relational cues in work settings. *Journal of Personality and Social Psychology, 83,* 919–929.

Sandoval, V. A., & Adams, S. H. (2001). Subtle skills for building rapport: Using neuro-linguistic programming in the interview room. *FBI Law Enforcement Bulletin,* 1–5.

Schreiber Compo, N., Gregory, A. H., & Fisher, R. (2012). Interviewing behaviors in police investigators: A field study of a current US sample. *Psychology, Crime & Law, 18*(4), 359–375.

Sellers, S., & Kebbell, M. R. (2009). When should evidence be disclosed in an interview with a suspect? An experiment with mock-suspects. *Journal of Investigative Psychology and Offender Profiling, 6*(2), 151–160.

Seps, K. (1997). *Werkalliantie: Literatuuroverzicht en herziening van de WAV* [Literature overview and revision of the WAI]. Unpublished dissertation. Leuven: Katholieke Universiteit Leuven.

Sharpley, C. F., & Guidara, D. A. (1993). Counsellor verbal response mode usage and client-perceived rapport. *Counselling Psychology Quarterly, 6*(2), 131–143.

Sharpley, C. F., & Ridgway, I. R. (1992). Development and field-testing of a procedure for coached clients to assess rapport. *Counselling Psychology Quareterly, 5*(2), 149–151.

Sharpley, C. F., Guidara, D. A., & Rowley, M. A. (1994). Psychometric evaluation of a 'standardized client' procedure with trainee counselors. *Counselling Psychology Quarterly, 7*(1), 69–83.

Sharpley, C. F., Halat, J., Rabinowicz, T., Weiland, B., & Stafford, J. (2001). Standard posture, postural mirroring and client-perceived rapport. *Counselling Psychology Quarterly, 14*(4), 267–280.

Shawyer, A., Milne, B., & Bull, R. (2009). Investigative interviewing in the UK. In T. Williamson, B. Milne, & S. P. Savage (Eds.), *International developments in investigative interviewing* (pp. 24–38). Cullompton: Willan Publishing.

Shepherd, E. (2007). *Investigative interviewing: The conversation management approach.* Oxford: Oxford University Press.

Shepherd, E., & Milne, R. (2006). Have you told management about this?: Bringing witness interviewing into the twenty-first century. In A. Heaton-Armstrong, E. Shepherd, G. Gudjonsson, & D. Wolchover (Eds.), *Witness testimony: Psychological, investigative and evidential perspectives* (pp. 131–151). Oxford: Oxford University Press.

Snook, B., Eastwoord, J., Stinson, M., Tedechini, J., & House, J. C. (2010). Reforming investigative interviewing in Canada. *Canadian Journal of Criminology and Criminal Justice, 52*(2), 203–217.

Stokoe, E. (2009). "I've got a girlfriend": Police officers doing 'self-disclosure' in their interrogations of suspects. *Narrative Inquiry, 19*(1), 154–182.

St-Yves, M. (2006). The psychology of rapport: Five basic rules. In T. Williamson (Ed.), *Investigative interviewing: Rights, research and regulation* (pp. 87–105). Devon: Willan Publishing.

St-Yves, M. (2009). Police interrogation in Canada: from the quest for confessions to the search for the truth. In T. Williamson, B. Milne, & S. P. Savage (Eds.), *International developments in investigative interviewing* (pp. 92–110). Cullompton: Willan Publishing.

St-Yves, M., & Deslauriers-Varin, N. (2009). The psychology of suspects' decision-making during interrogation. In R. Bull, T. Valentine & T. Williamson (Eds.), *Handbook of psychology of investigative interviewing. Current developments and future directions* (pp. 1–15). Chichester: Wiley-Blackwell.

Tickle-Degnen, L. (2002). Client-centered practice, therapeutic relationship, and the use of research evidence. *American Journal of Occupational Therapy, 56*(4), 470–474.

Tickle-Degnen, L., & Rosenthal, R. (1987). Group rapport and non-verbal behaviour. In C. Hendrick (Ed.), *Group processes and intergroup relations* (pp. 113–136). Newbury Park: Sage Publications.

Tickle-Degnen, L., & Rosenthal, R. (1990). The nature of rapport and its nonverbal correlates. *Psychological Inquiry, 1*(4), 285–293.

Vallano, J. P., & Schreiber Compo, N. (2011). A comfortable witness is a good witness: Rapport-building and susceptibility to misinformation in an investigative mock-crime interview. *Applied Cognitive Psychology, 25,* 960–970.

Vallano, J., Schreiber Compo, N., Wood, S., Perry, A., Lobos, A. M., Villalba, D., Kemp, D., & Cochran, J. (2008). Rapport-building and susceptibility to misinformation in an investigative mock crime interview. Paper presented at the annual meeting of the American Psychology-Law Society, 5th March 2008.

Van Amelsvoort, A., Rispens, I., & Grolman, H. (2010). *Handleiding verhoor* [Interrogation manual]. 's Gravenhage: Elsevier.

Van De Plas, M. (2007). *Handboek politieverhoor: Basistechnieken.* [Manual of police interviewing: Basic techniques]. Brussel: Politeia.

Vanderhallen, M. (2007). *De werkalliantie in het politieverhoor* [The working alliance in police interviewing]. Unpublished PhD thesis. Leuven: Katholieke Universiteit Leuven.

Vanderhallen, M., & Lei, C. (2012). Skills for interrogating criminal suspects. In C. Weidong & T. Spronken (Eds.), *Three approaches to combating torture in China* (pp. 203–236). Cambridge: Intersentia.

Vanderhallen, M., Vervaeke, G., & Holmberg, U. (2011). Witness and suspect perceptions of working alliance and interviewing style. *Journal of Investigative Psychology and Offender Profiling, 8*(2), 110–130.

Vanderhallen, M., Vervaeke, G., & Michaux, E. M. (2013). Experiences from training and supervision in real (video-recorded) suspect interviews in Belgium: Pitfalls and opportunities. *iIIRG-Bulletin, 5*(1), 36–45.

Volckaert, M. (2005). *Verhoor in de basisopleiding voor inspecteur van politie* [Interviewing in the basic training for police officers]. Unpublished dissertation. Leuven: Katholieke Universiteit Leuven.

Vrij, A., Mann, S., & Fisher, R. (2006). Information-gathering vs accusatory interview style: Individual differences in respondents' experiences. *Personality and Individual Differences, 41*, 589–599.

Walsh, D. W., & Bull, R. H. (2010a). What really is effective in interviews with suspects? A study comparing interview skills against interview outcomes. *Legal and Criminological Psychology, 15*, 305–321.

Walsh, D., & Bull, R. (2010b). Interviewing suspects of fraud: An in-depth analysis of interviewing skills. *The Journal of Psychiatry & Law, 38*, 99–135.

Walsh, D., & Bull, R. (2012a). Examining rapport in investigative interviews with suspects: Does its building and maintenance work? *Journal of Police and Criminal Psychology, 27*, 73–84.

Walsh, D., & Bull, R. (2012b). How do interviewers attempt to overcome suspects' denials? *Psychiatry, Psychology and Law, 19*(2), 151–168.

Walsh, D. W., & Milne, R. (2008). Keeping the PEACE? A study of investigative interviewing practices in the public sector. *Legal and Criminological Psychology, 13*, 39–57.

Watson, J. C., & Geller, S. M. (2005). The relation among the relationship conditions, working alliance, and outcome in both process-experienced and cognitive-behavioral psychotherapy. *Psychotherpy Research, 15*, 25–33.

Weidong, C., Lei, C., & Spronken, T. (2012). A three-way approach to the fight against torture. Procedural sanctions, prevention in places of detention, and improvement of police interrogation techniques. In C. Weidong, & T. Spronken (Eds.), *Three approaches to combating torture in China* (pp. 1–7). Cambridge: Intersentia.

Yeschke, C. L. (2003). *The art of investigative interviewing*. Burlington: Butterworth-Heinemann Elsevier Science.

Chapter 5
Interview Techniques in International Criminal Court and Tribunals

Melanie O'Brien and Mark Kebbell

Introduction

The largest number of serious crimes such as murder and rape occur during conflicts and wars. For this reason, for justice to be achieved, those responsible must be held accountable. This has been done on an international level, for example, with the International Military Tribunal at Nuremberg after the end of the Second World War. More recently, tribunals such as the International Criminal Tribunal for Rwanda (ICTR) and the International Criminal Court (ICC) have conducted investigations and prosecutions for war crimes, crimes against humanity, and genocide. Much of the evidence in these trials is elicited from witnesses, victims, and suspects, and therefore, the way in which they are interviewed is critical to successful prosecutions of the guilty. In this chapter, we consider research interviews with interviewers in ICC and tribunals concerning their approach to interviewing and the training they have received. The challenges faced by this group of interviewers are discussed here.

In domestic law enforcement and legal systems, police and lawyers generally come from the same or similar cultural, educational, and professional backgrounds. However, in the ICC and other international criminal courts and tribunals, people who conduct interviews of suspects and witnesses come from a variety of cultural and educational backgrounds, and backgrounds that are often very different from the interviewees. International criminal investigators and prosecutors are likely to be influenced by their national training and experience. Such differences may impact substantially on interview processes and techniques used. The qualitative research data presented in this chapter are based on and were obtained by the first author via interviews conducted with former and current staff of the ICC and other international criminal courts and tribunals. These interviews were conducted one on one, in Sydney, Lyon, or The Hague, and based on a two-part questionnaire. The first

M. O'Brien (✉) · M. Kebbell
Griffith University, Queensland, Australia
e-mail: melanie.obrien@griffith.edu.au

R. Bull (ed.), *Investigative Interviewing*, DOI 10.1007/978-1-4614-9642-7_5,
© Springer Science+Business Media New York 2014

part of the questionnaire contained open-ended questions regarding the background and experience in interviewing of the investigator or lawyer. The second part was a set response questionnaire to determine the frequency of the use of particular interview techniques. Unless otherwise noted, all such information comes from these sources. She interviewed a total of 14 current and former staff: seven investigators, five lawyers, one investigator with a legal background, and one lawyer with a police background. Additional information came from interviews with legal advisors in the Office of the Prosecutor (OTP) of the ICC. The majority of participants currently works at the ICC or the Special Tribunal for Lebanon (STL), or are former investigators from the International Criminal Tribunal for the former Yugoslavia (ICTY). Some participants have worked in more than one international court or tribunal; therefore, there were some participants who formerly worked at the ICTR, the Kosovo Tribunal, and the Special Court for Sierra Leone (SCSL). Interviews were also undertaken with the Interpol Fugitive Investigative Support Sub-Directorate (specialising in suspects of international crimes), as well as staff at the Institute for International Criminal Investigations (IICI) in The Hague.

A meaningful body of work on interviewing vulnerable witnesses of international crimes has been produced by scholars and nongovernmental organisations, on topics such as victims (in particular, victims of sexual and gender-based violence), and children (Bergsmo and Wiley 2008, pp. 18–21). Handbooks and guides have also been produced on the investigation of international crimes (Bergsmo and Wiley 2008; Groome 2011; Nystedt et al. 2011). However, little research has looked at the investigative interviewing of suspects of international crimes. Interviewing of suspects is as important as interviewing victims and witnesses, as this can assist with information gathering and the process towards establishing the truth (or at least partial truth) of these horrendous crimes and their surrounding context (Goldstone 1996; Rauxloh 2010). While this chapter refers to 'suspects and witnesses', the witnesses referred to are 'insider witnesses'; that is, people who may not be considered for trial at the ICC or a tribunal, but who may well have perpetrated war crimes, crimes against humanity and/or genocide. The insider witnesses often provide the critical evidence of war crimes. For example, while surviving victims of war crimes may be able to identify the crimes perpetrated against them, they are usually unable to identify who gave orders for war crimes to be committed. Consequently, insider witnesses are used to determine who, if anyone, authorised war crimes. Even if insider witnesses are not at risk of prosecution (or at least, may not be at first, but perhaps at a later stage), it is still important to consider interview techniques for them in the same way as 'full' suspects, as their crimes form part of the larger pattern of mass participation. Perpetrators have generally committed multiple crimes, sometimes thousands of crimes. They are also often either military personnel (whether they be regulated state military or rebel militia), police, or politicians. Thus, perpetrators of international crimes are different to those whom police and lawyers may encounter in a domestic investigation.

Background to International Criminal Courts and Tribunals

The first international criminal tribunal to be founded was the ICTY, in 1993, to seek to ensure accountability for crimes committed in the territory of the former Yugoslavia since 1 January 1991. This was followed by the ICTR in 1994 for crimes committed during the Rwandan genocide of 1994 (Schabas 2006). Two hybrid courts were also set up. The SCSL was set up in 2000 to try alleged perpetrators of crimes, which were committed in armed conflicts after 30 November 1996, and the Extraordinary Chambers in the Courts of Cambodia (ECCC, formed in 2003), prosecuting senior leaders of Democratic Kampuchea, and those believed to be most responsible for grave violations of national and international law committed in Cambodia between 17 April 1975 and 6 January 1979. Far less prominent, are the 'Regulation 64' Panels in the Courts of Kosovo (the Kosovo Tribunal), established in 2000 to try alleged perpetrators responsible for atrocities committed during the armed conflict in Kosovo in 1999.

The Rome Statute of the permanent ICC was completed in 1998, and the ICC began operation in 2002 (Schabas 2007). The ICC has jurisdiction over war crimes, crimes against humanity, and genocide committed since 1 July 2002, within the territory of state parties, by nationals of state parties, or in any situation referred to the Court by the UN Security Council. These three categories of crimes are considered 'international crimes' (Cryer et al. 2007).[1]

Educational and Professional Backgrounds of Investigators and Lawyers

There are two main categories of personnel who undertake investigative interviews of suspects and witnesses in ICC and tribunals who were interviewed for this chapter. While in domestic systems it is most commonly the law enforcement officers such as police who undertake this type of interviewing, at the international courts and tribunals, this is done by both investigators and lawyers. Investigators usually come from a law enforcement background, commonly national police force services. All the police interviewers have previously experienced police training, the majority including specialist detective training. Some investigators also have tertiary education diplomas or degrees, such as a Masters in Law and Policing, an Associate Diploma in Justice Administration, or an Advanced Diploma of Government (Investigation Management). One investigator had trained and worked as a lawyer, but then changed careers to become a government investigator, before transferring to the ICC.

Lawyers ordinarily have a background in domestic law practice (typically criminal). All lawyers have a law degree (for example, Bachelor of Laws or Juris Doctor)

---

[1] The crime of aggression, which has now been defined under the Rome Statute, but is not yet an enforceable crime.

from their home country or another country. Some lawyers also had a second undergraduate degree (for example, Bachelor of Arts in Political Science) or a graduate
degree (such as a Master of Laws in Human Rights Law). The majority of lawyers
had practical experience in domestic legal practice, usually public prosecution. Some
lawyers surveyed had extensive experience at the same or a variety of international
courts and tribunals. For example, one lawyer had worked at the ICC for 7 years; one
STL lawyer had previously spent 5 years at the ICTY and 5 years at the ICC; another
working at the STL had previously also worked at the ICTR, Kosovo Tribunal, the
ICTY, and the SCSL; and a senior ICTY lawyer has been at the Tribunal since 1996.

Interview Training

The ICC's OTP has an Operations Manual (OM), finalized in September 2011, which
is not available publicly.[2] The OM has a general section on interviews, which includes
a chapter on witness interviews. This is broken down into various components: ap-
proaching the witness, security issues, screening of potential witnesses, preparation,
conduct of interview (for example, vulnerable witnesses, minors, or other trauma-
tized witnesses), record of interview,[3] and closing procedures (how to complete the
interview, interviewer's obligations). A general section on interviews examines in
more detail each category of the witness and the different statements that need to
be made to each type of witness with respect to their specific rights. Witness categories covered here include minors, victims of sexual violence, and suspects. There
is very limited detail on interview process, although there is a general reference to
open-ended questions (a point to which we will return later).

Basic training conducted by the OTP is based on the Manual, and emphasizes
the legal structure of interviews rather than any particular techniques (that is, how
the interviews are informed by the Rome Statute and the Rules of Procedure and
Evidence). Specialized training by external consultants is conducted on interviewing
sexual and gender-based violence victims and witnesses, cross-examination trial
strategies, and the examining of witnesses and experts in court. It is not clear what
this training is or how it is delivered. With regards to interviewing suspects, there are
no interview technique training courses required, nor are there interview technique
guidelines available for staff at the ICC.[4]

Interviews of suspects are undertaken not just by investigation personnel, but
also by prosecution lawyers. Training of investigation personnel is dependent on
their background. Police officers are more likely to have been trained in interview
techniques, but these techniques will vary greatly depending on the background of

---

[2] Interview with ICC Legal Assistant, The Hague, November 2011.

[3] Under Rules 111 and 112 of the Rules of Procedure and Evidence.

[4] There are also not any guidelines at the ICTY, ICTR, or STL. Training on interviewing concentrates
on procedures such as recording of interviews. Interview with ICTY Senior Trial Attorney, The
Hague, May 2011; Interviews with STL Senior Trial Attorneys, The Hague, November 2011.

the officer. For example, law enforcement participants who had received training in the UK or Australia were trained in and use the PEACE approach as well as cognitive interview techniques (for more on these see Milne and Bull 1999). In contrast, law enforcement participants from countries such as Bulgaria and Italy were not aware of and/or did not use such techniques. The only lawyer who was trained in and used such techniques is in fact employed as an investigator, and trained with the UK law enforcement, and thus is a hybrid category of law enforcement lawyer. Investigators and lawyers from the USA had been trained in the Reid Technique (Inbau et al. 2001). Past training by domestic institutions of lawyers in investigative interviewing techniques was largely found to be nonexistent. Instead, lawyers are trained in court-questioning techniques, such as cross-examination of expert witnesses (Evans 1995).

For participant interviewers in the international courts and tribunals, training was inconsistent. Some had experienced training on interviewing, while others had not. Of the lawyers surveyed, many had received some training whether it was basic interviewing, examining vulnerable witnesses (including, for example, child soldiers), and courtroom orientated advocacy. All investigators surveyed had some kind of interview training during their domestic career. This varied from specific courses on PEACE or intelligence interviewing, to on-the-job practical interview training. However, no investigator who participated had undergone any interview-related training at any of the international courts or tribunals at which they worked. This was particularly the case with the ICTY, where the assumption was that if you were employed as a senior investigator, you should know what you are doing (one investigator went into the field heading an investigation after only 2 weeks at the Tribunal).

Interview Techniques Reported to be Used

Caution must always be exercised when extrapolating from what people say they do to what they do, as there is often a discrepancy between these. This seems to be particularly the case with regards to interviewing (Kebbell et al. 1999). Nevertheless, we report here the respondents' comments concerning how they interview.

Rapport

One common thread was the need to create a rapport with the interviewee, regardless of other techniques used. This is consistent with what most academics and clinicians would recommend in other interviewing arenas (Milne and Bull 1999; Powell and

Lancaster 2003). One lawyer described the creation of rapport as having such importance, that in the process of doing so, you develop a mental relationship with the interviewee, that amounts almost to a 'reverse Stockholm syndrome'.[5]

This rapport is created in many different ways. One former ICTY investigator depicted an interview he had conducted in a motel room, rather than a police station.[6] This helped the investigator to create rapport, which was increased by going slowly through facts, starting with the bigger picture rather than targeting the conduct of the interviewee, and not taking an adversarial position. As a consequence, although the interviewee did not go into the interview with the express intention of admitting his role in the murder of civilians, that confession was the end result of the interview.

The creation of rapport can be the deciding factor not only in eliciting a confession, but in whether or not a suspect even speaks to court or tribunal investigators. When the ICTY sought to try Naser Orić, quite an effort was made to reach out to him in order to interview him.[7] After 18 months of investigation, contact was made with Orić through a solicitor that knew him. Orić did not reject the interview outright, but was concerned about being arrested. Therefore, it was agreed to meet him on 'neutral ground', at the US Embassy. At this meeting, it was agreed that he would later come for an interview, giving his version first, then he would answer questions. The initial interview, held at the ICTY's Sarajevo field office, lasted for 5 days. Following this, another interview was scheduled for a month's time. This second interview lasted 14 days. The investigator who conducted the interviews believes Orić would not have spoken to the ICTY if investigators had not made the effort to go and meet with him, to put the interview at a personal level through making contact and thus creating rapport. In addition, the approach and techniques used by investigators took into account the charisma of Orić's personality, playing to his egotism. Of course 14 days of interviewing is a long time and lengthy interviews have been associated with false confessions (Gudjonsson 2003). Nevertheless, as the alleged crimes are often numerous and committed over long periods of time, one would expect interviews for mass murders, for example, to take longer than for a single murder. Indeed it is quite common that interviews of suspects, witnesses, and victims of international crimes have lengthy durations of multiple days.

Rapport creation may be dependent on the gender or age of the interviewer and the interviewee. This can be particularly important with male military personnel, who inhabit a hypermasculine, hierarchical world (Higate 2003), and may refuse to speak with a female investigator or lawyer, particularly if she is younger.[8] One tactic employed for an egotistical military or police witness or suspect is to frequently refer to the witness or suspect by rank. In former Yugoslavia, high-level commanders would often be charming and interesting, gentlemanly, and polite making communication, at least on a superficial level, relatively easy. Other words used by investigators and lawyers to describe ICTY suspects include 'sophisticated', 'educated', 'stylish',

---

[5] Interview with ICC Associate Trial Lawyer, The Hague, November 2011.

[6] Interview with former ICTY Senior Investigator, Sydney, January 2012.

[7] Interview with former ICTY Senior Investigator, Sydney, January 2012.

[8] Interview with former ICC Investigator, Lyon, November 2011.

'egotistical', and 'charismatic'. Another lawyer revealed that a fellow female lawyer had succeeded in creating a rapport with a senior military suspect by playing to his vanity and flirting with him, for a very successful interview.[9] This demonstrates the difficulty in creating a standard guideline for a particular category of person, and also the relatively unregulated use of potentially unethical tactics that would not be permissible in many jurisdictions. Therefore, there would appear to be a need for training of investigators and lawyers concerning what techniques to use for the successful creation of rapport with different suspects in various situations and for ethical guidelines.

Use of Evidence

The next most popular technique mentioned by the investigators and lawyers is the use of evidence during the interview. This is consistent with the literature on reasons for confessions in interviews by domestic police agencies. Positive associations have been found between confession rates and strength of the evidence of guilt as judged by the interviewing officer (Cassell and Hayman 1996; Moston et al. 1992; Sellers and Kebbell 2011). Among the most common reasons given for confessing by prison inmates is their belief that the evidence against them is strong (e.g. Gudjonsson and Petursson 1991), and this has also been found in experimental simulation (e.g. Kebbell et al. 2006).

Evidence used in international investigative interviews includes documents, photographs, and maps. Evidence is most often used as a method of challenging statements made by a suspect or witness, or for eliciting information from a suspect (by asking the suspect to comment on the piece of evidence). Documents are particularly effective: in a military context, they can challenge a statement by proving the existence of an order. They can help to increase engagement in an interview with a public servant, who works with documents regularly, enabling them to see a common ground with the investigator or lawyer (helping to contribute to the rapport). Using evidence in an interview can elicit information, which can itself in turn become evidence (Nystedt et al. 2011).

However, in some situations under investigation at the ICC, evidence can be difficult to obtain. For example, evidence gathering in ICC investigations in Libya was hampered by ongoing armed conflict.[10] Therefore, the use of evidence as an interview technique may not always be possible. In some circumstances, interviewees create the evidence, by drawing or sketching. It may be an image that is drawn (e.g. an aerial view of a military compound), or a map (e.g. the location of a compound relative to a village). Any drawings made by a suspect or witness will be introduced into evidence or presented to the defence in discovery.

---

[9] Interview with former ICTY Senior Investigator, Sydney, January 2012.

[10] Interview with ICC Investigator, The Hague, November 2011.

Question Styles

Despite the lack of interview training of lawyers, reported styles of questioning used remain consistent across investigators and lawyers. Open-ended questions and free recall were reported to be used frequently. The elicitation of a free narrative has been argued to be a fundamental principle to best practice in suspect interviews (Read, Powell, Kebbell, Milne, and Steinberg, in press), which provides the interviewee with an opportunity to report what has happened at his or her own pace, without interruption (Fisher 1995; Powell et al. 2005). Free recall is best elicited in two ways: firstly, through the use of open-ended questions, and secondly, by not interrupting. Free recall by the suspect or witness was used by a number of investigators and lawyers. This was generally applied through initial broad scene setting to capture the overall flow of events, before engaging the interviewee with more questions in order to focus on specific events or times. One tactic often used to elicit information from a suspect of international crimes, such as Orić, in free recall, is to encourage them to 'tell their side of the story'. This is particularly useful in the context of international crimes, which are often committed within a setting of opposing groups, in which one group may perceive themselves as not having been 'heard' (by the court or tribunal, but also by the global community at large). Therefore, a political leader or military commander may well be enthusiastic about explaining their own perspective and situation, as well as their actions and the reasons behind them.

The use of free recall for broad scene setting is extremely important in the context of international crimes. An investigation of international crimes is different to that of a domestic 'ordinary' crime investigation. For example, the facts and information that an interviewer seeks to prompt from an interviewee must cover not only one event, but all things leading up to that event, the whole (usually military or political) context. The scale of the crimes being investigated is enormous; the crimes and events take place over days, weeks, and even years. Therefore, the context prior to and around the event(s) is crucial. In addition, there are different modes of perpetration for international crimes, including superior and command responsibility.[11] There are also the 'chapeau elements' of each crime that do not exist in domestic crimes. For example, to prove a war crime, in addition to the elements of the particular crime (e.g. murder—causing the death of a person), there must be a nexus to the armed conflict, and the victim must be a protected person (civilian).[12] Consequently, much more has to be proven in court than in a domestic crime (Bergsmo and Wiley 2008, pp. 6–7).[13] Accordingly, such investigative interviews are more in depth and are conducted with the goal of seeking a vast amount of information from a suspect or witness. Free recall can thus allow an interview to cover events over long periods of time.

---

[11] Articles 25 and 28 Rome Statute of the International Criminal Court.

[12] Elements of Crimes of Article 8 Rome Statute.

[13] Another consequence is that, whereas domestic interviews will last for a matter of hours, interviews of suspects and witnesses of international crimes will be lengthy, lasting for days. One investigator undertook an interview that lasted about 25 days.

If need be, closed questions are also used, more specifically if an interview is not progressing well and questions are being avoided. Indeed a smaller proportion of survey participants also referred to using both clarification questions and challenge questions. Clarification questions are used throughout the interview, whereas challenge questions are generally used later in the interview. Again, these types of questions are essential in order for court and tribunal staff to clarify knowledge and deepen understanding of events, processes, or structures (e.g. military hierarchies), and also to enable them to obtain the information necessary to build a case and prove the commission of a large number of crimes.

Challenges of Cultural Differences

ICC investigators and lawyers, and former ICTR investigators and lawyers, discussed the difficulties faced while conducting interviews in some areas of Africa. Several reasons were given. Firstly, investigators and lawyers faced a significantly high proportion of interviewees with little to no formal education. This resulted in a completely different challenge than with educated and sophisticated suspects (as mentioned above under the heading 'Rapport').

Secondly, the method of storytelling and concepts of time differ in some parts of Africa from those in western cultures. Techniques such as cognitive interviewing have been very largely developed in Western, Anglo countries, seeking successfully to develop a rich and detailed narrative by the suspect or witness. However, a story in Africa may not be told chronologically, in any telling. Time is not measured by a clock or calendar, but in reference to events. For example, a person in the UK might recount an event as occurring on 7 April 2009, whereas an event in the Democratic Republic of Congo or Rwanda might be mentioned relative to the rains. This has resulted in difficulty for interviewers being able to understand what the suspect means.

Another aspect to the African style of storytelling is to blend facts, events, and sources. For example, a witness might recount an event as if they were there, without revealing in fact that they were not there but are simply relaying what they heard from another person. Therefore, investigators and lawyers have had to adopt the technique of telling interviewees to start sentences with specific phrases such as 'I saw', 'I heard', or 'Someone told me'.

Conclusion

It is evident from the data collected through these interviews that to some extent, interview issues in the international context seem to be somewhat similar to those in conventional domestic interviews. For example, techniques used in the domestic environment such as rapport building and using evidence in interviews are also commonly used in international investigative interviews. However, there are also significant differences such as the sheer scale of the crimes and therefore the extensive time span of the interviews, difficulties in obtaining evidence in conflict zones, and perhaps most importantly, cultural disparities that may create problems for interviewers in achieving successful results using techniques trained and utilized in other cultures/countries.

What is clear from the interviews conducted for this chapter is that training at the ICC and other international criminal courts and tribunals with regards to interview techniques is piecemeal, and generally focuses on victims. With lawyers and investigators having such a diverse background of training and experience, and with lawyers in particular not having any prior training in investigative interviewing, it is important that the courts, particularly the ICC, adopt a comprehensive and court-wide training program. In addition, there is a need of guidelines for investigators and lawyers that include ethical principles for the interviewers to follow, with clear instructions as to what conduct is and is not acceptable. This is vital for the court, given the differing standards that exist around the world: for example, in the USA, deception is an acceptable technique to employ, whereas this would not be permitted in the UK or Australia. These kinds of specific issues need to be covered in guidelines and training.

All new investigators and lawyers are likely to benefit from being required to participate in a standard training program of techniques such as PEACE and cognitive interviewing. However, in addition to the standard training, separate training could be conducted pre-deployment for staff according to which country they are investigating a situation in. This training could include cultural awareness, in order to better understand how locals communicate, and also training from local law enforcement officials to give an idea of what techniques are used successfully, locally. A comprehensive training program at the international courts and tribunals will help substantially to standardize the conduct of investigators and lawyers, and ensure a set level of competency and abilities when it comes to investigative interviewing.

Acknowledgments The author would like to thank all participants in the research survey, and the International Criminal Court (ICC) and the Special Tribunal for Lebanon for granting permission to interview current staff members. Particular thanks go to John Ralston and Greg Townsend, who facilitated a number of interviews.

References

Bergsmo, M., & Wiley, W. H. (2008). Human rights professionals and the criminal investigation and prosecution of core international crimes. In S. Skåre, I. Burkey & H. Mørk (Eds.), *Manual on human rights monitoring: An introduction for human rights field officers*. Oslo: Norwegian Centre for Human Rights University of Oslo.

Cassell, P. G., & Hayman, B. S. (1996). Police interrogation in the 1990s: An empirical study of the effects of Miranda. *University of California Law Review, 43,* 839–931.

Cryer, R., Wilsmhurst, E., Friman, H., & Robinson, D. (2007). *An introduction to international criminal law and procedure*. Cambridge: Cambridge University Press.

Evans, K. (1995). *Advocacy in court: A beginner's guide* (2nd ed.). London: Blackstone.

Fisher, R. P. (1995). Interviewing victims and witnesses of crime. *Psychology, Public Policy, and Law, 1,* 732–764.

Goldstone, R. J. (1996). Justice as a tool for peace-making: Truth commissions and international criminal tribunals. *NYU Journal of International Law and Politics, 28,* 485–503.

Groome, D. (2011). *The handbook of human rights investigation* (2nd ed.) CreateSpace.

Gudjonsson, G.H. (Ed.). (2003). The Psychology of Interrogations and Confessions: A Handbook. Chichester: John Wiley & Sons.

Gudjonsson, G. H., & Petursson, H. (1991). Custodial interrogation: Why do suspects confess and how does it relate to their crime, attitude and personality. *Personality & Individual Differences, 12,* 295–306.

Higate, P. (Ed.). (2003). *Military masculinities: Identity and the state.* Westport, CT: Praeger.

Inbau, F. E., Reid, J. E., Buckley, J. P., & Jayne, B. C. (2001). *Criminal interrogation and confessions* (4th ed.). Gaithersberg, MD: Aspen.

Kebbell, M.R., Hurren, E.J., & Roberts, S. (2006). Mock suspects' decisions to confess: Accuracy of eyewitness evidence is crucial. *Applied Cognitive Psychology, 20,* 477–486.

Kebbell, M. R., Milne, R., & Wagstaff, G. F. (1999). The cognitive interview: A survey of its forensic effectiveness. *Psychology, Crime and Law, 5,* 101–115.

Milne, R., & Bull, R. (1999). *Investigative interviewing: Psychology and practice.* Chichester: Wiley.

Moston, S., Stephenson, G. M., & Williamson, T. (1992). The effect of case characteristics on suspect behaviour during police questioning. *British Journal of Criminology, 32,* 23–40.

Nystedt, M., Nielsen, C. A., & Kleffner, J. K. (Eds.). (2011). *A handbook on assisting international criminal investigations.* Stockholm: Folke Bernadotte Academy.

Powell, M. B., Fisher, R. P., & Wright, R. (2005). Investigative interviewing. In N. Brewer & K. D. Williams (Eds.), *Psychology and law: An empirical perspective (11–42).* New York, NY: Guilford Press.

Powell, M., & Lancaster, S. (2003). Guidelines for interviewing children during child custody evaluations. *Australian Psychologist, 38,* 46–54.

Rauxloh, R. E. (2010). Negotiated history: The historical record in international criminal law and plea bargaining. *International Criminal Law Review, 10,* 739–770.

Read, J. M., Powell, M. B., Kebbell, M. R., Milne, R., & Steinberg, R. (2013). Evaluating police interviewing practices with suspects in child sexual abuse cases. *Policing and Society.* doi:10.1080/10439463.2013.784297.

Schabas, W. A. (2006). *The UN International Criminal Tribunals: The former Yugoslavia, Rwanda and Sierra Leone.* Cambridge: Cambridge University Press.

Schabas, W. A. (2007). *An introduction to the International Criminal Court* (3rd ed.). Cambridge: Cambridge University Press.

Seller, S., & Kebbell, M. (2011). The role of evidence in the interviewing of suspects: An analysis of Australian police transcripts. *British Journal of Forensic Practice, 13,* 84–94.

Chapter 6
A Training Program for Investigative Interviewing of Children

Makiko Naka

Introduction

In 2010, the Prevention of Child Abuse Act (Kodomo Gyakutai Boshi Ho) was issued in Japan. People have since become more aware of neglect as well as physical, psychological, and sexual abuse against children. The number of referrals to child guidance centers, where social workers and psychologists seek to protect children, increased from 17,725 in 2000 to 66,807 in 2012 (Ministry of Health, Labor and Welfare 2013). However, not all of these referrals are treated as "cases" by the police. According to an annual report by the National Police (National Police Agency 2013), only 472 cases were investigated in 2012. Moreover, even if a case went to court, the child's testimony may be disregarded. In one case, the court dismissed a child's testimony by saying that "(in the child's testimony) no concrete or clear features are described to identify a perpetrator among others" (Hiroshima High Court 2005). In another case, a child's testimony was considered "not good enough due to the limitation of the child's understanding and expression. The testimony was strongly affected by her father who disliked the man (defendant)" (Sankei Shinbun 2010).

The credibility of a child's testimony considerably depends on the quality of the interview. In this chapter, we will first describe cases where the credibility of a child's testimony or the quality of interviews was questioned. Upon investigating these problems, the author realized that objective investigation is necessary in Japan. Therefore, the second part of the chapter describes how we introduced, and are implementing, forensic interviews in Japan, focusing on the development of a training program. Finally, the training program will be evaluated.

In terms of interviews, Japan is backward: We have no formal guidelines or legal systems for video recordings of child testimony. In 2010, the UN advised us to "... urgently review, in consultation with experts in the field, its procedures for the provision of support and assistance to child victims who are witnesses, with a view to ensuring that children are not subjected to additional trauma as a result of being

M. Naka (✉)
Hokkaido University, Hokkaido, Japan
e-mail: mnaka@let.hokudai.ac.jp

R. Bull (ed.), *Investigative Interviewing*, DOI 10.1007/978-1-4614-9642-7_6,
© Springer Science+Business Media New York 2014

required to testify repeatedly and consider, to this end, the use of video evidence rather than oral testimony in such proceedings" (Convention on the Rights of the Child, Committee on the Rights of the Child 2010, p. 39-a). Although little progress has been made in connection with the UN advice, minor changes are being made among child guidance centers and the police. The author hopes that this chapter will prove helpful for others in non-English-speaking countries to progress toward implementing forensic interviews.

Cases and Research

My research area is cognitive development in children, especially the comprehension and production of utterances in conversation. I study parent–child dialogue on past events, how people interpret indirect requests, how children learn vocabulary through conversation (e.g., Naka 1999), and memory in real-life contexts (e.g., Naka 1998). In 1992, I was asked to give an opinion on adult eyewitness testimony in a criminal case (Naka et al. 1996, 2002). After providing opinions on several adult cases, I was asked to act as an expert witness on a child witness' testimony. At the time, few people in Japan were studying this topic, but I was greatly attracted to it. The following are some cases I observed and studies I conducted, which were inspired by the cases. Specific information has been modified to preserve anonymity, but the wording remains unchanged.

Case 1

In this case, a 4-year-old girl testified against a man X, who allegedly injured a man Y to steal money (Sapporo District Court 1997). As previously stated, a problem in Japanese investigation is that no video or audio recordings of interviews are made. Statements are typically written down as a first-person narrative, even though the statement is obtained through conversations. However, uniquely, this statement was written in "question and answer" form, and thus I thought that it might have been recorded verbatim. The following is the main part of the dialogue ("I" denotes the interviewer and "C" denotes the child witness).

I: Why did Y fall down?
C: X is bad.
I: Why is X bad?
C: X is bad because Y fell down.
I: What did X do when Y fell?
C: Tripped with a foot.
I: Did X pick up a wallet?
C: No, X put it in the river.
I: Do you know where he put the wallet?
C: I know.

This may suggest that the child witnessed X tripping Y to take his wallet, which he threw away after taking the money. However, there were some problems. First the child did not say that X *was* bad, only that "X *is* bad." She replied "No" to the question asking whether X picked up the wallet. Further, her mother, who was present at the girl's interview, said in her own interview, "In my daughter's interview, she said X *don-shita*. For her, this means 'pushed'." *Don* is an onomatopoeic word meaning "thud" or "bump." Therefore, *don-shita* means "Did thud." "Tripped with a foot" must be the investigator's interpretation, because it did not appear in the child's statement. In addition, although the child said she knew where X had put the wallet, the wallet was never found there. Eventually, although the girl's competence was admitted, her testimony was dismissed.

Case 2

An 8-year-old girl told her mother, Mrs. A, that her classmate might be harassed by Mr. X, a teacher in the after-school program. Mrs. A spoke with the child's mother, Mrs. B, over the phone about her suspicion. Mrs. B was concerned and began asking her child about Mr. X. Their conversation was never recorded, but later in court, Mrs. B explained how she had asked her child about Mr. X. According to the stenographic court record, Mrs. B asked her child as follows:

"I (Mrs. B) said, 'I may be asking strange things. Is there any time that Mr. X touched you?' She said, 'Who said that?' and didn't say anything. So I told her about the phone call from Mrs. A. I asked her, 'Your name was on it. Tell me and I won't blame you.' I asked, 'Did Mr. X touch you?' Again I asked, 'Did Mr. X touch you?' Then she said, 'Yeah'. I asked, 'About where?' She showed about here with her hand. I asked her, 'Did he touch you when playing?' She was hesitating, but I told her again, 'Tell me clearly.' Then she said, 'Bumped into the shoulder and arm.' So I asked her, 'When?' Then she said, 'play time.' I asked, 'About when?' Then she said, 'Before summer holiday.' I asked again, 'This is the last time. Tell me. Did Mr. X really touch you?' She said, 'Yeah.' I asked her, 'Did Mr. X really touch you?' She said, 'Bumped into shoulder and arm. It hurt a bit'."

Again, it may appear that the child was being touched by Mr. X, but she did not mention touching. She only said "Yeah" and "Bumped". In addition, it was problematic that the mother repeated closed questions, suggested that the child was involved in an incident ("your name is on it"), and pressured the child ("Tell me and I won't blame you").

Case 3

Children are not well regarded in court either. In the following case, we have analyzed a stenographic record of examination in court. Walker (1993) analyzed a court document and found that 73 % of adults' questions (i.e., examination in chief and cross examination) were closed questions and 88 % of children's responses were one- or two-word short answers. She also indicated that lawyers especially ask inadequate questions such as multi-faceted or embedded questions (e.g., "Did you tell your dad that you saw it?"), questions with pronouns and anaphora (e.g., this, that), and grammatically complex (i.e., typically long) questions. Brennan (1995) described 15 characteristics of lawyers' questions, referring to them as negative rhetorical, multi-faceted, lacking grammatical/semantic connection, juxtapositioning topics, and so on. Indeed, questions phrased by lawyers (i.e., negative, double-negative, multi-faceted, grammatically complex, tagged or containing difficult words) are hard to understand and answer not only for children but also for undergraduates (Perry et al. 1995; Kebbell and Johnson 2000).

Following these studies, Naka (2001) analyzed a court case involving a child. There were 1,603 utterances in which a judge, a prosecutor, and a lawyer asked 229, 348, and 220 questions, respectively. Instead of categorizing each utterance into exclusive categories, we counted the indices of inadequate questions (i.e., negative terms (e.g., not, never), pronouns, embedding, and tagging), as well as indices of adequate questions (such as wh questions) and the Japanese grammatical marker KA, which indicates that a sentence requires an answer for each utterance. The results showed that inadequate indices occurred more frequently in lawyers' questions than in judges or prosecutors' questions. Furthermore, the incidence of children's multi-word answers was significantly higher in response to questions with adequate indices than those with inadequate indices. Finally, the number of multi-word answers was inversely proportional to the length of the questions. As the UN Committee on the Rights of the Child recommends (Convention on the Rights of the Child 2010, p. 38-c), we should "ensure that judges, prosecutors, police and other professionals working with child witnesses receive training on child-friendly interaction with victims and witnesses..."

Laboratory Studies

Such cases triggered research into child testimony (see Naka 2006 for an English review). For instance, in the Kabutoyama case, children with learning disabilities gave detailed testimony after repeated interviews. Inspired by this case, Yamamoto and his colleagues conducted a study showing that after repetitive interviews, children said untrue things (Takaoka et al. 2002; Yamamoto et al. 2013).

Inspired by another case, we too conducted a study to clarify the importance of interviewing (Naka 2012). In this study, we presented 249 children, aged 7–8 or 10–11, with a video recorded event. In the first session, they were asked to recall the content of the video either by use of (a) free recall, (b) free recall with context reinstatement (closing eyes and remembering the content of the video for 1 min), (c) recall with closed questions that contain accurate and inaccurate information, or (d) interviews that mainly utilized open-ended and wh questions, and closed questions were asked if necessary. In the second session, children were verbally presented with 20 sentences depicting scenes (e.g., The girl in the video wore a white shirt);

however, 15 out of the 20 scenes were not in the video (i.e., false sentences). Children were instructed to respond to each sentence with either "I saw it with my own eyes," "I didn't see it," or "I don't know."

Results from the first session revealed, as predicted, that children recalled more accurate information in the interview condition than in other conditions. Context reinstatement was effective only for older children. In the second session, younger children answered "I saw it with my own eyes" for false scenes more often than did older children. More importantly, younger children in the context reinstatement and question conditions chose "I saw it" for false scenes more frequently than those in the other conditions. Close examination showed that children in the context reinstatement condition more frequently confirmed false scenes that included incorrect attributes such as colors (e.g., "green bin" instead of "blue bin"), whereas those in the question condition tended to confirm false scenes with incorrect items suggested by misleading questions (e.g., lady's apron), suggesting that children's memories are affected not only by external information (i.e., the adult's questions) but also by internal information (i.e., images that the child might create).

Introducing Forensic Interviews to Japan

Start-up

Interviews conducted without proper training jeopardize the validity of the child's testimony. After providing opinions on several cases, I realized that merely criticizing the interviews does not improve the situation. In 2000, there was a Psychology and Law Conference in Dublin. On my way there, I joined a group of Japanese lawyers visiting the Institute of Criminal Justice Studies at the University of Portsmouth. There I met Ray Bull, the editor of this book and, at the time, a professor at that university. He was the coauthor of the pioneering Memorandum of Good Practice (MOGP), the official guidance in England and Wales for forensic interviewing of children (Home Office 1992).

Obtaining the MOGP from the UK Home Office, we translated and published it with additional explanatory chapters (Home Office 1992; Naka and Tanaka 2007). Similar treatment was given to *Interviewing children: A guide for child care and forensic practitioners* (Aldridge and Wood 1998; Naka et al. 2005), which analyzed interviews conducted by the UK police. We also translated *Investigative Interviewing: Psychology and practice* (Milne and Bull 1999; Hara 2003). Meanwhile, a committee of the Japanese Society for Law and Psychology published guidelines for witness testimony and identification (2005), in which this chapter's author along with Kotaro Takagi wrote a chapter about child witnesses.

However, simply publishing guidelines is not enough: professionals must be trained to use their knowledge and skills in real-world cases. In 2007, with Ray Bull's help, I attended a 2-week course on joint investigative interviewing organized by the London Metropolitan Police. Based on what I learned there as well as discussion and practice with graduate students in our department, I began formulating a course. In February 2008, I was able to conduct a pilot course for professionals from the child guidance center, lawyers, and law school students.

In April 2008, we applied to the Japan Science and Technology Agency for a grant to conduct research into interviews and develop a program to train interviewers. When awarded the 4-year grant, we set up a "forensic interview support office" where three staff (two researchers, one technician) supported training and real-world application, and we conducted research relevant to forensic interviews (e.g., children's vocabulary when discussing events, the use of dolls, camera perspectives). Then, we entered into a contract with Hokkaido prefecture, which enabled 22 professionals to attend our 4-day training course each year.

In the following years, we also attended the American Professional Society for Abused Children (APSAC) in the USA for forensic interview training, Children's Justice Center of Salt Lake County in the USA for the National Institute of Child Health and Human Development (NICHD) protocol training, CornerHouse, Minneapolis in the USA for RATAC[TM] interview training, and Sussex Police in the UK for the PEACE model suspect interview training. The fund helped us visit Child Abuse and Response Evaluation Services (CARES) Northwest in Oregon, USA; I. Hershkowitz at Haifa University, Israel; one stop centers in Korea and Melbourne; and B. Mirabal at the University of Puerto Rico, to investigate forensic interview methodologies.

Guidelines

In 2008, we trained lawyers, law school students, and social workers at the child guidance center in the MOGP and its successor the ABE (Home Office 2002) phased approach. The phased approach consists of Establishing Rapport, Free Narrative Account, Questioning, and Closure. Establishing Rapport includes discussing neutral topics, explaining the ground rules, establishing the purpose of the interview, etc. The Free Narrative Account may start with the interviewer telling the child "Tell me why you are here today." It emphasizes asking the child to provide as much information in his/her own words as possible. The Questioning phase includes open-ended, wh, and closed questions, and if absolutely necessary, leading questions that should be followed up by open-ended questions. Finally, in Closure, the interviewer summarizes what the child said, then asks the child if she/he would like to add anything, answers the child's questions, thanks the child, provides a contact number, and then discusses a neutral topic to try to ensure that the child does not leave the room feeling depressed (Home Office 1992, 2002). This guidance provides the important basics and examples of questions and utterances. However, we found that novice trainees had difficulties in formulating open-ended questions.

Reviewing the trainees' performance in 2008, we introduced the NICHD protocol, which was developed by Michael Lamb and his colleagues at the USA NICHD

(Lamb et al. 2007). Its structure and elements are similar to those of MOGP and ABE, but the sequence of the interviewer's utterances is given verbatim in the NICHD protocol.

The protocol consists of (a) Introduction (including self-introduction), the purpose of the interview, and ground rules such as requiring the truth, to say "I do not understand" if the child does not understand the question, to say "I don't know" if the child does not know the answer, to correct the interviewer if he/she makes a mistake, etc.; (b) Rapport Building, where the interviewer asks the child to discuss things he/she likes doing; (c) Training in Episodic Memory, where the interviewer asks the child to report what happened on the day of a special event (e.g., birthday) and yesterday or today; (d) Transition to Substantive Issues, wherein the interviewer invites the child to discuss substantive issues, focusing on the last, or the first, or the most remembered incident if it may have occurred multiple times; (e) Investigating the Incidents, where interviewer collects additional information using open-ended questions and wh questions that focus on information previously provided by the child; (f) Break, where interviewer checks with his/her staff for any missing information; (g) Eliciting Information that has not been mentioned, where the interviewer obtains necessary information using wh and open-ended questions; (h) Information about Disclosure, where the interviewer asks about the child's previous disclosure (if any); and (i) Closing, where the interviewer thanks the child, addresses any questions the child may have, and provides a contact number.

As mentioned, the NICHD protocol renders exact wording. For instance, the first utterance is "Hello, my name is _____ and I am a police officer. [Introduce anyone else in the room; ideally, nobody else will be present.] Today is _____ and it is now _____o'clock. I am interviewing _____ at _____." (Lamb et al. 2007, p. 1217) Although some may consider using such determined utterances to be too rigid, according to others, it may reduce the interviewer's cognitive load. Four types of open-ended question, i.e., the invitation ("Tell me what happened"), time-segmenting cues ("Tell me what happened from time point A to time point B"), cued invitation ("Tell me more about [what the child said]"), and follow up ("And then"), and facilitators ("hum, hum") and echoing (echoing what the child said last), if practiced well, would enable the interviewer to allocate more resources to listening than planning open-ended questions.

With Michael Lamb's permission, we translated the protocol into Japanese and began using it. The protocol's length (15 pages) and the fact that it branches depending on a child's response presented difficulties. Therefore, we created a sheet to demonstrate the structure, (a)–(i) of the protocol, and had trainees become familiar with it before delving into the protocol's details.

Training

The training program was designed to make trainees aware of (a) the obstacles in collecting accurate information, such as problematic questions, pressures, suggestions, and repeated interviews (i.e., system variables), and problems on the part of children, such as limited cognitive abilities (e.g., memory, verbal skills, source monitoring, awareness to the self), suggestibility, and acquiescence due to social immaturity (estimator variables); (b) the elements and structure of forensic interviews; and (c) the skills to conduct interviews in real cases. Since we started training in 2008, we have modified the training program. Initially, we emphasized conversation analysis to make trainees more sensitive to question types and being capable of formulating open-ended questions. However, after we started to use the NICHD protocol, where open-ended questions are explicitly provided, we could allocate more time to the process of obtaining information (i.e., the event from beginning to end), and identifying the information to collect (i.e., checkable facts that would lead to corroborative evidence). The lectures and work/role plays are shown in the Appendix. The program is provided in a 16 to 24-h course, which can be conducted over 2–4 days, depending on the time available to professionals.

The following are some important points to meet professionals' needs. These may benefit those who are planning to introduce forensic interviews in their countries.

Team Approach

A consensus in forensic interviewing is to have a multidisciplinary approach in which police officers and social workers *work together* (Children's Act 1989/2004). A multidisciplinary approach prevents a child from being interviewed repeatedly by different kinds of professionals, which may cause memory distortions and mental damage to the child. Although there is no framework for working together in Japan, we adopted a team approach, hoping that such principle may be possible in the future. We allocate four trainees to a team and assign an ID (A, B, C, and D) to each member, which can be used in group work and role plays. For instance, a trainer can say "Now A plays the interviewer, B plays the interviewee, and C and D are the support staff." In the role play, the support staff also have assignments. For instance, C takes notes and checks for missing information and D is in charge of positioning a camera, a wireless microphone, and chairs as well as checking the time and missing information.

We have observed that the team approach functions well. First, each member systematically experiences different roles. Second, it instills in the trainees that an interview should be conducted by a team, with each member having a different role. Third, it reduces tension and prevents members from criticizing one another. Fourth, the members, usually attending from different parts of Japan, get acquainted and maintain their relationships after the training. Finally, assigning IDs and specifying roles works well in Japanese culture, where people tend to be shy. If a trainer would ask *someone* to present the result of a group discussion in front of others, they may look to one another to speak. In such a situation, "Now C should present the result." would work well. Thus, all in all, even if a multidisciplinary approach is not yet accomplished, working as a team provides good results and seems to fit in our collective culture.

The Difference Between Counseling/Therapy and Forensic Interview

Although the MOGP clearly shows that forensic interviews are different from therapy (Home Office 1992), our trainees found this idea difficult to grasp. In almost all training events, trainees asked about the difference between clinical and forensic interviews. Some criticized the idea of investigative interviewing, thinking that it may lack therapeutic elements such as sympathy and compassion to support victims. The confusion may arise from our culture, which puts a great value on emotional bonds and social relationships (Markus and Kitayama 1991; Wang 2004). Indeed, investigators' traditional practice has been a "counseling approach," in which an interviewer sees an alleged victim repeatedly to build a close interpersonal relationship with him/her, and then, the investigator gradually elicits information from the child piece by piece. However, in such a practice, a child may feel like to please the investigator by telling what the investigator would like to hear.

Therefore, at the beginning of course, we emphasize that a forensic interview aims to collect objective information that is necessary to acquire facts. We explain that an extremely close relationship may cause the child to acquiesce and thus harm objectivity. We also state that both counseling and investigation are necessary to help children, but it is inappropriate for one person to conduct both. In fact, an experienced police officer reported that assuming both roles causes her a dilemma, i.e., she wants more details to resolve the case but she also does not want to ask more questions as this may hurt the child. A frequently mentioned concern is "But we do not have the human resources. We cannot afford a counselor and an investigator for a child." To such questions, we recommend switching children, i.e., a social worker who takes care of a particular child conducts a forensic interview with another child, and vice versa.

Distinguishing Open-ended Questions

Another aspect that needs addressing is communication style. There are two types of reminiscing styles, elaborative and pragmatic (Fivush and Fromhoff 1988; Haden et al. 1997; Harley and Reese 1999). Elaborative mothers attempt to elicit a story and seek elaboration, whereas pragmatic/repetitive mothers tend to ask many wh questions. Asian parents seem to be more pragmatic/repetitive. Takahashi (1995) presented a film clip to Japanese 4 to 6-year olds, and then their mothers asked the children about the content. They mostly used wh and closed questions. Jin and Naka (2002) studied how Chinese parents talk to their 3 to 5-year old children about past events. The results showed that they also used wh and closed questions to elicit information, and this tendency increased when talking to young children. Fujisaki and Muto (1985) studied how nursery school teachers helped 3 to 5-year old children discuss personal events. They were found to use wh questions to elicit children's narratives, although they asked a few "Tell me" questions to 5-year olds. Thus, wh and closed questions seem to be prevalent when talking to children in our culture. In fact, many trainees believe that an "open-ended question" is equivalent to a wh question.

Therefore, before we introduce the interview protocol, we demonstrate the four types of open-ended questions, facilitators and echoing mentioned above, and ask trainees to practice role play in pairs. In the first role play, we pair up A and B, assigning them the roles of an interviewer and interviewee, respectively. In the same way, we pair up C and D, assigning them to be an interviewer and interviewee, respectively. In the second role play, we assign B to be an interviewer and C to be an interviewee, and D to be an interviewer and A to be an interviewee, so each member can talk to two members in the team.

In the first role play, we instruct interviewers (trainees) to interview the interviewee on what happened on their way to the training site. We display a horizontal line representing time and ask interviewers to elicit information that covers the entire time period (from one end to the other end of the line). If an interviewee provides only partial information (e.g., I came by bus), the interviewers are encouraged to expand it by asking, "Tell me more about coming by bus" (cued recall) or "Tell me what happened from the time of getting on the bus until the time of getting off the bus" (time segmentation). We explain that invitation, cued recall, and time segmentation can elicit significant information from the interviewee without introducing any information from the interviewer. We also explain that information given by the interviewee should be elaborated by follow ups ("And then"), facilitators ("Um, um"), and echoing.

In the second role play, interviewers ask interviewees about a recent purchase ("Tell me about your recent shopping"). Purchasing something consists of a series of events. Further, an interviewer needs to collect information about the stage (i.e., place), stage settings (e.g., shelves, carts), stage properties (e.g., other commodities), and personae (e.g., shop clerks, other customers). Even though they may have to resort to wh questions to elicit information, we instruct them to follow these up with open-ended questions (e.g., "Where was the shop?" and if an interviewee says "A convenience store," then "Tell me more about the convenience store") (Lamb et al. 2007).

In 2011, we introduced the Griffith Question Map (GQM) (Griffiths and Milne 2005). This tool facilitates the use of appropriate questions. On the original sheet, there are eight lines representing questions: Open questions ("Tell me. . ."), probing (wh questions), appropriate closed questions (yes–no questions after exhaustive probing), inappropriate closed questions (early yes–no questions), leading questions (questions that suggest answers), multiple questions (questions including multiple concepts), forced choice (A or B questions), and opinion statements. The "good" questions are at the top and the "bad" questions are at the bottom. Thus, each question asked by an interviewer can be plotted on the GQM. As shown in Fig. 6.1 (top), we modified the map with an invitation at the top, and the follow-up (e.g., "And then"), time segmentation and cued invitation, and wh questions at the bottom. The good questions are shown in thick lines. Below these are closed questions (yes–no questions and A or B questions), suggestive, and tagged questions ("The car was black, wasn't it?"), which are shown in thin lines. Using this map, we encourage trainees to stay on the thick lines and return to them if they employ inappropriate questions. We have found that practicing with this tool helps trainees to understand and use open-ended questions.

The Difference Between a Unique Episode and a Script, or an Event and a Routine

It is known that Asian children, compared to Western children, typically provide less specific and less information about past events (Wang 2004). In addition, because abuse is often repeated, children tend to discuss abusive incidents as routine (e.g., "Father hits me whenever he drinks") rather than specific episodes (e.g., "Father was drunk and hit me twice") (Lamb et al. 2008). Even in the training, we sometimes observe that an interviewee playing a child's role discusses an event in the present tense as routine. Therefore, it is important to explain the difference between episodic and semantic memories or a unique episode and a script, and emphasize that forensic interviewing is used to establish that a specific event occurred at certain time and place.

In the NICHD protocol, there is a question to try to separate specific incidents, i.e., "Did that happen once or more than once?") (Lamb et al. 2008). This question helps the interviewer as well as the interviewee to focus on an event rather than a routine. If an interviewee says "It occurred more than once," then the interviewer asks the child to focus on the most recent time, the first time, or the time he/she remembers best.

In addition, SE3R, a tool devised by Eric Shepherd, is effective for distinguishing event information from background information such as settings, details of objects, persons, routines, and other knowledge (Shepherd 2007; Fig. 6.1). SE3R consists of a horizontal line representing time and knowledge bins (boxes) below the line. The line includes a written account of a sequence of events as they occurred. If an interviewee provides information that is not on the line, that information is written in the bin. For instance, if a child Jane (J) said "Uncle Bob (UB) picked up a nearby newspaper and hit me with it," one can consider the incident as "UB picks up newspaper," followed by "UB hits J with newspaper" (events are written in the active voice and present tense, with the subject's initials). If the child explained that Uncle Bob was her mother's older brother and he lived with her, this would be written in a bin called "Uncle Bob." If the child described details of the newspaper, this information would be written in a bin called "newspaper."

Practicing the interview with this tool helps not only to distinguish the event and knowledge but also to assist an interviewer to understand that eliciting event information should be prioritized. At the initial phase of training, interviewers tend to interrupt whenever an interviewee mentions new information. For instance, if a child says "Uncle Bob. . . ," an interviewer immediately feels like asking about Uncle Bob, and the same is the case with the "newspaper." Thus, the interviewer diverts the

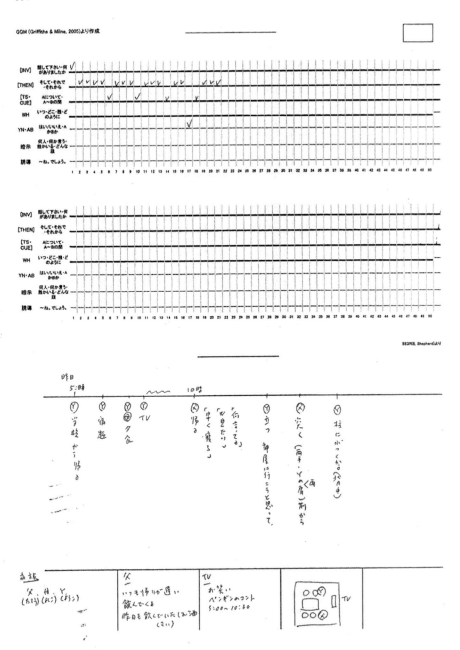

Fig. 6.1 Tools used in training: GQM (Griffiths and Milne 2005) and SE3R (Shepherd 2007). *Note*: In both, fictional contents are shown

child's attention from talking about the event to Uncle Bob, the newspaper, and so on, which is information that the interviewer can actually collect later in the interview. In real interviews, the tool could also be used by the support staff. It is useful to find a gap between what a child has said and not said, or a conflict between what the child said and what others, if they were available, have said.

Planning an Interview: Checkable Facts

Finally, information that would lead to corroborative evidence should be collected. In investigative interviews, it is essential to ask open-ended questions, because, compared with other types of information, open-ended questions are known to elicit less (or no) information contradictory to what the child had said previously in the interview, and thus considered to be more accurate (e.g., Lamb and Fauchier 2001; Orbach and Lamb 2001). However, in reality, in some jurisdictions it is difficult to prosecute someone with only witness evidence. In Japanese criminal courts, judges require the exact time and place, and corroboration even from young children. Therefore, it is essential to obtain the maximum possible information that leads to corroboration, i.e., checkable facts.

To elicit checkable facts, one needs to be sufficiently sensitive to information and to what may corroborate it. To identify a person, his/her name, how he/she is addressed, and a description of the person (e.g., build, clothing, accessories) would be important. A child's calling a person "Dad" is not enough, because he/she may have more than one father figure. As for the place, aspects such as whether it was outside or inside, how far/long one walked/drove, scenery, surroundings, and objects in the place would be important. A child's referring to a place as a "patio" is not enough, because a child may have the wrong name for the place. As for time, whether it was a school day or holiday, before or after a specific meal, TV programs, sales slips, etc. may lead to corroboration. Again, a child's "Three o'clock on Saturday" should not be assumed to be what we adults understand by this phrase unless there is something to corroborate the statement.

We plan an interview as a group: Trainees list information that may lead to or provide corroboration. Not every question should be asked to elicit such information. Rather, if a child mentions any of them, an interviewer or support staff should be sensitive enough to check it, enabling a follow up with evidence.

Evaluation

Overview

So far, we have trained more than 1,000 professionals since we started the program 5 years ago and evaluated the training using three different trainee samples in the years 2009 ($N = 12$), 2010 ($N = 36$), and 2010 ($N = 32$) (Naka et al. 2010; Naka

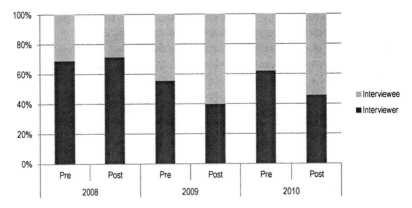

Fig. 6.2 The ratio of utterances (in letters and characters) by interviewer and interviewee before (Pre) and after (Post) the training

2011). The trainees were social workers or psychologists working at child guidance centers and related institutes.

The evaluation is conducted by analyzing mock interviews. A few weeks prior to training, the trainees receive a package that contains instructions, a DVD of a 1-min film clip, an IC recorder, and an envelope in which to return the materials. After perusing the instructions, a trainee asks *any* individual (preferably a child but could be an adult if necessary) to be an interviewee. After obtaining consent, the trainee explains the task; asks the interviewee to talk about his/her breakfast (for episodic memory training); and shows the DVD, during which the trainee stays outside the room (i.e., the trainee does not watch the DVD). The trainee then returns and conducts an interview on the DVD content, following which he/she sends the audio recording of the interview to us. After training, the trainees receive a package with a different DVD. They then conduct another interview and send the audio recording to us.

The training aims to elicit more information from interviewees. Figure 6.2 shows the percentage of utterance by the interviewer and by the interviewee both before and after the training, measured by the number of letters (i.e., the number of Hiragana, Katakana, and Kanji letters). We did not observe a significant increase in interviewees' utterances in the 2008 sample, although the length of narratives became longer after the training. In the 2009 and 2010 samples, we found significant differences. We will describe below the results from 2010 in more detail.

2010 sample

The sample comprised 32 professionals (nine males and 23 females) aged 27–54 years old (M = 40.06, SD = 8.79), who had 1–337 months' experience of working at a Child Guidance Center (M = 69.09, SD = 81.74). The average total interview time was 999 s and 1,070 s for pre- and post-interviews, respectively; this difference was not significant. Dependent variables were the amount of information elicited

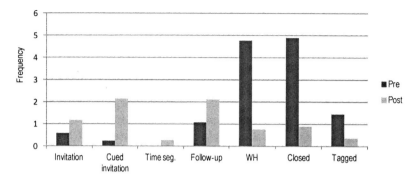

Fig. 6.3 The interviewers' utterances before (Pre) and after (Post) the training

from the interviewee and the types of utterances by interviewers before and after training. Besides the effect of training, we also looked at the effects of gender, age, and trainees' experience.

There was no difference in the number of letters pre- and post-training interviews, but the interaction of (interviewer (i.e., trainee)/interviewee) × (pre-/post-) × interview phases was significant. In the episodic memory phase, no difference was found between the interviewer and interviewee. However, in the substantive phase, aimed at eliciting information about the DVD, the interviewer talked more than the interviewee in the pre-training interview, whereas the interviewee talked more than the interviewer in the post-training interview. Also, the interviewer spoke less in the post-training interview than in the pre-training interview, whereas the opposite was true for the interviewee. There were no significant effects of gender, age, or experience.

In addition, we looked at the differences in the types of pre- and post-training interview questions. As shown in Fig. 6.3, the number of wh questions, closed questions, and tag questions decreased, whereas the number of time segmentation questions and cued invitations increased from pre- to post-training interviews, suggesting that the change in utterance types was responsible for increase in the interviewer's utterances in the post-training interview. Invitations, time segmentation, cued invitation, and follow ups elicited longer utterances compared to other type of utterances.

In addition, we looked at variations in the Japanese expressions for "Tell." In Japanese, the imperative form of "Tell" is "Hanashi-te" or "Hanashi-te-kudasai." In the pre-training interviews, interviewers used a variety of expressions, including polite interrogative forms that may be translated as "Would you please tell..." (e.g., "Hanashi-te-kure-masu-ka?," "Hanashi-te-morae-masu-ka?," and "Hanashi-te-itadake-masu-ka?"), and euphemistical interrogative forms with negation that are even more polite ("Hanashi-te-kure-masen-ka?," "Hanashi-te-morrae-masen-ka?," and "Hanashi-te-itadake-masen-ka?"). However, in the post-training interview, these variations converged into a simple form of "Tell."

Finally, the preliminary analysis showed that the accuracy of information obtained increased from 24.06 or 84 % in pre-training interviews to 29.09 or 92 % in post-training interviews, the latter being significantly greater than the former without increasing errors. Although continued follow up and practice are necessary, attending the training in itself does seem to facilitate improvements in interviewing style.

Final Remarks As mentioned before, this is the fifth year since we started the training. Due to support from the Japan Science and Technology Agency and later from the Japanese Ministry of Education, Culture, Sports, Science and Technology, and in collaboration with other researchers and practitioners, we have provided training not only in Hokkaido but also in other parts of Japan. Trainees have expanded from social workers and psychologists to family court investigators, police officers, and prosecutors. According to Yamamoto (2012), the number of child guidance centers that use such forensic interviews increased from 8 % in 2007 to 44 % in 2010. There are at least four facilities that now have suites for forensic interviews. Although there is significant room for improvement in the implementation of forensic interviews in the legal system and a multi-disciplinary approach, the changes are encouraging. At CARES Northwest in Oregon, USA, I overheard that "It started from a closet." In Salt Lake County and Israel, implementation of the NICHD protocol began as an "experiment." I hope this chapter will benefit those who, like us, are working to implement forensic interviews.

Appendix: The Training Program

Training is conducted in groups. Each group consists of four people with the IDs A, B, C, and D. [ ] indicates approximate time in minutes.

1. Lecture: Problems in Child Testimony [90] Difficulties in interviewing children and problems in children's testimonies in a forensic and social work context:

1. It is emphasized that multiple interviews, pressures, and leading questions can not only cause to alteration of memory but also to secondary trauma, as suggested by the UN.
2. Children's cognitive development, especially regarding communication skills, memory, and suggestibility.

2. Lecture and Work: Open-ended Questions and Free Narratives [30]

1. Introduction to the four types of open-ended questions, i.e., invitation, time segmentation, cued invitation and follow up, and facilitator and echoing.
2. Trainees practice how to use the four types of open-ended questions, and facilitator and echoing as shown in Sect. 3.3.

3. Lecture and Work: Introduction to Forensic Interviews and the NICHD Protocol [60]

1. Forensic interviews (aim and structure) in general and worldwide trend toward a multidisciplinary approach.

2. Introduction to the NICHD protocol, showing a simple structure.
3. A mini-interview: A is assigned as an interviewer, B is assigned as an interviewee, and C and D are support staff. B is shown a 1-min film clip, based on which A as an interviewer, and C and D as support staff, conduct an interview. The interview follows the protocol, i.e., (a)–(i) in Sect. 2.2.

4. Lecture and Work: Planning an Interview [70]

1. The entire procedure for conducting an interview: When (immediately after a plan is made), where (warm but not distracting), by whom (a trained interviewer), settings, and apparatus, etc.
2. Planning an interview: In a group, trainees discuss information that is missing from what has already been obtained and information along with the corresponding facts that corroborate it.
3. Planning how to start an interview: When a child says "I don't know" to an invitation "I want to talk about why [you are here] today" (Lamb et al. 2007), it could be that the child does not understand the purpose or topic of the interview, does not know how to start, or is reluctant.

5. Role Plays and Reviews (105 for Each Role Play and Review) Each member rotates roles among interviewer, interviewee, support staff 1 (taking notes, looking for missing information), and support staff 2 (positioning, time management, looking for missing information from the overview). A scenario for an interview is provided to an interviewer, based on which the interviewer and support staff plan an interview. Meanwhile, the interviewee is given detailed instruction outside the room. The planning and interview take approximately 30 min. Each interview is video recorded and reviewed immediately after the role play. Usually, the interviews are reviewed consecutively. The role plays are repeated four times with each member rotating among the roles. The GQM and SE3R are used in later reviews, although these tools have not been used for evaluated interviews.

6. Lecture and Work: Reluctant Children [50]

1. The trend of children being reluctant is shown with reference to Aldridge and Wood (1998), Hershkowitz, Orbach, Lamb, Sternberg, and Horowitz (2006), Hershkowitz, Horowitz, and Lamb (2005), and so on. We then discuss the approach to reluctant children.
2. A short (i.e., 2–3 min) role play is conducted, with one trainee being an interviewer and another being a reluctant interviewee. The role plays are repeated twice.

7. Lecture: Corroboration and Checkable Facts [50] Information that may lead to corroboration is discussed. See Sect. 3.5.

8. Lecture and Work: Difficult Questions [30] The necessity of using "taboo words" is discussed. The trainees are paired and practice how to reply to a difficult but sensitive question such as "Do you have sex?," which a child may abruptly ask. How to listen to and elicit information from a child is also discussed. The work was adopted from a joint investigation training provided by the London Metropolitan Police in the UK.

9. Interviewing Children [60] In addition to the training, we provide an interview with a real child and conversation analysis (transcription of conversation and analysis using a computer) at Hokkaido University. Children take part in some activities (such as playing games in the room or walking around the campus) and are then interviewed on their activities.

References

Aldridge, M., & Wood, J. (1998). *Interviewing children: A guide for child care and forensic practitioners.* Chichester: Wiley. [Aldridge, M., & Wood, J. (1998). Translated by Naka, M., Satio, K., & Wakinaka, H. (2004). Kodomo no mensetsuhou Shihou tetsuzuki ni okeru kodomo no kea gaido Kyoto Kitaojishobo] (Child interview A guideline for childs carecriminal proceedings).

Brennan, M. (1995) The discourse of denial: Cross-examining child victim witnesses. *Journal of Pragmatics, 23,* 71-91.

Convention on the Rights of the Child Committee on the Rights of the Child. (2010). *Consideration of reports submitted by states parties under article 12(1) of the optional protocol to the convention on the rights of the child on the sale of children, child prostitution and child pornography—concluding observations.* Japan, 25 May–11 June 2010.

Fujisaki, H., & Muto, T. (1985). Helping young children with acquisition of conversation skill: An analysis of teaching scenes. *Showa 57, 58 & 59th Kagakukenkyuhi Hojokin Tokutei Kenkyu Report "Gengo no Hyojunka", 1,* 157–176. (In Japanese).

Fivush, F., & Fromhoff, F. A. (1988). Style and structure in mother-child conversations about the past. *Discourse Processes, 11,* 337–355.

Griffiths, A., & Milne, R. (2005). Will it all end in tiers? In T. Williamson (Ed.), *Investigative interviewing: Research, rights and regulation* (pp. 167–189). Cullompton: Willan.

Haden, C. A., Haine, R. A., & Fivush, R. (1997). Developing narrative structure in parent-child reminiscing across the preschool years. *Developmental Psychology, 33,* 295–307.

Harley, K., & Reese, E. (1999). Origins of autobiographical memory. *Developmental Psychology, 35,* 1338–1348.

Hershkowitz, I., Horowitz, D., & Lamb, M. E. (2005). Trends in children's disclosure of abuse in Israel: A national study. *Child Abuse & Neglect, 29,* 1203–1214.

Hershkowitz, I., Orbach, Y., Lamb, M. E., Sternberg, K. J., & Horowitz, D. (2006). Dynamics of forensic interviews with suspected abuse victims who do not disclose abuse. *Child Abuse & Neglect, 30,* 753–769.

Hiroshima High Court. (2005). *Heisei 16 (U) No. 106.* (in Japanese).

Home Office. (1992). *Memorandum of good practice on video recorded interviews with child witnesses for criminal Proceedings.* London: The Stationery Office. [Home Office (1992). Translated by Naka, M., & Tanaka, S. (2007). Kodomo no shiho mensetsu: Bideo rokuga mensetsu gaidorain. Tokyo: Seishin Shobo] (Child forensic interview: A guideline for video recorded interview).

Home Office. (2002). *Achieving the best evidence in criminal proceedings: Guidance for vulnerable and intimidated witnesses, including children.* Home Office Communication Directorate.

Japanese Society for Law and Psychology. (2005). *Mokugeki kyoujutsu and shikibetu tetsuzuki ni kansuru gaidorain.* Tokyo: Gendaijinbun-sha. (A guideline for eyewitness testimony and identification procedure, In Japanese).

Jin, J. A., & Naka, M. (2002). Elicitation of children's narratives about past events by Chinese mothers and fathers. *Japanese Journal of Developmental Psychology, 13,* 274–283. (In Japanese.)

Kebbell, M. R., & Johnson, S. D. (2000). Lawyers' questioning: The effect of confusing questions on witness confidence and accuracy. *Law and Human Behavior, 24,* 629–641.

Lamb, M. E., & Fauchier, A. (2001). The effects of question type on self-contradictions by children in the course of forensic interviews. *Applied Cognitive Psychology, 15*, 483–491.

Lamb, M. E., Hershkowitz, I., Orbach, Y., & Esplin, P. W. (2008). *Tell me what happened: Structured investigative interviews of child victims and witnesses.* Chichester: Wiley.

Lamb, M. E., Orbach, Y., Hershkowitz, I., Esplin, P. W., & Horowitz, D. (2007). A structured forensic interview protocol improves the quality and informativeness of investigative interviews with children: A review of research using the NICHD Investigative Interview Protocol. *Child Abuse & Neglect, 31*, 1201–1231.

Markus, H. R., & Kitayama, S. (1991). Culture and the self: Implications for cognition, emotion, and motivation. *Psychological Review, 98*, 224–253.

Milne, R., & Bull, R. (1999). *Investigative interviewing: Psychology and practice.* Chichester: Wiley. [Milne, R., & Bull, R. (1999). Translated by Hara, S. (2003). Torishirabe no shinrigaku Jijitsu choshu no tameno sousa mensetsuho Kyoto Kitaojishobo] (Psychology of investigation Investigative interviewing methods for searching for facts).

Ministry of Health, Labour and Welfare, (2013). http://www.mhlw.go.jp/stf/houdou/2r98520000037b58-att/2r98520000037ban.pdf. Accessed 1 Oct 2013. (In Japanese).

Naka, M. (1998). Repeated writing facilitates children's memory for letters and characters. *Memory & Cognition, 26*, 804–809.

Naka, M. (1999). The acquisition of Japanese numerical classifiers by 2–4-year-old children: The role of caretakers' linguistic inputs. *Japanese Psychological Research, 41*, 70–78.

Naka, M. (2001). Child interview in court: A case study of Lawyerese. *Japanese Journal of Law and Psychology, 1*, 80–92. (In Japanese).

Naka, M. (2006). Memory talk and testimony in children. In R. Mazuka, et al. (Eds.), *Handbook of East Asian psycholinguistics* (pp. 123–129). Cambridge: Cambridge University Press.

Naka, M. (2011). The effect of forensic interview training based on the NICHD structured protocol. *Japanese Journal of Child Abuse and Neglect, 13*, 316–325. (In Japanese).

Naka, M. (2012). The effect of different ways of interviewing on children's reports and subsequent memories of an eyewitnessed event. *Japanese Journal of Psychology, 83*, 303–313. (In Japanese).

Naka, M., Futakuchi, Y., & Koyama, K. (2010). *A training program on investigative interviewing with children: Three-day training and its effect on the interview.* Poster presented at the 3rd International Investigative Interviewing Research Group Annual Conference, Stavern, Norway, 22–24 June.

Naka, M., Itsukushima, Y., & Itoh, Y. (1996). Eyewitness testimony after three months: A field study on memory for an incident in everyday life. *Japanese Psychological Research, 38*, 14–24.

Naka, M., Itsukushima, Y., Itoh, Y., & Hara, H. (2002). The effect of repeated photo identification and time delay on the accuracy of the final photographic identification and the rating of memory. *International Journal of Police Science and Management, 4*, 53–61.

National Police Agency. (2013). Jidou gyakutai oyobi fukushihan no kenkyojoukyou tou: Heisei 24nen 1 gatsu-12 gatsu. (The situations of arrested cases of child abuse and welfare crime: January to December, 2012). (In Japanese).

Orbach, Y., & Lamb, M. E. (2001). The relationship between within-interview contradictions and eliciting interviewer utterances. *Child Abuse & Neglect, 25*, 323–333.

Perry, N. W., McAuliff, B. D., Tam, P., Claycomb, L., Dostal, C., & Flanagan, C. (1995). When lawyers question children: Is justice served? *Law and Human Behavior, 19*, 609–629.

Sankei Shinbun [Sankei Newspaper] (2010). http://sankei.jp.msn.com/affairs/trial/100520/trl1005201406001-n1.htm. Accessed 6 June 2010. (In Japanese).

Sapporo District Court. (1997). *Heisei 9 (WA) No. 347.* (In Japanese).

Shepherd, E. (2007). *Investigative interviewing: The conversation management approach.* New York: Oxford University Press.

Takahashi, N. (1995). Mother-child communication in preschoolers: The relationship between mothers' extraction style and their children's explanation. *Japanese Journal of Educational Psychology, 43*, 32–41. (In Japanese).

Takaoka, M., Saito, K., Wakinaka, H., & Yamamoto, T. (2002). False memories in children created through a series of interviews. Who took a boy away? *International Journal of Police Science and Management, 4*, 62–72.

Walker, A. G. (1993). Questioning young children in court: A linguistic case study. *Law and Human Behavior, 17*, 59–81.

Wang, Q. (2004). The emergence of cultural self-constructs: Autobiographical memory and self-description in European American and Chinese children. *Developmental Psychology, 40*, 3–15.

Yamamoto, T., Wakinaka, H., Saito, K., Takaoka, M., & Takagi, K. (2003). *Umidasareta monogatari: Mokugeki shogen, kioku no henyo, enzai ni shinrigaku wa dokomade semareruka*. Kyoto: Kitaojishobo. (Produced stories: To what extent can psychology access to eyewitness testimony, memory distortion, and miscarriage of justice? In Japanese).

Yamamoto, T. (2012). *Kateinai seibouryoku higaiji (jido gyakutai, jido poruno tou) no hakken, shien ni okeru kaku kankeikikan no taiou to renkei ni kansuru chosa kenkyu*. Tokyo: Kodomo Mirai Zaidan. (Survey on actions and cooperation of relevant organizations in finding and supporting the victimized children in intra-familial sexual abuse (child abuse and child pornography) in Japanese).

Chapter 7
Success Within Criminal Investigations: Is Communication Still a Key Component?

Martin O'Neill and Becky Milne

Introduction

This chapter discusses whether good communication skills are still considered a key component of investigative success in the modern era. Various studies of the past indicate the importance of good communication skills, but most are from at least a decade ago or even more distant. The chapter draws upon two studies undertaken between 2008 and 2011 as part of the first author's doctoral research. We begin by defining what constitutes a criminal investigation, as this is fundamental to an understanding of the context of this research, followed by a discussion of what success means within a criminal investigation.

Criminal Investigation

Criminal investigation has been a part of much of modern society's identity for centuries, both in real life and in fiction. Yet, the term means different things to different people. It has been posited as being: 'a reconstruction of the past' (Osterburgh and Ward 2000) and 'a social construction of meaning' (Innes 2003). However, in the UK, legislation has provided a statutory definition that will suffice for the present discussion:

> For the purposes of this Part a criminal investigation is an investigation conducted by police officers with a view to it being ascertained—whether a person should be charged with an offence, or whether a person charged with an offence is guilty of it.

(Section 22, Criminal Procedure and Investigations Act (CPIA) 1996)

M. O'Neill (✉) · B. Milne
University of Portsmouth, Portsmouth, United Kingdom
e-mail: noneill5@port.ac.uk

B. Milne
e-mail: becky.milne@port.ac.uk

R. Bull (ed.), *Investigative Interviewing*, DOI 10.1007/978-1-4614-9642-7_7,
© Springer Science+Business Media New York 2014

The CPIA codes of practice go on to describe that this will include investigations begun in the belief that a crime is about to be committed as well as those reported as already having happened (CPIA Codes of Practice, Home Office 1997).

Understanding the definition is crucial to investigators, as they need to know when any particular investigation has begun in order to comply with other duties assigned to them by the Act and associated codes of practice. Interestingly, the Act and codes do not make a distinction between detectives and others within a police investigation. They distinguish the roles of investigator (wide enough to encompass both detectives and others), disclosure officer, and officer in the case. Each is identified as having duties once a criminal investigation has begun. Amongst the most important are: the need to record, retain, and ultimately reveal (to the prosecutor) relevant material, as well as the necessity to pursue all reasonable lines of enquiry whether they point towards or away from the suspect. Much of the legislation was enacted to combat fears that police historically withheld important information, ignored exonerating facts, and simply constructed cases against people who were sometimes innocent. High profile miscarriages of justice often demonstrated these failings in abundance (such as the Guilford four, the Birmingham six, the case of the Taylor sisters, and Stefan Kiszko, see Savage and Milne 2007).

Each criminal investigation may involve solely one officer managing the investigation to a successful conclusion. Nowadays, that may not be a trained detective who manages such investigations because uniformed officers also manage a large proportion of volume crime cases (Chatterton 2008). What is clear is that within each criminal investigation at whatever level, if the case is to progress, there will invariably be a need to collect relevant information, engage with colleagues, engage with potential experts, interview witnesses, interview suspects, engage with CPS, and provide evidence in the form of a written case file in order to bring the case to a conclusion (Innes 2003).

Each of these facets of an investigation will require effective communication skills, most importantly, in the armoury of the officer in the case. That person has to bring all parts of the investigation together in order to assist in identifying the most suitable outcome to the investigation, be it no further action (no crime or insufficient evidence to be able to assign liability), or whether any individual should be assigned liability for the crime (be it by fine, caution, reprimand, summons, or charge). Deficiencies in any of these areas of effective communication could hinder any such quest.

The Nature of Success

But what exactly constitutes success in the modern era? Few studies exist in the twenty-first century relating to officers' perceptions of what constitutes a successful investigator. We examined criminal investigation textbooks and the research literature in order to identify what traits and characteristics had previously been highlighted as important to investigative success. The two lists below were distilled from these sources.

List 1 (Text Books)

Intelligence, energy, training, ingenuity, experience, self-discipline, reasoning ability, objectivity, vigilance, curiosity, courage, memory, observation, tact, communication, knowledge of people, resourcefulness, perseverance, sensitivity, ethical, honest, report writing skills, good thief taker (Svensson and Wendel 1955; Jackson 1962; Thorwald 1965; Deinstein 1968; O'Hara 1970; Osterburgh and Ward 2000; Swanson et al. 2002).

List 2 (Research)

Intelligence, approachable, stable, persistent, reasoning ability, patient, motivated, teamwork, objectivity, initiative, empathy, independence of thought, creative, tenacious, decision-making, good judgement, communication skills, commitment, dedication, leadership, experienced, training, listening, knowledge of legal requirements, education, street intelligence, nose for the job, planning, integrity, strategic awareness (Greenwood et al. 1977: Cohen and Chaiken 1987; Morgan 1990; McGurk et al. 1992; Maguire et al. 1991; Smith and Flanagan 2000; Innes 2003).

Common themes that emerged from both sets of sources were: communication skills/ability, intelligence, training, experience, decision-making/reasoning ability, motivation, perseverance, empathy, integrity, nose for the job/good thief taker, experience, and creativity/ingenuity.

Communication as a Key to Investigative Success

Thus, communication skills have been highlighted by research studies as fundamental to success within criminal investigations. Some of the most relevant research is described below.

Cohen and Chaiken (1987) concentrated entirely upon the issue of investigator's effectiveness. Their study, commissioned by the US Department of Justice, conducted wide-ranging interviews with existing investigators and police staff, collected data and materials relating to detective selection procedures, and observed police psychologists and selection personnel. It was found that police administrators could indeed identify better performing investigators. These authors also noted that a small proportion of officers were responsible for the majority of successful convictions.

These authors also identified personal traits that were believed, both by interviewees and enforcement agencies, to identify good investigative performance. These were: motivation, stability, persistence, intelligence, perseverance, initiative, judgement, teamwork, involvement, and dedication. They went further and considered that for good performance as an investigator officers required qualities in the following areas: gathering information, field operation, arrests, public and victim satisfaction, prosecution, personal performance, and qualifications (in terms of education, training, and previous assignments within the department). Cohen and Chaiken (1987, p. 17) noted that:

The most striking finding is that written civil service examinations best predicted arrest activity and investigative skills, including gathering evidence and crime scene management.

They went on to state:

> The civil service tests are designed to measure cognitive abilities or the capacity to know, perceive, and think. These traits lead in turn to creativity, abstract reasoning, memory and intelligence, all of which are considered vital for recreating crime scenes, pursuing crime leads, and organising crime information logically and clearly.

In concluding their report, these authors suggested key indicators of future detective performance as being: numbers of arrests, investigation skills, supervisory ratings, and communication ability. They contended that these could themselves be predicted by performance in the civil service exam, verbal ability tests, police academy scores, and oral interviews. Prior work experience, age, education, and IQ should, in their view, also be taken into account.

In the UK, Morgan (1990) conducted a study in an attempt to answer the question, 'How do detectives solve crimes and what can be done to improve performance?' He interviewed 52 police officers through group discussions and a questionnaire; in both of which, he asked questions related to crime investigation and in particular volume crime investigations such as burglary, thefts, and assaults. Firstly, he asked detectives, 'How are crimes actually solved?' A large percentage responded by stating that information from victims, witnesses, and the public was most important to the successful outcome of a case. 'Spadework' was given as an example in a small number of responses, with little definition of the term. Local knowledge, communication of information, personal qualities of the detective, time to pursue investigations, and luck were also highlighted by some detectives as reasons why crimes were solved. Detectives were also asked, 'What skills are necessary for an investigator to solve crime?' Their responses included: an ability to communicate, being approachable, knowledge of the local area, patience, persistence, tenacity, objectivity, time to pursue enquiries, and gut feelings. Morgan (1990, p. 66) stated:

> The individual interviews of police officers and detectives in the previous chapter showed little or no identification of discernible individual skills in the process of criminal investigation. Attributes identified were more concerned with organisational skills, the ability to seek and obtain information. The ability to communicate was the most frequently identifiable attribute.

It is interesting to note that in both the USA and the UK the ability to communicate was cited as most important by practitioners. This has also been found to be fundamental to the ability to interview in various studies of police investigative interviewing (Baldwin 1994; Soukara et al. 2002). For instance, identified how more skilled interviewers demonstrated greater flexibility, better empathy and compassion towards an interviewee, and better communication skills.

Maguire et al. (1991) asked CID officers to define the special skills that characterised a good investigator. They received a variety of responses, most of which were similar to those described above. For example, their study identified that good detectives were thought to possess a complex set of personal qualities such as: intelligence, common sense, initiative, inquisitiveness, independence of thought, commitment, persistence, ability to talk to people, and an innate ability such as a 'nose' for the job or 'thief-taking ability'.

According to Maguire et al. (1991), and consistent with Morgan's study (1990), the most frequently mentioned ability was the ability to communicate. As well as identifying personal qualities, Maguire et al. (1991) went on to list a set of (possibly) learned skills that detectives also felt contributed to being a good investigator, these being: knowledge of the law, local knowledge, communication skills, interview techniques, file construction skills, cultivating informants, presenting evidence, and the ability to recognise and extract relevant information from documents.

McGurk et al. (1992) also provided a list of detectives' beliefs of what personal characteristics were required for detective work. The most identified areas were: 'coping with separation for long periods of time from family and home'; 'working with people for their benefit'; 'interpreting feelings, ideas and facts'; 'empathy—seeing matters from another's viewpoint'; 'tolerating/evaluating uncertain and conflicting information', 'influencing other people's behaviour, ideas and opinions', and 'dealing with people'. Their study also provided a list of the most identified specific abilities required for detective work, which included being able to: produce ideas, produce unusual or clever responses to a problem, generate new solutions to problems, communicate ideas in a spoken or written format, select the most appropriate solution to specific problems, articulate ideas fluently, listen to what is said, understand the meaning of words and ideas, and organise/unify disorganised information. Finally, their study identified attributes identified by detectives as required for the investigation of critical incidents. These consisted of: getting information, critically appraising information, combining information, organisational skills, practical problem solving, applying specialist knowledge, personality attributes, remembering facts, and doing clerical work.

Bull and Cherryman (1995) studied specialist interviewing skills by asking police officers to rate the importance of a set of skills, abilities, and behaviours. Respondents rated compassion as 'very important' and empathy as 'important' skills of a specialist interviewer. Milne and Bull (1999), when discussing the use of enhanced cognitive interviewing, identified rapport building as important to investigative interviewing, and they equated being able to communicate empathy as central to rapport.

Fahsing and Gottschalk (2008) asked investigators in Norway to identify the top five skills of an effective Senior Investigating Officer (SIO). Many (55 %) responded that creativity is important, it being the most popular reply amongst them. The next highest was professionalism (24 %), followed by objectivity, structure, organisation, and communication (20 %). However, empathy was identified only three times as important to investigative success.

Little *modern* research exists on the investigative tasks and the skills, abilities, and characteristics required to achieve success in volume crime investigations. Almost nothing is known about the main activities of volume crime investigators and what they do on a day-to-day basis. What do they consider amounts to success within volume crime investigations? How do they think success should be measured? What, in their view, makes a good or successful volume crime investigator? All of these important questions remain as yet unanswered. In relation to the skills, abilities, and characteristics required to be successful, what do volume crime investigators in the modern era think? Previous research and textbooks gave us an understanding of what is possibly required to be a successful investigator, but are these areas still relevant today? Are communication skills *still* considered a key component of investigative success?

The aims of the two new studies herein were to attempt to answer these questions, and more, by asking current volume crime investigators for their views. Study 1 specifically asked: What is success and how *should* it be measured? What makes a successful investigator? How important to success are the 30 skills, abilities, and characteristics, derived from the research in list two? Why do investigations go wrong? And why do miscarriages of justice occur? Study 2 asked investigators to select successful investigators from amongst their peers and rate them for the same 30 skills, abilities, and characteristics derived from prior research.

Study 1

Method

Participants

Police forces in England and Wales were asked to participate in the research. Those who agreed were Kent, Thames Valley, Lancashire, Devon and Cornwall, West Midlands, and North Wales. They were asked to allow access to one of their Basic Command Unit (BCU) volume crime investigation teams so that a number of potential respondents could participate. All forces in the UK divide themselves into Basic Command Units or equivalent (these are called Boroughs in the Metropolitan Police Service), each of which is commanded by a Chief Superintendent. The BCU can be made up of several towns or geographical areas, and these may in turn have their own volume crime investigation teams. Each participating force, having identified a specific BCU for the study, then allocated one of its volume crime teams for the research. This resulted in teams of various sizes, responsibilities, and personnel being nominated. All allocated teams contained a mixture of 'plain-clothed' police constables and detective constables, supervised by uniformed police sergeants and detective sergeants, and managed by either a uniformed inspector or detective inspector. For the study, each force was visited for a week in 2008. Table 7.1 identifies each participating force together with staff numbers allocated to the study, and the main make-up of its volume crime team.

Table 7.1 Possible participant distribution by force together with teams studied

Force	Team numbers	Volume crime structure
Kent	42	One area crime unit dealing with the majority of volume crime
Thames Valley	39	Separate units dealing with general crime and priority crime
North Wales	32	Two units dealing with all volume crime
Lancashire	28	One proactive unit dealing with burglaries and vehicle crime
Devon and Cornwall	30	One unit dealing with all volume crime, plus burglary and motor vehicle unit
West Midlands	42	Separate units dealing with motor vehicle crime, burglaries, robberies, and general crime

It can be seen from Table 7.1 that potentially a total of 213 individuals could have participated. Some early demographic details were obtained in relation to the 213 potential respondents. Firstly, the gender distribution was 58 females (27.2 %), and 155 males (72.8 %). Secondly, in terms of ethnicity, one officer (0.46 %) was non-White. Thirdly, the rank distribution was 169 at police constable or detective constable level (79.3 %), 35 at sergeant or detective sergeant level (16.4 %), eight at inspector or detective inspector level (3.8 %), and one civilian (0.5 %). Finally, 111 (52.1 %) had attended an Initial Crime Investigator Development Programme (ICIDP) course or equivalent, whilst 102 (47.9 %) had not. This programme (ICIDP) replaced the old Trainee Investigator course, utilised for trainee detectives. Students embark upon the programme when they wish to qualify as a full-time plain-clothed investigator. In modern parlance, this role is no longer referred to as that of detective but is indistinguishable from the same.

Individuals

A total of 64 completed questionnaires were obtained from the site visits (out of a possible 213) (no questionnaires were returned that had been left for respondents to fill in and send through the post). Thus, the response rate was 30 %. This response rate may have been low due to the amount of time it would take to complete the rather extensive questionnaire. This was not assisted by the high workload and time constraints upon the officers. Whilst each force generously stated that it would allow officers to fill in the questionnaires in duty time, many officers commented that due to workload this was impractical and, in some cases, impossible. The nature of volume crime investigative work (and indeed any kind of investigative work) is that planned events often have to come second to responding to new incidents, arrests, and situations. The distribution of returned questionnaires by force is in Table 7.2.

The age range of the respondents was from 25 to 64 years (mean of 36.58). The gender distribution was 73.4 % male and 26.6 % female. In terms of current rank, 68.8 % ($N = 44$) were police constables or detective constables, 26.6 % ($N = 17$)

Table 7.2 Distribution of completed questionnaires per force

Rank	Force	Distributed	Returned	Percent
1	Kent	38	20	52.6
2	Thames Valley	39	6	15.3
3	North Wales	30	7	23.3
4	Lancashire	28	16	57.1
5	Devon and Cornwall	31	8	25.8
6	West Midlands	42	7	16.3

were of police sergeant or detective sergeant rank, 3.1 % ($N = 2$) were of inspector or detective inspector rank, and 1.6 % ($N = 1$) was a civilian employee working within the volume crime environment. Thus, as expected, a large proportion of the respondents were of constable rank. Respondents were asked to indicate their lengths of service in years, which ranged between 3 and 33 years (mean of 12.0), yielding a representative sample in this regard.

In terms of educational level, respondents were asked to state their educational level upon leaving full-time education. The distribution was: 4.7 % 'CSE level' or equivalent ($N = 3$), 31.3 % 'GCSE/O level' or equivalent ($N = 20$), 28.1 % 'A level' or equivalent ($N = 18$), 29.7 % 'degree level' ($N = 19$), 1.6 % 'postgraduate level' ($N = 1$), and 3.1 % 'other' (City and Guilds etc.) ($N = 2$). One person reported no qualifications upon leaving school ($N = 1$). A few respondents indicated that they had achieved only 'CSE level' or lower (i.e. none) at school, but nevertheless were able to obtain entry to the police service. It is not known whether these individuals later went on to achieve the minimum police entry standards (believed to be five 'GCSE/O levels' or equivalent), or whether passing the entry examination alone was sufficient. The distribution of respondents in terms of having received detective training was: 40 (62.5 %) trained detectives and 23 (35.9 %) non-trained detectives (including the one civilian member of staff).

Materials

A six-section questionnaire was designed which contained closed- and open-ended questions, the contents of which were informed by previous research (Greenwood et al. 1977; Innes 2003; MaGuire et al. 1993; McGurk et al. 1992; Sanders 2008). Section 1 asked respondents for their views on the role and aims of a volume crime investigator. It also asked respondents to list their main activities and rate them in relation to frequency of occurrence. Section 2 asked respondents questions about the investigation of crime. These included whether they utilised any kind of process or structure within their investigations, whether they felt that investigation could be taught, and whether they felt investigation was an art, craft, or science, a mixture of them all, or something else. Section 3 asked respondents to consider investigative success. What did they think amounted to success? Did they feel that it could be measured? What were their thoughts on the best ways in which to measure success?

In the final part of this section, they were also asked their views on why some investigations were substandard as well as why they felt that miscarriages of justice occur. Section 4 asked them to consider the skills, abilities, or characteristics of a successful investigator. They were firstly asked to identify the top ten skills, abilities, or characteristics that they felt were needed in order to be successful. They were then asked to identify how important they felt some of the attributes, identified by previous research, were to being a successful investigator. Thirty attributes were provided from research (List two above). Section 5 asked investigators to consider the selection and training of investigators, specifically how they felt investigators should be selected, how they should be trained, and whether they felt training could contribute to success. Section 6 asked investigators to respond to demographic questions regarding age, gender, ethnicity, length of service, previous experience, current rank, educational level, previous letters of satisfaction or letters of appreciation, and national investigator training.

Procedure

The researcher visited each of the forces for a week in order to administer the questionnaires personally to as many of the designated staff as possible. Forces were asked to permit their staff to spend time filling in the questionnaire in small groups. The intention was for the researcher to explain personally the nature of the research, obtain informed consent, and then administer the questionnaire. It was felt that the personal touch would yield a greater response rate than sending out the questionnaires to designated representatives. Some officers were absent through sickness, on leave, or were too busy to attend on some of the times and dates identified. New times and dates were scheduled for some. Those who were sick, on leave, or unable to set aside time during the week were left questionnaires to fill in and send to the researcher at a specified address. Each participating respondent was provided with a unique code in order to protect their identity and the confidentiality of the information provided. All participants were informed of the anonymous nature of the questionnaire and of the fact that the collated answers would form part of future publications. Each questionnaire included instructions and request for consent prior to the respondent completing the questionnaire.

Results

The findings are presented below in sections that deal with: what respondents think about modern volume crime investigation; how they perceive their role; what they view as success; how they think success should be measured; what attributes are required to be successful; what factors make cases fail; and their perceptions as to why miscarriages of justice occur.

Table 7.3 Most frequent volume crime investigator activities

Rank	Activity	Number	Percentage
1	Interviewing suspects	35	54.6
2	Case file preparation	31	48.4
3	Attending scenes	28	43.7
4	Attending court	28	43.7
5	Interviewing witnesses	16	25.0
6	Statement taking	16	25.0
7	Meetings	10	15.6
8	Administration	10	15.6
9	Research	9	14.0
10	Proactive targeting	9	14.0

Table 7.4 Officers' perceptions of what success means

Rank	What amounts to success?	Frequency	Percentage
1	Victim satisfaction	25	39.0
2	Convictions	19	29.6
3	Detections	16	25.0
4	Thoroughness	15	23.4
5 =	Getting to the truth	9	14.0
5 =	Justice	9	14.0
7 =	Arresting/identifying offender	7	10.9
7 =	Ensuring all leads pursued	7	10.9
9 =	Good case papers	5	7.8
9 =	Appropriate sentence	5	7.8
9 =	Crime reduction	5	7.8

Respondents were asked to provide a list of the most frequent activities they performed, in no particular order. Table 7.3 identifies the top ten.

Success in Volume Crime Investigation: What Is It?

Respondents were asked to state what in their view amounted to success in volume crime investigation. This was an open question, and content analysis was conducted on the subsequent responses. The different responses were classified into most frequently recurring themes (see Table 7.4).

In Table 7.4, there is a mixture of topics that arguably can be achieved on an individual basis (for instance arrest or good case papers) and those that an individual alone is less likely to be able to control (for instance, convictions or justice).

Measurement of Success

Respondents were then asked whether they felt it was possible to measure the success of investigative work: 43 (66 %) indicated 'yes' and 17 (26 %) indicated 'no', whilst 5 (8 %) indicated *both* 'yes' and 'no'. Those answering 'yes' to this question were

Table 7.5 Officers' perceptions of how best to measure success

Rank	Measure identified	Frequency chosen	Percentage
1	Detections	27	42.1
2	Convictions	12	18.7
3	Victim satisfaction	7	10.9
4	Thoroughness	6	9.3
5	Crime reduction	4	6.2
6	Team detections	3	4.6

Table 7.6 Officers' perceptions of how best to measure success of individuals

Rank	Measurement	Frequency	Percentage
1	Detections	29	45.3
2	Convictions	16	25.0
3	Victim satisfaction	15	23.4
4	Tutor/supervisor assess	11	17.1
5	Qualitative review	9	14.0
6	Arrest rate	6	9.3
7 =	Thoroughness	5	7.8
7 =	All RLEs followed	5	7.8
9	Teamwork	4	6.2
10 =	Types of investigations	3	4.6
10 =	Interview skills	3	4.6

Table 7.7 Officers' perceptions on how best to measure success of investigations

Rank	Measure	Frequency	Percentage
1	Detections	26	40.6
2	Thoroughness	16	25.0
3	Convictions	13	20.3
4	Victim satisfaction	12	18.7
5	Review	7	10.9
6	Supervisor assessment	6	9.3
7	Amount of effort expended	4	6.2
8	Meets expectation of all parties	4	6.2

then asked to elaborate on their response to the question and to state what they felt the best measures were. Table 7.5 identifies the measures indicated and the frequency with which they were chosen.

Respondents were also asked what they felt the best ways to measure the success of an individual *investigator* were. Table 7.6 shows the responses in order of frequency.

Respondents were then asked what they felt the best ways to measure the success of an individual *investigation* were. The results are summarised in Table 7.7, where each of the potential measures received at least four nominations (all the other measures received only one or two nominations).

Of the respondents who answered this question, over 50 % identified more than just detection rates as being the most appropriate method to use.

Respondents answering 'yes' to the question of whether it was possible to measure success were asked to identify in what ways it was possible to measure it.

	Rank	Skill, ability or characteristic	Frequency	Percentage
Table 7.8 Top skills, abilities, and characteristics of a successful investigator	1	Communication skills	48	75.0
	2	Enthusiasm/motivation	35	54.6
	3	Tenacity	22	34.3
	4	Teamwork	21	32.8
	5	Objectivity	21	32.8
	6	Organisational	19	29.6
	7	Knowledge of the law	18	28.1
	8	Honesty and integrity	17	26.5
	9	Decision-making	15	23.4
	10	Listening	14	21.8
	11	Creativity	14	21.8
	12	Thoroughness	13	20.3
	13	Paperwork	13	20.3
	14	Flexibility	13	20.3
	15	Experience	13	20.3

Skills, Abilities and Characteristics of Successful Investigators

All respondents were asked to identify the top ten skills, abilities, or characteristics they felt an investigator would need to possess in order to be successful at volume crime investigation (they were asked to do so prior to having sight of the list of 30 qualities identified by previous work). The top 15 responses to the question are listed in Table 7.8 (more than 20 % of respondents chose them). Choices such as intelligence (7.8 %), empathy (4.68 %), 'street intelligence' (4.68 %) and 'nose for the job' (3.12 %) received little support.

Respondents were then provided with the list of the 30 skills, abilities, and characteristics previously identified as being important qualities for an investigator to possess in order to be successful. Alongside each quality was a scale ranging from 1 to 5.

Respondents were asked to rate each of the qualities in terms of how important they felt them to be in order for an investigator to be successful. The mean score is presented for each quality at the right-hand side of Table 7.9.

In relation to the topics of communication, motivation, commitment, dedication, initiative, and decision-making, all were ranked quite important or very important by at least 90 % of respondents. In contrast, in the areas of education, strategic awareness, training, empathy, and leadership, over 50 % of respondents felt they were moderately important or lower. Listening skills ranked ninth out of the 30 skills indicating that respondents thought this was a key trait. A Kendal's coefficient of concordance showed that officers were consistent with their use of the rankings (W $(29, N = 64) = .249$, $p < .001$), although the effect is only weak to moderate.

When Things Go Wrong

Respondents were asked the question, 'What *stops* investigations going wrong?' The most frequent responses are presented in Table 7.10.

Table 7.9 Officers' ratings of previous research attributes

Rank	Attribute	1 Not very important	2 Not too important	3 Moderately important	4 Quite important	5 Very important	Mean (SD)
1	Communication	0.0	1.6	4.7	25.0	68.8	4.6 (0.6)
2	Motivation	0.0	1.6	4.7	29.7	64.1	4.5 (0.6)
3	Commitment	0.0	0.0	6.3	31.3	60.9	4.4 (0.8)
4	Dedication	0.0	0.0	7.8	31.3	59.4	4.4 (0.8)
5	Persistence	0.0	0.0	14.1	32.8	53.1	4.3 (0.7)
6	Initiative	0.0	3.1	6.3	43.8	46.9	4.3 (0.7)
7	Decision-making	0.0	1.6	6.3	48.4	43.8	4.3 (0.6)
8	Reasoning	0.0	1.6	10.9	46.9	40.6	4.2 (0.7)
9	Listening skills	0.0	3.1	17.2	31.3	48.4	4.2 (0.8)
10	Integrity	0.0	9.4	9.4	20.3	59.4	4.2 (1.1)
11	Judgement	1.6	1.6	10.9	46.9	39.1	4.2 (0.8)
12	Tenacity	0.0	3.1	20.3	43.8	32.8	4.0 (0.8)
13	Legal knowledge	0.0	3.1	23.4	37.5	35.9	4.0 (0.8)
14	Teamwork	0.0	4.7	21.9	37.5	35.9	4.0 (0.8)
15	Approachable	1.6	7.8	15.6	39.1	35.9	4.0 (0.9)
16	Objectivity	0.0	1.6	21.9	54.7	21.9	3.9 (0.7)
17	Patience	1.6	3.1	28.1	43.8	23.4	3.8 (0.8)
18	Independence of thought	0.0	3.1	31.3	37.5	26.6	3.8 (0.9)
19	Street intelligence	0.0	9.4	23.4	42.2	25.0	3.8 (0.9)
20	Planning	0.0	1.6	21.9	60.9	14.1	3.8 (0.8)
21	Creativity	0.0	6.3	35.9	35.9	21.9	3.7 (0.8)
22	Experience	1.6	9.4	32.8	28.1	28.1	3.7 (1.0)
23	Nose for the job	1.6	6.3	32.8	37.5	21.9	3.7 (0.9)
24	Intelligence	1.6	4.7	25.0	48.0	20.3	3.6 (1.0)
25	Stability	4.7	9.4	29.7	34.4	21.9	3.5 (1.0)
26	Empathy	0.0	10.9	45.3	31.3	12.5	3.4 (0.8)
27	Training	1.6	10.9	43.8	31.3	12.5	3.4 (0.9)
28	Leadership	6.3	6.3	40.6	39.1	7.8	3.3 (0.9)
29	Strategic awareness	3.1	21.9	35.9	34.4	4.7	3.1 (0.9)
30	Education	6.3	28.1	45.3	20.3	0.0	2.8 (0.8)

Table 7.10 Officers' perceptions on what prevents failure

Rank	Area identified	Frequency	Percentage
1	Good supervision	23	36.0
2	Thoroughness	12	19.0
3	Structure	10	16.0
4	Sufficient time to deal	9	14.0
5	Good teamwork	9	14.0
6	Keeping victim updated	8	12.5
7	Reviews	7	11.0
8	Good planning	6	9.0
9	Good communication	6	9.0
10	Efficiency	5	7.0

Table 7.11 Officers' perceptions on why cases fail

Rank	Problem	Frequency	Percentage
1	Lack of time	12	19.0
2	Heavy workload	9	14.0
3	Lazy investigator	9	14.0
4	Poor time/organisation	8	12.5
5	Lack of attention to detail	5	8.0
6	Poor communication	5	8.0
7	Lack of witness cooperation	5	8.0
8	Poor supervision	4	6.2
9	Lack of motivation	4	6.2
10	Poor case files	3	4.5

Respondents were then asked to consider what *makes* an investigation go wrong. Table 7.11 identifies the topics most commonly cited.

Whilst lack of time and heavy workload were the most cited causes, the choices of laziness, lack of organisation, lack of attention to detail, and lack of motivation demonstrate that the officers were not afraid to criticise the working practices of themselves and their peers.

Study 2

The same crime groups were utilised for this second study, the aim of which was to try to identify successful volume crime investigators by using peer nomination. This method was utilised successfully by Smith and Flanagan (2000) when attempting to study the skills, abilities, and characteristics of an effective Senior Investigating Officer (SIO) within major crime investigations. In that study, the researchers asked officers to nominate effective SIOs. As a result, ten were nominated. These were then interviewed in conjunction with other officers. Smith and Flanagan (2000) were able to compare the general group with the peer-nominated group in order to identify consistent themes. There are of course drawbacks to using subjective nominations. Firstly, there is little to prevent respondents choosing people for inappropriate reasons (i.e. friendship, popularity, etc.). Secondly, their choice might be influenced by

	Rank	Force	Distributed	Returned	Percentage
Table 7.12 Questionnaire B response rates by force	1	Kent	38	17	44.7
	2	Thames Valley	39	29	74.3
	3	North Wales	30	19	63.3
	4	Lancashire	28	16	57.1
	5	Devon and Cornwall	31	16	51.6
	6	West Midlands	42	24	57.1

incorrect knowledge of the person, or little knowledge of their professional practices. Despite these potential drawbacks, it has been identified how useful peer nominations can be (Cohen and Chaiken 1987; Smith and Flanagan 2000). Indeed, police officers themselves have often cited peer assessment as one of the best methods to determine success (Maguire et al. 1993).

As a result, it was considered appropriate to gauge *who* current volume crime investigators identified as successful from within their midst, and how they rated them against the 30 skills, abilities, and characteristics derived from previous research. Study 1's results suggested that they would choose investigators whom they believed to possess better communication skills, be more highly motivated, with better reasoning and decision-making skills, and that topics such as training, education, intelligence, and empathy would be rated lower.

Method

Design

It was felt that the best means of gathering respondents' thoughts on good and bad practice, plus their ratings of chosen successful peers would be in the form of a questionnaire. The questionnaire was piloted to a small group of investigators and, following minor amendments, took the form of open-ended questions for good and bad practice, plus scale ratings for the 30 attributes (drawn from previous research).

Participants

The same forces and crime departments utilised for Study 1 took part in this study. All individuals approached to take part in the study were working within their respective volume crime teams at the time and were thus likely to have known of and worked regularly with their peers.

Of the 213 questionnaires distributed, a total of 121 were completed and returned. Thus, compared to that in Study 1, an overall response rate of 56.8 % was recorded. The response rates per force are itemised in Table 7.12.

Of the 121 respondents, 85 (70.2 %) were male and 36 (29.7 %) were female. In terms of age, the respondents ranged from 22 to 64 years (mean of 35.83). The length of service of the respondents ranged from 3 to 33 years (mean of 11.45). In terms of rank distribution, 70.2 % were PC/DC rank, 25.6 % were PS/DS rank, and 3.3 % were Insp/DI rank, whilst 0.8 % were civilian staff. This distribution was the expected outcome because forces were asked to provide a whole volume crime investigation team for the study. Each team would be expected to have a number of constable investigators supervised by a number of sergeants who in turn would be managed by one or two inspectors. The distribution in terms of educational levels was 4.1 % 'CSE', 28.1 % 'GCSE/O level', 27.3 % 'A level', 28.9 % 'degree level', 5 % 'postgraduate level', 5.8 % 'other', and 0.8 % 'no qualifications at all'. In relation to national investigator training (ICIDP), 50 (41 %) had not received it, whilst 71 (58 %) had. As discussed earlier, this programme of study leads to students becoming nationally accredited as investigators. The distribution here reflects how more officers work within crime groups who do not go on to qualify in this way.

Materials

Section 1 of the questionnaire asked respondents to identify five people in their volume crime investigation teams who in their opinion were the most successful. Having selected them, they were asked to rate each of their individual choices according to the 30 qualities identified by research as being essential to investigative success. Section 2 asked respondents to provide some of their own personal details, such as age, gender, length of service, previous experience, current rank, educational level, previous letters of satisfaction or letters of appreciation, and whether they had received national training in the form of an investigator course or equivalent.

Procedure

It is well documented that the culture of detectives can include being suspicious of outsiders (Skolnick 1966; Innes 2003). There was little reason to suggest that the culture of volume crime investigation teams, mixed as they were with detectives and non-detectives, would be any different. It was felt that the best way in which to approach the situation was with the personal touch: attending each crime group personally and demonstrating within introductions that the researcher himself was a serving police officer genuinely interested in researching issues important to them. It was hoped that this might help to allay any potential fears and encourage more people to participate. It was stressed that the study was for the purposes of doctoral research and that as such strict confidentiality rules and procedures were in place. Respondents were informed that what they wrote within the questionnaire would be anonymous, and that any subsequent written report would not be able to identify participants by name. It was explained that each individual would be given a separate code to ensure anonymity. From the introductions, conducted at each force site, it was clear that initially there was a degree of mistrust regarding the project. Once the research was described to individuals, including the fact that the researcher was an 'insider', many accepted that there was no hidden agenda and willingly participated. Only one person throughout the visits to all of the forces refused to be involved.

Respondents were asked to find somewhere quiet, away from distractions, in order to complete the questionnaire. They were told that the instructions hopefully were self-explanatory, but that they could ask questions at any stage. They were informed that it would take them around 30 min to complete the questionnaire. In terms of choice of the five most successful investigators, the only restrictions upon respondents' choices were that the individual's chosen had to be from the list of officers provided. Thus, each participant was provided with a list of officers *currently* working within that crime group (obtained by the researcher from the crime manager of each individual station, usually of detective chief inspector rank). Officers were told that they were required to actually *name* their choices not to discuss their choices with their peers. The importance of having named individuals was in order for the researcher to be able to identify them from this study and later subject a number of them to further research and analysis. It was stressed within the introduction and within the questionnaire itself that choices were restricted to successful performance as an investigator, and should not be determined by popularity or friendship. No definition of successful was provided to respondents. Thus, in effect, their decisions were based upon their own opinions of what success meant.

The first author originally intended to ask respondents to rate both their chosen top five and bottom five investigators. However, it was decided that this was inappropriate and could cause potential distress to officers if they felt that they were being identified by their peers as being in the low success set. It was felt that the resultant nomination system itself would be adequate to identify a low choice set by the absence of nominations from peers.

Once the questionnaires had been analysed, a high choice set was identified within each force (as well as a low choice set). Comparisons were then made between the 'high choice' set and the 'low choice' set. Further analysis was conducted regarding the successful investigators' attributes.

Each of the individual respondents within participating crime groups was allocated a unique reference number to ensure anonymity. Only the researcher was aware of the codings and thus the identity of the individuals involved. Those with the most votes were placed in ascending order and a percentage allocated to them based upon the number of people who could have chosen them against the number of people who did choose them. As a result, the high choice set comprised 32 individuals, and the low choice set, for the purpose of balance, also comprised 32 individuals, all of whom had taken part in the study thus far.

Respondents' ratings of the presence of the 30 attributes in successful peers are set out in Table 7.13.

Table 7.13 Officers' perceptions of the presence of the 30 attributes in peers

Rank	Attribute	Never	Rare	Sometimes	Frequent	Always	Mean
1	Persistence	0.00	0.73	8.82	40.80	49.63	4.39
2	Integrity	0.00	1.12	14.23	30.71	53.93	4.37
3	Commitment	0.00	0.74	10.48	40.82	47.94	4.35
4	Decision-making	0.00	0.73	7.32	49.08	42.85	4.34
5	Nose for the job	0.00	1.12	13.53	36.46	48.87	4.33
6	Judgement	0.00	0.73	9.52	48.35	41.39	4.30
7	Dedication	0.00	0.72	12.04	43.43	43.79	4.30
8	Experience	0.36	3.64	13.86	30.65	51.45	4.29
9	Motivation	0.00	2.52	12.27	40.43	44.76	4.27
10	Teamwork	0.00	7.35	18.75	22.79	51.10	4.17
11	Independent	0.00	2.57	16.91	41.17	39.33	4.17
12	Streetwise	0.37	1.85	16.35	42.75	38.66	4.17
13	Reasoning	0.36	2.18	14.96	47.81	34.67	4.14
14	Communication	1.09	5.09	17.45	37.45	40.00	4.13
15	Tenacity	0.00	1.48	17.77	47.03	33.70	4.12
16	Initiative	0.00	1.86	15.29	51.11	31.71	4.12
17	Approachable	2.93	6.95	14.65	27.10	48.35	4.10
18	Legal knowledge	0.00	2.91	17.91	51.23	27.91	4.04
19	Planning	0.00	3.28	21.16	46.35	29.19	4.01
20	Stability	1.11	7.03	17.03	39.25	35.55	4.01
21	Intelligence	0.36	4.34	17.75	53.98	23.55	3.96
22	Patience	0.36	4.34	18.11	54.34	22.82	3.94
23	Objectivity	0.36	4.37	20.43	51.09	23.72	3.93
24	Listening skills	1.10	3.67	23.89	43.75	27.57	3.93
25	Leadership	0.72	8.30	24.18	37.90	28.88	3.85
26	Creativity	0.00	4.90	35.09	36.98	23.01	3.78
27	Strategic	3.06	9.57	27.96	33.71	25.67	3.69
28	Training	0.40	12.1	35.36	37.80	14.22	3.53
29	Empathy	4.46	12.2	26.76	39.03	17.47	3.52
30	Education	2.32	13.4	38.13	37.20	8.83	3.36

Results

The 30 Skills, Abilities and Characteristics Identified in Previous Research

Table 7.13 contains a final mean score (on the five-point scale) of those qualities or attributes. When making their choices and scoring the areas below, respondents were asked only to score areas they felt able to from personal knowledge of the individuals chosen. Where they had little knowledge, they were asked to leave that particular area blank. In Table 7.13, 'independent' represents independence of thought, 'streetwise represents' street intelligence, and 'strategic' represents strategic awareness.

Table 7.14 compares the mean ranking of the importance of the 30 skills from Study 1 (as in Table 7.13), with the mean ranking of their presence within perceived successful investigators.

In both studies, it is clear that the following were rated as important and more evident amongst successful practitioners: commitment, persistence, decision-making,

Table 7.14 Ranking comparison of attribute importance vs. presence in peers

Study 1 rankings ($N = 64$)	Study 2 presence ($N = 605$)
1 Communication	1 Persistence
2 Motivation	2 Integrity
3 Commitment	3 Commitment
4 Dedication	4 Decision-making
5 Persistence	5 Nose for the job
6 Initiative	6 Judgement
7 Decision-making	7 Dedication
8 Reasoning	8 Experience
9 Listening skills	9 Motivation
10 Integrity	10 Teamwork
11 Judgement	11 Independence of thought
12 Tenacity	12 Street intelligence
13 Legal knowledge	13 Reasoning
14 Teamwork	14 Communication
15 Approachable	15 Tenacity
16 Objectivity	16 Initiative
17 Patience	17 Approachable
18 Independent thought	18 Legal knowledge
19 Street intelligence	19 Planning
20 Planning	20 Stability
21 Intelligence	21 Intelligence
22 Creativity	22 Patience
23 Experience	23 Objectivity
24 Nose for the job	24 Listening skills
25 Stability	25 Leadership
26 Empathy	26 Creativity
27 Training	27 Strategic awareness
28 Leadership	28 Training
29 Strategic awareness	29 Empathy
30 Education	30 Education

motivation, dedication, integrity, communication, judgment, reasoning, initiative, and teamwork. Those seemingly less important and less evident were: patience, planning, intelligence, stability, creativity, leadership, training, empathy, strategic awareness, and education.

Investigative Success

Respondents were also asked a series of questions relating to success. Firstly, they were asked whether they felt that success could be measured. If they answered this first question affirmatively, they were asked to describe how it could best be measured. They were then asked the best ways in which to measure the success of individual investigators and individual investigations (separate questions). The top four measures identified consistently were detections, convictions, victim satisfaction, and thoroughness. Further analysis of the qualitative responses, however, found that whilst some participants appeared to be pragmatic and accept that detection figures alone could identify success (perhaps over a long period of time), many others identified detection figures as but one of a number of measures to be utilised to identify success. This perhaps echoes the dissatisfaction with the clear-up rate alone as a measure of success identified in previous studies (Maguire et al. 1992; Tong 2004).

Respondents suggesting that it was *not* possible to measure investigative success raised some important issues in their responses. If detection rates alone are measured, there has always been a problem relating to seriousness of a crime versus complexity. The Home Office Counting Rules have never distinguished crimes in this way. Each crime gets one individual reference number. An £ 88,000 robbery has the same detected score as a robbery of a phone. Every murder, based purely upon clear-up figures, counts exactly the same as the theft of a bar of chocolate. Investigators felt that the complexity, time, and effort required for the more serious cases deserve more recognition within such figures. If officer A has dealt with 30 cases and detected them all, and officer B has dealt with 60 and detected them all, who is more successful? On paper, it will of course be officer B. Our opinion might change when we find out that officer B deals only with shoplifters, whilst officer A deals with assaults, burglaries, and sexual offences. Such latter cases will indeed be more serious, complex, and time consuming than almost all of the shoplifting cases. Finally, it was identified that an investigator could conduct a thorough, meticulous investigation, but could have little to show for it in the end due to lack of evidence. Detection figures do not describe the amount of work and effort put into cases that do not obtain a positive disposal, nor do they identify the quality of the investigation.

Main Activities

The respondents were asked to identify their main activities. Interviewing suspects ranked highest, with case file preparation second. In terms of interviewing suspects, it is no surprise that it was rated the most frequent activity (Burrows and Tarling 1987). With regard to case file preparation, whilst it has been a constant finding that police officers have a negative attitude towards paperwork and administration (Ericson 1993; Sanders 1977), it has repeatedly been evident that case file preparation is an essential element in successfully bringing an offender to justice (Hobbs 1988; Smith 1997; Stelfox 2011). Once again, it is not surprising that respondents rated this as a frequent activity. Ranked third was attending scenes, and attending court was ranked fourth. These tasks were also identified as being the most difficult and important in the McGurk et al. (1992) study. Administration ranked low, as did attending meetings. Issues such as completing pocket books, driving, giving advice to colleagues, typing tape transcripts, and reading documents that appeared in the McGurk et al.'s study (1992) were replaced with areas such as attending crime scenes, statement taking, meetings, administration, research, and proactive targeting. In relation to administration, this could of course replace in respondents' minds the categories of reading, completing diaries, and perhaps even liaison with colleagues (although this is not evident in the responses). However, the fact that typing tape transcripts is no longer amongst the top activities could be due to the fact that many forces now have administrative units able to perform such functions (Tong 2004).

Interviewing witnesses and taking statements ranked fifth and sixth, respectively. The fact that they rated fairly low on the list could represent a further change in working practices, where administrative staff (such as civilian investigators) regularly conducts statement-taking duties on behalf of investigators. They would also interview witnesses when tasked to do so. Respondents still felt, however, that both these tasks were frequent activities undertaken by modern investigators.

Based upon the list of responses, it is fair to say that at least the top eight of the ten activities would require good communication skills on the part of the investigator in order to effectively carry them out.

Skills, Abilities, and Characteristics of a Successful Investigator

Respondents were also asked to identify what they felt were the top ten skills, abilities, and characteristics that a successful investigator should possess. The most frequently highlighted was good communication skills, again consistent with previous studies (Cohen and Chaiken 1987; Maguire et al. 1993; McGurk et al. 1992; Morgan 1990). Motivation was close behind in second. This is also consistent with previous studies (Morgan et al. 1990; McGurk et al. 1992). Listening skills appeared high on the list, and these are clearly a facet of good communication skills. It is interesting to note that the old favourites such as 'nose for the job' and 'street intelligence' (identified in the list of 30 traits from previous research) were not at the forefront of investigators' minds when asked to describe their top ten. Creativity also ranked surprisingly low considering recent research that suggests its importance to investigation (Fahsing and Gottschalk 2008).

Respondents were then provided with the list of 30 skills, abilities, and characteristics identified by previous research and asked to rate them in terms of importance. Respondents indicated that education, strategic awareness, leadership, and empathy were not as important to success as were good communication skills, motivation, commitment, dedication, and persistence. In fact, education received the lowest mean score, indicating that investigators do not believe that educational level of an investigator is as important to success, contrary to previous research (Cohen and Chaiken 1987; Greenwood et al. 1977; Smith and Aomodt 1997). Respondents' answers were consistent with the previous open question, as good communication skills and motivation were the top two choices in both. Other areas receiving a mean score of four or over were: commitment, dedication, integrity, listening skills, good judgement, decision-making ability, tenacity, initiative, teamwork, reasoning ability, and persistence. Scores for empathy were surprisingly low. Previous studies have identified the importance of empathy to investigators (McGurk et al. 1992), and to interviewers (Griffiths and Milne 2006; Holmberg and Christianson 2002).

Surprisingly, whilst respondents in Study 1 chose communication skills as the most important of the 30 skills, abilities, and characteristics, in Study 2 such skills came midway (rank 14; mean = 4.13). It should be remembered, however, that each set of respondents was asked a somewhat different question. The first study asked respondents to identify the traits in relation to their importance to success, whilst respondents in the second study were asked to rate individuals they had picked in terms of how frequently those traits were *demonstrated* by them. Perhaps even successful investigators are assessed by their peers as not having perfect communication skills (though the peer rating on the five-point scale was 'good' at 4.13).

Investigative Failure and Miscarriages of Justice

Consistent themes were identified when respondents answered the questions concerning what makes an investigation go wrong and why some investigations are substandard, such as lack of time, high workload, lack of motivation, poor supervision, and laziness. In terms of what makes an investigation go wrong, issues such as poor organisational skills, lack of attention to detail and poor communication featured near the top of officers' beliefs.

Finally, respondents were asked why they felt miscarriages of justice occur. It was not surprising that detection culture and corrupt practices were the most frequent responses. It was somewhat reassuring that officer mistakes also featured in the top three. It was quite striking that some respondents felt that miscarriages of justice were a thing of the past and simply did not occur in the modern era. This is contrary to the evidence that is emerging. For example, the Taylor sisters 1993; Sally Clarke 2003; Donna Anthony (2005); Angela Cannings (2004), and Suzanne Holdsworth (2008). One could argue that this displays a rather naive view of the criminal justice system or, on a more positive note, that such things are not even within the contemplation of modern investigators because old assumptions, biases, and value systems have gone. A final, more sobering, possibility is that those officers simply do not understand exactly what miscarriages of justice are, adding power to a recent argument that investigative training should include training on miscarriages of justice (Savage and Milne 2007).

Some respondents cited lack of objectivity as a reason why miscarriages of justice occur. Without further exploration, it is difficult to assess whether this encompasses the premature closure type situations identified by Shepherd and Milne (1999), where officers come to their own pre-emptive conclusions either prior to interview or at any time during an investigation, in effect closing their mind to any other possibilities. Such a state of mind can lead to potential miscarriages of justice. Either way, there is scope for consideration as to whether investigative training includes enough training in areas such as where cases go wrong and hypothesis testing. Whilst Core Investigative Doctrine (2005) discusses hypotheses, it does so somewhat negatively, suggesting they should be utilised only when all information is known. More detailed training on their usefulness might be beneficial.

Discussion

The two new studies reported here demonstrate some consistency with previous research in relation to officer's beliefs concerning the attributes required for success, particularly the importance of good communication skills. However, some interesting anomalies have presented themselves. Respondents appear to value education, training, stability, and intelligence less than areas such as persistence, motivation, and decision-making. Good communication skills ranked highly as a desired attribute of a successful investigator, but appeared somewhat less evident in those investigators chosen as successful by their peers. In addition, the list of main activities identified by respondents (such as suspect interviewing, case file preparation, statement taking, and witness interviewing) contained activities that require good communication skills. It would be fair to say that based upon these two studies good communication skills are indeed considered a key component to investigative success in the modern era. Indeed, they appear fundamental to almost every facet of the investigative role.

References

ACPO, Centrex. (2005). *Practice advice on core investigative doctrine*. Camborne: National Centre for Policing Excellence.

Baldwin, J. (1994) Police interrogation: what are the rules of the game? In D. Morgan and G. Stephenson (Eds). *Suspicion & Silence: The Right to Silence in Criminal Investigations*. Blackwell: London.

Bull, R., & Cherryman, J. (1995). *Helping to identify skills gaps in specialist investigative interviewing*. London: Home Office.

Burrows, J., & Tarling, R. (1987). The investigation of crime in England and Wales. *British Journal of Criminology, 27*, 229–251.

Chatterton, M. (2008). *Losing the detectives: Views from the front line*. Leatherhead: The Police Federation of England and Wales.

Cherryman, J., & Bull, R. (2000). Reflections on investigative interviewing. In F. Leishman, B. Loveday & S. Savage (Eds.), *Core issues in policing* (pp. 194–210). Harlow: Longman.

Cohen, L., & Chaiken, J. (1987). *Investigators who perform well*. Corporate Author: Abt Associates, Inc., United States, Washington, D.C.: U.S. Dept. of Justice, National Institute of Justice, Office of Communication and Research Utilization.

Criminal Procedure and Investigations Act 1997 Codes of Practice. (1997). London: Home Office.

Deinstein, W. (1968). *Technics for the crime investigator*. 6th edition, Springfield Illinois: Charles C. Thomas.

Ericson, R. (1993). *Making crime a study of detective work* (2nd ed.). Toronto: Toronto University Press.

Fahsing, I. A., & Gottschalk, P. (2008). Characteristics of effective detectives: a content analysis for thinking styles in policing. *International Journal of Innovation and Learning, 5*, 651–663.

Greenwood, P., Chaiken, J., & Petersilia, J. (1977). *The criminal investigation process*. Lexington, Mass: D.C. Heath.

Griffiths, A., & Milne, R. (2006). Will it all end in tears? Police interviews with suspects in Britain. In T. Williamson (Ed.), *Investigative interviewing: rights, research regulation* (pp. 167–189). Oregon: Willan Publishing.

Hobbs, D. (1988). *Doing the business: entrepreneurship, the working class and detectives in the East End of London*. Oxford: Oxford University Press.

Holmberg, U, & Christianson, S. A. (2002). Murderers' and sexual offenders' experiences of police interviews and their inclination to admit or deny crimes. *Behavioural Sciences and the Law, 20*, 31–45.

Home Office. (1993). *Circular 17/93: Performance indicators for the police*. London: Home Office.

Home Office. *Police and Criminal Evidence Act 1984 (s 66 (1))*. London: The Stationery Office.

Home Office. *Statistical Bulletin*. 2008, London: Home Office.

Innes, M. (2003). The process structures of police homicide investigations. *British Journal of Criminology, 42*, 669–88.

Innes, M. (2003). *Investigating murder: detective work and the police response to criminal homicide.* Oxford: Clarendon Press.

Jackson, R. (1962). *Criminal investigation: A practical textbook for magistrates, police officers and lawyers, 5th edition.* London: Sweet and Maxwell.

McGurk, B., Gibson, R., & Platten, T. (1992). *Detectives: A Job and Training Needs Analysis.* Harrogate: Central Planning Unit

Maguire, M., Noaks, C., Hobbs, R., & Brearley, N. (1991). *Assessing Investigative Performance.* Cardiff: School of Social and Administrative Studies, University of Wales.

Milne, R. & Bull, R. H. (1999). *Investigative interviewing, psychology and practice.* Chichester: Wiley Press.

Morgan, B. (1990). *The police function and the investigation of crime.* London: Gower.

National Policing Plan–2004 to 2008. (2004). Harrogate: Centrex.

O'Hara, C. E. (1970). *Fundamentals of criminal investigation, 2th edition.* Illinois: Charles C. Thomas.

Osterburg, J. W., & Ward, R. (2000). *Criminal Investigation—a method for reconstructing the past.* Cincinnati: Anderson Publishing.

R v Cannings (2004) EWCA Crim 1.

R v Donna Anthony (2005) EWCA Crim 952.

R v Taylor (Michelle Ann) and Anor (1993), (1994) 98 Crim App R 361.

R v Sally Clark (2003) EWCA Crim 1020.

R v Suzanne Holdsworth (2008) EWCA Crim 971

Sanders, W. A. (1977). *Detective work: a study of criminal investigations.* New York: The Free Press.

Sanders, B. A. (2008). Using personality traits to predict police officer performance. *Policing: An International Journal of Police Strategy and Management, 31*, 129–147.

Savage, S., & Milne, R. (2007) Miscarriages of justice, the role of the investigative process, In T. Newburn, T. Williamson & A. Wright (Eds.), *The handbook of criminal investigation.* Cullompton: Willan Publishing.

Shepherd, E., & Milne, R. (1999). Full and faithful, ensuring quality practice and integrity of outcome in witness interviews. In A. Heaton-Armstrong, E. Shepherd & D. Wolchover (Eds.), *Analysing witness testimony: a guide for legal practitioners and other professionals.* London: Blackstone Press Ltd

Skolnick, J. (1966). *Justice without trial.* New York: Wiley.

Smith, D. (1997). Case construction and the goals of criminal process. *British Journal of Criminology, 37*(3), 319–346.

Smith, S.M, & Aomodt, M. G. (1997). The relationship between education, experience and police performance. *Journal of Police and Criminal Psychology, 12*(2), pp.7–14.

Smith, N., & Flanagan, C. (2000). *The effective detective: Identifying the skills of an effective SIO.* Police Research Series Number 122. London: Home Office.

Soukara, S., Bull, R., Vrij, A. (2002). Police detectives' aims regarding their interviews with suspects: any change at the turn of the millennium. *International Journal of Police Science and Management, 4*.

Stelfox, P. (2011). Criminal investigation: Filling the skills gap in leadership, management and supervision. *Policing, 5*.

Svensson, A., & Wendel, O. (1955). *Crime Detection: Modern Methods of Criminal Investigation.* Amsterdam: Elsevier Publishing Company.

Swanson, C. R., Chamelin, N. C., & Territo, L. (2002). *Criminal investigation.* New York: McGraw-Hill.

Thorwald, J. (1965). *The Century of the Detective.* New York: Harcourt.

Tong, S. (2004). *Training the effective detective.* Unpublished PhD thesis, Cambridge University.

Chapter 8
Investigative Interviewing and Training: The Investigative Interviewer Apprentice

Lotte Smets and Imke Rispens

Introduction

Interviewing individuals, be they witnesses, victims, suspects or minors, is crucial in policing. Within the context of investigation and for many decades, a great deal of research has been done into police interviewing. So far, the focus of this research has been on revealing the truth, the objective of the interview and generating reliable and valid information (Williamson 1993; Baldwin 1994; Milne and Bull 1999; Gudjonsson 2003; Holmberg 2004; Powell et al. 2009).

This research has increased our knowledge about which investigative interview techniques and attitudes are more likely to lead to accurate information. In turn, this has led to an increased emphasis on the importance of thorough training that concentrates on learning these well-founded interview techniques, as well as on structural training (i.e. evaluating and coaching of people's investigative interview practices). Recent research has shown that coaching police officers in investigative interview competences can lead to an improvement of interpersonal investigative interview skills (Smets 2012).

Several other researchers have also studied the importance of supervision for police interview practices. Their findings show that these types of coaching can improve the quality of interviews (Fisher et al. 1989; George and Clifford 1992; Sternberg et al. 1999; Orbach et al. 2000; Sternberg et al. 2001a, b; Lamb et al. 2002; Powell and Wright 2008; Smets 2012). Interview evaluation and coaching is, therefore, recommended. It enables us to distil aspects that need to be learned from the practice of investigative interviewing, so that the professionalism of the investigative interviewer can be enhanced and future interview performance can be optimised.

L. Smets (✉)
Training, Coaching en Counselling, Lanista
Antwerp, Belgium
e-mail: Lotte.smets@icloud.com

I. Rispens
School of Detectives, Graduate School for Investigation,
Police Academy, Apeldoorn, The Netherlands
e-mail: Imke.Rispens@politieacademie.nl

R. Bull (ed.), *Investigative Interviewing*, DOI 10.1007/978-1-4614-9642-7_8,   147
© Springer Science+Business Media New York 2014

In practice, there are various kinds of coaching, such as supervision, intervision (this is discussing practice with peers), evaluation, group and individual coaching. These different methods share a common and explicit aim: to improve quality by evaluating an individual's performance and through giving and receiving feedback.

Currently, supervision and coaching initiatives are being organised within the police organisation in both the Netherlands and Belgium. The usefulness and effect of these various kinds of coaching will be discussed in this chapter. In the first part, we will explain why working with coaching, both group and individual, is a necessary aspect of optimising investigative interview competences. By way of introduction, we then go on to concentrate on the various kinds of coaching methods—supervision and intervision are terms that are used a lot these days—and why generating and processing feedback should be an essential daily practice for investigative interviewers. Finally, we conclude the introductory section by reporting on the findings of recent research showing that coaching has a positive learning effect on interviewers.

The second part of this chapter discusses coaching opportunities and their potential for police investigative interview practice in greater depth. What is interviewing coaching? Why is it advisable to use it? And what does an interviewing coach's job profile look like? We go on to give practical tips for giving and receiving feedback. Our objective is to work towards integrated coaching practices and optimal interview techniques.

Intervision and Supervision

Interpersonal Investigative Interviewing Competences

Those involved in its daily practice, as well as those in the academic world, suggest that investigative interviewing is a police technique, in which suspects, witnesses, victims or minors are questioned, which is not every police officer's strong suit (Bockstaele 2002; Gudjonsson 2002). Gathering case information in order to establish the truth is the primary goal of investigations, and is the reason why investigative interviewing is a frequently used investigative technique. The relevance and value of this information in relation to the issue of guilt goes on to be the subject of the subsequent legal investigation. This is an important next step in the judicial system. Teaching detectives an interview style that allows them to gather information such as applying standardised investigative interviewing protocols is, thus, an essential first step. This is also true if one takes a bottom-up approach. Learning empirical investigative interviewing methods and techniques is even more important given that suspects can now invoke their right to have a lawyer present.[1] But it is not the only important factor.

---

[1] In Belgium, suspects who are eligible for legal aid are persons who are suspected of committing crimes with a sentence of at least 1 year (as referred to in the Salduz Act). The Salduz Act appeared in the Belgian Official Journal (*Belgisch Staatsblad,* B.S.) on 5 September 2011 (B.S. 05 Sep 2011). Officially, the Salduz Act is called the Amendment of the Code of Criminal Procedure Act (*Wet tot wijziging van het Wetboek van strafvordering*) and the Act of 20 July 1990 concerning remand

Interviewing is a reflection of a dynamic process in which the investigative interviewer must take various aspects into account (such as material, procedural and technical issues) all at the same time (De Fruyt et al. 2006a). Bearing in mind the aim of investigative interviewing (i.e. to gather information), it is crucial that these aspects are carried out correctly. This demands the professional application of acquired investigative interviewing techniques. In addition to this, there are several psychological processes[2] that are responsible for the specific dynamics during the investigative interview that determine the relationship between the interviewer and the person being questioned. For this reason, no two interviews are alike, because each interview is steered by the communication and interaction processes taking place at the time. Therefore, alongside investigative interviewing methods and techniques, being able to adapt is also necessary.

Practice involves investigative interviewers continually adapting themselves depending on the kind of investigation, the person being questioned and the circumstances. Often, this propensity to adapt aids the interview. Moreover, it is the interviewer's flexibility that has led to interviews being a popular police investigative technique that at all times can be used (Köhnken 1995).

Neither can we expect every interviewer to be infallible, nor can we expect every interviewer to adapt in the right way to every possible interview situation, given that persons being interviewed could be suspects and witnesses, as well as victims and/or minors (Smets 2009). We have to assume that being able to adapt properly to a given interview situation depends on individual skills and interpersonal interview competences: What is a person good at? What is an interviewer's strength? What capacities does this person have? What kind of interview (suspect, victim or witness) is an interviewer better suited to?

Evaluating interpersonal interview competences and then coaching the interviewer are useful if we want to give interviewers insight into their professional interviewing behaviour: both their strengths and their weaknesses (i.e. those investigative interviewing skills that they are not so good at). This chapter is an argument for introducing evaluation and coaching of several investigative interviewing competences, alongside integrating structural interview courses, into investigation work so that interviewers' personal effectiveness and the quality of investigative interviewing can be optimised.

The Various Kinds of Coaching

There are various coaching types and methods that can be integrated into organisations, and which enable employees to optimise specific professional activities, such as investigative interviewing. The best known and those that have been used traditionally

---

in custody to give rights to all those who are interrogated and all those who are deprived of their freedom. These rights include the right to consult a lawyer and the right to be represented by a lawyer.

[2] Such as the interaction between the interviewer and the person being interviewed, constructions and the interviewer's frame of reference.

in social sciences for the training of psychologists and social workers are intervision and supervision. More recently, staffs at large commercial businesses are also being coached, in line with the company's philosophy and mission. But what do these various coaching methods consist of and how do they differ? In order to point out the difference between the concepts of intervision, supervision, coaching and evaluation, what follows is a short description of the methods and objectives of these principles.

- Intervision: Intervision is a method in which colleagues (or interviewers) come together to discuss specific work situations or problems (GG Werkmagazine 2012). Anyone in the group can put forward a work situation. These are first listed and then one is chosen for further discussion. If interviewers are involved, the topic may be a specific interview. The interviewer in question relates the circumstances and the rest ask questions. This encourages insight and self-reflection on the part of the interviewer, while at the same time, it uses the expertise of the other interviewers. The situations will often be familiar to the other people in the group and, by discussing them, interviewing expertise and quality can be enhanced. Intervision usually takes place on several occasions across a substantial period of time with a small group of the same participants. Beforehand, agreements are made about the rules, the objectives and the way the intervision is performed. The process requires the participants to have basic skills. Intervision can be done independently or under supervision.

There is no hierarchy within an intervision group. Intervision promotes expertise by encouraging staff to call on one another's expertise and experience. It is based on the principle of learning from and with one another: 'The whole is more than the sum of its parts' and combining forces can empower. When the individual knowledge of various colleagues is combined to find solutions to given problems, often more valuable solutions emerge. This principle is primarily driven by the power of autonomy and independence among employees. An employer or organisation that puts such methods in place demonstrates great trust in employees.

- Supervision: Supervision is usually an individual learning process, under the guidance of a supervisor, involving a method that addresses the personal, work-related learning issues (GG Werkmagazine 2012). It is a form of reflection on one's own style of working. With regard to interviewing, it provides insights into the situations that present problems for the interviewer, the underlying causes, how they can be handled and what the alternatives are. The supervisor could be an investigative interviewing coach, superior, or behavioural specialist. The focus in supervision is on learning, also for future situations.

With supervision, a learning process is offered under the guidance of a 'supervisor', which is not the case with intervision (in the latter, employees are seen as intelligent students who learn and accrue expertise from their practical and educational experiences). During the supervision process, the aim is to consolidate the learning process through conscious participation. The supervisor encourages the student to reflect about his or her personal learning process. The supervisor is generally an individual who is more skilled and experienced than the employee in training. In this way, expert knowledge is also transferred.

A Canadian study (Cyr et al. 2012) investigated the usefulness of supervision and receiving written feedback. Interviewers followed a 5-day course on the questioning of vulnerable witnesses (according to the NICHD protocol). In the months following the course, half of the interviewers were given detailed, individual written feedback about their interviews. This feedback was discussed with the interviewer. For each interview, a score was given for the kind of questions asked (open, closed, targeted, multiple choice, leading and invitations for free recall), whether paraphrasing had been used (short summary of what had already been said), the number of core and peripheral details (object, person and actions) mentioned by the witness, and whether the investigative interviewing protocol had been followed. The interviewers that were given feedback were more inclined subsequently to interview according to the investigative interviewing protocol than those who were not given feedback. They were also more inclined to invite the witnesses to give free explanations and the witnesses offered more core details. Once supervision and written feedback stopped, on the other hand, the interviewers were less inclined to ask open questions, and they got less information from the witnesses.

- Coaching: Coaching is a more in-depth type of supervision, which allows what has been learned to sink in and focuses on optimal performance. It is usually done on an individual basis, but is often temporary: The coach helps the person to gain insight into his or her own professional performance. The work is done with certain learning objectives in mind and the coach pays attention to the emotional wellbeing of the individual. Using self-knowledge and reflection, the focus is on the optimal execution of certain tasks or assignments, such as investigative interviewing technique. Personal capacities and competences serve as a frame of reference in this. Given that we consider coaching as a more in-depth type of training, supplementary to intervision and supervision methods, we will also be considering, at greater length, the practical applications of coaching as a concept later in this chapter.

The Importance of Feedback

In intervision, supervision and coaching, individual performance is evaluated and feedback is given. Giving and receiving feedback plays a prominent role. Feedback has therefore been found to be important for instilling development and optimising investigative interviewing capacities.

Sternberg et al. (1997, 1999, 2001a, b), Orbach et al. (2000) and Lamb et al. (2000, 2002) all studied the learning effect from feedback and follow-up supervision after an initial, short-duration interview course. Sternberg et al. (1997) investigated in particular whether using a fixed interviewing protocol during the rapport-building phase had any impact on the amount of information that is gathered when minors are questioned. In this, these researchers differentiated between protocols consisting of open as opposed to leading questions. Their results show that asking open questions during the introductory phase leads to more words and significantly more details about criminal acts being revealed during subsequent questioning than when leading questions are asked. Given that this course consisted only of learning various protocols (a one-off protocol training course), Sternberg et al. (1999) later studied the effect of a 5-day intensive course, supplemented by follow-up sessions and individual expert feedback. The findings showed that, regardless of the script used (open versus leading protocol), the six investigative interviewers being trained asked fewer direct and leading questions after the follow-up and feedback sessions. The coaching comprised the following interventions:

- Learning and practicing two investigative interviewing protocols to facilitate contact with the persons being questioned (script with open versus leading questions)
- Formal information about how memory works, aspects of child language and the susceptibility of young individuals to being influenced, as well as how to apply phased investigative interviewing methods
- Film showing fragments of investigative interviews using effective and less effective investigative interviewing methods
- Feedback on the participants' everyday investigative interviewing practice
- Supervision in small groups every 2 months
- Written expert feedback on investigative interviewing performances and telephone feedback sessions between the expert and the interviewer (from Powell et al. 2005, p. 26)

This course made constructive use of educational and interactive techniques, such as a bimonthly supervision and providing expert feedback. Yet, it should be noted that scant attention was paid to the personal development of interviewers, such as creating insight into personal performance and growth potential. While there is individual feedback, this took place by telephone. Telephone contact is a good alternative to, but probably less effective than a one-to-one situation where the coach and the interviewer meet each other in a safe setting. In this setting, the communication between the coach and the interviewer is much more direct and clear because eye contact and body language play a role in communication (Smets and Pauwels 2010).

Lamb et al. (2002) also came to the conclusion that organising feedback and follow-up sessions leads to better investigative interviewing. During the supervision, interviewers used half as many non-leading invitations and interventions, and the number of multiple choice questions rose significantly. Additionally, the interviews that were carried out after the supervision sessions produced 50 % less case information and details than the interviews conducted during the supervision phase (Lamb et al. 2002).

These results suggest that learned investigative interviewing skills regressed drastically once the supervision sessions ended. This also points out the need for repeated or ongoing feedback and supervision. Despite the positive effect of expert feedback and supervision sessions on interviews, not a single study has succeeded in showing enduring structural behavioural changes after the training has ended (Smets 2012). Lamb et al.'s results (2000, 2002) show that interviewers, be it consciously or not, revert to their old interviewing habits in the absence of supervision and expert feedback. These findings suggest that organising supervision sessions and providing feedback on the basis of best practice guidelines or protocols is not sufficient.

Investigative interviewers may not be able to differentiate their own interviewing behaviour from undesirable interviewing skills because they have limited insight into their personal professional performance. Insight into professional performance is essential, both on the part of the trainer and the interviewer, before interview behaviour can be optimised and professionalised permanently. This can be achieved through evaluating and coaching interview competences. Initially, interviewers can be confronted with their professional performance, and then go on to recognise the need to adjust some of their behaviour. The authors of this chapter are, therefore, of the opinion that new opportunities must be explored and that a more fundamental approach is needed in the form of coaching interpersonal interviewing skills.

Experimental Coaching

A recent research programme found that individual coaching of interviewers optimised interpersonal investigative interview competences (Smets 2012).

Inspired by intervision and supervision principles, two new coaching techniques were specially developed for police interview practices. The effect of both techniques was subsequently studied quasi-experimentally in the police investigative practice of five local and federal Dutch language police forces in Belgium. The two coaching techniques comprised a one-off group coaching session versus a longer-term, individual coaching procedure. The coaching effect of both procedures was studied and evaluated using the Police Interview Competency Inventory (PICI, De Fruyt et al. 2006b; Smets 2009). The PICI is a questionnaire and observation outline used to reveal and measure investigative interviewer skills.

The PICI is a five-dimensional instrument that measures interview competences in an objective and standardised way. The instrument comprises 40 different interviewing competences such as being empathetic, motivated, careful, aggressive, patient, authoritarian, understanding and so on. These competences can be subdivided into five general dimensions, namely 'careful-tenacious', 'controlled-tolerant', 'dominant-insisting', 'sensitive-verbal' (communicative), and 'benevolent' (empathetic). Using a five-point Likert scale, self-evaluations and evaluations by others can be carried out.

For the first training method, the 1-day group coaching, 31 experienced detectives were coached for 1 day, in small groups of four to six, using a simulated suspect interview (a role-play done by a professional actor), during which the interviewers were asked to give feedback on one another's interview behaviour. For the second training method, the individual coaching lasting over a period of 6 months, during which the interviewer and coach participated in three to four individual sessions. Thirty-two detectives were given personal and individual coaching by an interviewing coach. The coach was a detective who had built up special investigative interviewing expertise during his career.

The effect of both coaching techniques was studied using a pre- and post-coaching design. Using the PICI questionnaire, the participants' individual coaching performances were evaluated before and after the various training interventions.

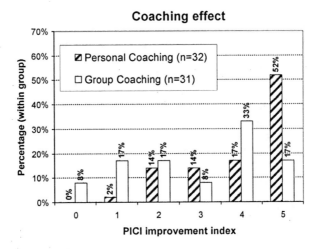

Fig. 8.1 Coaching effect

The results show that the interpersonal interviewing skills of the interviewers who participated improved after both training methods. From the comparison between both coaching methods and the analyses of the progress that the interviewers made, it emerged that the individual coaching of interviewers has a stronger effect than one-off participation in group coaching (Smets 2012).

The results show (see Fig. 8.1) that after having individual coaching, 52 % of the participating interviewers demonstrated improvements in all five PICI competences (not only in the competences for which they had been coached). There was also evidence of improvement among the group of interviewers who had only experienced the one-off group coaching session, in that 33 % of the participants demonstrated a significant improvement in four of the five PICI interview competences.

Furthermore, the investigative interviewers showed improvement in empathetic and communications-related PICI competences in particular. These results suggest that the so-called soft interview characteristics can be coached better and more easily compared to changing habits related to so-called coercive interview characteristics. This is promising because previous research has shown that it is these soft characteristics in particular that are necessary for an information-gathering investigative interview style (i.e. open and non-leading questions and assuming a neutral interview attitude). This is important, given the presence of lawyers in the post-Salduz era. Moreover, these characteristics help to avoid unwarranted pressure during questioning. Empathy and communicative skills may well be important ingredients for ascertaining the truth. Questioning is, after all, more than just seeking a meaning; getting to the truth is fundamental.

During the long-term individual coaching course, it is possible to work much more intensely on preset learning goals than it is during one-off group coaching. It emerged, however, that giving and receiving feedback from the interviewing coach and colleagues was much more instructive than expected.

It should be noted that the group that was not given long-term coaching knew that the other group was getting long-term coaching and that they would both be evaluated at a later date. Perhaps, because of this, the one-off coaching group tried harder. In addition, it is likely that the interviewers exchanged views informally across the two groups about their experiences and by doing so learned from one another, even after the coaching session was finished. Also, the coaching intervention platform had broken down the 'taboo' that accompanies the giving and receiving of feedback, probably resetting in the sharing experiences across the two groups.

Evaluation and Coaching

Realisation and Integration

In the preceding section, we discussed the motivation for intervision and supervision and the effect of coaching on individual interview competences. However, how can interviewers be coached best? How does one structure a coaching course and how is it integrated into daily police practice?

Coaching of investigative interviewers aims at facilitating personal growth through increasing awareness of professional behaviour and by stimulating existing potential. Coaching is enabling an interviewer to release his or her potential so that he/she can perform to the best of his ability. It involves making changes from within and this includes personal autonomy. During the coaching, the interviewing coach and the interviewer together seek out personal capacities and learn to apply these consciously during professional interview situations.

In short, coaching of individuals aims at personal development by heightening awareness of the interviewer's behaviour. The aim is to motivate the interviewer. Coaching is teaching the other person to learn. In this, the interviewer invokes the capacity for self-reflection so that the interviewer becomes more self-aware and self-confident. It is a process of personal guidance and evaluation in which the one being coached learns while the coach supports and guides. A coaching process is generally organised according to a process in which specific objectives are predetermined. In this, the intention is to realise these objectives within a particular period and make them apparent within the organisation.

It is essential to have an evaluation phase prior to the coaching course. During this, interpersonal investigative interviewing competences are first listed and then evaluated. On the basis of this, personal learning goals are then formulated and later effected.

Form, Timing and Coaching Setting

It is possible to integrate evaluation and coaching before, during, and after an interview. In this, investigative interviewing performance can be evaluated at both a content and personal level. For the latter, an assessment can be performed to check (1) whether the interviewer has combined and integrated the interviewing techniques and (2) whether competences are well developed or not. Coaching of content, on the other hand, is more case-oriented and focuses on the successful completion of a specific dossier.

Coaching an interviewer is a kind of supervision and aims at improving the quality of the interview by supporting the interviewer. Evaluation and coaching generally take the form of feedback. This feedback may relate to the interviewer's behaviour and interaction with the suspect (personal coaching) or to the interview itself (content coaching). Both content and personal coaching can be organised in various ways, depending on the practical requirements (i.e. real life, individual or group coaching).

In *real life coaching*, the coach watches the interview as it actually takes place and may give feedback during the interview (e.g. from the observation room). Similar to the Dutch application, the focus here is generally on content- or case-oriented coaching, although personal coaching may also be useful in this setting. To be able to give good feedback, the coach must be able to follow the interview properly, for instance, by using audio-visual equipment. The coach must also be able to pass feedback on to the interviewer, for instance, through a personal intercom (i.e. the interviewer has an earpiece through which the coach communicates) between the observation room and the interviewing room. Another way to do it is for the coach to write notes with instructions that are passed through to the interviewing room. Alternatively, breaks can be instigated for interim discussions between the interviewer and coach.

For real-life coaching, it may well be useful to organise a preliminary discussion between the coach and the interviewer(s). This will allow for investigative interview experience, coaching experience, expectations, learning points and arrangements about the coaching methods and times, as well as the circumstances to be thoroughly discussed beforehand. During this discussion, it is also helpful to come to proper agreements about the degree and types of instructions as well as the feedback that can be expected.

In *individual coaching*, the coach can support the interviewer to prepare prior to the interview and/or only gives feedback after the interview. A feedback session would then normally take place in a one-on-one setting, or during an individual coaching discussion. Such a discussion could be part of a coaching course in which personal investigative interviewing competences in particular are evaluated and coached. If the focus and objectives are on case-oriented interview evaluation, a one-off individual coaching session is organised. An individual coaching course could follow on from a one-off case-oriented coaching discussion and vice versa.

Coaching sessions can also be undertaken *in groups*. The advantage of this is that interviewers can learn from one another. The focus is on giving and receiving feedback, not only from the interviewing coach but also from other interviewers. After, for example, a simulated interview (this can be a role play in which an actor plays the suspect, for instance), interview performances can be evaluated and interview competences can be inventoried. This type of coaching makes particular use of the available know-how and expertise of the experienced interviewers who take part.

What these three different coaching settings have in common is that they coach the interviewer in applying his/her investigative interviewing knowledge and skills, according to the organisation's needs. The various coaching settings make it possible to choose the best setting for a given situation and objective depending on requirements, for instance, case-oriented support or personal coaching.

Case Study 1: Individual Coaching

If an investigative interviewer is given personal coaching, and during individual coaching discussions is made aware of the fact that he/she, for instance, is becoming impatient while questioning a pompous businessman who is suspected of committing fraud, individual coaching may lead to various scenarios that will improve the quality of the interview.

Interview scenario 1: During coaching, the interviewer can learn to adapt his/her behaviour to this type of suspect and develop suitable interview behaviour, such as learning to be patient and to remain empathic.

Interview scenario 2: During the coaching session, the interviewer develops self-confidence from which he/she can create options, such as interrupting the interview temporarily when he/she becomes aware of the fact that he/she is reacting impatiently to the interviewee, and that this is being expressed as resentful behaviour towards the suspect.

Interview scenario 3: Finally, the interviewer may anticipate such possible impatience prior to the interview and decide, for instance, to conduct the interview with the help of an empathic colleague.

In other words, the objective of investigative interviewing competence coaching is to conduct investigative interviews professionally by reflecting about one's own personal professional investigative interviewing competences and learning to anticipate these.

The timing of coaching also is important. The type and organisation of the coaching setting depends on its timing. The timing in turn depends on integration and practical opportunities, which may vary according to each police force or station.

The interviewer can call on the interviewing coach prior to the interview. The coach can then support the interviewer when making the interview plan and preparing the questions by adopting a critical attitude, and by asking questions that make the interviewer aware of the steps that must be taken and are necessary for a thorough preparation. The coach helps the interviewer to reflect on things instead of saying how things should have been handled. In this, the coach primarily takes the role of initiator. If required, the coach can advise the interviewer or give suggestions if the interviewer overlooks things. These suggestions should enable the interviewer to plan the interview himself/herself. The interviewing coach takes care of supervision and explains things. This type of coaching focuses mainly on the content of the interview and evaluating it from a case point of view.

Case study 2: Coaching prior to the interview

To be able to ask the right questions, the coach must be familiar with the broad outlines of what the interviewer did and how it went. The coach does not need to know the details. The interviewer is the one who prepares for the interview and takes care of the details; the coach only asks questions like: 'What approach are you going to use for the interview? What are you hoping to achieve with that?'

Obviously, it is possible to have personal coaching before a specific interview. The coach and the interviewer then agree beforehand which competences they want to put the spotlight on during the interview: What is the interviewer good at and what does he/she need to look out for?

During the actual investigative interviewing process, the coach can also support the interviewer, both from a content and case point of view, by giving instructions and feedback. (Case study 3). This can be done using a personal intercom or during interim consultations.

Case study 3: Coaching during to the interview

During interim consultations, the coach and the interviewer look back at how the interview has gone so far, and try to learn from it. The interviewer is first given the opportunity to let off a bit of steam. After this, the coach gives feedback and asks questions that reflect on the process, like: 'How do you think it went? Why do you think that happened? What impact do you think that action had? What were you trying to achieve?' The coach and interviewer then go on to consider what might happen next and how the interview should proceed.

If the interviewing coach and the interviewer agree to specific things beforehand during individual sessions, then the coach would remind the interviewer of these and coach him/her in those specific investigative interviewing competences.

After the interview, an individual postmortem can be held between the coach and the interviewer. The same strategy is followed during the postmortem as during the interim discussions: the postmortem can focus on the content and/or personal coaching aspects.

During this phase, a great deal of attention is paid to coaching by asking questions and giving feedback. The coach's observations regarding the interview or his/her reflections about it, as formulated by the interviewer, will guide the postmortem. For individual evaluations, the coach does not necessarily have to be present during the interview. In the postmortem, the discussion can turn to the interviewer's personal learning needs and expectations.

After the interview, it is instructive to not only consider the interview in terms of facts and content revealed. It is also useful to look at the way the interviewer handled it: the personal aspects. In this, one can evaluate the investigative interviewing techniques that were applied: What worked well, what did not, how did the suspect respond, how did the interviewer respond to the suspect? One can also analyse the discussion skills that were used, for instance, the kind of questions asked and how they were asked: Did the interviewer use paraphrasing, summarising and confrontational language? In addition to this, the interviewer's bearing and competences can also be evaluated, for example, by using PICI. In this way, interviewers can get more insight into the strengths and weaknesses of their interviewing skills.

Research shows that the image people have of themselves (self-image) and the image that others have of them normally differ as self-descriptions are often disposed to a number of self-presentation biases (Allport 1961; Greenberg et al. 1982; Marshall et al. 2005). People can describe themselves as more or less favourable, and their self-estimated effectiveness may be different from the perception of their peers and supervisors. Thus, while it is true that investigative interviewers are capable of evaluating their own interviews, a valuable supplement to this are evaluations by an interviewing coach, a colleague or a superior. Generally speaking, these give a more objective idea of how the interview was carried out.

Internal and External Investigative Interviewing Coaches

Investigative interviewing coaches should have extensive empirical knowledge at their disposal related to investigative interviews and interview techniques, and they must be able to motivate interviewers to act according to this knowledge (Van Amelsvoort et al. 2012). Coaches also draw on large reserves of patience, which enables them to work at the coachee's tempo. The coach and the interviewer must trust each other. It is important for the coach to be able to adjust his/her style of coaching to suit the level of the interviewer being coached. This requires flexibility and expertise on the part of the coach.

The advantage offered by interviewing coaches is that they do not have to carry out the interview themselves and are, therefore, in a more objective position to oversee the process, both during and after it is complete. It is often more difficult for interviewers to analyse the process because they are part of it.

The literature shows that police officers strongly prefer trainers and experts with extensive experience and those who come from a background of working in investigative interviewing (Memon et al. 1994; Powell et al. 2005). A coach's profile is therefore best considered at length.

An investigative interviewing coach should be a person who has a great deal of experience in (1) the questioning of suspects, victims and/or witnesses, and (2) coaching, motivating and stimulating individuals. Depending on an 'evidence-based' versus 'best practices' approach, two profiles can be defined, namely an internal versus external investigative interviewing coach:

- An internal interviewing coach is an extremely experienced interviewer with an extensive background in the field. This is a person who is part of the police organisation and prepared to share his/her expertise through evaluation and/or coaching initiatives. An internal coach is expected to have the proper coaching skills.
- An external coach is someone from outside the police organisation. Someone with special coaching expertise, who at the same time is familiar with the empirical knowledge and theory related to interview and how to apply this knowledge in practice.

An internal investigative interviewing coach is, first and foremost, an experienced interviewer who has undergone training to be a coach. An external coach is, first and foremost, an experienced coach who has undergone training to become an interviewer or has some knowledge of investigative interviewing techniques.

The literature describes police culture as being a typical and dynamic phenomenon that is characterised among other things as having an 'anti-intellectual attitude' (Van der Torre 1999) that embodies the opinion that 'real' police work cannot be learned 'in the classroom'. This refers to the notion that, once integrated into the field, police officers generally (be it under pressure from their colleagues or not) prefer to learn on the beat (Chan et al. 2008). A consequence of this is that in difficult situations, officers are more inclined to rely on their common sense and accrued expertise rather than what was discussed during specialised investigative interviewing training course. This is sometimes evidenced by a kind of resistance to experts and academics when it comes to taking part in training courses or evaluation initiatives (Memon et al. 1994; Van der Torre 1999; Powell et al. 2005).

Moreover, it seems that investigative interviewers will not use prescribed guidelines and/or certain investigative interview techniques before they are convinced of their practical use and effectiveness. This is demonstrated in a 'what works' approach versus an 'empirically-based' approach. With a view to ensuring the success of a coaching session, making a well-deliberated choice in terms of the investigative interviewing coach's profile is therefore important.

Although we could argue that receiving feedback from a fellow interviewer is more difficult to accept, we see in practice—and this is backed up in the literature—that there is a strong preference for internal investigative interviewing coaches (Smets 2012). This probably has to do with the fact that experienced experts or internal coaches, as opposed to theoretically schooled experts, can fall back on their own anecdotes and practical experience. This puts the investigative interviewing coach and the interviewer on the same communication level, which has three advantages.

First, the coach's ability to empathise with the interviewer is beyond question: He/she knows what the interviewer is talking about. Second, the interviewer can identify with the coach and will understand more readily what the coach means. Third, through his/her own expertise, the internal coach finds it easier to make clear what he/she is talking about, which means that the interviewer is more inclined to act on the feedback. Moreover, using internal interviewing coaches has the advantage that the coach is on site and that the interviewer can call on the coach unannounced, if he/she feels the need, to get advice before a complex investigative interview, for example.

An internal investigative interviewing coach and the interviewer who needs coaching share common ground, i.e. the same background, the same frame of reference and the same way of communicating. The downside is that internal interviewing coaches, as opposed to external interviewing coaches, have not undergone training in and do not have professional experience in coaching and supervising people. It is, therefore, important that internal coaches first undergo training in formulating, giving and receiving feedback and that they themselves are coached by experts. A train-the-trainer approach has much to offer in this respect.

Table 8.1 Tips for giving feedback

Tip	Example
Mention concrete facts and possible consequences. Do not make value judgments	Correct: 'You are not responding to the suspect's answer, which may make him feel like you have not heard what he said.' Not: 'You are arrogant.'
Usefulness	If someone has a stammer, they cannot change this behaviour. Giving feedback about stammering is therefore not useful. It is even frustrating because the person is reminded that they cannot do anything to control this behaviour
Descriptive and specific instead of judgmental	Correct: 'I notice that you don't have much eye contact with the suspect.' Not: 'Your behaviour is arrogant.'
Use the first person Speak for yourself, you are the one who made the observation. If you take responsibility for your message, it will be less threatening	Correct: 'I see that you are not probing the suspect for information, which means you may be missing out on information.' Not: 'You should have probed a lot more than you did.'
Restrict the number of things you point out. Too much feedback will be disheartening for the person and that is precisely the opposite of what you are trying to achieve. Acquiring skills and changing behaviour takes time	
Give them tops and tips Be constructive: First mention what you thought went well (tops) before you start mentioning areas for improvement (tips). Do not give compliments if you do not mean them, and certainly not as a way of softening the blow that is about to come. Never put a compliment in front of a comma followed by 'but'	
Give feedback step by step otherwise you will give the impression that you are only mentioning areas for improvement or that you immediately brush aside every compliment with an area for improvement	
Give the other person space to react. Check whether your feedback is recognisable and understood	
Make it known that you mean well. After all, you would never give feedback for the sake of criticising someone	

Table 8.2 Tips for receiving feedback

Tips	Example
Ask for specific suggestions and alternatives	'What do you mean?'
	'How would you do it?'
	'How would you do it differently?'
Don't argue and be defensive.	Not: 'Yes but...'
See feedback as an opportunity to learn.	Not: 'That's because...'
Listen carefully and openly. Do not go on the defensive; rather think about what the information that the person is giving can teach you	
Probe.	'Could you explain?'
Ask for clarification about things you don't understand.	'Can you give me an example?'
Ask for examples and clarification	
Thank the person giving you feedback	'Thanks for your feedback. I can put it to good use.'

Tips for Giving and Receiving Feedback

Given that our research results show that giving and receiving feedback from interviewers leads to further and personal development of investigative interviewing skills, we encourage organisations to elaborate their coaching initiatives and to integrate them into their daily practice.

Expert organisation of feedback sessions is based on a number of important premises. First, there must be an atmosphere of mutual trust and confidence. Second, it is essential to recognise the importance of evaluating investigative interviewing performances by way of feedback; the person receiving the feedback and the person giving the feedback both must have the feeling that feedback is an important tool for, for instance, improving investigative interviewing techniques, conversational skills or attitude.

For this reason, there are conditions and rules attached to giving and receiving feedback. Coaching individuals is pre-eminently a matter of working with people, which entails taking the necessary care when embarking on it. Organising and giving feedback to interviewers should therefore preferably be done by professionals in the field of policing who have experience and expertise in the coaching of individuals. They could be either internal or external coaches.

As a way of preparing to integrate coaching sessions, we highly recommend sending interviewing coaches on a training course for the efficient and resolute application of coaching communications when giving feedback. It is important that the feedback is formulated clearly and plainly so that the interviewer is not left with questions about his/her performance. In research carried out by Warren et al. (1999), interviewers indicated that the feedback they were given by instructors was not specific enough for them to be able to practice their newly acquired skills properly. Giving feedback is only useful when it is done according to certain 'rules'. If not, the feedback may be misunderstood and/or have the opposite effect (Tables 8.1 and 8.2).

Conclusion

There are many kinds of supervision that embody elements of coaching: intervision, supervision, individual coaching and group coaching. Coaching encompasses various aspects and evaluation is possible depending on the timing, the type of coaching, the objective and the setting. Depending on the situation in the police station, customised work can be done; its objective is to improve the quality of investigative interviewing. Nowadays, more and more emphasis is being brought to bear on the quality of interviews. In addition to this, with audio-visual recording and legal assistance during questioning, the investigative interviewing process is becoming increasingly transparent. Interviewer skills are visible, as is the effect that they have on ascertaining the truth. Educating and training investigative interviewers forms the basis for enhancing investigative interviewer competences. Some investigative interviewers are not able to differentiate their own interviewing behaviour from undesirable interviewing skills because they have no insight into their personal professional performance. Insight into professional performance is essential, both on the part of the trainer and the interviewer, before interview behaviour can be optimised and professionalised permanently. Evaluating interviews combined with coaching is, therefore, necessary so that the level of interview competences can be maintained and so that interviewers are given the opportunity to further develop their skills. The structural implementation of coaching initiatives in police interview practice is, therefore, necessary.

References

Allport, G. W. (1961). *Pattern and growth in personality*. New York: Holt, Rinehart & Winston.

Baldwin, J. (1994). Police interviewing techniques: Establishing truth or proof? *British Journal of Criminology, 33*, 325–352.

Bockstaele, M. (Ed.) (2002). *Politieverhoor en personality-profiling*. Brussels: Politeia

Chan, J. (2008). Studying life on Mars: Police culture into the future. In A. Collier, E. Devroe, & E. Hendrickx (Eds.), *Cahiers Politiestudies: Politie en cultuur* (pp. 95-109). Brussels: Politeia.

Cyr, M., Dion, J., McDuff, P., & Trotier-Sylvain, K. (2012). Transfer of skills in the context of non-suggestive investigative interviews: Impact of structurered interview protocol and feedback. *Applied Cognitive Psychology, 26*, 516–524.

De Fruyt, F., Bockstaele, M., & De Greef, K. (2006a). Competenties in het politieverhoor: structuur, meting en het verband met persoonlijkheid. *Panopticon, 1*(1), 12–30.

De Fruyt, F., Bockstaele, M., Taris, R., & Van Hiel, A. (2006b). Police interview competences: Assessment and associated traits. *European Journal of Personality, 20*, 567–584.

Fisher, R. P., Geiselman, R. E., & Amador, M. (1989). Field test of the cognitive interview: Enhancing the recollection of actual victims and witnesses of crime. *Journal of Applied Psychology, 74*, 722–727.

George, R., & Clifford, B. (1992). Making the most of witnesses. *Policing, 8*, 185–198.

GG Werkmagazine. (2012) http://www.goedgezien.nl/supervisieintervisieofcoaching.html. Accessed Oct 2012

Greenberg, J., Pyszczynski, T., & Solomon, S. (1982). The self-serving attributional bias: Beyond self-presentation. *Journal of Experimental Social Psychology, 18*, 56–67.

Gudjonsson, G. H. (2002). Who makes a good interviewer? Police interviewing and confessions. In M., Bockstaele (Ed.), *Politieverhoor en personality-profiling* (pp. 93-102). Brussels: Politeia.

Gudjonsson, G. H. (2003). *The psychology of interviews and confessions: A handbook.* Chichester: Wiley.

Holmberg, U. (2004). *Police interviews with victims and suspects of violent and sexual crimes: Interviewees' experiences and interview outcomes* (Doctoral thesis). Stockholm University, Stockholm, Sweden.

Köhnken, G. (1995). Interviewing adults. In R. Bull & D. Carson (Eds.), *Handbook of psychology in legal contexts* (pp. 215–233). Chichester: Wiley.

Lamb, M. E., Sternberg, K. J., Orbach, Y., Hershkowitz, I., Horowitz, D., & Esplin, P. W. (2000). The effects of intensive training and ongoing supervision on the quality of investigative interviews with alleged sex abuse victims. *Applied Developmental Science, 6,* 114–125.

Lamb, M. E., Sternberg, K. J., Orbach, Y., Esplin, P. W., & Mitchell, S. (2002). Is ongoing feedback necessary to maintain the quality of investigative interviewers with allegedly abused children? *Applied Developmental Science, 6,* 35–41.

Marshall, M., De Fruyt, F., Rolland, J.-P., & Bagby, R. M. (2005). Socially desirable responding and the factorial stability of the NEO-PI-R. *Psychological Assessment, 17,* 379–384.

Memon, A., Milne, R., Holley, A., Koehnken, G., & Bull, R. (1994). Towards understanding the effects of interviewer training in evaluating the cognitive interview. *Applied Cognitive Psychology, 8,* 641–659.

Milne, R., & Bull, R. (1999). *Investigative interviewing: Psychology and practice.* Chichester: Wiley.

Orbach, Y., Hershkowitz, I., Lamb, M. E., Sternberg, K. J., Esplin, P. W., & Horowitz, D. (2000). Assessing the value of structured protocols for forensic interviews of alleged child abuse victims. *Child Abuse and Neglect, 24,* 733–752.

Powell, M. B., & Wright, R. (2008). Investigative interviewers' perceptions of the value of different training tasks on their adherence to open-ended questions with children. *Psychiatry, Psychology and Law, 15,* 272–283.

Powell, M. B., Fisher, R. P., & Wright, R. (2005). Investigative interviewing. In N. Brewer, D. Kipling, & D. Williams (Eds.), *Psychology and law: An empirical perspective* (pp. 11-42). New York: Guilford.

Powell, M. B., Wright, R., & Clark, S. (2009). Improving the competency of police officers in conducting investigative interviews with children. *Police Practice and Research, 11,* 211–226.

Smets, L. (2009). Reliability and correlational validity of police interview competences: Assessing the stability of the police interview competency inventory. In M. Cools, S. De Kimpe, B. De Ruyver, M. Easton, L. Pauwels, P. Ponsaers, G. Vande Walle, T. Vander Beken, F. Vander Laenen, & G. Vermeulen (Eds.), *Governance of security research papers series II: Readings on criminal justice, criminal law and policing* (pp. 311–328). Antwerpen: Maklu.

Smets, L. (2012). *Police investigative interviewing – A new training approach,* Reeks Politiestudies nr. 3, Antwerpen: Maklu.

Smets, L., & Pauwels, C. (2010). The feasibility and practicability of police training: Investigative interviewers' perceptions towards coaching. *Policing: An International Journal of Police Strategies & Management, 33,* 664–680.

Sternberg, K. J., Lamb, M. E., Hershkowitz, I., Yudilevitch, L., Orbach, Y., Esplin, P. W., et al. (1997). Effects of introductory style on children's abilities to describe experiences of sexual abuse. *Child Abuse and Neglect, 21,* 1133–1146.

Sternberg, K. J., Michael, E. L., Esplin, P. W., & Baradaran, L. P. (1999). Using a scripted protocol in investigative interviews: A pilot study. *Applied Developmental Science, 3,* 70–76.

Sternberg, K. J., Lamb, M. E., Davies, G. M., & Westcott, H. L. (2001a). The memorandum of good practice: Theory versus application. *Child Abuse and Neglect, 25,* 669–681.

Sternberg, K. J., Lamb, M. E., Orbach, Y., Esplin, P. W., & Mitchell, S. (2001b). Use of a structured investigative protocol enhances young children's responses to free-recall prompts in the course of forensic interviews. *Journal of Applied Psychology, 86,* 997–1005.

Van Amelsvoort, A., Rispens, I., & Grolman, H. (2012). *Handleiding verhoor. 5e, herziende druk.* The Hague: Stapel and De Koning.

Van der Torre, E. J. (1999). *Politiewerk: Politiestijlen, community policing, professionalisme.* Rotterdam: Samson.

Williamson, T. M. (1993). From interview to investigative interviewing. Strategic trends in police questioning. *Journal of Community and Applied Social Psychology, 3,* 89–99.

Warren, A., Woodwall, C. E., Thomas, M., Nunno, M., Keeney, J. M., Larson, S. M., et al. (1999). Assessing the effectiveness of a training program for interviewing child witnesses. *Applied Developmental Science, 3,* 128–135.

Chapter 9
When in Interviews to Disclose Information to Suspects and to Challenge Them?

Ray Bull

This chapter commences with an overview of recommendations made since the 1980s concerning how to reduce the resistance some suspects (especially guilty ones) may feel about talking in interviews with investigators. Then, recent research on what guilty suspects have actually said about their pre-interview willingness to admit/confess will be described. Following this, advice given over the decades in several countries about how to confront suspects in interviews with information that may incriminate them will be presented. The ensuing sections of the chapter will review some of our recent research on when in interviews it seems best to do this. The chapter will end with a brief account of one of the best interrogators of all time.

In 2002, Holmes (formerly of the Miami Police Department) published a book entitled *Criminal Interrogation: A Modern Format for Interrogating Suspects* in which he stated that 'When you finish reading this book, I hope you have one predominate thought, "You don't obtain confessions by asking the suspect questions. You have to convince a suspect to confess by the use of persuasive interrogational arguments."' Holmes continued that 'The primary purpose of questioning is to determine that the transition to accusatory interrogation should be made' (p. 16).

One of the major assumptions underlying justification for the use of coercive interrogation techniques are the pervasive/common-sense beliefs that (1) '... suspects almost never confess spontaneously but virtually always in response to police pressure' (Leo 2008, p. 162) and (2) 'Confessions, especially to serious crimes, are rarely made spontaneously. Rather they are actively elicited ... typically after sustained psychological pressure' (Leo 2008, p. 119). Leo himself does not hold such beliefs but the general public may well do and thus may also many investigators (e.g. Alison et al. 2008), unless they read chapters such as the current one.

R. Bull (✉)
University of Derby, Derby, UK
e-mail: rhb10@leicester.ac.uk; ray.bull@le.ac.uk

R. Bull (ed.), *Investigative Interviewing*, DOI 10.1007/978-1-4614-9642-7_9,
© Springer Science+Business Media New York 2014

The Role of Resistance

In contradiction to such beliefs, over 20 years ago Gudjonsson and Clark's then-new (1986) theory focussed on the three main factors that they considered likely to influence suspects in police interviews. The suspects' coping strategies would affect whether suspects became suggestible or resistant. If interviewers provided 'negative feedback' (e.g. as part of their 'psychological pressure') some suspects might well respond to this with resistance rather than compliance (also see Gudjonsson 2006). Many years ago, Gudjonsson also pointed out that among the main reasons why some suspects confess is their perception of the strength of the incriminating evidence/information held by the interviewer/investigator (Gudjonsson and Bownes 1992; Gudjonsson and Petursson 1991). Bearing in mind this seminal work by Gudjonson and colleagues, I would like here to emphasise (and to discuss in this chapter) that of high importance to the successful interviewing of guilty suspects is a skilled combination of (1) avoidance of the use of 'negative feedback' (e.g. repeatedly accusing a person of lying) and (2) appropriate revelation of the incriminating information.

Of course, if an interviewer lies to a guilty suspect about aspects of the 'evidence'—which still seems to be permitted in some countries—this runs the risk of such a suspect, who of course 'was there', now believing that the actual evidence against them must be weak. Until recently, however, developments regarding the interviewing/interrogating of 'persons of interest'/suspects lacked substantial contributions regarding the beliefs of suspects themselves.

The Beliefs of Suspects

In a 'ground-breaking' study of actual suspects' comments on their police interviews, Holmberg and Christianson (2002) analysed the questionnaire responses of men convicted in Sweden of murder or of serious sexual offences. Just over half (52 %) of the 182 prisoners agreed to fill in an extensive questionnaire and 83 of these questionnaires were appropriate for analysis (the completed questionnaires were sent in sealed envelopes by these prison inmates directly to Holmberg at his University). Within the questionnaire, 22 items focussed on how the interviewers had behaved when interviewing these men as suspects and a further 16 items on the men's reactions. Another question asked about the extent to which the prisoners had admitted to (or denied) the crime during the police investigation (around half had admitted).

Analysis of the data regarding how the interviewers had interviewed revealed that some of them were reported to have behaved largely in a dominating way and others in a humane way. Analysis of the interviewees' reports of their own reactions revealed that some of them had been obliging, friendly, and felt respected whereas others had been frightened, stressed, and felt insulted. Whether denial or admittance occurred was then related by Holmberg and Christianson to the reported style of interviewing. They found a relationship between the interviewees' reactions and denial/admittance, in that those who reported being frightened, stressed, or insulted were less likely to have admitted. These researchers concluded that a 'dominant interviewing style is associated with suspects denying crime' (p. 42). This style involved a 'superficial case-oriented approach, characterised by impatience, aggression, a brusque and obstinate condemning approach, presumably aiming to extort a confession' (p. 42).

Research critical of the police may sometimes be judged by investigators as being biased if the researcher 'is not one of us'. However, this research study was conducted by a person (Holmberg) who had decades of experience of being a police officer. This important, innovative study has a number of possible limitations. One of these is that the prisoners completed the questionnaires some considerable time after the interviews—the average length of time between the relevant (alleged) offences and completing the questionnaire was 32 months (the actual dates of the interviews were not available). Another is that whether the prisoners had denied or admitted could have biased their reports of how the interviews had been conducted. Another issue that needs to be considered when assessing the implications of this study is that interviewee denial may possibly have caused a dominant interviewing style.

In 2005, in the USA, O'Connor and Carson (both highly experienced professional interviewers) found that the predominant reason offenders who confessed (to child molestation) gave for why they confessed was the respect shown to them by the interviewers. Of the one-third who did not confess/make any admissions, many said that this was because of the way they were interviewed/interrogated by the police (e.g. in a demeaning and/or coercive manner). These authors recommended on the basis of their research that an investigator/interviewer needs to demonstrate to the interviewee an understanding of the latter's view of the world, develop rapport, communicate in a nonthreatening and nonjudgmental way while showing understanding, empathy, and respect for the interviewee as a human being. Some of the offenders commented that in their police interviews it had been made obvious to them that the interviewers felt negative towards them, which caused them not to provide information that otherwise they may well have provided.

The following year in Australia, Kebbell, Hurren, and Mazerolle (2006) arrived at similar conclusions. They made the important point that until recently most of the psychological (and other) research concerning the obtaining of information from people who may be involved in wrongdoing had focussed on false confessions rather than on how best to obtain information from actual wrongdoers. In their first study, convicted sex offenders were asked about their interviews with the police and suggestions for improving such interviewing. Of great importance was their remarkable finding that prior to their police interview only 16 % said that they had planned to deny. One-third had planned to give an account of wrongdoing/confess and half said that prior to being interviewed they had not yet decided whether to give an account/confess or not (somewhat similar findings were also found in a Canadian study—see Deslauriers-Varin and St-Yves 2006, below). Their finding concerning the few who had already decided not to provide relevant information flies in the face of common sense, which was aptly summarised by Leo (2008, see above).

The Australian inmates' consensual suggestions for improving investigators' interviewing skills (also reported in Kebbell et al. 2010) fell into the categories of compassion, neutrality, honesty, being clear, and nonaggressive. Those regarding what would make interviewees less likely to provide accounts/confess were aggressive behaviour, bias, and pressurising. When asked 'What do you think are the most important characteristics for an interviewer to have?' The consensual replies focussed on an interviewer being capable, approachable, understanding, calm, nonaggressive, neutral, respectful, assertive, honest, professional, empathic, good listener, and interpersonally skilled.

In the second study of Kebbell et al. (2006), a different sample of incarcerated male 'sex' or 'violence' participants provided information (via a 35-item questionnaire) concerning how their interviews were conducted by the police. Some of the sex offenders had confessed and some had denied. The confessors indicated that their interviews had been more ethical, humane, and less domineering than did the deniers, and had involved the interviewer using more 'evidence-presentation strategies'. Interestingly, when asked to compare the interviews that they had experienced with how they thought the police should interview for both types of offending (i.e. sex or violence), the largest differences were for 'evidence-presenting strategies' and 'ethical', followed by 'humanity' and less 'dominance'.

In this second study, each sex offender also read a number of vignettes in which the description of the police interview varied, and they were asked to indicate the likelihood of each of the suspects confessing (also reported in Kebbell et al. 2008). This likelihood was found to be significantly greater in the 'humanity' condition than in the 'dominant' or 'cognitive distortion' conditions (and in the control condition). From these studies, Kebbell et al. concluded that 'improving ethical interviewing and displays of humanity may increase the likelihood of confessions' (p. 59) and that 'dominance may reduce the likelihood of a confession' (p. 59).

In their final study, Kebbell et al. asked experienced police interviewers how those suspected of being involved in wrongdoing should be interviewed, and found a strong consensus regarding the importance of rapport and empathy, '. . . the most common opinion amongst the participants was that a humane approach is typically preferable to a dominant or aggressive approach . . .' (p. 82). In addition, Kebbell et al. importantly noted that '. . . some participants argued that catching a suspect out in a lie could be equally as effective as obtaining a confession . . .' (p. 89) via '. . . presenting evidence which conflicted with what the offender has said previously . . .' (p. 91). However, they also noted that 'we still do not know the best way of doing this' (p. 109) (this is a topic to be returned to later in this chapter).

Kebbell et al. also (though rather briefly) mentioned the concept of 'reactance' (see Gudjonsson 2003), noting that a lack of effectiveness of a domineering interrogating/interviewing style may well be due to the psychological reaction of defiance this may well create within the interviewee. Their substantial report's concluding sentence was 'Based on these results, it seems that the most ethical approach to police interviewing may also be the most effective' (p. 110).

On a similar topic, Vanderhallen and Vervaeke (2014) provide an overview of some of the new findings presented in Vanderhallen's Belgian doctoral thesis. In her study, 126 people who had just been interviewed by the police in relation to various offences agreed to fill in a number of questionnaires relating to (1) their perception of the interviewers' empathy and interviewing style, (2) their own feelings of hostility, anxiety, and of being respected, (3) their satisfaction with the interview, and (4) the 'working alliance' (which these researchers state consists of three subcomponents: 'an *agreement* on the goal, an *agreement* on the tasks of both participants, and an emotional bond of mutual trust and acceptance . . . The working alliance is fostered and fed by an attitude of empathy, unconditional positive regard and authenticity' (p. 16)). They found that interviewees' interview satisfaction ratings were significantly related to their evaluations of the strength of the 'working alliance' and to a 'humanitarian' interviewing style.

In the same year as Kebbell et al. submitted their report, Deslauriers-Varin and St-Yves, 2006 (also see St-Yves and Deslauriers-Varin 2009) reported that in Canada 44 % of their sample of convicted persons said they had, in fact, been ready just before their interrogation/interview commenced to confess/provide an incriminating account. However, one-quarters of these changed their mind during the interrogation. Similarly, of the 32 % who were not already prepared to confess at the beginning of their interviews one-quarter also changed their mind.

In their more recent publication, Deslauriers-Varin, Lussier, and St-Yves (2011) reported on their survey of a large number of incarcerated offenders whose official files contained information concerning whether (45 %) or not (55 %) they had confessed. Included in the survey was a question concerning the offenders' perceptions at the time of interrogation/interview of the strength of the police evidence against them, and it was found that the confessors' perception of this was significantly stronger than the non-confessors'. Indeed, of the many factors examined in this complex study, '. . . offenders' perception of police evidence emerged as one of the strongest predictors of confession . . .' (p. 130). These authors concluded that 'These results highlight the importance of case preparation and gathering evidence against a suspect prior to the police interrogation' (p. 142).

Confronting Suspects with Information

A year or two after the 1983 publication of our book *Psychology for Police Officers* (Bull et al. 1983), in the mid 1980s, I organised in London an innovative 1-day conference on police interviewing at which a small number of psychologists made presentations to a large audience (mostly of police officers). One of these presenters was Dr. Eric Shepherd (a former Royal Marine and Intelligence Corps officer) who outlined his new 'Conversation Management' approach. This seemingly novel approach to the interviewing of suspects/persons of interest emphasised techniques designed to facilitate the resistant, and the possibly willing, to converse on relevant topics. It contrasted directly with the then-traditional approach of confronting the suspect with the incriminating information while accusing him/her and using a rapid 'question-and-answer' approach (which is still practiced in several parts of the world). Instead, Shepherd stressed (to an audience then of sceptics) that an effective interviewer/interrogator, initially in (and throughout) the interview, has to set up (and maintain) what in the past I have referred to as 'rapport' with the interviewee (see Milne and Bull 1999; Vanderhallen and Vervaeke 2014; Walsh and Bull 2012a). This 'ethical' (as Shepherd (1991) called it) or 'humane' approach (e.g. see the crucial study mentioned above by Holmberg and Christianson 2002) was designed to encourage the interviewee to talk. Of course, only if the suspects can be encouraged to talk/provide relevant information can the interviewers compare what the suspects say with what the interviewers already know. Thus, one aim of 'Conversation Management' those decades ago was (and still is) to reveal contradictions, gaps, and so on regarding suspects' accounts. Shepherd (1991) wisely recommended this years before relevant research was published (see below) demonstrating the efficacy of this method (e.g. in detecting inconsistencies, contradictions, and lying/truth telling). Although, the major emphasis (and achievement) of 'Conversation Management' was in terms of the importance of treating the interviewee as a conversational partner, the benefit of doing this to the detection of possible deception/truth should not be underestimated. Indeed, in their 1999 chapter, Shepherd and Mortimer devoted a page to the topic of 'deception' (p. 285), but they noted that while the 'PEACE model of police interviewing (National Crime Faculty 1996) requires' the interviewer to note 'any unresolved inconsistency', this was 'rarely done' at that time.

This conclusion was supported by one of the (very few) then available studies of what actually happens in police interviews with suspects. In 1992, the Home Office (part of the Government in England and Wales) published the pioneering research by Baldwin that it had commissioned to examine how interviews were conducted in the late 1980s after audio-tape recording of them became mandatory in 1986 in England and Wales. Of the 600 recorded interviews that Baldwin (1993) analysed, '... most were short and surprisingly amiable discussions in which it often seemed that officers were rather tentative in putting allegations to a suspect... Indeed in almost two-thirds of all cases... no serious challenge was made by the interviewers to what the suspect was saying' (p. 331). 'Even when the suspect denied the allegation, no challenge was made by the interviewers in almost 40 % of cases' (p. 331). In only 20 of the 600 interviews that Baldwin examined did suspects 'change their story in the course of an interview. In only nine of these cases was the change of heart attributable to the persuasive skills of the interviewer, and even here only three involved offences of any seriousness... The great majority of suspects stick to their starting position—whether admission, denial, or somewhere in between—regardless of how the interview is conducted' (p. 333).

Similarly, Moston, Stephenson, and Williamson (1992) also found that in the majority of several hundred taped interviews the police spent little time, if any, trying to obtain the suspects' accounts of events. Instead, they accused the suspects of the offence and asked for their response to such accusations. Typically, suspects were straightaway accused of the crime and informed, early on, of the evidence/information implicating them. Moston et al. found, not surprisingly, that when the evidence was strong, confessions were more likely. However, when the police evidence was not strong, the suspects soon became aware of this and, understandably, did not confess. If the suspect refused to confess and the evidence was weak, the interviewers seemed not to know what to do next.

Early revelation to suspects of incriminating information/evidence runs the risk, especially in vulnerable people (Gudjonsson 2003), of suspects then involuntarily or voluntarily including some of this information in their subsequent accounts/confessions.

More recently in Taiwan, in their survey of several hundred detectives/interviewers, Tsan-Chang Lin and Chih-Hung Shih (2013) found that a substantial proportion (especially of those who had not received training) indicated that they usually commenced their interrogations/interviews by revealing 'evidence of guilt'. For recent laboratory-based research on the importance of such evidence/information disclosure see Horgan, Russano, Meissner, and Evans (2012) who concluded that '... guilty participants were driven to confess based on the perceived amount of proof the interrogator had against them ...' (p. 76).

In several countries (e.g. the USA), suspects have the right to be made aware of the incriminating evidence against them from the outset (DePaulo and Bond 2012). However, in many investigations relevant information known to the investigators/police is not necessarily, in and of itself, incriminating if the suspect in his/her initial free account offers an appropriate explanation of it (e.g. freely volunteers being present near to the scene of the crime for a good reason).

One of the most important studies ever published concerning what actually happens when the police interview suspects was by Leo (1996). This seminal study, conducted in the USA, is deserving of wider and deeper attention around the world than it has heretofore received. Leo noted that the Court (Justice Earl Warren) in *Miranda v. Arizona* (1966) commented on the absence of first-hand knowledge of what actually takes place during police interviews with suspects and that it called for research on this topic. In the ensuing 30 years, little such research was conducted. Leo's own study was based on his 9 months of 'fieldwork' with the Criminal Investigation Division of a large, urban police department (thought by many, Leo reports, to be one of the leading police forces in the USA). He sat in on 122 interviews (involving 45 detectives) and he also watched video recordings of a further 60 interviews conducted by two other police organisations. In his 1996 publication, Leo demonstrated good awareness of the possible influence his presence had on the 122 live interviews and he was able to compare these with the 60 recorded interviews (where he was not present). He noted that he tended to be excluded from the more serious cases, though this was not always so. Leo coded each of the interviews for the 25 potential tactics/techniques which he derived from those (1) advocated in police manuals, (2) taught on training courses, and (3) used in popular culture. Leo reported (as had Moston et al. in England in 1992) that the detectives usually began by confronting the suspects with evidence suggesting guilt, either real/true evidence (85 % of interrogations) or false evidence (30 % seemingly permitted in the USA but not in some other countries such as England); then the detectives attempted (in 43 %) to undermine the suspects' denials.

Leo also noted that the detectives:

- Often appealed to the suspects' self-interest in confessing (in 88 %)
- Mentioned the importance of the suspect cooperating (in 37 %)

- Offered moral justifications or psychological excuses (in 34 %)
- Used praise/flattery (in 30 %)
- Mentioned the detectives' expertise (in 29 %)
- Minimised the seriousness of the offence (in 22 %)
- Appealed to the suspects' conscience (in 22 %)

Leo defined an interrogation as 'successful' if the suspect provided during it some incriminating information (around two-thirds met this definition). Significant associations were found between some of the tactics and the suspects providing incriminating information, for example:

- Identifying contradictions (in 91 % of the interrogations in which this tactic was used the suspect provided some incriminating information)
- Offering the suspect a moral justification or psychological excuse (in 91 %)
- Praise/flattery (in 91 %)
- Appealing to the suspect's conscience (in 97 %)

From Leo's seminal study, one can conclude (for the purposes of the current chapter) that Shepherd's belief in the importance of interviewing in a way that can identify contradictions received empirical support.

Apparently, independent of Shepherd's contribution, in the Netherlands some years later, emphasis was placed on the interviewer/interrogator 'confronting the suspect with story inconsistencies' (cf. Komter 2003; de Keijser et al. 2012, p. 616). This Dutch approach of not revealing all of the possibly incriminating information at the beginning (see van den Adel 1997; van Amelsvoort et al. 2005) reached an international audience with the publication in English of an overview by van der Sleen in 2009 who noted that 'At the beginning of the 1990s the Police Academy in The Netherlands developed a model that could be used to structure the questioning of suspects' (p. 38). This model places emphases on (1) minimising suspect resistance, (2) the interviewer asking questions relating to the available 'evidence'/relevant information without yet having revealed this to the suspect, and (3) only then pointing out to the suspect how each of the suspect's responses to the questions is consistent with or in contradiction to the 'evidence'.

In 2002, updated training in Norway also emphasized the obtaining from suspects of a 'free account' and then challenging or seeking clarification regarding the contents of such an account (Rachlew 2002). Similarly, in England and Wales, national guidance updating the PEACE model (see Milne and Bull 1999) also emphasized this (Centre For Investigative Skills 2004). van der Sleen finished her chapter with a quotation from a man convicted of killing his girlfriend in which he said that (1) he was caught out by his own words, (2) the police could have arrested him earlier but instead used time to prepare, and (3) the police were skilful and never aggressive.

When in Interviews it Seems Best to Confront/Challenge

In her 2005 doctoral dissertation, Stavroula Soukara (whom I had the pleasure of supervising) reported our empirical study (see Bull and Soukara 2010) of a special sample of 40 police tape-recorded interviews in which suspects actually 'shifted' from denial to admission/confession. In that study, we were particularly interested in what the interviewers were doing in the minutes that led up to the time of 'shift', and we innovatively found that they were 'disclosing evidence' and 'asking open questions'. However, during our data analyses (in around 2003), we also noted that in these particular interviews the 'disclosing of evidence' had been going on for considerable periods of time prior to the 'shifts'. This led me to think that it may be the gradual/incremental disclosure of information/evidence that is crucial, but it was only several years later that I was able to obtain research funding to empirically examine this notion (Dando and Bull 2011; Dando et al., in press, see later in this chapter). In 2005, Hartwig, Granhag, Stromwall, and Vrij suggested that research be conducted on 'different drip-feeding procedures in which parts of the evidence are disclosed throughout the interrogation' (p. 483), and Maria Hartwig more recently co-authored a study along these lines (Sorochinski et al., in press).

In 2006/2007, in Sweden, Professor Par Anders Granhag and colleagues noted (Granhag et al. 2007; Hartwig et al. 2006) that investigative interviewers often have available to them some potentially incriminating information regarding the suspect whom they are about to interview (indeed, we might add that this is one of the main reasons why people become suspects), However, they pointed out that (1) little research has been conducted on how such information is, or could be, used during interviews and (2) most interviewing and interrogation manuals were silent on this issue.

Following on from Soukara's study, we, more recently, again found 'disclosing evidence' to be associated with admitting/confessing (Walsh and Bull 2012b). In recordings of 'benefit fraud interviews', of the 22 'skills/tactics' we examined, there were 13 that significantly differentiated between interviews in which suspects (a) 'shifted' to/towards confessing or (b) did not 'shift', these being:

- Disclosure of evidence
- Emphasising contradictions
- Encouraging account
- Gentle prods
- Open questions
- Persistence
- Positive confrontation
- Probing questions
- Providing appropriate structure
- Regular summarising
- Repetitive questioning
- Showing concern
- Silence

Since 2006, Par Anders Granhag and his former colleague Maria Hartwig have conducted several studies concerned with the possible effects of the timing of evidence/information disclosure. Their initial studies compared early with late disclosure of (relatively small amounts of) information. Their more recent studies are described in Jordan, Hartwig, Wallace, Dawson, and Xhihani (2012), Hartwig, Granhag, Strömwall, Wolf, Vrij, and Roos af Hjelmsäter (2011), and briefly in Hartwig, Meissner, and Semel, (2014).

In 2009, Sellers and Kebbell published a study comparing the effects of early versus late disclosure of either strong or weak evidence. They mentioned that '... whilst a consensus is emerging that evidence is vital in the eliciting of confessions, there is disagreement about how and when it should be used in suspect interviews' (p. 151). They noted that some prior work had found police officers to commence interviews by confronting suspects with evidence/information, and they commented on some of the problems this might cause, especially if that information contained errors (i.e. that a guilty suspect would react to). Theirs was a laboratory study, 'Due to legal and ethical constraints research on evidence disclosure strategies cannot be conducted with real criminal suspects' (p. 153). In this study, undergraduates were asked to carry out a mock theft. Later, they were interviewed with strong or weak eyewitness information being revealed early or late and asked to confess. Not surprisingly, the stronger evidence was associated with more confessions. Also, late disclosure was associated with more confessing. In fact, few confessed when weak evidence/information was revealed early in interviews. Sellers and Kebbell importantly pointed out that early disclosure cannot be undone. They also noted that 'Allowing suspects to provide their own accounts also means that the guilty may attempt to portray themselves in a positive light by emphasising mitigating factors, and this might make them more likely to confess' (p. 158, the effects of such self-generated 'minimization' is worthy of research attention). The timing of evidence/information disclosure was also briefly mentioned by Read, Powell, Kebbell, and Milne (2009) who commented that early disclosure allows suspects to create a false version incorporating such information.

Two years later, Sellers and Kebbell (2011) published their analyses of a sample of Australian police interviews with suspected sex offenders. In this, they found that in 60 % of interviews these officers employed a strategy that involved encouraging suspects initially to provide a 'free account' and if a confession did not then occur they then disclosed some of the evidence implicating the suspects. In only 20 % of these interviews (conducted since 2001) did the evidence disclosure precede the request for an account. They noted, of course, that '... once a suspect believes there is enough evidence to prove their guilt, they conclude that a confession is more likely to create a favourable impression with the police and the courts than a denial would' (p. 84). Indeed, in many countries an 'early plea' of guilty/a confession prior to court results in a substantially reduced sentence (however, such (non-early) disclosures appeared to have little effect on the proportion who confessed). Indeed, similar to what Baldwin (1993) earlier found in England, '... no suspect who began an interview with firm denials changed their position substantially, even when confronted with evidence of their guilt' (p. 91, but see the study by Walsh and Bull (2012b) described above which, in contrast to Sellers and Kebbell's finding of no suspect changing/shifting from denying to confessing, found that a considerable proportion did so). It would be interesting, in light of the findings of Dando and Bull's two studies (see below), to examine whether Sellers and Kebbell's firm deniers' lying/truth telling could be better determined from the 'later' revelation interviews.

In our own work, in both studies (Dando and Bull 2011; Dando et al., in press), we found that gradual revelation by experienced interviewers to (mock) terrorists or builders of information resulting from covert observation of their activities enabled much better determination of which interviewees were lying (the terrorists) or truth telling (the builders) than did late or early revelation. In addition, the gradual disclosure put significantly greater cognitive load on the terrorist interviewees.

Such findings support an interviewing approach that I had been developing since looking at Soukara's data in 2003 (mentioned above). I have been calling this the 'GRIMACE' approach (a grimace can be the facial expression made when caught out in a lie) and it emphasises:

1. *G*athering *R*eliable *I*nformation prior to interview, then
2. *M*otivating an *A*ccount, then
3. *C*hallenging *E*ffectively

The comparing of what the interviewee says in interview with the information that should normally have been gained prior to interview is of vital importance, especially when such information has not been divulged early on in the interview (also see Blair, Levine, and Shaw's (2010) study 4 for some benefits of this; Park, Levine, McCormack, Morrison, and Ferrera (2002) for an interesting study of how people really detect if someone has been lying by using information gained from elsewhere; and Roberts (2011) for an updated account of the 'conversation management' approach's timing of challenges).

A new topic that we have recently commenced research on is concerned with (1) what investigators/interviewers consider to be strong or weak types of (forensic) evidence/information, (2) whether they receive any training regarding this, and (3) whether their perceived strength of such information/evidence influences when they decide to reveal it to suspects. Our study (Smith and Bull, in press) involved 398 experienced police interviewers from various countries who completed a questionnaire about their experience of using various types of forensic information in interviews with suspects, as well as their perceptions regarding the strength of various sources of forensic information, and how this may affect their interviewing strategy. The results indicated that although the participants have forensic information available in a large proportion of their interviews with suspects, the vast majority of them had received no training concerning how to interpret or use such forensic information. However, the perceived strength of it was reported by some participants to affect their interview strategy in terms of the timing of the revelation of such information/evidence during an interview.

I would like to end this chapter by mentioning relevant advice made available several decades ago. In his 1997 book, Toliver provides a fascinating account of the interview/interrogation strategies used during the Second World War by Hans-Joachim

Scharff of the German Luftwaffe, one of Germany's most successful 'interrogators'. Scharff's role was to interview pilots of the US Air Force who had been captured by the Germans (e.g. after they had bailed out of their stricken aircraft over Europe). In his preface, Toliver said that Scharff '...was always professional in his job and he always got the information he was seeking from each POW' (i.e. Prisoner of War, p. 6). Thinking of some of the many interrogative atrocities that took place during that war (some still practised nowadays), one might wonder how Scharff achieved this. Toliver tells us that '...it all happened because he was gentle and believed he could get more information from an interrogatee through kindness rather than by bullying and threats' (p. 6). He commented that 'Scharff's superiors recognized that he was perhaps the most effective...man on the staff. His...completely organized approach...coupled with his studious and thorough preparation...' (p. 311). He notes that Scharff himself pointed out that 'I will collect...a stifling amount of information and evidence beforehand, and by its display along with persuasion mainly appealing to common sense, I will make him tell me the things I have not heard before' (p. 56). Scharff would often reveal/disclose gradually to the airman aspects of this collected information.

In the book, Toliver provides reminiscences from those interviewed by Scharff which demonstrate that he deliberately treated them with dignity and respect. Toliver reports (p. 138) one of the US airmen as saying '...I was led to...my interrogator...I did not know what to expect and when he courteously greeted me and...offered me a cigarette...I admit I was caught off base because I fully expected to be bullied and threatened and perhaps even tortured'. This airman also said '...He knew everything...even where I went to college and my mother's maiden name....' Another airman said of Scharff '...he treated me fairly. He is a cunning devil and could extract a confession of infidelity from a nun. He could have been...a sadist...or a student of Oriental torture, but he was not. He was a professional...full of compassion for his fellow man' (p. 178). Another commented 'Scharff listened to my story about my very ill mother and sent a radio message to her that I was alive and okay but a POW' (p. 233). Yet another said 'Scharff was not pushy or arrogant at all, just talked as if we were passing the time of day...he never did force an issue...' (p. 261). Towards the end of his book, Toliver noted that '...Scharff and others...deplored the actions of one of the interrogators who insisted on using bullying tactics and coercion...' (p. 308) and that 'In Scharff's opinion one of the worst characteristics an interrogator could have would be bitterness towards the prisoners he interrogates. His nasty aggressions cause the POW to clam up and nothing is gained' (p. 309).

I hope that you have gained some useful investigatively relevant information from reading this chapter.

References

Alison, L., Sarangi, S., & Wright, A. (2008). Human rights is not enough: The need for demonstrating efficacy of an ethical approach to interviewing in India. *Legal & Criminological Psychology, 13*, 89–106.

Baldwin, J. (1992). *Video-taping of police interviews with suspects—An evaluation*. Police research series paper No. 1. London: Home Office.

Baldwin, J. (1993). Police interview techniques. Establishing truth or proof? *British Journal of Criminology, 33*, 325–352.

Blair, P., Levine, T., & Shaw, A. (2010). Content in context improves detection accuracy. *Human Communication Research, 36*, 423–442.

Bull, R., & Soukara, S. (2010). A set of studies of what really happens in police interviews with suspects. In G. D. Lassiter & C. Meissner (Eds.), *Interrogations and confessions*. Washington: American Psychological Association. 81–95.

Bull, R., Bustin, R., Evans, P., & Gahagan, D. (1983). *Psychology for police officers*. Chichester: Wiley.

Centre for Investigative Skills. (2004). Practical guide to investigative interviewing (4th ed.). CENTREX (Central Police Training and Development Authority).

Dando, C., & Bull, R. (2011). Maximising opportunities to detect verbal deception: Training police officers to interview tactically. *Journal of Investigative Psychology and Offender Profiling, 8*, 189–202.

Dando, C., Bull, R., Ormerod, T., & Sandham, A. (In press). Helping to sort the liars from the truth-tellers: The gradual revelation of information during investigative interviews. *Legal and Criminological Psychology*.

de Keijser J., Malsch, M., Kranendonk, R., & de Gruijter, M. (2012). Written records of police interrogation: Differential registration as determinant of statement credibility and interrogation quality. *Psychology, Crime and Law, 18*, 613–629.

DePaulo, B., & Bond, C. (2012). Beyond accuracy: Bigger, broader ways to think about deceit. *Journal of Applied Research in Memory and Cognition, 1*, 120–121.

Deslauriers-Varin, N., & St-Yves, M. (2006). *An empirical investigation of offenders' decision to confess their crime during police interrogation*. Paper presented at the Second International Investigative Interviewing Conference, July, Portsmouth.

Deslauriers-Varin, N., & St-Yves, M. (2009). The psychology of suspects' decision-making during interrogation. In R. Bull, T. Valentine, & T. Williamson (Eds.), *Handbook of psychology of investigative interviewing* (pp. 1–16). Chichester: Wiley-Blackwell.

Deslauriers-Varin, N., Lussier, P., & St-Yves, M. (2011). Confessing their crime: Factors influencing the offender's decision to confess to the police. *Justice Quarterly, 28*, 113–145.

Granhag, P. A., Strömwall, L.A., & Hartwig, M. (2007). The SUE-technique: The way to interview to detect deception. *Forensic Update, 88*, 25–29.

Gudjonsson, G. (2003). *The psychology of interrogations and confessions: A handbook*. Chichester: Wiley.

Gudjonnson, G. (2006). Sex offenders and confessions: How to overcome their resistance during questioning. *Journal of Clinical Forensic Medicine, 13*, 203–207.

Gudjonsson, G., & Bownes, I. (1992). The reasons why suspects confess during custodial interrogation: Data for Northern Ireland. *Medicine, Science, and the Law, 32*, 204–212.

Gudjonsson, G., & Clark, N. (1986). Suggestibility in police interrogation: A social psychological model. *Social Behaviour, 1*, 83–104.

Gudjonsson, G., & Petursson, H. (1991). Custodial interrogation: Why do suspects confess and how does it relate to their crime, attitude and personality? *Personality and Individual Differences, 12*, 295–306.

Hartwig, M., Granhag, P. A., Strömwall, L., & Vrij, A. (2005). Detecting deception via strategic disclosure of evidence. *Law and Human Behavior, 29*, 469–484.

Hartwig, M., Granhag, P. A., Strömwall, L. A., & Kronkvist, O. (2006). Strategic use of evidence during police interviews: When training to detect deception works. *Law and Human Behavior, 30,* 603–619.

Hartwig, M., Granhag, P. A., Strömwall, L., Wolf, A., Vrij, A., & Roos af Hjelmsäter, E. (2011). Detecting deception in suspects: Verbal cues as a function of interview strategy. *Psychology, Crime, & Law, 17,* 643–656.

Hartwig, M., Meissner, C., & Semel, M. (2014). Human intelligence gathering and interrogation: Assessing the challenges of developing an ethical, evidence-based approach. In R. Bull (Ed.), *Investigative interviewing.* New York: Springer.

Holmberg, U., & Christianson, S-A. (2002). Murderers' and sexual offenders' experiences of police interviews and their inclination to admit or deny crimes. *Behavioral Sciences and the Law, 20,* 31–45.

Holmes, W. (2002). *Criminal interrogation: A modern format for interrogating criminal suspects based on the intellectual approach.* Springfield, Ill: C.C. Thomas.

Horgan, A., Russano, M., Meissner, C., & Evans, J. (2012). Minimization and maximization techniques: Assessing the perceived consequences of confessing and confession diagnosticity. *Psychology, Crime & Law, 18,* 65–78.

Jordan, S., Hartwig, M., Wallace, B., Dawson, E., & Xhihani, A. (2012). Early versus late disclosure of evidence: Effects on verbal cues to deception, confessions, and lie catchers' accuracy. *Journal of Investigative Psychology and Offender Profiling, 9,* 1–12.

Kebbell, M., Hurren, E., & Mazerolle, P. (2006). *An investigation into the effective and ethical interviewing of suspected sex offenders. Final report to the Australian Criminology Research Council.*

Kebbell, M., Alison, L., & Hurren, E. (2008). Sex offenders' perceptions of the effectiveness and fairness of humanity, dominance, and displaying an understanding of cognitive distortions in police interviews: A vignette study. *Psychology, Crime and Law, 14,* 435–449.

Kebbell, M., Alison, L., Hurren, E., & Mazerolle, P. (2010). How do sex offenders think the police should interview to elicit confessions from sex offenders? *Psychology, Crime and Law, 16,* 567–584.

Komter, M.L. (2003). The interactional dynamics of eliciting a confession in a Dutch police interrogation. Research on Language and Social Interaction, 36, 433–470.

Leo, R. (1996). Inside the interrogation room. *Journal of Criminal Law and Criminology, 86,* 266–303.

Leo, R. (2008). *Police interrogation and American justice.* Boston: Harvard University Press.

Milne R., & Bull, R. (1999). *Investigative interviewing: Psychology and practice.* Chichester: Wiley.

Moston, S., Stephenson, G., & Williamson, T. (1992). The effects of case characteristics on suspect behaviour during police questioning. *British Journal of Criminology, 32,* 23–40.

National Crime Faculty. (1996). *Investigative interviewing: A practical guide.* Bramshill: Police Staff College.

O'Connor, T., & Carson, W. (December 2005). Understanding the psychology of child molesters: A key to getting confessions. *The Police Chief, 72,* 1–7.

Park, H., Levine, T., McCormack, S., Morrison, K., & Ferrea, M. (2002). How people really detect lies. *Communication Monographs, 69,* 144–157.

Rachlew, A. (2002). *Oslo Police investigative interviewing programme: KREATIV—Based on the PEACE approach.* Paper presented at the Seventh Investigative Psychology Conference, Liverpool.

Read, J., Powell, M., Kebbell, M., & Milne, R. (2009). Investigative interviewing of sex offenders: A review of what constitutes best practice. *International Journal of Police Science and Management, 11,* 442–459.

Roberts, K. (2011). Police interviews with terrorist suspects: Risks, ethical interviewing and procedural justice. *British Journal of Forensic Practice, 13,* 124–134.

Sellers, S., & Kebbell, M. (2009). When should evidence be disclosed in an interview with a suspect? An experiment with mock-suspects. *Journal of Investigative Psychology and Offender Profiling, 6,* 151–160.

Sellers, S., & Kebbell, M. (2011). The role of evidence in the interviewing of suspects: An analysis of Australian Police transcripts. *British Journal of Forensic Practice, 13,* 84–94.

Shepherd, E. (1991). Ethical interviewing. *Policing, 7,* 42–60.

Shepherd, E., & Mortimer, A. (1999). Identifying anomaly in evidential text. In A. Heaton-Armstrong, E. Shepherd, & D. Wolchover (Eds.), *Analysing witness testimony: A guide for legal practitioners and other professionals* (pp. 267–320). London: Blackstone.

Smith, L., & Bull, R. (In press). Exploring the disclosure of forensic evidence in police interviews with suspects. *Journal of Police and Criminal Psychology.*

Sorochinski, M., Hartwig, M., Osborne, J., Wilkins, E., Marsh, J., Kazakov, D., & Granhag, P. A. (In press). Interviewing to detect deception: When to disclose the evidence? *Journal of Police and Criminal Psychology.*

Soukara, S. (2005). *Investigative interviewing of suspects: Piecing together the picture.* Doctoral dissertation, University of Portsmouth.

St-Yves, M., & Deslauriers-Varin, N. (2009). The psychology of suspects' decision-making during interrogation. In R. Bull., T. Valentine, & T. Williamson (Eds.), *Handbook of psychology of investigative interviewing.* (pp. 1–16). Chichester: Wiley.

Toliver, R. (1997). *The interrogator: The story of Hans-Joachim Scharff—master interrogator of the Luftwaffe.* Atglen: Schiffer Military History.

Tsan-Chang, L., & Chih-Hung, S. (2013). *A study of police interrogation practice in Taiwan.* Paper presented at the Asian Conference of Criminal and Police Psychology, Singapore.

Van Amelsvoort, A., Rispens, I., & Grolman, H. (2005). *Handleiding Verhoor* (Revised editions in 2006, 2007, 2010 & 2012). Amsterdam: Stapel & De Koning.

van den Adel, H. (1997). *Handleiding Verhoor.* 's-Gravenhage: Vuga.

Vanderhallen, M., & Vervaeke, G. (2014). Between investigator and suspect: The role of the working alliance in investigative interviewing. In R. Bull (Ed.), *Investigative interviewing.* New York: Springer.

van der Sleen, J. (2009). A structured model for investigative interviewing of suspects. In R. Bull., T. Valentine, & T. Williamson (Eds.), *Handbook of psychology of investigative interviewing.* (pp. 35–52). Chichester: Wiley.

Walsh, D., & Bull, R. (2012a). Examining rapport in investigative interviews with suspects: Does its building and maintenance work? *Journal of Police and Criminal Psychology, 27,* 73–84.

Walsh, D., & Bull, R. (2012b). How do interviewers attempt to overcome suspects' denials? *Psychiatry, Psychology and Law, 19,* 151–168.

Chapter 10
The Inconsistent Suspect: A Systematic Review of Different Types of Consistency in Truth Tellers and Liars

Annelies Vredeveldt, Peter J. van Koppen and Pär Anders Granhag

Introduction

"Today you stated that you were home all night on the night in question, but in your first interview with the police, you said that you went out to get cigarettes." This kind of statement is often used in court to cast doubt on the trustworthiness of witnesses and defendants. Pointing out inconsistencies is considered to be one of the most powerful courtroom tactics at a lawyer's disposal (e.g., Aron and Rosner 1985). Its success is likely due to the fact that many people believe that inconsistency is indicative of lying, and conversely, that consistency is a sign of truth telling. These beliefs have been expressed by lay people and legal professionals alike (Brewer et al. 1999; Granhag and Strömwall 2000b; Greuel 1992; Potter and Brewer 1999; Strömwall and Granhag 2003).

The present chapter reviews the available empirical evidence on the diagnostic value of consistency to predict truth telling, and of inconsistency to predict lying. We cover four different types of consistency, namely: (a) within-statement consistency (i.e., the level of consistency between details within the same statement), (b) between-statement consistency (i.e., the level of consistency between statements made by the same suspect), (c) within-group consistency (i.e., the level of consistency between statements made by different suspects), and (d) statement-evidence consistency (i.e., the level of consistency between the suspect's statement and other pieces of evidence). Before reviewing the empirical evidence, we will explain three

A. Vredeveldt (✉)
VU University Amsterdam, Amsterdam, The Netherlands
e-mail: a.vredeveldt@vu.nl

P. J. van Koppen
VU University Amsterdam, Amsterdam, The Netherlands
e-mail: p.j.van.koppen@vu.nl

Maastricht University, Maastricht, The Netherlands

P. A. Granhag
University of Gothenburg, Göteborg, Sweden
e-mail: pag@psy.gu.se

R. Bull (ed.), *Investigative Interviewing*, DOI 10.1007/978-1-4614-9642-7_10,
© Springer Science+Business Media New York 2014

theory-driven interview approaches designed to amplify differences in consistency between liars and truth tellers.

In light of the variability in the use of terms in the literature on deception, allow us to define the terms used throughout this chapter. For the sake of economy of expression, the term "suspect" will be used as an umbrella term for any person who is asked to provide a statement in experiments (i.e., including witnesses). The term "liar" and "lying" will be used for a person who is instructed not to tell the truth, either via a direct instruction to lie, or via an instruction to discuss an "imagined" experience. The term "statement" will be used to refer to the statement or interview as a whole, whereas "detail" will be used to refer to a specific detail or response within the statement.

Interview Approaches

One of the most frequently reported subjective cues to deception is consistency (e.g., Strömwall and Granhag 2003; Strömwall et al. 2003). Furthermore, both legal professionals and lay people seem to agree on how the consistency cue should be used, namely, consistency is seen as a sign of truth telling, whereas inconsistency is considered to be indicative of lying. However, what we know about memory might suggest exactly the opposite pattern. Probably the most influential approach regarding the relationship between consistency and deception is the "repeat versus reconstruct hypothesis" proposed by Granhag and Strömwall (1999, 2000a). The hypothesis consists of two important propositions. First, the authors highlight the French philosopher Montaigne's argument that a liar should have a good memory. Thus, good liars know that they need to keep track of their lies to avoid being unmasked, and will attempt to carefully repeat the same story. Second, research shows that memory is a reconstructive process (e.g., Baddeley et al. 2009; Loftus 2003). Therefore, when truth-telling suspects rely on their memory for an event, their testimony is likely to contain various types of inconsistencies. In short, it is predicted that the "repeat" strategy used by liars will promote consistency, whereas the "reconstructive" strategy used by truth tellers will undermine consistency. As a consequence, consistency may be a sign of lying, rather than truth telling.

A number of interview approaches have been designed to maximize differences between liars and truth tellers. Most of these approaches take advantage of the cognitive differences between liars and truth tellers specified in the repeat versus reconstruct hypothesis. Here, we review three cognitive approaches most commonly discussed in the literature on consistency, namely, asking unanticipated questions, imposing cognitive load, and strategic use of evidence (see Vrij and Granhag 2012; Vrij et al. 2010a, 2011 for more elaborate reviews).

Unanticipated Questions

Liars are often able to appear consistent because they are likely to have prepared for the interview. Indeed, Hartwig et al. (2007) found that liars were significantly more likely than truth tellers to have a strategy prior to the interview (see also Hartwig et al. 2010), and that one of their most frequent strategies was to "stick with the story". Preparation is particularly important when there is another suspect involved, in which case the suspects need to "get their stories straight" (Vrij et al. 2009). In contrast, truth tellers are less likely to prepare for an interview. Kassin (2005) argues that innocence puts innocents at risk because (a) people tend to believe in a just world (Lerner 1980), in which innocent people do not get convicted, and (b) people believe that their true feelings and intentions will be apparent to the interviewer, a fallacy referred to as the "illusion of transparency" (Gilovich et al. 1998). Due to the reconstructive nature of memory, truth tellers' unprepared stories may thus appear less consistent than liars' prepared stories.

Vrij et al. (2009) point out that investigators can exploit liars' preparation strategies by asking questions that liars did not anticipate prior to the interview. For instance, Vrij et al. asked questions that included spatial shifts (e.g., "In relation to the front door, where did you and your friend sit?") or temporal shifts (e.g., "In which order did you discuss the different topics you mentioned earlier?"). In response to these questions, liars will likely have no prepared answers ready. This increases the likelihood that they will have to think on the spot, thereby showing signs of cognitive load (cf. Lancaster et al. 2012; Liu et al. 2010). Furthermore, during subsequent interviews, liars may not remember the answers they fabricated hastily during the interview as accurately as the answers they had prepared extensively prior to the interview (Leins et al. 2012). Finally, in the case of multiple suspects, liars will be more likely to contradict each other in response to unanticipated questions than in response to anticipated questions (Vrij et al. 2009). Later in the chapter, we will review how asking unanticipated questions during the interview affects different types of consistency in liars and truth tellers.

Cognitive Load

A related interviewing approach is asking questions that impose cognitive load on the suspect (Vrij et al. 2008a). An important assumption of this approach is that lying involves a number of mentally taxing processes, including the creation of the lie, suppression of the truth, and monitoring one's own and others' behavior. Because lying is usually a more cognitively demanding task than telling the truth (Buller and Burgoon 1996; Zuckerman et al. 1981), lying suspects should typically have fewer cognitive resources available during the interview than truth-telling suspects. This assumption has been supported by findings that liars perform worse than truth tellers on secondary tasks during interviews (Lancaster et al. 2012). Furthermore, liars are not always able to suppress subtle signs of cognitive load. For instance, liars typically move their hands and fingers less than truth tellers due to high cognitive load (Caso et al. 2006; Vrij 2006; Vrij et al. 1997, 2008b; but see DePaulo et al. 2003). Nevertheless, these subtle signs are generally not sufficient for observers to detect deception—both trained and untrained lie-catchers tend to perform only slightly above chance level (Bond and DePaulo 2006; DePaulo et al. 2003; Hartwig and Bond 2011).

The investigative interviewer can amplify observable differences between liars and truth tellers by providing instructions that require complex mental operations. For instance, Vrij et al. (2008b) found that suspects who were instructed to tell their story in reverse chronological order showed significantly more signs of cognitive load (e.g., more speech hesitations and increased mention of cognitive operations) than suspects who told their story in normal chronological order. Furthermore, observers were significantly better at distinguishing between lying and truth-telling suspects when judging the reverse-order statements compared to the chronological-order statements. In a similar vein, Vrij et al. (2010b) found that an instruction to maintain eye contact with the interviewer (which imposes cognitive load; cf. Glenberg et al. 1998; Markson & Paterson 2009; Vredeveldt et al. 2011) amplified cues to deception compared to a control condition, and increased observers' ability to distinguish between liars and truth-tellers. In sum, imposing additional cognitive load during the interview has the potential to highlight observable differences between liars and truth tellers.

Strategic Use of Evidence

A third approach to amplifying differences between lying and truth-telling suspects involves the strategic use of evidence. When investigators have independent evidence available (e.g., fingerprints or witnesses), they can make a strategic decision about how to use that evidence in the investigation. Hartwig et al. developed the Strategic Use of Evidence (SUE) technique (Hartwig et al. 2005, 2006), which involves a strategic and a tactical level. The strategic, more abstract level concerns general cognitive principles involved in interviews, such as the tendency for truth tellers to be more forthcoming than liars (see Granhag and Hartwig 2008, for more on the strategic level of the SUE technique).

The tactical level of the SUE technique is case-dependent, and involves concrete interview tools derived from the conceptual framework underlying the SUE technique. SUE tactics can be categorized into three groups: (1) *evidence tactics*, used to evaluate the evidence during preinterview planning; (2) *question tactics*, used to exhaust potential alternative explanations that may account for the evidence; and (3) *disclosure tactics*, used to disclose the evidence in the most effective way. For instance, one tactic that was the focus of the earlier work on the SUE technique (e.g., Hartwig et al. 2005, 2006) is late disclosure of evidence. By disclosing the evidence at the end of the interview rather than at the beginning, the interviewer gives suspects the opportunity to contradict such evidence or their earlier statements. Late disclosure of evidence has proven effective in improving the detection of deception; in one study, police recruits trained in this tactic achieved 85 % deception detection accuracy, compared to 56 % accuracy achieved by their untrained colleagues (Hartwig et al. 2006).

In more recent work, Granhag et al. (2012a, 2012b) have further developed the tactical level of the SUE technique. Based on the Evidence Framing Matrix

(Granhag 2010), they designed a revised SUE technique, referred to as SUE-Incremental (as opposed to SUE-Basic). The Evidence Framing Matrix specifies two important dimensions for each piece of evidence, namely, the strength of the source of the evidence, and the degree of precision of the evidence. In their disclosure of evidence, interviewers can frame the source of the evidence as weak (e.g., "we have information") or strong (e.g., "we have video footage"), and the precision of the evidence as low (e.g., "you were seen in the neighborhood") or high (e.g., "you were seen entering the house"). The SUE-Incremental technique advocates a gradual approach of evidence disclosure, starting with the vaguest phrasing (weak source/low specificity) and gradually moving on to the most precise phrasing (strong source/high specificity). The incremental disclosure of evidence is expected to cause suspects to change their story in order to fit the evidence presented to them, thus eliciting inconsistencies. The SUE-Incremental technique allows for interviewers to make optimal use of the evidence, even when there is only one piece of evidence available in a case.

Another potentially useful addition to interviewers' tactical toolbox is the Tactical Use of Evidence (TUE) approach proposed by Dando et al. (Dando and Bull 2011; Dando et al. 2013). In line with the principles underlying the SUE-Incremental technique, TUE also advocates a "drip-feeding" approach to revealing evidence. However, the empirical evidence on the effectiveness of TUE is currently limited to two studies (Dando and Bull 2011; Dando et al. 2013), and these studies did not assess cues to deception. Hence, it remains to be seen whether TUE can maximize differences in (verbal) behavior between liars and truth tellers.

In sum, the tactical interview tools derived from the conceptual framework underlying strategic use of evidence can improve observers' ability to detect deception. Later in this chapter, we will review how these interview tactics affect different types of consistency.

Consistency and Deception

We now turn to a review of the empirical evidence on the relationship between consistency and deception. The purpose of this review is not only to determine whether there are significant differences in consistency between liars and truth tellers, but also to provide an estimate of the predictive value of consistency cues. To this end, we provide effect sizes for all studies in this review (see Tables 10.1 and 10.2). Because the predictive value of consistency cues depends heavily on the interview technique employed, we report effect sizes separately for the different interview conditions within each study.

In the empirical literature, "consistency" has been operationalized in different ways. One way of assessing consistency is by rating the extent to which a statement as a whole overlaps with another statement (provided at a different time or by a different suspect) or with another piece of evidence (e.g., fingerprints found at the scene of the crime), on a scale ranging from "inconsistent" to "consistent," or vice versa. For studies reporting such ratings of overall consistency, we calculated the standardized mean difference (SMD) between liars and truth tellers (see Appendix 1 for more information on calculations). An overview of these differences is provided in Table 10.1.

An alternative approach to operationalizing consistency is to count the number of consistent and inconsistent details appearing in statements provided by liars and truth tellers, respectively. For studies reporting this measure, we calculated three measures commonly used to compare effect sizes (see Table 10.2). First, to evaluate the common beliefs that (a) consistency is predictive of truth telling and (b) inconsistency is predictive of lying, we assessed diagnostic values for each of these beliefs. Second, we calculated the odds ratio (OR), which compares the odds of consistency when a suspect is telling the truth with the odds of consistency when a suspect is lying (see Appendix 1 for more information). Third, we provide the natural log of the OR—a measure derived from the OR that is frequently used in meta-analytic comparisons because it is normally distributed and less sensitive to small frequencies than the OR.

Within-Statement Consistency

We define "within-statement consistency" as the correspondence between details provided by a suspect in the space of one statement. Some researchers have examined within-statement consistency in terms of the number of consistent and inconsistent details appearing in the statement (e.g., Walczyk et al. 2009), whereas others have evaluated it in terms of consistency ratings for the statement overall (e.g., Granhag et al. 2012b).

Walczyk et al. (2009) instructed one group of participants to lie and another group to tell the truth in response to questions about their biographical information and recent activities. In their first experiment, they found that the odds of consistency were nearly seven times higher in the truth-telling condition than in the lie condition (see Table 10.2). In their second experiment, Walczyk et al. gave one group of liars the opportunity to rehearse their lies prior to questioning. Rehearsal made the liars somewhat more consistent, but not dramatically so: the odds of consistency for truth tellers were ten times higher than for unrehearsed liars, and still eight times higher than for rehearsed liars. In a follow-up study (Walczyk et al. 2012), participants were asked to answer questions about witnessed videotaped events, instead of their own recent activities. In this study, the odds of consistency were nearly eight times higher for participants who told the truth compared to unrehearsed liars, and 6.5 times higher compared to participants who had rehearsed their lies. In sum, the findings reported by Walczyk et al. suggest that truth tellers are substantially more likely to provide consistent responses within the same interview than liars.

A somewhat more nuanced picture is provided by studies using more realistic methodologies and different interview approaches. For instance, Leins et al. (2011) asked participants to come to the laboratory in pairs. The experimenter sent half of the pairs to lunch together (innocent condition). The remaining pairs did not go to lunch, but were instructed to steal money from a purse in a nearby room (guilty

Table 10.1 Summary statistics for studies reporting consistency ratings

Consistency type	Study	Condition	Truth tellers		Liars		SMD
			M	SD	M	SD	
Within-statement	Leins et al. (2011)		5.6	1.5	3.8	1.6	0.2
	Granhag et al. (2012a)	Early disclosure	4.0	0.0	4.0	0.0	0.0
		SUE-Basic	4.0	0.0	3.6	1.1	0.5
		SUE-Incremental	4.0	0.0	3.0	1.2	1.2
	Granhag et al. (2012b)	Early disclosure	4.0	0.0	3.9	0.6	0.3
		SUE-Basic	4.0	0.0	3.7	0.7	0.7
		SUE-Incremental	4.0	0.0	3.4	0.9	1.0
Between-statement	Granhag et al. (2003)		7.8	1.9	8.7	1.0	−0.1
	Leins et al. (2012)[a]	Same-mode	1.0	0.1	0.9	0.1	0.1
		Different-mode	0.9	0.1	0.7	0.2	0.5
Within-pair	Granhag et al. (2003)	Statement 1	7.5	1.5	8.7	0.7	−0.3
		Statement 2	7.6	1.5	8.1	1.2	−0.1
	Vrij et al. (2009)	Anticipated	4.3	1.4	4.4	1.6	0.0
		Unanticipated[b]	4.4	1.4	3.2	1.4	0.2
Within-triad	Roos af Hjelmsäter et al. (2012)	Anticipated[c]	4.6	1.1	4.4	1.3	0.0
		Unanticipated[d]	4.2	1.4	3.1	1.5	0.2
	Granhag et al. (2012a)	Early disclosure	4.0	0.0	3.6	0.8	0.7
		SUE-Basic	4.0	0.0	2.9	1.2	1.2
		SUE-Incremental	4.0	0.0	2.7	1.4	1.2
Statement-evidence	Hartwig et al. (2005)	Early disclosure	2.8	0.4	2.6	0.6	0.2
		Late disclosure	3.9	0.4	2.2	0.7	1.1
	Jordan et al. (2012)	Early disclosure	5.9	0.3	3.9	2.3	1.0
		Late disclosure	5.2	1.9	1.1	1.8	0.7
	Clemens et al. (2010)	Early disclosure	3.0	0.2	2.5	0.8	0.4
		Late disclosure	2.9	0.3	2.1	0.8	0.5
	Hartwig et al. (2006)	Untrained	1.8	0.3	1.3	0.5	0.4
		SUE	1.9	0.2	0.9	0.5	0.9
	Granhag et al. (2012a)	Early disclosure	4.0	0.0	3.9	0.4	0.5
		SUE-Basic	4.0	0.0	3.3	1.3	0.7
		SUE-Incremental	4.0	0.0	2.5	1.8	1.2
	Granhag et al. (2012b)	Early disclosure	4.3	1.5	1.6	1.4	0.3
		SUE-Basic	4.2	1.3	0.9	1.0	0.4
		SUE-Incremental	5.3	0.7	1.5	1.5	0.9
	Hartwig et al. (2011)	Free recall	2.8	0.2	2.5	0.3	0.4
		Probes	3.0	0.0	2.1	0.5	2.4
		Free recall + probes	2.9	0.3	2.2	0.5	0.7

Means and standard deviations for truth tellers and liars, respectively, and the standard mean difference between truth tellers and liars, by interview condition. *M* mean, *SD* standard deviation, *SMD* standard mean difference

[a] The consistency proportions were treated as scores on a scale from 0 to 1
[b] Averaged over four unanticipated questions
[c] Averaged over four anticipated description questions
[d] Averaged over six unanticipated drawing questions

Table 10.2 Summary statistics for studies reporting frequencies

Consistency type	Study	Consistency	Truth tellers N		Liars N		DV	OR	Log(OR)
Within-statement	Walczyk et al. (2009, Exp. 1)	Consistent	1339	98.3%	1,220	89.6%	1.1	–	–
		Inconsistent	23	1.7%	142	10.4%	6.2	–	–
		Odds (consistency)	–	58.2	–	8.6	–	6.8	1.9
	Walczyk et al. (2009, Exp. 2)[a]	Consistent	881	98.9%	1,615	90.6%	1.1	–	–
		Inconsistent	10	1.1%	167	9.4%	8.4	–	–
		Odds (consistency)	–	88.1	–	9.7	–	9.1	2.2
	Walczyk et al. (2012)[a]	Consistent	884	99.0%	1,684	93.2%	1.1	–	–
		Inconsistent	9	1.0%	122	6.8%	6.7	–	–
		Odds (consistency)	–	98.2	–	13.8	–	7.1	2.0
	Vrij et al. (2012)[b]	Consistent	29	93.5%	23	74.2%	1.3	–	–
		Inconsistent	2	6.5%	8	25.8%	4.0	–	–
		Odds (consistency)	–	14.5	–	2.9	–	5.0	1.6
Between-statement	Granhag and Strömwall (2003)	Repeated[c]	144	45.7%	64	41.6%	1.1	–	–
		Omissions[c]	171	54.3%	90	58.4%	1.1	–	–
		Commissions[d]	81	36.0%	74	53.6%	1.5	–	–
		Odds (repeated)	–	0.8	–	0.7	–	1.2	0.2
		Odds (omissions)	–	1.2	–	1.4	–	0.8	-0.2
		Odds (commissions)	–	0.6	–	1.2	–	0.5	-0.7
	Granhag et al. (2003)	Repeated[c]	127	69.8%	107	62.6%	1.1	–	–
		Omissions[c]	55	30.2%	64	37.4%	1.2	–	–
		Commissions[d]	76	37.4%	41	27.7%	0.7	–	–
		Odds (repeated)	–	2.3	–	1.7	–	1.4	0.3
		Odds (omissions)	–	0.4	–	0.6	–	0.7	-0.3
		Odds (commissions)	–	0.6	–	0.4	–	1.6	0.4

Table 10.2 (continued)

Consistency type	Study	Consistency	Truth tellers N	Truth tellers %	Liars N	Liars %	DV	OR	Log(OR)
	Strömwall and Granhag (2005)	Repeated[a]	76	33.6%	97	43.1%	0.8	–	–
		Omissions[c]	150	66.4%	128	56.9%	0.9	–	–
		Commissions[d]	106	58.2%	70	41.9%	0.7	–	–
		Odds (repeated)	–	0.5	–	0.8	–	0.7	-0.4
		Odds (omissions)	–	2.0	–	1.3	–	1.5	0.4
		Odds (commissions)	–	1.4	–	0.7	–	1.9	0.7
Within-pair	Wagenaar and Dalderop (1994)[e]	Consistent	–	39.0%	–	79.0%	0.5	–	–
		Inconsistent	–	61.0%	–	21.0%	0.3	–	–
		Odds (consistency)	–	0.6	–	3.8	–	0.2	-1.8
	Strömwall and Granhag (2007)	Consistent	97	88.2%	84	76.4%	1.2	–	–
		Inconsistent	13	11.8%	26	23.6%	2.0	–	–
		Odds (consistency)	–	7.5	–	3.2	–	2.3	0.8
	Vredeveldt and Wagenaar (2013)	Consistent	96	72.7%	50	36.2%	2.0	–	–
		Inconsistent	36	27.3%	88	63.8%	2.3	–	–
		Odds (consistency)	–	2.7	–	0.6	–	4.7	1.5

Number and percentage of consistent and inconsistent details provided by truth tellers and liars; diagnostic values of consistency to predict truth-telling and of inconsistency (including omissions and commissions) to predict lying; the odds of consistency for truth tellers and liars, respectively; the odds ratio; and the natural log of the odds ratio. DV diagnostic values, OR odds ratio, Log(OR) natural log of the odds ratio

[a] Because there were only minor differences between unrehearsed and rehearsed liars, frequencies were summed across both lie conditions

[b] Vrij et al. counted the number of participants who contradicted themselves rather than the number of responses

[c] The numerator consists of the total number of details reported in the former of the two interviews

[d] The numerator consists of the total number of details reported in the latter of the two interviews

[e] Reflecting proportions of explicit details. Frequencies were not reported

condition). When the latter pairs returned, they were instructed to fabricate an alibi of having had lunch together during the time of the theft. Subsequently, all participants were informed that they were suspected of theft and interviewed individually (either ten minutes or a week later). During the interview, suspects were asked a number of general (anticipated) questions, as well as a number of unanticipated questions, including questions about the spatial layout of the restaurant. Furthermore, they were asked to draw a sketch of the layout of the restaurant. Leins et al. coded the level of consistency between the drawing and the verbal answers about the spatial layout of the restaurant, and found that truth tellers were significantly more consistent than liars (see Table 10.1).

In another recent study, Vrij et al. (2012) sent participants on a mission, during which they were intercepted by one interviewer from a friendly organization and one interviewer from a hostile organization (in counterbalanced order). Each interviewer asked four questions, two of which required participants to describe their route in chronological order, and two of which asked for a description of the route in reverse order. Participants were instructed to tell the truth about their mission to the interviewer from the friendly organization, but to lie to the interviewer from the hostile organization. Vrij et al. found that suspects were substantially more likely to contradict themselves within an interview when they were lying than when they were telling the truth (see Table 10.2).

Granhag et al. (2012b) examined the impact of three interviewing techniques on the levels of within-statement consistency displayed by innocent and guilty suspects. They instructed participants to go into a bookstore, where some participants stole a book (guilty condition), whereas others merely checked the price of the book (innocent condition). Subsequently, participants were accused of theft and interviewed. All participants were instructed to deny stealing the book. During the interview, the evidence was disclosed either before suspects provided their statement (Early Evidence), at the end of the interview (SUE-Basic), or in increments of strength and precision (SUE-Incremental). In the Early Evidence condition, there was no significant difference in within-statement consistency between liars and truth tellers. In contrast, in both SUE conditions, liars were significantly less consistent than truth tellers. The difference was most pronounced in the SUE-Incremental condition (see Table 10.1).

In a follow-up study, Granhag et al. (2012a) examined within-statement consistency in groups of three suspects. All groups were instructed to go into a room, where half of the groups checked some reference numbers and stole something from one of the packages, whereas the other groups only checked the reference numbers. Subsequently, all participants were accused of theft and interviewed individually, using one of the three interview techniques discussed above. In the Early Evidence condition, ratings of within-statement consistency were at ceiling for both truth-telling and lying suspects. When interviewed with SUE-Basic, lying suspects were slightly less consistent than truth-telling suspects, though the difference was not significant. When interviewed with SUE-Incremental, however, lying suspects were significantly less consistent than truth-telling suspects (see Table 10.1).

In sum, it seems that interview techniques may be used to improve the predictive value of within-statement consistency cues. Studies using artificial experimental set-ups, in which the "interview" task is automated (Walczyk et al. 2009, 2012), typically find that truth tellers are substantially more consistent than liars. In more naturalistic settings, on the other hand, in which suspects are interviewed by a trained interviewer (Granhag et al., 2012a, b), there seem to be smaller differences in within-statement consistency between liars and truth tellers. However, these differences can be amplified by asking unanticipated questions that are likely to impose additional cognitive load (Leins et al. 2011; Vrij et al. 2012), and by strategic disclosure of evidence, preferably in an incremental fashion (Granhag et al. 2012a, b).

Between-Statement Consistency

Another approach is to evaluate the consistency between two consecutive statements provided by the same suspect. Between-statement consistency can be evaluated not only in terms of the number of contradictions between statements, but also in terms of the extent to which two statements overlap. When looking at repeated statements over time, the degree of overlap of two statements is typically broken down into measures of "repetitions" (i.e., details that are mentioned during all statements), "omissions" (i.e., details that are mentioned in an earlier statement but not in a later statement), and "commissions" (i.e., details that are mentioned in a later statement but not in an earlier statement). For instance, Granhag and Strömwall's (2002) participants viewed a staged violent event and were interviewed on three occasions over a period of 11 days (see also Granhag and Strömwall 2001). Half of the participants were instructed to tell the truth about the witnessed event, whereas the other half were instructed to lie in order to cover up for the perpetrators. For 50 % of truthful and 50 % of deceptive participants, the frequencies of repetitions, omissions, commissions, and contradictions between the three statements were coded for four forensically relevant categories of information (e.g., which factor triggered the conflict). There were no direct contradictions in any of the statements, and there was no significant difference between liars and truth tellers in the proportion of details repeated or omitted (see Table 10.2). However, liars were significantly more likely than truth tellers to add details to later statements that they had not mentioned in earlier statements (i.e., commissions; see Table 10.2).

In a follow-up study conducted by Granhag et al. (2003), participants arrived at the laboratory in pairs. Half of the pairs had lunch together and were subsequently interviewed about the lunch (truth tellers). The remaining pairs did not have lunch together, but were instructed to state that they had had lunch together (liars). Granhag et al. included several measures of between-statement consistency. First, they assessed the number of repetitions, omissions, commissions, and contradictions between the two consecutive statements. There were only three contradictions in total, which were not analyzed further. There were no significant differences between liars and truth tellers in the number of repetitions and omissions, but this time it was the truth tellers who included significantly more new information than liars (see Table 10.2). In addition, Granhag et al. asked 120 independent participants to rate the consistency of statements on a scale from 1 (very low degree) to 10 (very high degree; see also Strömwall et al. 2003). Liars' statements tended to be rated as more consistent than truth tellers' statements, but this difference was not significant (see Table 10.1).

Strömwall and Granhag (2005) investigated the consistency between repeated statements made by 11-year old children. The children participated in two interviews, 1 week apart, about a magician show that they had either experienced (truth tellers) or imagined ("liars"). Strömwall and Granhag coded the number of repetitions, omissions, commissions, and contradictions in the children's statements, and found that the statements about real events contained significantly more omissions and commissions than the statements about imagined events, and slightly fewer repetitions (see Table 10.2). In other words, lying children were more consistent than truth-telling children.

Taken together, the findings reported by Granhag, Strömwall, and colleagues suggest that differences in between-statement consistency between liars and truth tellers are modest at best. When differences exist, the evidence suggests that consistency is indicative of lying rather than truth telling. This finding is in line with the repeat versus reconstruct hypothesis (Granhag and Strömwall 1999, 2000a), but at odds with popular beliefs about the relationship between consistency and lying (e.g., Potter and Brewer 1999). One exception to this general pattern of findings was that Granhag and Strömwall (2002) found that liars were significantly more likely to add new details to later statements than truth tellers. The reason for this exception is unclear, but it may have been due to methodological differences between the studies. For instance, Granhag and Strömwall's (2002) truth-telling participants were given extensive time to prepare their story, whereas truth-telling participants in the other studies (Granhag et al. 2003; Strömwall and Granhag 2005) did not receive time to prepare. Therefore, truth tellers in the latter studies may have had to "reconstruct" more than truth tellers in Granhag and Strömwall's (2002) study, resulting in less consistent testimony.

To the authors' knowledge, only one study has assessed between-statement consistency using a nonstandard interview approach. Leins et al. (2012) instructed half of their participants to perform a number of tasks (e.g., turn on the radio, complete a puzzle). The remaining participants did not perform the tasks but were instructed to convince the interviewer that they had. Participants were interviewed twice, reporting about the items in the room either verbally or by drawing a sketch. There were four interview conditions: verbal–verbal, pictorial–pictorial, verbal–pictorial, or pictorial–verbal. Overall, consistency between the two interviews was significantly higher for truth tellers than for liars. Furthermore, the difference between liars and truth tellers was larger when participants were asked to report in different response modes (verbal–pictorial or pictorial–verbal) than when they were asked to report in the same response modes (verbal–verbal or pictorial–pictorial; see Table 10.1). Leins et al. explain this finding in terms of cognitive flexibility. Truth tellers experienced the event perceptually, allowing them to draw on a rich memory trace when reporting the event in different ways. In contrast, liars likely only had a conceptual representation of the imagined events, reducing their flexibility in reporting the event in various modalities. In sum, it seems that differences in between-statement consistency between liars and truth tellers may be amplified by asking suspects to provide reports in varied response modes.

Within-Group Consistency

When there are multiple suspects in a case, it becomes possible to evaluate the degree of consistency between statements made by different suspects. Wagenaar and Dalderop (1994) were the first to assess this type of consistency. In their study, six pairs of participants went to the zoo, and six other pairs were asked to invent a story about going to the zoo together. Subsequently, all participants were interviewed individually about the zoo visit. In line with the repeat versus reconstruct hypothesis, Wagenaar and Dalderop found that lying pairs were significantly more consistent than truth-telling pairs (see Table 10.2). In a similar vein, in the previously discussed study involving pairs of suspects providing statements about a lunch meeting, Granhag et al. (2003) assessed the extent to which the two suspects' statements overlapped. The statements of lying suspects were found to contain significantly more overlapping themes than the statements of truth-telling suspects (see Table 10.1).

Two studies to date have examined the impact of nonstandard interview approaches on within-group consistency in adult suspects. First, Vrij et al. (2009) used a similar methodology as Granhag et al. (2003), in which pairs of suspects either had lunch together or invented a story about having lunch. However, Vrij et al. introduced a number of unanticipated questions during the interview (e.g., "Who finished his food first?") in addition to the more standard, anticipated questions (e.g., "What did you do in the restaurant?"). For the anticipated questions, there was no significant difference in correspondence between lying and truth-telling pairs. In response to the unanticipated questions, however, lying pairs of suspects contradicted each other significantly more than truth-telling pairs (see Table 10.1). Second, Granhag et al. (2012a) extended previous research on within-group consistency by assessing consistency for groups of three suspects (i.e., within-triad consistency), and by evaluating the impact of three interview techniques (Early Evidence, SUE-Basic, and SUE-Incremental). They used a mock theft paradigm, after which suspects were interviewed individually. Overall, within-triad consistency was significantly higher for truth-telling groups of suspects than for lying groups. Furthermore, the difference between lying and truth-telling triads was significant for the SUE-Basic and the SUE-Incremental conditions, but not for the Early Evidence condition (see Table 10.1).

In addition, three studies to date have investigated within-group consistency for younger participants. Strömwall and Granhag (2007) recruited pairs of adolescents (aged 12–13), half of whom experienced an encounter with an unknown man, whereas the other half were instructed to imagine and discuss such an encounter. All adolescents were interviewed individually. Truth-telling pairs of adolescents were found to be significantly more consistent than lying pairs (see Table 10.2). Vredeveldt and Wagenaar (2013) conducted a similar study with pairs of children aged 8–10. Again, it was found that truth-telling pairs provided significantly more consistent responses than lying pairs (see Table 10.2)—a finding at odds with Granhag et al.'s (2003) findings for adult pairs. Finally, in Roos af Hjelmsäter et al.'s (2012) study, adolescents aged 13–14 participated in groups of three. They experienced or imagined the same event as Strömwall and Granhag's (2007) participants, after which they were interviewed individually. In addition to the anticipated questions used by Strömwall and Granhag, adolescents in Roos af Hjelmsäter et al.'s study were given an unanticipated task, namely, drawing the positions of the actors on a spatial layout. Subsequently, adult observers rated the truth-telling triads as significantly more consistent than the lying triads. Interestingly, the difference between liars and truth tellers was only significant for the unanticipated task.

In sum, in "standard" interview settings, lying groups of adult suspects are often found to be either more consistent (Granhag et al. 2003; Wagenaar and Dalderop 1994) or equally consistent (Granhag et al. 2012a; Vrij et al. 2009) as truth-telling groups of suspects. In contrast, lying groups of children or adolescents are typically found to be *less* consistent than their truth-telling counterparts (Roos af Hjelmsäter et al. 2012; Strömwall and Granhag 2007; Vredeveldt and Wagenaar 2013). The difference between adults and children might be explained in light of developmental differences in social and cognitive functioning. Children are typically less aware of their own and other's mental states than adults are (Gallup 1998; Johnson et al. 2005), which makes them less likely to grasp the importance of appearing consistent with their group members in order to convince others of their truthfulness. Furthermore, even if children are aware of the importance of appearing consistent, they may be less skilful at controlling the verbal content of their statements than adults are (cf. Talwar & Lee 2002). Finally, children typically behave more egocentrically than adults (Epley et al. 2004), and hence may be less successful in collaborating with their peers to create a mutually coherent story.

Regardless of age, certain interview techniques have been found to increase differences between lying and truth-telling groups of suspects. Thus, when the interviewer poses unanticipated questions (Roos af Hjelmsäter et al. 2012; Vrij et al. 2009) or uses evidence strategically (Granhag et al. 2012a), more inconsistencies between lying suspects may be exposed.

Statement-Evidence Consistency

In cases in which police interviewers have access to evidence that is independent from the statements provided by suspects, they have the opportunity to examine an additional index of consistency, namely the extent to which the statement is consistent with the other evidence.

Hartwig et al. (2005) were among the first to examine consistency in a scenario in which other evidence was available. They used a mock crime paradigm, in which participants in the guilty condition were instructed to steal a wallet from a briefcase in a video store, whereas participants in the innocent condition only looked for a particular movie (moving the briefcase during their search) and left the store empty-handed. After a week, all participants came back to the laboratory and were informed that they would be interviewed due to suspicions of theft. During the interview, they were presented with three pieces of evidence (e.g., fingerprints on the briefcase), which could be viewed as incriminating, but could also be explained by the innocent task alibi. The evidence was disclosed either early or late in the interview. To measure statement-evidence consistency, Hartwig et al. coded the extent to which suspects contradicted the evidence when they were asked questions about the event. In the early-disclosure condition, liars and truth tellers were found to be equally consistent with the evidence. In the late-disclosure condition, however, liars were significantly less consistent than truth tellers (see Table 10.1).

Jordan et al. (2012) used the same experimental paradigm as Hartwig et al. (2005) and found that truthful statements were significantly more consistent with the evidence than deceptive statements in both the early- and late-disclosure conditions. However, in line with Hartwig and colleagues' findings, the absolute difference between liars and truth tellers was larger in the late-disclosure condition than in the early-disclosure condition (see Table 10.1).[1] In a similar mock crime paradigm, Clemens et al. (2010) examined the effect of late disclosure of evidence on statement-evidence consistency in statements provided by adolescents aged 12–14. Overall, truth-telling adolescents were more consistent with the evidence than lying adolescents (see Table 10.1). Furthermore, for the most incriminating piece of evidence, liars in the late disclosure condition were significantly less consistent with the evidence than liars in the early-disclosure condition.

Hartwig et al. (2006) trained 41 police trainees in the use of the SUE technique, whereas 41 other police trainees were not trained. These trainees then interviewed participants suspected of a theft, in a similar mock theft paradigm as described above. Statement-evidence consistency was significantly higher for truth tellers than for liars. Moreover, lying suspects interviewed by the SUE trainees displayed significantly lower statement-evidence consistency than lying suspects interviewed by the other trainees, whereas SUE training had no significant impact on the degree of statement-evidence consistency displayed by truth tellers (see Table 10.1). In short, the use of SUE amplified differences in statement-evidence consistency between liars and truth tellers.

Granhag et al. (2012b) also examined the impact of interviewing techniques (Early Evidence, SUE-Basic, and SUE-Incremental) on the degree of statement-evidence consistency displayed by innocent and guilty suspects accused of stealing a book. Across all interview conditions, truth tellers displayed significantly higher statement-evidence consistency than liars, but the size of the difference between liars and truth tellers was largest in the SUE-Incremental condition (see Table 10.1).[2] In a similar vein, Granhag et al. (2012a) examined statement-evidence consistency for guilty and innocent suspects interviewed with one of the same three interview techniques. Statement-evidence consistency tended to be higher for truth

---

[1] Note that the SMD was larger for the early-disclosure condition due to the small standard deviation for innocent suspects in that condition (the accuracy of which was confirmed with the authors of the article).

[2] It should be noted that the large difference between liars and truth tellers in the SUE-Incremental condition was due to the relatively high level of statement-evidence consistency observed for truth tellers in this condition. Contrary to expectations, deceptive statements in the SUE-Incremental condition were nearly as consistent with the evidence as those in the Early Evidence condition.

tellers than for liars in all conditions, but the difference was only significant in the SUE-Incremental condition. Table 10.1 shows that liars in this condition displayed substantially lower statement-evidence consistency than truth tellers.

In most of the studies on statement-evidence consistency, interviewers used a combination of open- and closed-ended questions. Hartwig et al. (2011) examined which of these types of questions is most effective in differentiating between liars and truth tellers based on statement-evidence consistency. They hypothesized that free-recall questions would allow lying suspects to evade mentioning any incriminating evidence, whereas closed-ended probing questions would cause them to contradict the evidence. In a mock-theft paradigm, suspects were assigned to one of three interview conditions: (a) free-recall questions only, (b) closed-ended questions only, or (c) a combination of free recall and closed-ended questions. Overall, deceptive statements were found to be significantly less consistent with the evidence than truthful statements. Furthermore, there was a significant interaction between veracity and interview condition: the difference in statement-evidence consistency between liars and truth tellers was smallest when suspects were only asked free-recall questions, and largest when they were only asked closed-ended probes (see Table 10.1). Thus, closed-ended questions allow for better differentiation between liars and truth tellers based on statement-evidence consistency than free-recall questions.

In sum, empirical findings suggest that truthful statements are typically either equally or more consistent with the other available evidence than deceptive statements are. Furthermore, differences in statement-evidence consistency between liars and truth tellers can be amplified by strategic use of the available evidence (e.g., Hartwig et al. 2006; Hartwig et al. 2005; Jordan et al. 2012). In this respect, incremental disclosure of evidence seems to be even more effective than late disclosure (Granhag et al. 2012a, 2012b), and closed-ended questions seem to be more effective than free-recall questions (Hartwig et al. 2011).

Conclusions and Future Directions

Consistency and Deception

The literature on the relationship between consistency and deception paints a relatively coherent picture. In terms of within-statement, between-statement, and within-group consistency, most studies employing standard face-to-face interviews have found that adult suspects who are lying are typically either equally consistent or more consistent than their truth-telling counterparts. This is in line with the repeat versus reconstruct hypothesis, which suggests that the "repeat" strategy employed by liars results in more consistent statements than truth tellers' "reconstruct from memory" strategy. However, in terms of statement-evidence consistency, liars' statements are typically either equally consistent or *less* consistent with the evidence than truth tellers' statements. Despite the differences depending on the type of consistency under investigation, the accumulative evidence seems to suggest that there is little empirical basis for the commonly held belief that truth-telling suspects are always more consistent than lying suspects.

Inspection of the effect sizes in Tables 10.1 and 10.2 confirms that differences in consistency between liars and truth tellers tend to be modest. Under "standard" conditions (in which the questions were anticipated or the evidence was disclosed early), the standardized mean differences (displayed in Table 10.1) ranged from negative to positive, and most were small (.20) to medium (.50) in size (as defined by Cohen 1992). In terms of diagnostic values (displayed in Table 10.2), consistency was not very diagnostic of truth telling in any of the studies included in this review, with DVs ranging from 0.5 (Wagenaar and Dalderop 1994) to 2.0 (Vredeveldt and Wagenaar 2013). In contrast, inconsistency was somewhat diagnostic of lying in some of the studies. It should be noted, however, that all studies with relatively high DVs for inconsistency (between 4.0 and 8.4) either employed artificial methodologies (Walczyk et al. 2009, 2012), or imposed cognitive load on the suspects (Vrij et al. 2012). Furthermore, even the highest DV in Table 10.2 does not seem very impressive in light of findings that properly conducted eyewitness identifications have DVs of around 15 (De Jong et al. 2005; Wagenaar and Van Der Schrier 1996). In sum, the popular belief that consistency is predictive of truth telling has not received empirical support, and the belief that inconsistency is predictive of lying has to date only received modest support, in experiments that were rather unrealistic.

Interview Approaches

In light of the relative lack of consistency differences between liars and truth tellers, several interview approaches have been developed to try to improve differentiation between liars and truth tellers. First, asking unanticipated questions during the interview has been found to elicit inconsistencies in liars' statements, in terms of within-statement consistency (Leins et al. 2011), between-statement consistency (Leins et al. 2012), and within-group consistency (Roos af Hjelmsäter et al. 2012; Vrij et al. 2009). Even though the unanticipated-question technique significantly increased differences in consistency between deceptive and truthful statements, the differences between lying and truth-telling suspects who were asked unanticipated questions were still only small to medium in size (see Table 10.1; Leins et al. 2012; Roos af Hjelmsäter et al. 2012; Vrij et al. 2009).

The strategic use of evidence during interviews has also been found to amplify differences between liars and truth tellers in terms of within-statement consistency (Granhag et al. 2012a, b), within-group consistency (Granhag et al. 2012a), and statement-evidence consistency (Granhag et al. 2012a, 2012b; Hartwig et al. 2006; Hartwig et al. 2005; Jordan et al. 2012). Moreover, when evidence was disclosed late in the interview, SMDs between liars and truth tellers were increased to medium (.50) to large (.80) in size, and when evidence was disclosed incrementally, all SMDs were above .80 (see Table 10.1). Thus, based on the evidence to date, strategic use of evidence seems to be the most effective way of increasing differences between liars and truth tellers.

One important unanswered question is the impact of imposing cognitive load during the interview on various types of consistency. We know from previous research that imposing cognitive load can amplify other cues to deception, such as increases in speech hesitations and decreases in spatial and auditory details in liars' statements (Vrij et al. 2008b; Vrij et al. 2010b). However, none of these studies have assessed consistency. Although Vrij et al. (2012) examined the impact of imposing cognitive load on consistency, they only analyzed contradictions that emerged *between* the chronological-order and reverse-order responses. Future investigations should compare consistency within statements provided under conditions of high cognitive load to consistency within statements provided in control conditions. Interestingly, Vrij et al. (2008b) state that they "have been told by several American investigators who used the reverse-order instruction when interviewing suspects, that suspects frequently gave themselves away with obviously non-credible stories that were replete with inconsistencies" (p. 263). This anecdotal evidence should be assessed more systematically in future research.

Limitations

These recent developments in investigative interviewing approaches provide some promising prospects for deception detection in the real world. Nevertheless, it should be noted that many of the studies on which these approaches are based have limited ecological validity (cf. Van Koppen 2012). First, most studies recruit undergraduate students as participants, a group that is unlikely to be representative of real criminal suspects. In addition, the "crimes" committed by these participants are trivial, and do not have any real consequences for the participants. In fact, in the typical experimental setup, the "liar" is asked to lie by the experimenter. Thus, lying is desired in these experiments, whereas it is usually considered wrong in real police interviews. The conditions for truth tellers may be exactly the other way around. In real police interviews, truth telling is considered desirable and relatively easy to do, whereas truth telling in experiments may sometimes be more demanding than lying. Truth tellers can make mistakes, whereas liars can "win the game" by beating the experimental interviewer. In that sense, the results of research to date may, with a little exaggeration, reflect the psychology of a game played by relatively intelligent students rather than what really goes on in the mind of the average suspect during police interviews.

Although ethical considerations prohibit researchers from alleviating some of these concerns about ecological validity, future research should make every attempt to approach real-world conditions as much as possible. For example, several researchers have evaluated the verbal and nonverbal behavior of individuals pleading for the return of a missing relative, half of whom were subsequently convicted of murdering the relative themselves (Ten Brinke and Porter 2012; Ten Brinke et al. 2012; Vrij and Mann 2001). This line of research is a step in the right direction toward more realistic deception detection research, and consistencies in such statements could be examined.

Another problem with the research on deception detection pertains to the issue of base rates. Typically, studies in this area employ base rates of 50 % guilty participants and 50 % innocent participants. In real life, however, suspects at the police station are typically there for a reason; that is, they are often suspects because there is strong or reasonable evidence against them. Although the true base rate of guilty suspects can never be known, legal-psychological scholars have estimated that the guilty base rate might be closer to 95 % than 50 % (Clark 2012; Crombag et al. 1992; Van Koppen 2012; Wagenaar 2005). The effectiveness of interview methods is heavily dependent on guilty base rates: if 95 % of suspects are guilty, investigators will achieve higher deception detection accuracy by using methods that are biased towards guilt than by using methods that are biased towards innocence. In fact, if a police officer uses any random method, valid or not, to assess the veracity of denying suspects, she is usually right if the method brings her to the conclusion that the suspect is lying. Of course, implementation of methods that are biased towards guilt is probably not desirable because society may place greater value on protecting the innocent than on convicting the guilty (cf. Clark 2012). Nevertheless, researchers should be more aware of the potentially skewed guilty base rate in the real world.

Conclusion

Taken together, the corpus of research on consistency and deception suggests that—contrary to beliefs held by lay people and legal professionals—consistency is not necessarily indicative of truth telling, and inconsistency is not necessarily a sign of lying. The research on interview approaches designed to amplify cues to deception has been immensely valuable in informing legal professionals about more effective methods of eliciting cues to deception. Nevertheless, the general literature on suspect interviewing to date has perhaps focused a little too much on the detection of deception and the elicitation of confessions.

Looking ahead, we would welcome more research exploring interviewing approaches that promote the elicitation of forensically relevant information from suspects. In the literature on witness interviewing, this issue has received ample attention (see e.g., Memon et al. 2010; Vredeveldt and Penrod 2012; Wagstaff et al. 2011), and Fisher and Perez (2007) have suggested that some interview methods designed for witnesses may also be effective for use with suspects (as recommended since 1992 by the PEACE approach used nationally in England and Wales; Milne and Bull 1999). Eventually, we hope that converging evidence from empirical research will inform the implementation of suspect interview techniques that improve deception detection, increase the diagnosticity of confessions, *and* provide important new leads for further police investigation.

Appendix 1: Effect Size Estimates

Standardized Mean Difference

For studies in which mean consistency scores were obtained, we examined the standardized mean difference (SMD) between liars and truth tellers as an indicator of effect size. Because this measure tends to be upwardly biased when based on small samples, we provide an unbiased estimate of the SMD throughout this chapter (using the correction provided by Hedges (1981), which is depicted in the second part of the equation below), calculated as:

$$\text{SMD} = \left(\frac{\bar{X}_T - \bar{X}_L}{s_p} \right) \left(1 - \frac{3}{4N - 9} \right),$$

where $\bar{X}_T$ is the mean consistency score for truth tellers, $\bar{X}_L$ is the mean consistency score for liars, N is the total sample size and s_p is the pooled standard deviation, calculated as:

$$s_p = \sqrt{\frac{(n_T - 1)s_T^2 + (n_L - 1)s_L^2}{(n_T - 1) + (n_L - 1)}},$$

where n_T is the number of truth tellers, n_L is the number of liars, s_T is the standard deviation for truth tellers, and s_L is the standard deviation for liars.

Odds Ratio

For studies that used frequencies of consistent and inconsistent details for liars and truth tellers as the dependent measure, we examined the odds ratio (OR) as an indicator of effect size. The odds ratio is calculated as:

$$\text{Odds ratio} = \frac{ad}{bc},$$

where a is the number of consistent details provided by truth tellers, b the number of inconsistent details provided by truth tellers, c the number of consistent details provided by liars, and d the number of inconsistent details provided by liars (cf. Lipsey and Wilson 2001). An OR of 1 would indicate no relationship between consistency and truth telling, an OR greater than 1 suggests that consistency is predictive of truth telling, and an OR between 0 and 1 suggests that consistency is predictive of lying. For example, an OR of 4 would indicate that the odds of consistency are four times greater for truth tellers than for liars, whereas an OR of 0.25 would indicate that the odds of consistency are four times *smaller* for truth tellers than for liars.

References

Aron, R., & Rosner, J. L. (1985). *How to prepare witnesses for trial*. Colorado Springs: Shepard's/McGraw-Hill.

Baddeley, A. D., Eysenck, M., & Anderson, M. C. (2009). *Memory*. Hove: Psychology Press.

Bond, C. F., & DePaulo, B. M. (2006). Accuracy of deception judgments. *Personality & Social Psychology Review, 10,* 214–234. doi:10.1207/s15327957pspr1003_2.

Brewer, N., Potter, R., Fisher, R. P., Bond, N., & Luszcz, M. A. (1999). Beliefs and data on the relationship between consistency and accuracy of eyewitness testimony. *Applied Cognitive Psychology, 13,* 297–313. doi:10.1002/(sici)1099-0720(199908)13:4<297::aid-acp578>3.0.co; 2-s.

Buller, D. B., & Burgoon, J. K. (1996). Interpersonal deception theory. *Communication Theory, 6,* 203–242. doi:10.1111/j.1468-2885.1996.tb00127.x.

Caso, L., Vrij, A., Mann, S., & De Leo, G. (2006). Deceptive responses: The impact of verbal and non-verbal countermeasures. *Legal and Criminological Psychology, 11,* 99–111. doi:10.1348/135532505x49936.

Clark, S. E. (2012). Costs and benefits of eyewitness identification reform: Psychological science and public policy. *Perspectives on Psychological Science, 7,* 238–259. doi:10.1177/1745691612439584.

Clemens, F., Granhag, P. A., Strömwall, L. A., Vrij, A., Landström, S., Roos af Hjelmsäter, E., & Hartwig, M. (2010). Skulking around the dinosaur: Eliciting cues to children's deception via strategic disclosure of evidence. *Applied Cognitive Psychology, 24,* 925–940. doi:10.1002/acp.1597.

Cohen, J. (1992). A power primer. *Psychological Bulletin, 112,* 155–159. doi:10.1037/0033-2909.112.1.155.

Crombag, H. F. M., Van Koppen, P. J., & Wagenaar, W. A. (1992). *Dubieuze zaken: De psychologie van strafrechtelijk bewijs* (4th ed.). Amsterdam: Uitgeverij Contact.

Dando, C. J., & Bull, R. (2011). Maximising opportunities to detect verbal deception: Training police officers to interview tactically. *Journal of Investigative Psychology and Offender Profiling, 8,* 189–202. doi:10.1002/jip.145.

Dando, C. J., Bull, R., Ormerod, T. C., & Sandham, A. L. (2013). Helping to sort the liars from the truth-tellers: The gradual revelation of information during investigative interviews. *Legal and Criminological Psychology,* Advance online publication. doi: 10.1111/lcrp.12016.

De Jong, M., Wagenaar, W. A., Wolters, G., & Verstijnen, I. M. (2005). Familiar face recognition as a function of distance and illumination: A practical tool for use in the courtroom. *Psychology, Crime & Law, 11,* 87–97. doi:10.1080/10683160410001715123.

DePaulo, B. M., Lindsay, J. J., Malone, B. E., Muhlenbruck, L., Charlton, K., & Cooper, H. (2003). Cues to deception. *Psychological Bulletin, 129,* 74–118. doi:10.1037/0033-2909.129.1.74.

Epley, N., Morewedge, C. K., & Keysar, B. (2004). Perspective taking in children and adults: Equivalent egocentrism but differential correction. *Journal of Experimental Social Psychology, 40,* 760–768. doi:10.1016/j.jesp.2004.02.002.

Fisher, R. P., & Perez, V. (2007). Memory-enhancing techniques for interviewing crime suspects. In S. A. Christianson (Ed.), *Offenders' memories of violent crimes* (pp. 329–354). Chichester, UK: John Wiley & Sons, Ltd.

Gallup, G. G. (1998). Self-awareness and the evolution of social intelligence. *Behavioural Processes, 42,* 239–247. doi:10.1016/s0376-6357(97)00079-x.

Gilovich, T., Savitsky, K., & Medvec, V. H. (1998). The illusion of transparency: Biased assessments of others' ability to read one's emotional states. *Journal of Personality and Social Psychology, 75,* 332–346. doi:10.1037/0022-3514.75.2.332.

Glenberg, A. M., Schroeder, J. L., & Robertson, D. A. (1998). Averting the gaze disengages the environment and facilitates remembering. *Memory & Cognition, 26,* 651–658. doi:10.3758/BF03211385.

Granhag, P. A. (2010). *The Strategic Use of Evidence (SUE) technique: A scientific perspective.* Paper presented at the High Value Detainee Interrogation Group (HIG, FBI). HIG Research Symposium: Interrogation in the European Union, Washington, D.C.

Granhag, P. A., & Hartwig, M. (2008). A new theoretical perspective on deception detection: On the psychology of instrumental mind-reading. *Psychology, Crime & Law, 14,* 189–200. doi:10.1080/10683160701645181.

Granhag, P. A., & Strömwall, L. A. (1999). Repeated interrogations—Stretching the deception detection paradigm. *Expert Evidence, 7,* 163–174. doi:10.1023/a:1008993326434.

Granhag, P. A., & Strömwall, L. A. (2000a). Deception detection: Examining the consistency heuristic. In C. M. Breur, M. M. Kommer, J. F. Nijboer & J. M. Reintjes (Eds.), *New trends in criminal investigation and evidence* (Vol. 2, pp. 309–321). Antwerpen: Intresentia.

Granhag, P. A., & Strömwall, L. A. (2000b). Effects of preconceptions on deception detection and new answers to why lie-catchers often fail. *Psychology, Crime & Law, 6,* 197–218. doi:10.1080/10683160008409804.

Granhag, P. A., & Strömwall, L. A. (2001). Deception detection based on repeated interrogations. *Legal and Criminological Psychology, 6,* 85–101. doi:10.1348/135532501168217.

Granhag, P. A., & Strömwall, L. A. (2002). Repeated interrogations: Verbal and non-verbal cues to deception. *Applied Cognitive Psychology, 16,* 243–257. doi:10.1002/acp.784.

Granhag, P. A., Strömwall, L. A., & Jonsson, A.C. (2003). Partners in crime: How liars in collusion betray themselves. *Journal of Applied Social Psychology, 33,* 848–868. doi:10.1111/j.1559-1816.2003.tb01928.x.

Granhag, P. A., Rangmar, J., & Strömwall, L. A. (2012a). Small cells of suspects: Eliciting cues to deception by strategic interviewing. *Manuscript submitted for publication.*

Granhag, P. A., Strömwall, L. A., Willén, R. M., & Hartwig, M. (2012b). Eliciting cues to deception by tactical disclosure of evidence: The first test of the Evidence Framing Matrix. *Legal and Criminological Psychology.* doi:10.1111/j.2044-8333.2012.02047.x.

Greuel, L. (1992). Police officers' beliefs about cues associated with deception in rape cases. In F. Lösel, D. Bender & T. Bliesener (Eds.), *Psychology and law —International perspectives* (pp. 234–239). Berlin: Walter de Gruyter.

Hartwig, M., & Bond, C. F. (2011). Why do lie-catchers fail? A lens model meta-analysis of human lie judgments. *Psychological Bulletin, 137,* 643–659. doi:10.1037/a0023589.

Hartwig, M., Granhag, P. A., Strömwall, L. A., & Vrij, A. (2005). Detecting deception via strategic disclosure of evidence. *Law and Human Behavior, 29,* 469–484. doi:10.1007/s10979-005-5521-x.

Hartwig, M., Granhag, P. A., Strömwall, L. A., & Kronkvist, O. (2006). Strategic use of evidence during police interviews. *Law and Human Behavior, 30,* 603–619. doi:10.1007/s10979-006-9053-9.

Hartwig, M., Granhag, P. A., & Strömwall, L. A. (2007). Guilty and innocent suspects' strategies during police interrogations. *Psychology, Crime & Law, 13,* 213–227.

Hartwig, M., Granhag, P. A., Strömwall, L. A., & Doering, N. (2010). Impression and information management: On the strategic self-regulation of innocent and guilty suspects. *The Open Criminology Journal, 3,* 10–16. doi:10.2174/1874917801003010010.

Hartwig, M., Granhag, P. A., Strömwall, L., Wolf, A. G., Vrij, A., & Roos af Hjelmsäter, E. (2011). Detecting deception in suspects: Verbal cues as a function of interview strategy. *Psychology, Crime & Law, 17,* 643–656. doi:10.1080/10683160903446982.

Hedges, L. V. (1981). Distribution theory for Glass's estimator of effect size and related estimators. *Journal of Educational Statistics, 6,* 107–128.

Johnson, A. K., Barnacz, A., Yokkaichi, T., Rubio, J., Racioppi, C., Shackelford, T. K., Fisher, M. L., Keenan, J. P. (2005). Me, myself, and lie: The role of self-awareness in deception. *Personality and Individual Differences, 38,* 1847–1853. doi:10.1016/j.paid.2004.11.013.

Jordan, S., Hartwig, M., Wallace, B., Dawson, E., & Xhihani, A. (2012). Early versus late disclosure of evidence: Effects on verbal cues to deception, confessions, and lie catchers' accuracy. *Journal of Investigative Psychology and Offender Profiling, 9,* 1–12. doi:10.1002/jip.1350.

Kassin, S. M. (2005). On the psychology of confessions: Does innocence put innocents at risk? *American Psychologist, 60*, 215–228. doi:10.1037/0003-066X.60.3.215.

Lancaster, G. L. J., Vrij, A., Hope, L., & Waller, B. (2012). Sorting the liars from the truth tellers: The benefits of asking unanticipated questions on lie detection. *Applied Cognitive Psychology.* doi:10.1002/acp.2879.

Leins, D. A., Fisher, R. P., Vrij, A., Leal, S., & Mann, S. (2011). Using sketch drawing to induce inconsistency in liars. *Legal and Criminological Psychology, 16*, 253–265. doi:10.1348/135532510x501775.

Leins, D. A., Fisher, R. P., & Vrij, A. (2012). Drawing on liars' lack of cognitive flexibility: Detecting deception through varying report modes. *Applied Cognitive Psychology, 26*, 601–607. doi:10.1002/acp.2837.

Lerner, M. J. (1980). *The belief in a just world.* New York: Plenum.

Lipsey, M. W., & Wilson, D. B. (2001). *Practical meta-analysis.* London: Sage Publications.

Liu, M., Granhag, P. A., Landström, S., Roos af Hjelmsäter, E., Strömwall, L. A., & Vrij, A. (2010). "Can you remember what was in your pocket when you were stung by a bee?": Eliciting cues to deception by asking the unanticipated. *The Open Criminology Journal, 3*, 31–36. doi:10.2174/1874917801003010031.

Loftus, E. F. (2003). Our changeable memories: Legal and practical implications. *Nature Reviews Neuroscience, 4*, 231–234. doi:10.1038/nrn1054.

Markson, L., & Paterson, K. B. (2009). Effects of gaze-aversion on visual-spatial imagination. *British Journal of Psychology, 100*, 553–563. doi: 10.1348/000712608X371762.

Memon, A., Meissner, C. A., & Fraser, J. (2010). The cognitive interview: A meta-analytic review and study space analysis of the past 25 years. *Psychology, Public Policy, and Law, 16*, 340–372. doi:10.1037/a0020518.

Milne, R., & Bull, R. (1999). *Investigative interviewing: Psychology and practice.* Chichester: Wiley.

Potter, R., & Brewer, N. (1999). Perceptions of witness behaviour-accuracy relationships held by police, lawyers and mock-jurors. *Psychiatry, Psychology and Law, 6*, 97–103. doi:10.1080/13218719909524952.

Roos af Hjelmsäter, E., Öhman, L., Granhag, P. A., & Vrij, A. (2012). 'Mapping' deception in adolescents: Eliciting cues to deceit through an unanticipated spatial drawing task. *Legal and Criminological Psychology.* doi:10.1111/j.2044-8333.2012.02068.x.

Strömwall, L. A., & Granhag, P. A. (2003). How to detect deception? Arresting the beliefs of police officers, prosecutors and judges. *Psychology, Crime & Law, 9*, 19–36. doi:10.1080/10683160308138.

Strömwall, L. A., & Granhag, P. A. (2005). Children's repeated lies and truths: Effects on adults' judgments and reality monitoring scores. *Psychiatry, Psychology and Law, 12*, 345–356. doi:10.1375/pplt.12.2.345.

Strömwall, L. A., & Granhag, P. A. (2007). Detecting deceit in pairs of children. *Journal of Applied Social Psychology, 37*, 1285–1304. doi:10.1111/j.1559-1816.2007.00213.x.

Strömwall, L. A., & Granhag, P. A., & Jonsson, A.-C. (2003). Deception among pairs: "Let's say we had lunch and hope they will swallow it!". *Psychology, Crime, and Law, 9*, 109–124. doi:10.1080/1068316031000116238.

Talwar, V., & Lee, K. (2002). Development of lying to conceal a transgression: Children's control of expressive behaviour during verbal deception. *International Journal of Behavioral Development, 26*, 436–444. doi:10.1080/01650250143000373.

Ten Brinke, L., & Porter, S. (2012). Cry me a river: Identifying the behavioural consequences of extremely high-stakes interpersonal deception. *Law and Human Behavior, 36*, 469–477. doi:10.1037/h0093929.

Ten Brinke, L., Porter, S., & Baker, A. (2012). Darwin the detective: Observable facial muscle contractions reveal emotional high-stakes lies. *Evolution and Human Behavior, 33*, 411–416. doi:10.1016/j.evolhumbehav.2011.12.003.

Van Koppen, P. J. (2012). Deception detection in police interrogations: Closing in on the context of criminal investigations. *Journal of Applied Research in Memory and Cognition, 1,* 124–125. doi:10.1016/j.jarmac.2012.04.005.

Vredeveldt, A., & Penrod, S. D. (2012). Eye-closure improves memory for a witnessed event under naturalistic conditions. *Psychology, Crime & Law.* doi:10.1080/1068316x.2012.700313.

Vredeveldt, A., & Wagenaar, W. A. (2013). Within-pair consistency in child witnesses: The diagnostic value of telling the same story. *Applied Cognitive Psychology.* doi:10.1002/acp.2921.

Vredeveldt, A., Hitch, G. J., & Baddeley, A. D. (2011). Eyeclosure helps memory by reducing cognitive load and enhancing visualisation. *Memory & Cognition, 39,* 1253–1263. doi:10.3758/s13421-011-0098-8.

Vrij, A. (2006). Challenging interviewees during interviews: The potential effects on lie detection. *Psychology, Crime & Law, 12,* 193–206. doi:10.1080/10683160512331331319.

Vrij, A., & Mann, S. (2001). Who killed my relative? Police officers' ability to detect real-life high-stakes lies. *Psychology, Crime & Law, 7,* 119–132. doi:10.1080/10683160108401791.

Vrij, A., & Granhag, P. A. (2012). Eliciting cues to deception and truth: What matters are the questions asked. *Journal of Applied Research in Memory and Cognition, 1,* 110–117. doi:10.1016/j.jarmac.2012.02.004.

Vrij, A., Akehurst, L., & Morris, P. E. (1997). Individual differences in hand movements during deception. *Journal of Nonverbal Behavior, 21,* 87–102. doi:10.1023/a:1024951902752.

Vrij, A., Fisher, R., Mann, S., & Leal, S. (2008a). A cognitive load approach to lie detection. *Journal of Investigative Psychology and Offender Profiling, 5,* 39–43. doi:10.1002/jip.82.

Vrij, A., Mann, S., Fisher, R., Leal, S., Milne, R., & Bull, R. (2008b). Increasing cognitive load to facilitate lie detection: The benefit of recalling an event in reverse order. *Law and Human Behavior, 32,* 253–265. doi:10.1007/s10979-007-9103-y.

Vrij, A., Leal, S., Granhag, P. A., Mann, S., Fisher, R., Hillman, J., & Sperry, K. (2009). Outsmarting the liars: The benefit of asking unanticipated questions. *Law and Human Behavior, 33,* 159–166. doi:10.1007/s10979-008-9143-y.

Vrij, A., Granhag, P. A., & Porter, S. (2010a). Pitfalls and opportunities in nonverbal and verbal lie detection. *Psychological Science in the Public Interest, 11,* 89–121. doi:10.1177/1529100610390861.

Vrij, A., Mann, S., Leal, S., & Fisher, R. (2010b). 'Look into my eyes': Can an instruction to maintain eye contact facilitate lie detection? *Psychology, Crime & Law, 16,* 327–348. doi:10.1080/10683160902740633.

Vrij, A., Granhag, P. A., Mann, S., & Leal, S. (2011). Outsmarting the liars: Toward a cognitive lie detection approach. *Current Directions in Psychological Science, 20,* 28–32. doi:10.1177/0963721410391245.

Vrij, A., Leal, S., Mann, S., & Fisher, R. (2012). Imposing cognitive load to elicit cues to deceit: Inducing the reverse order technique naturally. *Psychology, Crime & Law, 18,* 579–594. doi:10.1080/1068316x.2010.515987.

Wagenaar, W. A. (2005). De diagnostische waarde van bewijsmiddelen. In M. J. Sjerps & J. A. C. van Voorhout (Eds.), *Het onzekere bewijs: Gebruik van statistiek en kansrekening in het strafrecht* (pp. 3–26). Deventer: Kluwer.

Wagenaar, W. A., & Dalderop, A. (1994). *Remembering the zoo: A comparison of true and false stories told by pairs of witnesses.* Unpublished manuscript, Department of Experimental Psychology, Leiden University.

Wagenaar, W. A., & Van Der Schrier, J. H. (1996). Face recognition as a function of distance and illumination: A practical tool for use in the courtroom. *Psychology, Crime & Law, 2,* 321–332. doi:10.1080/10683169608409787.

Wagstaff, G. F., Wheatcroft, J. M., Caddick, A. M., Kirby, L. J., & Lamont, E. (2011). Enhancing witness memory with techniques derived from hypnotic investigative interviewing: Focused meditation, eye-closure, and context reinstatement. *International Journal of Clinical and Experimental Hypnosis, 59,* 146–164. doi:10.1080/00207144.2011.546180.

Walczyk, J. J., Mahoney, K., Doverspike, D., & Griffith-Ross, D. (2009). Cognitive lie detection: Response time and consistency of answers as cues to deception. *Journal of Business and Psychology, 24,* 33–49. doi:10.1007/s10869-009-9090-8.

Walczyk, J. J., Griffith, D. A., Yates, R., Visconte, S. R., Simoneaux, B., & Harris, L. L. (2012). LIE detection by inducing cognitive load: Eye movements and other cues to the false answers of "witnesses" to crimes. *Criminal Justice and Behavior, 39,* 887–909. doi:10.1177/0093854812437014.

Zuckerman, M., DePaulo, B. M., & Rosenthal, R. (1981). Verbal and nonverbal communication of deception. In L. Berkowitz (Ed.), *Advances in experimental social psychology* (Vol. 14, pp. 1–59). New York: Academic Press.

Chapter 11
Human Intelligence Interviewing and Interrogation: Assessing the Challenges of Developing an Ethical, Evidence-based Approach

Maria Hartwig, Christian A. Meissner and Matthew D. Semel

The purpose of this chapter is to review the available research on Human Intelligence (HUMINT) interrogations. We will argue that there has been a recent paradigm shift in the approach to HUMINT interrogations. We will describe the conceptual, methodological, and practical implications of this paradigm shift. The chapter will be structured as follows. First, we will describe the defining characteristics of HUMINT interrogations and outline the scope of our discussion. We will describe how the challenges of HUMINT interrogations may be similar as well as different from interrogations in criminal settings. Second, in order to provide a context for our claim of a paradigm shift, we provide a historical overview of practice and research on HUMINT interrogations. Third, we offer a review of the current state of knowledge about the psychology of HUMINT interrogations, with a particular focus on methods that have been shown to be effective. Finally, we will outline several challenges for future research in this domain, and discuss how research on HUMINT may proceed to fill the gap in current knowledge.

Interrogations in HUMINT and Criminal Contexts

Interviews and interrogations are major elements of intelligence gathering. The primary goal of intelligence collection from human sources is to elicit accurate and operationally useful information from another person. As straightforward as this may seem at first glance, HUMINT collection is associated with substantial difficulties,

M. Hartwig (✉)
John Jay College of Criminal Justice, New York, USA
e-mail: mhartwig@jjay.cuny.edu

C. A. Meissner
Iowa State University, Ames, Iowa, USA
e-mail: cmeissner@iastate.edu

M. D. Semel
e-mail: mds417@optonline.net

R. Bull (ed.), *Investigative Interviewing*, DOI 10.1007/978-1-4614-9642-7_11,
© Springer Science+Business Media New York 2014

involving for example, the complexities of cross-cultural interactions, the unreliable nature of human memory, and the inherent difficulties of distinguishing between true and false statements (Evans et al. 2010). In the last decade, the use of psychologically and physically coercive interrogation techniques that aim at reducing resistance and producing compliance has received considerable attention in the media, particularly the notorious so-called enhanced interrogation techniques employed under the Bush administration (e.g., Hersh 2004). Such techniques have been met with wide criticism, based on the arguments that they are ineffective and that they may violate international laws (Costanzo and Gerrity 2009). It is outside the scope of our chapter to provide a discussion of the legality and ethics of harsh interrogation techniques (for such discussions, see Abeles 2010; Boehm 2009; Zimbardo 2007). The point is simply that HUMINT policy and practice is now a common topic in the public discourse. However, the empirical body of work on HUMINT interrogations is still relatively small—an issue we will return to later in this chapter.

Interrogations are conducted in the realm of intelligence gathering. In the criminal justice systems, interviews and interrogations of suspects are important elements of criminal investigations. Recently, research has suggested that there may be substantial problems in current interrogation practice. More specifically, a wave of DNA exonerations has demonstrated that false confessions produced during a police interrogation are significant contributors to erroneous convictions (Cutler 2012; Drizin and Leo 2004). For example, data from the Innocence Project suggests that false confessions are involved in around 25 % of the known large number of erroneous convictions cases (www.innocenceproject.org; see also Sheck et al. 2000). A substantial proportion of these false confessions appear to stem from coercive and manipulative interrogation techniques (Kassin et al. 2010; Leo 2001). Partly as a function of the problem of false confessions, interrogations in criminal contexts have received considerable empirical attention in the last decades (Gudjonsson 2003; Kassin and Gudjonsson 2004).

Before we review the available research on interrogation, let us briefly outline the similarities and differences between HUMINT and criminal interrogations. First, how can interrogation be broadly defined? Evans et al. (2010) note that there is no consensus on a definition, after which they proceed to offer one definition of interrogation as "the systematic questioning of an individual perceived by investigators as noncooperative, within a custodial setting, for the purpose of obtaining reliable information in response to specific requirements" (p. 3). We rely on this definition here, with the exception that we do not consider interrogation to necessarily involve lack of cooperation on behalf of the individual being questioned.

Based on this definition, HUMINT and criminal interrogations have in common that they involve questioning of a suspect or source, with the particular aim of producing information. However, in our view, one of the critical differences between HUMINT and criminal interrogations is in the *kind* of information they aim at producing. Criminal interrogations typically focus on generating information about isolated, past events. Within this focus, there are some cultural differences in the focus of criminal interrogation. For example, interrogations in criminal investigations in the USA are heavily geared towards producing confessions (Kassin 1997).

In many western European legal systems, the focus is instead on generating objective facts about the crime in question (Bull and Milne 2004). Regardless of these differences, a characteristic element of criminal interrogations is that they are retrospective, closed-ended, and often confirmatory in nature, meaning that they typically attempt to produce information about single events in the past.

Compared to criminal interrogations, HUMINT interrogations may be more complex in nature. Generally speaking, HUMINT interrogations aim to map not only isolated past events, but also networks of people and events—i.e., large-scale operations. Moreover, they may be both retrospective and prospective in nature. That is, the goal of the interrogation may include not only mapping the past but also generating information about intentions, plans, and possible future events. It may be worth noting that the challenges of HUMINT are, in these respects, similar to those facing investigators of organized crime.

An additional difference between criminal and HUMINT interrogation is in the sociocultural dynamic between the interrogator and the source. In contrast to most criminal interrogations, HUMINT interrogations are frequently cross-cultural interactions. That is, the interrogator and the source may not share ethnicity, culture, or language. Because of this, HUMINT interrogations are sometimes conducted with the use of interpreters. Unfortunately, the dynamics of interviewing using interpreters have not been extensively mapped (Granhag et al. 2005).

A Historical Overview of HUMINT Interrogation Practice and Research

Before we turn to the current scientific research on HUMINT interrogations, we provide a brief historical overview of HUMINT interrogation. The purpose of this overview is to illustrate the fundamental change in the ethos of HUMINT interrogation policy, practice, and research. First, a note on the chronological scope of our review. We believe that a turning point in HUMINT policy and practice occurred in 2009, when President Obama signed Executive Order 13491, formally establishing the "United States Army Field Manual 2-22.3, Human Intelligence Collector Operations" as the norm for HUMINT interrogation (Brandon 2011). By simultaneously revoking order 13440, President Obama established that all HUMINT interrogation should conform to the Geneva convention, effectively banning the Bush regime's program of so-called enhanced interrogation techniques. Furthermore, the executive order called for the creation of a special task force, charged with the task of studying and evaluating current interrogation practice (i.e., the effectiveness of the techniques outlined in the Army Field Manual). Subsequently, the High-Value Detainee Interrogation Group (HIG) was formed. HIG's mission statement describes that it "will study the comparative effectiveness of interrogation approaches and techniques with the goal of identifying the most effective existing techniques and developing new lawful techniques to improve intelligence interviewing." Thus, an official research agenda to examine HUMINT interrogation techniques was put in place. In the section below, we aim to summarize the state of the field leading up to Obama's policy change.

Sources of Data. How might one find information about past interrogation policy and practice? There are several sources of data. A body of descriptive literature exists chronicling the experiences of HUMINT collectors and some of the techniques they have employed over the course of a number of conflicts. In addition, official manuals used in HUMINT interrogations are widely available both from booksellers and general sites on the Internet. Journalists have also reported extensively about HUMINT interrogations and have described practices sanctioned by the military as well as methods that the US military has not officially approved. Moreover, researchers have examined the behavior of American prisoners of war (POWs) during their internment and have sought to understand under what circumstances POWs become compliant and provide their captors with information. This early empirical work, designed to develop defensive interrogation strategies, or the ability to resist interrogations, ceased after the Korean War but still represents some of the most significant research to date about interrogations in the military context. In addition, individual interrogators, from World War II through the recent conflicts in Iraq and Afghanistan, have described their activities. Official information about the policies and practices of the Central Intelligence Agency (CIA) are more difficult to find. Reports generally consist of historical documents and books that use declassified material (McCoy 2006; Otterman 2007; Weiner 2007). Some declassified historical documents from the CIA are accessible via the Internet (e.g., Pribbenow, n.d.). Retired agents have written accounts of their service but these are subject to approval by the CIA (e.g., Scheuer 2007). Most significantly, the CIA sponsored much of the early scientific research about offensive and defensive interrogation strategies until alarm over the research caused the agency to cease its sponsorship (McCoy 2006).

Accounts from POWs: World War II and the Korean War. Accounts of the treatment of the US POWs in World War II and the Korean War suggest that the stresses of war and capture can make sources compliant, but have a negative effect on their ability to provide accurate and actionable intelligence (Biderman 1957, 1959). Isolation, sensory deprivation, and poor living conditions in prison camps were found to be negatively correlated with prisoners' ability to provide accurate intelligence, and would sometimes induce false confessions (Biderman 1960; Biderman and Zimmer 1961). With the advent of the Cold War, communist regimes frequently used interrogations to elicit false confessions or other propagandistic statements from captured US military personnel. For example, in the Korean War, 36 American airmen confessed to "a plot to bomb civilian targets" after undergoing what was then called "touchless torture" (Margulies 2006). High-value prisoners were isolated from all human contact, except for their interrogators, and at least one airman was held in solitary confinement for 10 months. The North Koreans and the Chinese subjected these prisoners to stress positions, such as standing for hours, and prolonged interrogation sessions during which questions were repeated over and over to disorient the subject. Guards threw food at the prisoners and forced them to defecate in public. According to Margulies, after being "exhausted and demoralized", the airmen's resistance was overcome and they eventually confessed. All the confessions elicited under these conditions were false.

Farber et al. (1957) also examined techniques to elicit false confessions, self-denunciations, or propagandistic statements used on American prisoners of war captured during the Korean conflict (see also Carlson 2002). During their captivity, American military personnel were subjected to extreme conditions including sleep deprivation, malnutrition, isolation, poor medical care, and continual threats of death or bodily harm. Farber et al. suggested that the prisoners' confinement included three overall elements (debility, dependency, and dread—DDD) that interacted to produce an overall, psychologically weakened effect on the prisoners. Debility was produced because prisoners were deprived of sleep, were denied consistent meals, and suffered from fatigue. In addition, prisoners were often in chronic pain resulting from untreated wounds and other medical problems that were ignored. As a result, captured personnel could not resist even minor physical abuse. Dependency was induced by the captives' weakened physical state and the fact that they were incapable of fulfilling their most basic needs. Dread resulted because prisoners were subjected to violence and continual threats of violence, loss of control, and even their inability to satisfy the demands of their interrogators.

In stark contrast to the approaches described above are the interrogation techniques employed by the legendary interrogator Hanns Joachim Scharff, who worked for the German Luftwaffe during World War II. Scharff was famed for his charm and his ability to extract information without coercion (Shoemaker 2008; Toliver 1997). His approach was characterized by two critical elements: First, he employed a humane approach to the people he interrogated. His style was conversational rather than adversarial, and he did not press the subjects for information (Scharff 1950). Instead, he learned as much as he could about the backgrounds of his subjects, including detailed personal information, before he started an interrogation. During the interrogations, he often told elaborate stories rather than bombarding the source with requests for information (Granhag et al. in press). Second, he approached interrogation strategically, viewing its purpose as gaining reliable information. In fact, his conversational style and tendency to tell stories (and allowing the subject to correct him or to confirm certain information in his stories) was a highly deliberate strategy, aimed at what is referred to as *information elicitation*. The goal of information elicitation was to produce information in such a fashion that the source remains unaware of the real aim of the exchange (Brandon et al. 2011). In other words, by creating an "I already know it all" illusion, sources would inadvertently supply information that Scharff did not previously know (Granhag et al. in press).

In sum, the evidence stemming from studies of POWs suggests that HUMINT interrogation during parts of the twentieth century were, with a few notable exceptions, characterized by psychological and physical coercion. Such methods certainly had powerful effects on subjects—they produced confessions and propaganda. However, such methods did not appear to be effective in generating reliable and actionable intelligence.

US Government Sponsored Research. The CIA directly or indirectly sponsored much of the research on offensive interrogation techniques until the 1970s (Kleinman 2006; McCoy 2005, 2006; Otterman 2007). Offensive interrogations are those designed to elicit information from a subject (in contrast to defensive interrogation techniques, which are designed to help military personnel withstand interrogation). A range of avenues were explored, including manipulation of the physical environment and psychological states through sensory deprivation isolation, and the use of psychoactive drugs. At its height, the research involved 80 institutions, 44 of them colleges or universities (Thomas 1977).

Sensory deprivation is aimed at drastically reducing the level of a person's normal sensory stimulation for a relatively prolonged period of time (Goldberger 1982). Anecdotal evidence from people who have experienced some form of sensory deprivation, such as prisoners, explorers, and the victims of ship wrecks, uniformly describe a craving for sensual stimuli as well as changes in thinking, feeling, and perception that can be accompanied by hallucination-like visions (Kubzansky 1961). Hinkle (1961) discussed experiments conducted by Hebb, another sometime CIA-funded researcher, on sensory deprivation. He concluded that within a few hours, sensory deprivation began to exact a toll on brain function, similar to the effects of beatings, starvation, or lack of sleep. In experiments where researchers reduced levels of perceptual sensation, primarily by restricting visual input, subjects experienced a generally disorganizing effect. In studies on general sensory deprivation (with the deprivation ranging from 3 min to 6 days), researchers observed a variety of cognitive and behavioral effects, including breakdown of visual-motor coordination, loss of accuracy in tactual perception and spatial orientation, difficulty in focusing, fluctuating curvature of lines and surfaces, and a general decrease in the efficiency of perceiving relevant stimuli (Kubzansky 1961).

Researchers also studied the psychological effects of isolation. Across studies, isolation negatively affected subjects' cognitive and decision-making capacities. Bexton et al. (1954) found that even after the experiment concluded, some subjects still experienced confusion. Overall, the predominant experiences after isolation were fatigue, drowsiness, confusion, loss of orientation, and a need to reorient oneself to the familiar aspects of reality (Kubzansky 1961). Kubzansky commented that depending on the relationship between interrogator and subject, the interrogator, in a case of isolation, might become associated with a relief from discomfort. As a result, a subject may be more willing to cooperate with the interrogator even though cognitive abilities and hence the ability to provide accurate information would be substantially impaired.

In addition, the CIA supported research on the effectiveness of psychoactive drugs to induce compliance and produce information. For example, the agency kept nine federal inmates high on LSD for 77 days to test the drug's effects (Weiner 2007). There were also experimental studies on other hallucinogenic drugs such as mescaline, as well as barbiturates (e.g., amobarbital). The conclusion from this work was that while subjects under the influence of drugs may produce information they otherwise would not, the reliability of this information was in serious doubt (Gottschalk 1961).

In sum, the CIA research corroborated the results of the POW studies and reinforced the conclusion that sensory deprivation and isolation, even for short periods, can seriously debilitate subjects. Hence, such techniques are not conducive to effective intelligence gathering. Although we acknowledge the glaring ethical problems this research raises, we will not discuss them here (see Skerker 2012 for an excellent and extensive treatment of these issues). Instead, we want to highlight the implicit model of HUMINT interrogation inherent in this research. It seems to be based on what we may a *compliance through stress model*. This model has at least three assumptions. First, sources will be reluctant to cooperate during interrogation. Second, by applying psychological (or physical) stress, such resistance will be broken down. And third, when resistance has been broken down, sources will be willing (and able) to produce reliable intelligence. As our review of current research will show, this model sharply contrasts with modern views on effective interrogation.

Relevant Research on Interviewing and Interrogation

As we note above, the modern scientific literature focusing specifically on HUMINT interrogation is slim. However, there is a large body of empirical work that has bearing on the challenges of HUMINT. Here, we review some of this research, and suggest important avenues for future research. First, we discuss the available literature on interview and interrogation techniques, focusing on approaches that both promote cooperation and effectively elicit information from memory. Second, we describe research on the challenges of assessing the credibility of information elicited during an interrogation, with a focus on recent research suggesting that certain interview approaches may facilitate the detection of deception. Finally, we identify several areas in need of further research with the goal of developing ethical, evidence-based approaches to HUMINT interrogation (see also Evans et al. 2010).

Methods of Intelligence Interviewing and Interrogation. At the heart of an effective HUMINT interview lies the methods used by an interrogator to break a subject's resistance, solicit and maintain their cooperation, and elicit from them detailed strategic information relevant to national-security interests. Much of the current training that both criminal investigators and intelligence personnel receive is based upon *customary knowledge*—interview practices that have developed over time through experience, that are handed down through observational learning and storytelling, and that are ultimately codified in manuals, policies, and regulations. Unfortunately, such knowledge lacks a systematic and unbiased perspective from which to determine causality. We propose that it is ultimately *scientific knowledge* that will improve the effectiveness of interview and interrogation methods—a perspective that is drawn from independent observation, is theory driven and empirically derived, and is founded upon the principles of replication and peer review. In this section, we briefly review the available research literature on methods of interviewing and interrogation, identifying those methods with the potential for improving HUMINT interrogations that seek to elicit critical intelligence information.

Empirical research on the efficacy of interview and interrogation approaches was initially motivated by claims of actual innocence in the US criminal justice system (e.g., Scheck et al. 2000). Over the past two decades, researchers have sought to understand how suspects may be led to falsely confess (see Gudjonsson 2003; Kassin et al. 2010), and the process by which memory may become contaminated through the interview process, leading witnesses and victims to misremember or misinterpret their experiences (see Brainerd and Reyna 2005; Loftus 2005). Much has been learned from this research that is relevant to the challenges of collecting HUMINT as a product of interview and interrogation methods (see Loftus 2011).

First, modern interrogation approaches often rely not upon physical coercion, but rather psychological manipulation of a source to elicit a statement or confirm available information—these approaches are often referred to as *accusatorial interrogation methods*. As described by Kassin and Gudjonsson (2004), accusatorial interrogations often involve three phases in which (a) a source is detained in a small room and left to experience the anxiety, insecurity, and uncertainty associated with police interrogation; (b) the source is then accused or confronted (sometimes falsely) with available information, is prevented from denying his/her involvement and is warned of the potential for significant consequences associated with their affiliations or actions (referred to as *maximization*); and finally (c) a now sympathetic interrogator attempts to gain the source's trust, offers face-saving excuses or justifications for their involvement, and implies more lenient consequences should the source provide information (referred to as *minimization*). Although customary knowledge (prior experience) leads experienced interrogators to purport that these methods are effective in producing confirmatory information from a source, scientific assessments suggest that accusatorial methods actually increase the likelihood of both true and false information when compared with a control (direct interview) condition (see Kassin et al. 2010; Meissner et al. 2012)—that is, these methods ultimately lead to confirmatory information gathering that is counterproductive to the HUMINT objective.

In contrast, several high-profile false confessions in England and Wales led to enactment of the Police and Criminal Evidence (PACE) Act of 1984 (Bull and Soukara 2010; Home Office 2003). This act prohibited the use of accusatorial methods and mandated the recording of custodial interrogations. In 1992, a new model of investigative interviewing was introduced in Great Britain (referred to as the PEACE model, see Milne and Bull 1999) that focuses on developing rapport, explaining the allegation and the seriousness of the offense, and emphasizing the importance of honesty and truth gathering. Individuals are provided the opportunity to offer their perspective without interruption, and only thereafter may interrogators engage using positive confrontation and identifying inconsistencies or contradictions. Ultimately, the goal of such *information-gathering methods* is one of "fact-finding" rather than that of obtaining a confirmatory statement (with an emphasis on the use of open-ended questions). In a recent systematic review of the available empirical literature on information-gathering approaches, Meissner et al. (2012) found that these approaches significantly increased truthful information from guilty individuals and significantly reduced the incidence of false information from innocent individuals when compared with accusatorial methods—in other words, information-gathering methods proved more diagnostic and productive to an investigation. Using a novel experimental paradigm that attempts to model the HUMINT interrogation context, Evans et al. (2013) recently replicated these findings and demonstrated that information-gathering approaches produced more information from guilty and innocent participants, including critical guilty knowledge that would further an intelligence investigation. Although further research and replication of these findings is warranted, the available research suggests that information-gathering approaches offer an effective alternative to modern accusatorial methods that pervade HUMINT training doctrine (i.e., customary knowledge).

Research has also highlighted the significant role of confirmatory hypothesis testing (or confirmation bias) on the elicitation of information in forensic settings. For example, compelling research by Loftus (2005, 2011) and others (e.g., Brainerd and Reyna 2005; Ceci and Bruck 1995) has detailed the ease with which human memory can become contaminated via suggestive and presumptive interview approaches, particularly for events in the distant past (Payne et al. 1994) and when the suggestive information is provided by another individual (Gabbert et al. 2003)—conditions that are relevant to the HUMINT interrogation context. Importantly, confirmation bias not only distorts the potential memory of the source, but it also has been shown to influence both perceptions of source veracity and the interrogation process itself. For example, as discussed below, Meissner and Kassin (2002) first demonstrated the role of investigator biases in judgments of truth and deception by showing that experience investigators demonstrate a proclivity to assume guilt or deception on the part of interviewees (see also Kassin et al. 2005; Meissner and Kassin 2004). This presumption of guilt has also been shown to influence the type of questions or interrogative approaches that investigators use in a suspect interview, leading to behavioral responses from the suspect that are consistent with this prior belief (including false information or confessions from innocent suspects)—a cycle of behavioral confirmation that only further increases an investigator's confidence in his/her hypothesis (see Kassin et al. 2005; Narchet et al. 2010).

A number of structured interview protocols have been developed to address the potential role of confirmatory hypothesis testing and memory contamination in the forensic setting, including protocols aimed at improving the recall of critical information from adults and children (cf. Lamb et al. 2008; Fisher and Geiselman 1992). Generally speaking, these interview protocols emphasize the importance of establishing rapport with the source, and encouraging the interviewer to introduce very little information during the interview but to instead allow opportunities for uninterrupted, free narrative responses from the individual. One interview protocol, the cognitive interview, further encourages the use of mnemonic prompts (such as context reinstatement, changing perspectives, or affording relevant retrieval cues) that have been shown to facilitate recall in basic memory research. A recent meta-analysis of the cognitive interview literature demonstrated a large and statistically significant increase in correct recall ($d = 1.20$) when the cognitive interview protocol was compared with that of a standard or structured interview protocol, with no significant effect on the accuracy of information elicited (Memon et al. 2010). Given the importance of eliciting event or person information from HUMINT sources, integration of the cognitive interview with a source that has been led to be cooperative is likely to significantly improve the amount of intelligence information elicited. As described below, use of the cognitive interview and its mnemonic prompts may also produce a corollary benefit—namely, enhancing interrogators' ability to distinguish between truth and deception.

Distinguishing between truth and deception in an interrogation. Veracity judgments are an important component of interrogations. Interrogators may face deception in many forms: For example, sources may misrepresent their identity, conceal information, or produce deliberately false information (Buller et al. 1994). Given that the aim of interrogation is to generate reliable information, it is critical for interrogators to assess the veracity of the information that is elicited during interrogation.

Psychologists have studied interpersonal deception and its detection for roughly half a century, and there is now a substantial body of research on the issue (for a comprehensive overview, see Vrij 2008). This research focuses on three primary questions. First, are there valid and reliable cues to deception? That is, do people behave differently when they provide false statements compared to when they are telling the truth? Second, how accurate are people at distinguishing between true and false statements? Third, are there ways in which people's ability to detect deception can be improved? Below we provide an overview of the major findings related to each of these questions.

There are hundreds of studies mapping the behavioral patterns of liars and truth tellers. Researchers have examined both verbal and nonverbal aspects of behavior in order to answer the question of whether there are cues to deception. This vast literature was synthesized in a meta-analysis by DePaulo et al. (2003), which incorporated 120 studies and 158 behavioral cues. Some cues were based on minute coding of behavior (e.g., the number of words spoken, the frequency of particular body movements), while others tapped into more global, impressionistic aspects of behavior (e.g., whether the communicator appeared positive, tense, or cooperative). Overall, the meta-analysis showed that the behavioral signs of deception are faint. That is, few of the 158 behaviors included in the meta-analysis were related to deception, and those that were actually associated with deception were only weakly linked. For example, contrary to widespread beliefs (Global Deception Research Team 2006), gaze aversion is not a reliable sign of deception, nor are frequent body movements and posture shifts (Strömwall et al. 2004). Behaviors that are most strongly linked to deception tend to be impressionistic cues—for example, liars appear more ambivalent and tense, they are perceived as less cooperative, and their speech seems less immediate and more uncertain.

How accurate are people at distinguishing between true and false statements? Researchers have examined human lie detection accuracy in a variety of ways (Frank 2005; Hartwig 2011). In the most typical approach, people are exposed to videotaped statements provided by participants in laboratory studies who generate either truthful statements or deliberately false statements about their opinions or attitudes, or about events that they have witnessed or participated in. In other studies, people are exposed to real life, high-stake lies in which others lie or tell the truth about serious crimes such as murder, rape or arson (Mann et al. 2004; Vrij and Mann 2001a, b). Summaries of this literature show that people obtain mediocre accuracy rates when facing this task—a meta-analysis of 206 lie detection studies showed an average accuracy rate of 54 %, which is far from impressive given that 50 % accuracy can be expected from chance alone (Bond and DePaulo 2006). Contrary to commonsense assumptions, meta-analytic results further show that lie detection accuracy rates are not higher when lies are told under high-stakes conditions. Instead, lie catchers are more prone to show a bias towards rendering lie judgments for statements told under high-stake conditions, suggesting that they may misinterpret the signs of pressure and motivation to convince emitted from both liars and truth tellers as signs of deception.

It is intuitively appealing to think that some people are better than others at detecting lies, due to some inherent skill, or as a function of training and "on-the job" experience (DePaulo and Pfeifer 1986, Garrido et al. 2004). Indeed, a large survey of US law enforcement officers showed a purported accuracy rate of 77 % (Kassin et al. 2007). There are two bodies of empirical evidence of relevance to this question. First, a meta-analysis of individual differences in lie detection accuracy showed that people differ no more in their ability to detect deception than what can be expected by chance (Bond and DePaulo 2008). This suggests that lie detection cannot readily be construed as a skill that some people possess to a greater extent than others (see also Leach et al. 2009). Second, comparisons of lay people and presumed lie experts such as police officers, customs officers, and prison guards show that they too obtain hit rates around the level of chance (Bond and DePaulo 2006; Hartwig et al. 2004; Kassin et al. 2005; Kraut and Poe 1980; Meissner and Kassin 2002, 2004). Thus, the self-reported accuracy rates of law enforcement officers reported by Kassin et al. (2007) appear to be substantial overestimates of their actual performance. Even though presumed lie experts achieve similar hit rates as lay people, it is worth noting that their decision making differs in critical ways: they demonstrate a bias towards rendering lie judgments, and they show overconfidence in these judgments when compared to lay people (Kassin et al. 2005; Meissner and Kassin 2002, 2004).

In sum then, a large body of empirical literature offers a rather robust conclusion that human lie detection accuracy is mediocre. This finding holds true for low- and high-stake lies and for lay people and presumed lie experts alike. Recently, Hartwig and Bond (2011) conducted a meta-analysis of the deception literature with the aim of understanding why lie detection accuracy rates are so consistently poor. Their analysis suggested the primary reason is that cues to deception are so weak—that is, lie catchers have little diagnostic material to rely on.

So far, we have painted a rather pessimistic picture of the possibilities of making accurate judgments of veracity. It seems that judgments of deception are error prone, even when made by experienced investigators who routinely assess credibility as part of their professional life. However, a wave of research produced in the last decade provides the basis for some optimism. This body of research is based on the premise that while liars might not automatically leak observable cues to deception, it may be possible to elicit cues to deception through strategic interview methods (Levine et al. 2010). That is, through strategic questioning it may be possible to magnify the behavioral differences between liars and truth tellers (Vrij and Granhag 2012), which in turn may lead to higher lie detection accuracy rates (Hartwig and Bond 2011). This line of research on interviewing to detect deception is of particular relevance for HUMINT interrogations, as it has clear practical implications for how such interrogations may be planned and carried out.

The methods to elicit cues to deception have in common that they emphasize cognitive rather than emotional differences between liars and truth tellers. That is, they assume that while liars may not necessarily be more nervous, uncomfortable, or anxious than truth tellers, they may differ in the amount of mental load they experience, and/or in the way they strategize and plan their statements (Vrij and Granhag 2012). For example, the *cognitive load approach* posits that lying is more mentally taxing than telling the truth, because liars face a more demanding task (for a discussion on cognitive load during lying, see Vrij et al. 2006, 2008). The cognitive load approach further suggests that by imposing additional cognitive load on liars and truth tellers, liars (who are already taxed by the mental burden of lying) may display more signs of being mentally burdened than truth tellers. Several studies support these assumptions. In brief, these studies show that when liars and truth tellers are asked to provide their statements under cognitively demanding conditions (e.g., by being asked to maintain eye contact with the interviewer, or by being asked to tell their story in reverse chronological order), liars display more cues to deception, and lie catchers are more accurate at distinguishing between true and false statements (e.g., Evans et al. 2013; Vrij et al. 2008).

Another approach to elicit cues to deception is based on the assumption that liars plan some, but not all of their responses. That is, they anticipate certain questions, and they prepare answers in response to these. This strategy makes sense—planning might make lying easier, and planned lies are generally associated with fewer cues to deception (DePaulo et al. 2003). However, the fact that liars only plan some of their responses can be exploited in order to produce cues to deception (Lancaster et al. 2013). In one study, researchers interviewed pairs of mock suspects, some of whom were telling the truth about going to lunch together, some of whom were lying about going to lunch in order to conceal a transgression. In response to the anticipated questions (e.g., regarding what they did in the restaurants), liars' responses were consistent with each other. In contrast, when asked questions they had not anticipated (e.g., when they were asked to provide a sketch of the outline of the restaurant), discrepancies between the liars' accounts emerged (Vrij et al. 2009). In another study, liars and truth tellers were interviewed about an upcoming trip (Warmelink et al. in press). Liars offered significantly less detailed responses to questions that were unanticipated (e.g., "What part of your trip was the most difficult to plan?") compared to questions that were anticipated (e.g., "What is the reason for your trip?"; for a related finding, see Sooniste et al. in press).

A third line of research, similarly anchored in the notion that liars plan and strategize prior to an interrogation is the Strategic Use of Evidence (SUE) technique (Hartwig and Granhag in press). More specifically, the SUE approach is based on the assumption that liars have different counter-interrogation strategies than truth tellers. In other words, while liars and truth tellers share the goal of convincing an interrogator of their story, they differ in the approaches they take to reach this goal (Granhag and Hartwig 2008). In particular, they differ in terms of information management strategies—in contrast to truth tellers, liars are by definition motivated to conceal certain information from an interrogator. For example, they may want to conceal information about their involvement in a transgression, or they may hold information about other people's identities and actions that they are motivated to keep the interrogator ignorant about. Indeed, research on liars' counter-interrogation strategies suggests that a primary focus concerns information management: their verbal strategies tend to be either avoidance (i.e., not mentioning being at a certain place) or escape/denial (i.e., denying being at a certain place when asked about it). The SUE approach exploits these information management strategies by using the available background information strategically in order to highlight liars' avoidance and escape strategies. For example, in the first study of the SUE approach, liars stole a wallet from the briefcase, while truth tellers merely moved the briefcase in order to look for an item. The interrogator had some relevant background information in the form of witnesses placing the suspect at the scene of the crime, as well as the suspect's fingerprints on the briefcase. When this information was strategically with-held during the interrogation, and the interrogator asked a series of questions about the suspect's whereabouts and actions (see Hartwig et al. 2011), liars' stories were inconsistent with the known facts (e.g., they tended to avoid mentioning being at the scene of the crime, and they often denied having seen or handled the briefcase). Furthermore, law enforcement trainees who were taught the SUE principles and tactics, obtained substantially higher hit rates in distinguishing between truths and lies than what is typically observed in the deception literature (Hartwig et al. 2006). For further discussion of the SUE approach and the tactics derived from it, see Granhag et al. (2012).

In conclusion, while detecting deception is a difficult task, recent research suggests that strategic interviewing methods may increase the chances of correct judgments of credibility. Such interview methods are based on an understanding of the challenges liars face, and the planning and strategizing they engage in order to successfully deceive. Taken together with recent empirical research on effective interview and interrogation approaches, we believe that a rather firm evidence base exists to begin moving HUMINT interrogation practice from a customary to a scientific basis.

Future Directions in HUMINT Interviewing and Interrogation

While recent research efforts in the areas of interviewing, interrogation, and cred-ibility assessment offer an empirical perspective that can be readily applied to the HUMINT context, a number of other issues, some unique to the intelligence gath-ering challenge, will require further scientific inquiry. Based upon our interactions and collaborations with intelligence interrogators, we discuss below a few areas that require further focus and consideration by researchers.

Facilitating Communication Between Researchers and Practitioners: A Com-mon Language. A grand challenge often faced in our attempts to share important research insights with practitioners has to do with the terminology used by researchers to describe the various interview and interrogation methods that we assess. Quite simply, our research will only have impact to the extent that we (a) accurately reflect the use of certain interview and interrogation approaches and contexts in our studies and (b) facilitate understanding of key concepts and interrogative methods in our communication with practitioners. Terms such as *minimization* versus *maximization, mnemonic cues, cognitive load,* or *positive confrontation* have meaning to psychologists in the investigative interviewing arena, but can be quite confusing and misinterpreted when shared with practitioners. As we have noted here and elsewhere (see Meissner et al. 2010), we believe that collaboration between scientists and practitioners is key to improving the practice of interviewing and interrogation—and the foundation of any successful collaboration is a shared conceptual and linguistic understanding of the topic area. It will be important for researchers and professionals to generate a common language from which to operate. A wonderful example of this can be seen in a recent paper by Kelly et al. (2012), in which the authors (researchers and a practitioner) propose a taxonomy of interrogation methods that is grounded in both psychological theory and operational experience.

Cross-Cultural Perspectives in the Booth. HUMINT interrogations often involve foreign national sources or high-value suspects who have knowledge of threats to the security of the government. Such interviews or interrogations present occasions that necessarily invoke cross-cultural (and intergroup) processes—including communication, person perception, and social influence among others. Unfortunately, there is only a small body of literature applying basic, cross-cultural research on such processes to the investigative interviewing context, despite the critical need for such research. Recent studies by Buene et al. (2011, 2010, 2009; Giebels and Taylor 2009) provide an excellent model for addressing this challenge. Further research on the role of culture in judgments of credibility is also warranted (see Bond and Rao 2004), including the potential influence of cultural biases (see Castillo and Mallard 2012).

Interviewing Through an Interpreter: Linguistic Challenges to Communication, Persuasion, and Credibility Assessment. A related characteristic of HUMINT interrogations is their frequent use of interpreters to facilitate communication with foreign nationals. As may be evident, the use of an interpreter presents many challenges to an already complex interaction between the source and the interrogator. Interpreters may influence the flow and accuracy of information that is communicated across the parties, and may hinder the use of certain interrogation strategies or approaches (see Lai and Mulayim in press). Interpreter expertise and prior experience/knowledge of interview and interrogation methods may moderate these effects. Further, the mode of interpretation (consecutive intervals vs. simultaneous translation) and placement of the interpreter within the interview context may further influence communication, rapport development, and the effectiveness of attempts at persuasion. Finally, the impact of language on judgments of credibility must also be considered, with recent research suggesting effects on both accuracy and response bias (see Da Silva and Leach 2011; Evans et al. 2013).

Conceptualizing and Measuring Rapport. Professional interrogators will often describe the importance of *rapport* in facilitating cooperation and eliciting information from suspects (see Kleinman 2006; St. Yves 2006). Although rapport has been more widely assessed in clinical and negotiation contexts (see Tickle-Degnen and Rosenthal 1990), there is a critical need to both conceptualize and assess rapport in the interview and interrogation context. An excellent review of the relevant basic research literature has been offered by Abbe and Brandon (2013), as the authors highlight the importance of developing our understanding of rapport in the investigative interviewing context. Recent empirical studies by Bull and Soukara (2010), Driskell et al. (2013), and Vallano and Schreiber Compo (2011) have demonstrated the importance of rapport in police interviews on the elicitation of quality information from sources or witnesses (see also Walsh and Bull 2012). Further research that provides a strong theoretical basis for conceptualizing and measuring the behavioral manifestations of rapport in both the interviewee and interviewer, including the influence of pseudo rapport (see DePaulo and Bell 1990), appears warranted.

Moving From the Laboratory to the Field: Empirically Assessing the Effectiveness of Evidence-Based Methods in the Training Academy and in the Field. Finally, generating data from experimental research will undoubtedly lead to a strong evidence base from which to inform training and practice; however, we should be careful about simply "handing off" our research findings with the assumption that our findings will generalize beyond the laboratory. It will be important for researchers to partner with training academies and agencies to support experimental evaluations of the methods we develop in the laboratory in comparison with those methods currently trained and used in the field. Over the past few years we have begun such a process of partnering with trainers to develop training assessments— experimental tests of our methods versus that trained by the academy. These studies help to inform trainers and operators about the scientific process and provide an empirical basis for a potential policy change in the academy's curriculum. Further, it will be important to monitor the effectiveness of the training materials that are developed, and to assess the effectiveness of our novel approaches when deployed into the operational environment.

Conclusions

In the current chapter, we have sought to provide a historical overview of HUMINT interrogation practices and to describe the contemporary challenges faced by interrogators in this context. We have also reviewed research in the investigative interviewing realm that can offer a scientific perspective to the current use of customary knowledge. We believe that ethical, evidence-based approaches can be developed that offer an effective alternative to the use of physical or psychological coercive methods. Ultimately, we hope that other researchers will join us in addressing the unique challenges offered by the HUMINT context.

References

Abeles, N. (2010). Ethics and the interrogation of prisoners: An update. *Ethics & Behavior, 20,* 243–249. doi:10.1080/10508421003798976.

Bexton, W. H., Heron, W., & Scott, T. H. (1954). Effects of decreased variation in the sensory environment. *Canadian Journal of Psychology, 8,* 70–76.

Beune, K., Giebels, E., & Sanders, K. (2009). Are you talking to me? Influencing behaviour and culture in police interviews. *Psychology, Crime & Law, 15,* 597–617. doi:10.1080/10683160802442835

Biderman, A. D. (1957). Communist attempts to elicit false confessions from Air Force prisoners of war. *Bulletin of the New York Academy of Medicine, 33,* 616–625.

Biderman, A. D. (1959). Effects of Communist indoctrination attempts: Some comments based on an Air Force prisoner-of-war study. *Social Problems, 6,* 304–313. doi:10.1525/sp.1959.6.4.03a00040.

Biderman, A. D. (1960). Social-psychological needs and "involuntary" behavior as illustrated by compliance in interrogations. *Sociometry, 23,* 120–147. doi:10.2307/2785678.

Biderman, A. D., & Zimmer, H. (Eds.). (1961). *The manipulation of human behavior.* New York, NY: Wiley.

Boehm, D. (2009). Waterboarding, counter-resistance, and the law of torture: Articulating the legal underpinnings of U.S. interrogation policy. *University of Toledo Law Review, 41,* 1–41.

Bond, C. F. Jr., & DePaulo, B. M. (2006). Accuracy of deception judgments. *Personality & Social Psychology Review, 10,* 214–234. doi:10.1207/s15327957pspr1003_2.

Bond, C. F. Jr., & DePaulo, B. M. (2008). Individual differences in judging deception: Accuracy and bias. *Psychological Bulletin, 134,* 477–492. doi:10.1037/0033-2909.134.4.477.

Bond, C.F., Jr., & Rao, S.R. (2004). Lies travel: Mendacity in a mobile world. In P.A. Granhag, & L.A. Strömwall (Eds.), The detection of deception in forensic contexts (pp. 127–147). Cambridge: Cambridge University Press.

Brainerd, C. J., & Reyna, V. F. (2005). *The science of false memory.* Oxford: Oxford University Press.

Brandon, S. (2011). Impacts of psychological science on national security agencies post-9/11. *American Psychologist, 66,* 495–506.

Brandon, S., Bhatt, S., Justice, B. P., & Kleinman, S. M. (2011). *Army field manual 2-22.3 interrogation methods: A scientific review.* (FOUO).

Buene, K., Giebels, E., & Sanders, K. (2009). Are you talking to me? Influencing behaviour and culture in police interviews. *Psychology, Crime & Law, 15,* 597–617. doi:10.1080/10683160802442835.

Buene, K., Giebels, E., & Taylor, P. J. (2010). Patterns of interaction in police interviews: The role of cultural dependency. *Criminal Justice and Behavior, 37,* 904–925. doi:10.1177/0093854810369623.

Buene, K., Giebels, E., Adair, W. L., Fennis, B. M., & Van Der Zee, K. I. (2011). Strategic sequences in police interviews and the importance of order and cultural fit. *Criminal Justice and Behavior, 38 (9),* 934–954.

Bull, R. (1999). Police investigative interviewing. In A. Memon & R. Bull (Eds.), *Handbook of the psychology of interviewing* (pp. 279–292). Chichester: Wiley.

Bull, R., & Milne, B. (2004). Attempts to improve the police interviewing of suspects. In G. D. Lassiter (Ed.), *Interrogations, confessions, and entrapment* (pp. 181–196). New York: Kluwer.

Bull, R. & Soukara, S. (2010). What really happens in police interviews. In G. D. Lassiter & C. A. Meissner (Eds.), Police interrogations and false confessions: *Current research, practice, and policy recommendations.* Washington, DC: American Psychological Association.

Buller, D. B., Burgoon, J. K., White, C. H., & Ebesu, A. S. (1994). Interpersonal deception: VII. Behavioral profiles of falsification, equivocation, and concealment. *Journal of Language & Social Psychology, 13,* 366–395. doi:10.1177/0261927X94134002.

Carlson, L. H. (2002). *Remembered prisoners of a forgotten war.* New York: St. Martin's Press.

Castillo, P. A., & Mallard, D. (2012). Preventing cross-cultural bias in deception judgments: The role of expectancies about nonverbal behavior. *Journal of Cross-Cultural Psychology, 43 (6)*, 967–978.

Ceci SJ, Bruck M. 1995. Jeopardy in the Courtroom: A Scientific Analysis of Children's Testimony. Washington, DC: *Am. Psychol. Assoc.*

Costanzo, M. A., & Gerrity, E. (2009). The effects and effectiveness of using torture as an interrogation device: Using research to inform the policy debate. *Social Issues and Policy Review, 3*, 179–210. DOI: 10.1111/j.1751-2409.2009.01014.x.

Cutler, B. L. (2012). *Conviction of the innocent: Lessons from psychological research*. Washington, DC: American Psychological Association. doi:10.1037/13085-000.

DePaulo, B. M., & Bell, K. L. (1990). Rapport is not so soft anymore. *Psychological Inquiry, 1*(4), 305–308. doi:10.1207/s15327965pli0104_6

DePaulo, B. M., & Pfeifer, R. L. (1986). On-the-job experience and skill at detecting deception. *Journal of Applied Social Psychology, 16*, 249–267.

DePaulo, B. M., Lindsay, J. J., Malone, B. E., Muhlenbruck, L., Charlton, K., & Cooper, H. (2003). Cues to deception. *Psychological Bulletin, 129*, 74–118. doi:10.1037/0033-2909.129.1.74.

Drizin, S. A., & Leo, R. A. (2004). The problem of false confessions in the post-DNA world. *North Carolina Law Review, 82*, 891–1007.

Evans, J. R., Meissner, C. A., Brandon, S. E., Russano, M. B., & Kleinman, S. M. (2010). Criminal versus HUMINT interrogations: The importance of psychological science to improving interrogative practice. *Journal of Psychiatry & Law, 38*, 215–249.

Evans, J. R., Michael, S. W., Meissner, C. A., & Brandon, S. E. (2013). Validating a new assessment method for deception detection: Introducing a Psychologically Based Credibility Assessment Tool. *Journal of Applied Research in Memory & Cognition, 2*, 33–41.

Farber, I. E., Harlow, H., & West, L. (1957). Brainwashing, conditioning, and DDD (Debility, Dependency, and Dread). *Sociometry, 20*, 271–285.

Fisher, R. P., & Geiselman, R. E. (1992). Memory enhancing techniques for investigative interviewing: *The cognitive interview*. Springfield, IL, England: Charles C Thomas, Publisher.

Frank, M. G. (2005). Research methods in detecting deception research. In J. A. Harrigan, R. Rosenthal, K. R. Scherer, R. Rosenthal, & K. R. Scherer (Eds.), *The new handbook of methods in nonverbal behavior research* (pp. 341–368). New York, NY: Oxford University Press.

Gabbert, F., Memon, A., & Allan, K. (2003). Memory conformity: Can eyewitnesses influence each other's memories for an event? *Applied Cognitive Psychology, 17*(5), 533–543.

Garrido, E., Masip, J., & Herrero, C. (2004). Police officers' credibility judgments: Accuracy and estimated ability. *International Journal of Psychology, 39*, 254–275. doi:10.1080/00207590344000411.

Giebels, E., & Taylor, P. J. (2009). Interaction patterns in crisis negotiations: Persuasive arguments and cultural differences. *Journal of Applied Psychology, 94*, 5–19. doi:10.1037/a0012953.

Goldberger, L. (1982). Sensory deprivation and overload. In L. Goldberger & S. Bretznitz (Eds.), *Handbook on stress: Theoretical and clinical aspects* (pp. 410–418). New York: Free Press.

Gottschalk, L. A. (1961). The use of drugs in interrogation. In O. Biderman & H. Zimmer (Eds.), *The manipulation of human behavior* (pp. 96–141). New York: Wiley.

Granhag, P. A., & Hartwig, M. (2008). A new theoretical perspective on deception detection: On the psychology of instrumental mind reading. *Psychology, Crime & Law, 14*, 189–200.

Granhag, P. A., Cancino Montecinos, S., & Oleszkiewicz, S. (in press). Eliciting intelligence from informants: The first scientific test of the Scharff-technique. *Legal & Criminological Psychology*.

Granhag, P. A., Strömwall, L. A., Willén, R., & Hartwig, M. (2012). Eliciting cues to deception by tactical disclosure of evidence: The first test of the Evidence Framing Matrix. *Legal & Criminological Psychology*.

Gudjonsson, G. H. (2003). *The psychology of interrogations and confessions: A handbook*. Chichester: Wiley.

Hartwig, M. (2011). Methods in deception research. In R. Barry & P. Steven (Eds.), *Research methods in forensic psychology*. Chichester: Wiley.

Hartwig, M., & Granhag, P. A. (in press). Strategic use of evidence. In T. R. Levine & J. G. Golson (Eds), *Encyclopedia of lying and deception*. London: Sage Publications.

Hartwig, M., & Bond, C. F. Jr. (2011). Why do lie-catchers fail? A lens model meta-analysis of human lie judgments. *Psychological Bulletin, 137,* 643–659.

Hartwig, M., Granhag, P. A., Strömwall, L. A., & Vrij, A. (2004). Police officers' lie detection accuracy: Interrogating freely versus observing video. *Police Quarterly, 7,* 429–456.

Hartwig, M., Granhag, P. A., Strömwall, L. A., & Kronkvist, O. (2006). Strategic use of evidence during police interviews: When training to detect deception work. *Law & Human Behavior, 30,* 603–619.

Hartwig, M., Granhag, P. A., Strömwall, L. A., Wolf, A., Vrij, A., Roos af Hjelmsäter, E. (2011). Detecting deception in suspects: Verbal cues as a function of interview strategy. *Psychology, Crime, & Law, 17,* 643–656.

Hersh, S. M. (2004). Chain of command. *New Yorker, 80*(12), 38–43.

Hinkle, J. E. (1961). The physiological state of the interrogation subject as it affects brain function. In O. Biderman & H. Zimmer (Eds.), *The manipulation of human behavior* (pp. 19–50). New York: Wiley.

Home Office (2003). Police and criminal evidence act 1984. Codes of practice A-E revised edition. HMSO: London, UK.

Kassin, S. M. (1997). The psychology of confession evidence. *American Psychologist, 52,* 221–233.

Kassin, S. M., & Gudjonsson, G. H. (2004). The psychology of confessions: A review of the literature and issues. *Psychological Science in the Public Interest, 5,* 33–67. doi:10.1111/j.1529–1006.2004.00016.x.

Kassin, S. M., Meissner, C. A., & Norwick, R. J. (2005). 'I'd know a false confession if I saw one': A comparative study of college students and police investigators. *Law & Human Behavior, 29,* 211–227. doi:10.1007/s10979–005-2416–9.

Kassin, S. M., Leo, R. A., Meissner, C. A., Richman, K. D., Colwell, L. H., Leach, A., & La Fon, D. (2007). Police interviewing and interrogation: A self-report survey of police practices and beliefs. *Law & Human Behavior, 31,* 381–400.

Kassin, S. M., Drizin, S. A., Grisso, T., Gudjonsson, G. H., Leo, R. A., & Redlich, A. D. (2010). Police-induced confessions: Risk factors and recommendations. *Law & Human Behavior, 34,* 3–38. doi:10.1007/s10979–009-9188–6.

Kelly, C. E., Miller, J. C., Redlich, A. D., & Kleinman, S. M. (2013). A taxonomy of interrogation methods. *Psychology, Public Policy, And Law, 19*(2), 165–178. doi:10.1037/a0030310

Kleinman, S. M. (2006). KUBARK counterintelligence interrogation review: Observations of an interrogator. In R. A. Fein, P. Lehner, & B. Vossekuil's (Eds.), *Educing information: Interrogation art and science* (pp. 95–139). Washington, DC: National Defense Intelligence College.

Kraut, R.E., & Poe, D. (1980). Behavioral roots of person perception: The deception judgements of customs inspectors and laymen. *Journal of Personality and Social Psychology, 39,* 784–98.

Kubzansky, P. E. (1961). The effects of reduced environmental stimulation on human behavior: A review. In O. Biderman & H. Zimmer (Eds.), *The manipulation of human behavior* (pp. 51–95). New York: Wiley.

Lai, M., & Mulayim, S. (in press). Interpreter linguistic intervention in the strategies employed by police investigative interviews. *Police Practice and Research*.

Lamb, M. E., Hershkowitz, I., Orbach, Y., & Esplin, P. W. (2008). Tell me what happened: Structured Investigative Interviews of Child Victims and Witnesses. Chichester, UK: Wiley.

Lancaster, G. L. J., Vrij, A., Hope, L., & Waller, B. (2013). Sorting the liars from the truth tellers: The benefits of asking unanticipated questions on lie detection. *Applied Cognitive Psychology, 27, 107–114.* doi:10.1002/acp.2879.

Leach, A., Lindsay, R. L., Koehler, R., Beaudry, J. L., Bala, N. C., Lee, K., & Talwar, V. (2009). The reliability of lie detection performance. *Law & Human Behavior, 33,* 96–109. doi:10.1007/s10979–008-9137–9.

Leo, R. A. (2001). False confessions: Causes, consequences, and solutions. In S. D. Westervelt & J. A. Humphrey (Eds.), *Wrongly convicted: Perspectives on failed justice*. New Brunswick: Rutgers University Press.

Leo, R. A., & Davis, D. (2010). From false confession to wrongful conviction: Seven psychological processes. *Journal of Psychiatry & Law, 38*, 9–56.

Leo, R. A., & Drizin, S. A. (2010). The three errors: Pathways to false confession and wrongful conviction. In G. Lassiter & C. A. Meissner (Eds.), *Police interrogations and false confessions: Current research, practice, and policy recommendations* (pp. 9–30). Washington, DC: American Psychological Association. doi:10.1037/12085-001.

Levine, T. R., Shaw, A., & Shulman, H. C. (2010). Increasing deception detection accuracy with strategic questioning. *Human Communication Research, 36*, 216–231. doi:10.1111/j.1468-2958.2010.01374.x.

Loftus, E. F. (2005). Planting misinformation in the human mind: A 30-year investigation of the malleability of memory. *Learning & Memory, 12*, 361–366. doi:10.1101/lm.94705.

Loftus, E. F. (2011) Intelligence gathering post 9/11. *American Psychologist. 66*, 532–541

Mann, S., Vrij, A., & Bull, R. (2004). Detecting true lies: Police officers' ability to detect suspects' lies. *Journal of Applied Psychology, 89*, 137–149.

Margulies, J. (2006, October 2). The more subtle kind of torment. *The Washington Post*.

McCoy, A. W. (2005). Cruel science: CIA torture and U.S. foreign policy. *The New England Journal of Public Policy*, 209–262.

McCoy, A. W. (2006). *A question of torture: CIA interrogation from the cold war to the war on terror*. New York: Owl Books.

Meissner, C. A., & Kassin, S. M. (2002). "He's guilty!": Investigator bias in judgments of truth and deception. *Law & Human Behavior, 26*, 469–480.

Meissner, C. A., & Kassin, S. M. (2004). "You're guilty, so just confess!": Cognitive and behavioral confirmation biases in the interrogation room. In D. Lassiter's (Ed.), *Interrogations, confessions, and entrapment* (pp. 85–106). Kluwer Academic: Plenum Press.

Meissner, C. A., Russano, M. B., & Narchet, F. M. (2010). The importance of a laboratory science for improving the diagnostic value of confession evidence. In G. D. Lassiter & C. Meissner's (Eds.), Police Interrogations and False Confessions: *Current Research, Practice, and Policy Recommendations* (pp. 111–126). Washington, DC: APA.

Meissner, C. A., Redlich, A. D., Bhatt, S., & Brandon, S. (2012). Interview and interrogation methods and their effects on true and false confessions. *Campbell Systematic Reviews, 13*, 1–53. doi:10.4073/csr.2012.13.

Memon, A., Meissner, C. A., & Fraser, J. (2010). The Cognitive Interview: A meta-analytic review and study space analysis of the past 25 years. *Psychology, Public Policy, And Law, 16*(4), 340–372. doi:10.1037/a0020518.

Narchet, F. M., Meissner, C. A., & Russano, M. B. (2011). Modeling the influence of investigator bias on the elicitation of true and false confessions. *Law & Human Behavior, 35*, 452–465.

Otterman, M. (2007). *American torture: From the cold war to Abu Ghraib and beyond*. Michigan: Pluto Press.

Payne, D. G., Toglia, M. P., & Anastasi, J. S. (1994). Recognition performance level and the magnitude of the misinformation effect in eyewitness memory. *Psychonomic Bulletin & Review, 1*, 376–382.

Pribbenow, N. (n.d.) The man in the snow white cell. *Center for the Study of Intelligence*. www.cia.gov.

Scharff, H. J. (1950). Without torture. *Argosy, 39*, 87–91.

Scheck, B., Neufeld, P., & Dwyer, J. (2000). *Actual innocence: Five days to execution and other dispatches from the wrongly convicted*. New York: Doubleday.

Scheuer, M. (2007). *Imperial hubris: Why the West is losing the war on terror*. Dulles: Potomac Books, Inc.

Shoemaker, D. P. (2008). Unveiling Charlie: U.S. Interrogator's creative success against insurgents. In National Defense Intelligence College (Ed.), *Interrogation: World war II, Vietnam and Iraq* (pp. 77–146). Washington DC: NDIC Press.

Skerker, M. (2012). *An ethics of interrogation*. Chicago: University of Chicago Press.

Sooniste, T., Granhag, P. A., Knieps, M., & Vrij, A. (in press). True and false intentions: Asking about the past to detect lies about the future. *Psychology, Crime & Law*.

St. Yves, M. (2006). Psychology of rapport: Five basic rules. In T. Williamson et al (Eds) Investigative Interviewing: *Rights, Research, and Regulation* (pp. 87–106). Willan Publishing.

Strömwall, L. A., Granhag, P. A., & Hartwig, M. (2004). Practitioners' beliefs about deception. In P. A. Granhag & L. A. Strömwall (Eds.), *The detection of deception in forensic contexts*. Cambridge: Cambridge University Press.

Tickle-Degnen, L., & Rosenthal, R. (1990). The nature of rapport and its nonverbal correlates. *Psychological Inquiry, 1,* 285–293.

The Global Deception Research Team. (2006). A world of lies. *Journal of Cross-Cultural Psychology, 37,* 60–74.

Thomas, J. (1977, September 13). CIA says it found more secret papers on mind control. *The New York Times*. http://select.nytimes.com/gst/abstract.html?res=F70C1EFA385A167493C1A 91782D85F438785F9&scp=10&sq=cia%20says%20it%20found%20more%20secret%20 papers%20on%20mind%20control&st=cse. Accessed 27 March 2013.

Toliver, R. (1997). *The interrogator*. Pennsylvania: Schiffer Publishing.

Vallan, J. P., & Schreiber Compo, N. (2011). A comfortable witness is a good witness: Rapport-building and susceptibility to misinformation in an investigative mock-crime interview. *Applied Cognitive Psychology, 25*(6), 960–970.

Vrij, A. (2008). *Detecting lies and deceit: Pitfalls and opportunities* (2nd ed.). New York, NY: John Wiley & Sons.

Vrij, A., & Mann, S. (2001a). Telling and detecting lies in a high-stake situation: The case of a convicted murderer. *Applied Cognitive Psychology, 15,* 187–203.

Vrij, A., & Mann, S. (2001b). Who killed my relative? Police officers' ability to detect real-life high-stake lies. *Psychology, Crime, & Law, 7,* 119–132.

Vrij, A., & Granhag, P. A. (2012). Eliciting cues to deception and truth: What matters are the questions asked. *Journal of Applied Research in Memory & Cognition, 1,* 110–117.

Vrij, A., Fisher, R. P., Mann, S., & Leal, S. (2006). Detecting deception by manipulating cognitive load. *Trends in Cognitive Sciences, 10,* 141–142. doi:10.1016/j.tics.2006.02.003.

Vrij, A., Fisher, R. P., Mann, S., & Leal, S. (2008). A cognitive load approach to lie detection. *Journal of Investigative Psychology & Offender Profiling, 5,* 39–43. doi:10.1002/jip.82.

Vrij, A., Leal, S., Granhag, P. A., Mann, S., Fisher, R. P., Hillman, J., & Sperry, K. (2009). Outsmarting the liars: The benefit of asking unanticipated questions. *Law & Human Behavior, 33,* 159–166. doi:10.1007/s10979–008-9143-y.

Vrij, A., Leal, S., Mann, S., & Fisher, R. P. (2012a). Imposing cognitive load to elicit cues to deceit: Inducing the reverse order technique naturally. *Psychology, Crime & Law, 18,* 579–594. doi:10.1080/1068316X.2010.515987.

Vrij, A., Mann, S., Leal, S., & Fisher, R. (2012b). Is anyone there? Drawings as a tool to detect deceit in occupation interviews. *Psychology, Crime & Law, 18,* 377–388. doi:10.1080/1068316X.2010.498422.

Walsh, D., & Bull, R. (2012). Examining rapport in investigative interviews with suspects: Does its building and maintenance work? *Journal of Police and Criminal Psychology, 27,* 73–84.

Warmelink, L., Vrij, A., Mann, S., Jundi, S., & Granhag, P. A. (in press). The effect of question expectedness and experience on lying about intentions. *Acta Psychologica*.

Weiner, T. (2007). *Legacy of ashes: The history of the CIA*. New York: Doubleday.

Zimbardo, P. G. (2007). Thoughts on psychologists, ethics, and the use of torture in interrogations: Don't ignore varying roles and complexities. *Analyses of Social Issues & Public Policy, 7,* 65–73. doi:10.1111/j.1530–2415.2007.00122.x.

Chapter 12
Prosecutors' Perceptions on Improving Child Witness Interviews About Abuse

Kimberlee S. Burrows and Martine B. Powell

Child sexual abuse (CSA) is a global health problem affecting millions of children worldwide (World Health Organisation 1999). Estimates of prevalence rates of CSA in developed countries are between 20 and 36 % (Price-Robertson et al. 2010); however, arrest and conviction rates are low. CSA cases are more than twice as likely as other offences to be declined for prosecution, and those cases referred to police are less likely to result in charges being filed compared to similar crimes involving adults (Cross et al. 1995). The consequence of low arrest rates is that many child victims who report abuse receive no major protective intervention from authorities.

Low prosecution rates of CSA cases are due in large part to insufficient quality of evidence obtained from witnesses who allege abuse (Office of Director of Public Prosecutions (ACT) and Australian Federal Police 2005; Powell and Wright 2009; Success Works 2011). The investigative interview with the child complainant, which forms the statement and is conducted by authorised police or human service workers soon after referrals of abuse are made, is the primary (and sometimes only) evidence available to secure a conviction. Prosecution must rely heavily on the child investigative interview in CSA cases because there is usually no physical evidence or other witnesses to the abuse and because (in some jurisdictions) the investigative interview is electronically recorded and played as evidence in chief at the trial (Corns 2001).

Insufficient evidence obtained from child witnesses is due in part to the fact that disclosing and remembering abuse is a complex process. Recollecting abuse is determined by a wide range of factors including the physical, mental, and emotional state of the child at the time of the event and the interview; the nature of the event being recalled and the child's involvement in it. In particular, the child's social skills and linguistic and cognitive capacity have a large impact on the ability to understand questions, remember details, and provide reliable answers (Powell et al. 2009). Limitations in the evidence obtained from child witnesses are also due in part to a mismatch

K. S. Burrows (✉) · M. B. Powell
Deakin University, Melbourne, Australia
e-mail: kburrows@deakin.edu.au

M. B. Powell
e-mail: martine.powell@deakin.edu.au

R. Bull (ed.), *Investigative Interviewing,* DOI 10.1007/978-1-4614-9642-7_12,   229
© Springer Science+Business Media New York 2014

in the questions known to maximise detail and minimise error in children's accounts compared to the questions typically used in investigative interviews. Decades of laboratory and field research has shown that to maximise the accuracy and detail of evidence, interviewers need to rely on non-leading open-ended questions whereas short-answer questions that narrow response options are more common (Aldridge and Cameron 1999; Lamb et al. 2000; Powell et al. 2005). The reason for the mismatch is that maintaining open-ended questions is a skill that requires extensive training with ongoing practice and expert feedback; this has been difficult for police and human service organisations to deliver on a global scale (see Powell 2008).

The issues driving low prosecution rates, however, are complex. As well as reflecting limitations in child witness capabilities and interviewer performance, low prosecution rates reflect legal process and the nature of the detail required by law to prove charges. Aside from the degree to which interviews accommodate children's memory and language capabilities, the *persuasiveness* and *usefulness* of the evidence contained in CSA interviews needs to be considered. There has been much less research on child testimony from a prosecution (as opposed to developmental memory) focus and most of this prosecution work has been qualitative in nature, focusing on eliciting prosecutors' perspectives of CSA interviews via surveys, focus groups, and in-depth interviews as opposed to examining the statistical association between interview process and trial outcomes. Further, the perspectives of prosecutors have been given little airplay in the literature, yet they provide an important foundation for improving interview process and justice outcomes.

Overall, prior research regarding the persuasiveness and usefulness of CSA interviews has resulted in four major conclusions. First, prosecutors support the system of electronically recording child witness interviews over the previous system which involved the taking of written statements. Second, prosecutors perceive that interviewers need to become better attuned to the evidential details required for successful prosecution of CSA cases. It appears that interviewers tend to overestimate rather than underestimate the amount of contextual and time-related information that is required. Third, interviewers need to prioritise the elicitation of a cohesive narrative account of the offending from the witness perspective as opposed to using mainly short-answer questions. Finally, whilst prosecutors support electronic recording of child witness statements as evidence in chief at the trial, they believe there needs to be scope to supplement these interviews with additional live witness evidence. In the remainder of this chapter, we elaborate on these conclusions and describe the research that has underpinned them.

Electronic Recording of Child Witness Interviews Is Preferable to Written Statements

Traditionally, police interviewers took written statements from children who alleged abuse and if, and when, the matter went to court, children gave their evidence in its entirety at trial. Over the last two decades, some jurisdictions (including Australia,

New Zealand, the United Kingdom, Israel, and Canada) have introduced legislation permitting the pre-trial recording, and admission into evidence of investigative interviews. Typically, when concerns of child abuse arise, trained interviewers (usually police) conduct and electronically record an interview with the victim. Where the case proceeds to prosecution, the interview is compiled with other evidence into a brief. At trial, the recorded interview of the child is available for use as evidence in chief. The specific provisions for use of interviews in court vary across jurisdictions in terms of, for example, the class of witness for whom the provision is available (e.g. 'vulnerable witnesses', children under 18 years old, adults with a cognitive impairment), and the extent to which the interview may be supplemented with live questioning in court (i.e. in some jurisdictions, the interview must be used as the entirety of the evidence in chief, whilst in other jurisdictions, the trial prosecutor can choose to lead additional evidence from the child). Following their evidence in chief, the child is cross-examined, and re-examined before the remainder of the evidence (if any) is presented and the judge directs the jury to reach a verdict.

In those jurisdictions where a system of using pre-recorded child witness interviews as evidence has been adopted and subsequently evaluated by eliciting the perspective of prosecutors, support has been unanimous. Specifically, prosecutors (as well as judicial officers) prefer the use of pre-recorded interviews over the traditional system whereby children gave their entire evidence live in court. There are several perceived benefits. First, recorded interviews improve the accuracy and completeness of children's statements because they capture the evidence closer in time to the complaint, whilst the events are fresher in the child's memory (Bala et al. 2001; Burton et al. 2006; Cashmore and Trimboli 2005; Hanna et al. 2010; McConachy 2002; Washington Association of Prosecuting Attorneys (WAPA) 2006). A video recorded statement made close to the time of complaint also captures the child's body language and demeanour at the time of disclosure, facilitating a more vivid and compelling account (Powell and Wright 2009).

Second, as well as being in the interest of justice by facilitating the highest quality evidence, the process of pre-recording child witness interviews is perceived to reduce the emotional burden of testifying for child witnesses (Davies et al. 1995; McConachy 2002; Richards et al. 2007). Using a recorded interview as evidence in chief minimises the child's exposure to the courtroom, and spares the child from having to repeat their evidence numerous times, including at trial and at any subsequent hearings or retrials (Corns 2001). Third, recorded statements assist prosecutors with trial preparation and decision-making by enabling them to better determine the appropriate charges, assess the strength of the case, and evaluate the child's ability to give evidence (Richards et al. 2007; WAPA 2006). Finally, pre-recorded child witness interviews are advantageous in the sense that they enable defence counsel to scrutinise the interview process, thereby promoting improvement in interview quality and providing a basis for prosecutors to rebut claims that the interviewer used coercive and leading questions (McConachy 2002; WAPA 2006).

Interviewers Need to be Better Attuned to the Legal Requirements

One of the most prominent concerns expressed by prosecutors when reflecting on the quality and usefulness of interviews about alleged child abuse relates to interview length and relevance of interview content. For example, Burrows and Powell (in press a), who conducted 36 in-depth interviews with 19 Australian prosecutors shortly before and after the verdict was delivered in child abuse trials, revealed widespread criticism that interviews with child witnesses were too long and should be more tightly contained around core offence details which legislation requires to be proven to secure a conviction. Essentially, interviewers need to establish beyond reasonable doubt *what* offence occurred, and *who* perpetrated it. These elements also need to be comprehensively established for another reason. If, at trial during crossexamination, the child divulges further information about the elements that they have not volunteered previously, then defence counsel will inevitably argue that the new information must be fabricated, or the child would have disclosed it earlier (Burrows and Powell 2013).

For fairness to the accused, who is entitled to know the allegations against him or her, the account also needs to have sufficient particularity to identify and distinguish one incident from any other (Burrows and Powell 2013). However, prosecutors have complained that there is excessive focus on many highly specific event details and that such details are elicited in an interrogative manner, using an abundance of short-answer (i.e. specific and closed) questions. Concerns about excessive interview length and questioning about irrelevant contextual details have been reported across different jurisdictions such as the UK (Criminal Justice Joint Inspection [CJJI] 2012; Stern 2010), New Zealand (Hanna et al. 2010) as well as numerous Australian jurisdictions (Cashmore and Trimboli 2005; McConachy 2002).

Prosecutors have identified various topics which they believe interviewers unnecessarily pursue with questioning, thereby undermining evidential quality by contributing to inappropriate length and content of interviews. For example, there is often extensive questioning about particulars (i.e. details such as time, place, or context of offending) that are required in most jurisdictions to ensure each act of abuse is adequately identified (Guadagno et al. 2006; *S v. R* 1989). Unnecessary questions are also often asked (a) about 'fine tune' descriptive details such as the colour of clothing, bedding, and furniture at the scene of the offence (Burrows and Powell under review a); (b) about the meaning of obscure terms for genitalia (Burrows and Powell under review b); (c) during the rapport-building phase (CJJI 2012; Mckenzie 1993); and (d) when interviewers attempt to establish whether the child can distinguish the concepts of truth and lies (CJJI 2012).

The perceived disadvantages of long interviews which are not tightly contained around the legal elements of the offence are as follows. With lengthy interviews, there is greater opportunity for errors and inconsistencies to arise in witness accounts. This is due in part to increased number of specific questions, as well as witness fatigue. Such interviewer-induced inconsistency and error, in turn, makes the child more vulnerable in crossexamination, as there is more content that can be used to challenge the child's credibility (Burrows and Powell in press a; Davies et al. 1995).

A tired child may also become distracted or irritable in the interview. Prosecutors have expressed concern that when jurors are faced with a video of a distracted or irritable child, they may judge the child to be a less reliable witness (Burrows and Powell in press a). Jurors, too, may become fatigued when watching the interview in court. Jury fatigue may impede the jury's ability to come to a fair decision (Burrows and Powell in press a; CJJI 2012).

So why do interviewers seek such extensive details from a child which (from a prosecution perspective) is unnecessary? Prosecutors attribute this to three issues: poor interview planning and case preparation (e.g. interviewers should elicit background information from informants who know the child prior to conducting the interview); inadequate engagement and active listening skills on the part of the interviewer; and limited understanding (on the part of the interviewer) of precisely what information is required for investigative and prosecution purposes (Burrows and Powell in press a). Support for the first two explanations comes from research critiquing the nature of the prompts typically used in investigative interviews and interviewers' adherence (or lack thereof) to best-practice interview guides (e.g. Aldridge and Cameron 1999; Lamb et al. 2000; Powell et al. 2005). Support for the third explanation comes from individual interview and focus group research where various professionals have discussed the requirements of the interview process and have critiqued actual CSA interviews (Guadagno et al. 2006; Powell et al. 2011). Irrespective of the research methodology, jurisdiction or participant sample, the work has shown that views about the information required in CSA interviews differs markedly between prosecutors and police interviewers. Police officers tend to perceive that highly specific details (such as the location, date, and time of the offence) are essential for particularisation to occur, and that maximising the number of separate offences, and specific details about each offence increases the chance of successful prosecution. In contrast, the prosecutors perceive that the primary goal of the police officers should be to elicit a free-narrative account of one or more offences.

The strong implication arising from the above-mentioned research, and that highlighted in several recent guides for reform (e.g. Hanna et al. 2010; Powell et al. 2011; Powell 2012), is that prosecutors need to play a much more integral role in the development of interviewer training guides. To date, interview protocol development has largely been left in the hands of experts (e.g. clinicians and academics) in child development, language, and memory[1]. If prosecutors' concerns about unnecessary questioning, inappropriate content, and excessive length of interviews is to be addressed, guidance is also required from prosecutors to establish the elements of the offence and the particulars of offending that need to be covered, and the manner in which certain details are best elicited from a prosecution perspective (Burrows and Powell in press a, 2013). Preliminary guidance about the evidential details required, resulting from recent qualitative research involving participant prosecutors, is discussed in the next section of this chapter.

---

[1] There has been some incorporation of legal professionals' expertise into interviewing protocols in the UK. The 'Memorandum of Good Practice' (1992) was drafted for the government by a psychologist and a law professor, and the recent revision, 'Achieving Best Evidence in Criminal Proceedings: Guidance on Interviewing Victims and Witnesses and using Special Measures' (Ministry of Justice 2011), included members of the Crown Prosecution Service on the writing team.

Interviewers Need to Focus on Eliciting a Coherent Narrative Account of the Abuse

As indicated earlier, best-practice interview protocols emphasise the importance of using open-ended questions to elicit a free-flowing, coherent narrative account of what happened with as little specific questioning as possible. Open-ended questions refer to those questions that encourage elaborate detail but do not specify what information needs to be recalled and contain only information that has previously been reported by the child. These questions tend to elicit narrative detail by asking the child to report another act or activity (e.g. 'What happened then?' or 'What else happened'), or by using previously reported information to invite further elaborate detail about the event (e.g. 'Tell me more about the part when . . . '). Specific questions, in contrast, generally start with 'Who', 'When', Where', 'How', and are more focused in nature. They include cued-recall questions, which ask the child to report certain information that is required, as well as closed questions that tend to elicit a one word answer (Powell and Snow 2007). Prosecutors, like academics in child witness memory, tend to highlight the importance of open-ended questions. Whereas the memory literature has focused on the utility of open-ended questions to elicit more accurate and detailed witness statements (Dent and Stephenson 1979; Sternberg et al. 1996; Orbach and Lamb 2007), research examining the perspective of prosecutors has highlighted the value of open-ended questions in eliciting persuasive and clear evidence (Burrows and Powell in press a; Guadagno et al. 2006).

Consider for example, the study by the Criminal Justice Joint Inspection (2012) who conducted a broad evaluation into the treatment of young victims and witnesses in the criminal justice system. The evaluation employed a mixed-methods approach, part of which involved eliciting feedback from legal professionals about the usefulness of child witness interviews as evidence in chief. The evaluation revealed that prosecutors, as well as members of the judiciary, found that children's accounts of abuse were often unclear and difficult to follow due to an over-abundance of specific questions about aspects of the child's initial story. Similarly, prosecutors in the study by Burrows and Powell (in press a) reported insufficient use of open-ended questions, questions they claimed were associated with more truthful and authentic testimony compared to when the testimony is broken up constantly into questions and answers.

From the perspective of prosecutors, the greater persuasiveness of open-ended (narrative-based) interviews is fourfold. First, overzealous questioning is perceived to result in confusing and repetitive accounts that are difficult for a jury to follow. If jurors struggle to follow a child's account, it may be difficult for them to be satisfied beyond reasonable doubt as to the guilt of the accused and acquittals may be more likely (Burrows and Powell 2013).

> What traditionally happens in interviews is the child gives a relatively long blanket answer with as much detail as he or she can, and then that answer is forensically 'chopped up' into many pieces and regurgitated, by way of asking the child questions about each piece of the story . . . I think there has to be great care in doing that . . . If it's clear what the child's allegations are, for example, a child says 'he touched me on my willy under my clothes', then that's the allegation! Why go over it?' . . . I think the ideal is to allow the child to give

his or her story. I mean, that's what it's all about at the end of the day. We are only seeking to allow the child to give his or her story. (Crown Prosecutor; Burrows and Powell 2013).

Second, a rapid question-and-answer approach creates more details and inconsistencies which the child may be cross-examined about (Davis et al. 1999). Irrespective of presence of error in the child's account, leading questions are of considerable concern to legal professionals and constitute the majority of objections to interviews in court (CJJI 2012; Davis et al. 1999; Hanna et al. 2010; Richards et al. 2007). Third, responses to open-ended questions assist in establishing the reliability of the complainant's account because for verbal evidence to be persuasive, it needs to be elicited in the person's own words, and in narrative format using open-ended questions. Responses to open-ended questions can enable juries and other decision-makers to see events through the witness's eyes and to establish 'an essence of criminality' (i.e. the *nature* of the acts committed). The following quote provided by a prosecutor and reported by Guadagno et al. (2006, p. 257) illustrates this well.

> I think what we really want to do is facilitate the voice of the child in a way that enables them to describe as accurately as they can their experiences. This is the best way of understanding the nature of the *criminality* alleged . . . We can become too overly focussed and lost in the minutiae . . . You've got to look at the child's experience as a whole . . . If the headset of the interviewer is 'I need to know X, Y and Z' well then they may not realise they've already got what they need in the narrative.

What the prosecutors are referring to is the coherence of the information presented (which is facilitated by storytelling) as opposed to disconnected event details in response to focused questions (see Klettke et al. 2010 for discussion of the impact on the trial process).

Finally, prosecutors also believe that focusing on eliciting the child's complete story in narrative format helps jurors to understand the offending 'relationship', and how the relationship developed and progressed into offending (Darwinkel et al. in press). There is currently major incongruence between people's expectations of how victims *would* or *should* respond during and after an incident of sexual assault and what actually happens in reality (Bouffard 2000; Frazier and Haney 1996; McLean and Goodman-Delahunty 2008). For example, two common misconceptions among community members and professionals are that victims will report abuse immediately to authorities and they will put up a physical struggle (Suarez and Gadalla 2010; Ullman 2010). As prosecutors are aware, victims whose behaviour is not consistent with these misconceptions are perceived as less credible. Therefore, the court needs to hear details about the relationship within which offending occurred in order to understand counterintuitive victim behaviour.

Interviewers tend to assume that specific questions are needed to elicit important elements such as the nature of the sexual act or children's meaning of obscure terms for body parts (Guadagno et al. in press; Wright and Powell 2006). Prosecutors disagree. They perceive that it is the contextual details contained in the narrative that assist in establishing penetration and in particularising the event. For example, rather than providing clarity for genitalia terms, specific questioning can undermine the evidential quality of the interview by frustrating or embarrassing the child, and risking error and inconsistency. A detailed narrative description of the offending can provide clarity about the meaning of obscure terms by indicating what body parts were involved in offending.

> We often see interviewers hounding the child about "what's the health name for this?" and "what do you use that for?" It's really frustrating to watch.... If you get a good narrative, the child will usually give good detail of what they're talking about in terms of the body parts and the position that they were in when the offending happened. For example, the child will usually indicate whether he or she was facing the offender, or facing away from him. That context will clarify what they mean by the term. (Crown Prosecutor; Burrows and Powell under review b).

Further, broader case evidence could be used to inform the meaning of a genitalia term as opposed to questioning the child. For example, rather than seeking clarification from the child, it may be possible to clarify the child's terms through discussion with a caregiver (Burrows and Powell under review b).

There Needs to be Scope to Allow Supplementary Live Questioning of the Witness in Court

A final theme that has emerged from the literature on prosecutors' perceptions of interviews is that, although pre-recorded interviews are generally favoured as evidence in chief in the trial, supplementary questioning of the child witness should be allowed in court. Four limitations associated with using recorded evidence have been noted. First, prosecutors have reported problems associated with poor technical quality of recordings (Powell and Wright 2009). Indeed, Cashmore and Trimboli (2005) reported that the technical quality of recorded interviews was often so poor that the interview could not be used as evidence. In particular, prosecutors were concerned that the size of the child's face was too small to enable the jury to observe the child's demeanour whilst accounting abuse, especially given that there is typically some distance between the jury and the TV screen. Prosecutors have suggested that the visual quality of interviews could be improved by ensuring the camera captures a clear, close image of the child's face. That is, prosecutors propose that the image on the screen should be a close-up of the child's upper torso, where facial expressions and hand gestures are clearly visible (Burrows and Powell in press b).

Similarly, prosecutors have expressed concern that jurors are often unable to adequately evaluate the evidence because of poor audio quality of the recordings. Specifically, the child's voice is often muffled, or cannot be made out because the volume of audio recorded on the tape is so low (e.g. Richards et al. 2007; WAPA 2005). Concerns with the technical quality of recorded interviews have been voiced consistently across jurisdictions, including Australia (e.g. Cashmore and Trimboli 2005), Canada (e.g. Bala et al. 2001), the UK, (e.g. Burton et al. 2006; CJJI 2012; Stern 2010), and the USA (e.g. WAPA 2005), and have persisted despite significant advancements in audio visual technology over the last decade. Prosecutors have suggested that audio quality could be improved by using clip-on (lapel) microphones to capture audio, particularly for younger children who move around a lot or who mumble (McConachy 2002).

A second limitation prosecutors have perceived with using pre-recorded evidence is that in some situations, recorded interviews may not be as compelling to a jury as a witness giving evidence live in court. McConachy (2002) found that prosecutors in New South Wales, Australia, rarely used interviews as evidence in chief because they believed that it was beneficial to the State's case for the jury to see the child give evidence in person. McConachy conducted an evaluation of the electronic recording of children's evidence to explore whether interviews were being used in court and why. Specifically, the evaluation sought to determine whether interviews increased the quality and completeness of children's evidence, and whether using interviews as evidence made appearing in court less stressful for children. Various methods were adopted to evaluate recorded interviews, including case tracking, court observation, and interviews with various stakeholders such as children and their parents, counsellors, and police. Legal representatives ($N = 74$) provided feedback about the use of recorded interviews as evidence in chief. A questionnaire elicited their perceptions of the benefits and limitations of recorded interviews, and their confidence about, and support for, the use of interviews as evidence in chief.

Forty percent of lawyers surveyed reported that playing a video recorded interview as evidence could be detrimental because, compared to live evidence, the video format distanced the child from the jury. In particular, the lawyers stated that recorded interviews could be disadvantageous because the court did not hear the child's story first hand, making it difficult for jurors to empathise with the child and assess the child's credibility. Prosecutors across the globe have expressed similar concerns about the persuasiveness of recorded evidence and some have stated that they believe that using interviews as evidence increases the likelihood that jurors will acquit the accused because interviews have less impact than a live witness in the courtroom (e.g. Davis et al. 1995; CJJI 2012). The detrimental effect to the State of the distance created between the jury and the child was believed to be exacerbated by the constant presence of the accused in the courtroom and the greater potential for the jury (as a result) to build a 'relationship' with the accused:

> The trouble with those interviews is that you've got the distance between the jury and the complainant because the child is just a face on a TV screen. As a juror, watching a screen is not as personal as someone sitting right next to you on a witness box. The accused sits in the court room the whole time. The accused and the jury get to know each other quite well because they're in court together for days. Jurors might start to feel like they know him and empathise with him. On the other hand, jurors only see the child on a TV screen for an hour or so. By the time they come to deliberate, they're not thinking about the child anymore (Crown Prosecutor; Burrows and Powell in press b).

The perception that recorded evidence is less persuasive to juries than a live witness has persisted despite evidence to suggest that juror decision-making is unaffected by the mode of evidence presentation (e.g. Davies 1999; Taylor and Joudo 2005). Whilst overall prosecutors are not denying that interviews are useful, there are concerns that need to be addressed about the persuasiveness of interviews in some situations. It may be that greater experience using recorded interviews as evidence may allay concerns about persuasiveness (McConachy 2002).

A third concern that prosecutors have with using recorded interviews rather than leading a live witness is that the child's demeanour in the interview may not be ideal for presentation in court. Prosecutors believe that the child's demeanour is important to the quality of evidence because it informs the jury's assessment of the child's credibility, and if the child exhibits a negative demeanour or behaviours whilst giving evidence, this may damage the jury's perception of the child's credibility and may in turn affect the jury's decision regarding the charges (Burrows and Powell in press a). Prosecutors in the study by Burrows and Powell (in press a) believed that the interview environment and the manner of interviewing often promoted undesirable child behaviour that may not have been exhibited if the child had given his/her evidence in chief in court. Negative behaviours, including opposition, frustration, confusion, or withdrawal by the child were believed to often result from inappropriate interviewing practices, such as asking the child incessant or confusing questions, or asking persistent or highly specific questions about sensitive issues. Prosecutors suggested that, to avoid inciting negative behaviour, interviewers should reflect on how their interviewing practice and manner may affect the child, and interact with the child in a way that promotes positive behaviour. Interviewing practices that may facilitate positive behaviour include minimising questioning and allowing the child breaks during the interview (Burrows and Powell in press a).

A fourth limitation that prosecutors have perceived with using pre-recorded interviews as evidence in chief is that children may be disadvantaged when they are called for live crossexamination (Bala et al. 2001; Burton et al. 2006; McConachy 2002). Burton and colleagues (2006) conducted a broad evaluation to determine the effectiveness of special measures available for vulnerable witness, including children, in England and Wales. Mixed methods were employed including agency surveys, practitioner interviews, case file tracking, and court observations. Prosecutor feedback about the quality of interviews was gathered through surveys ($N = 42$) and interviews ($N = 4$). Whilst prosecutors acknowledged the benefits of using recorded interviews rather than leading a live witness in evidence in chief, they voiced various concerns about interviews. Prosecutors reported that children whose evidence in chief is given via a recorded interview had little or no opportunity to become accustomed to the court's 'question-and-answer' process prior to crossexamination. Children may therefore be underprepared for crossexamination and perform poorly.

Children whose evidence in chief was given via recorded interview were also considered to be disadvantaged in crossexamination because of the typically long delay between the date of their interview and the date of trial. The lapse of time increases the likelihood of memory decay, and therefore increases the chance that the child may say something in crossexamination which is inconsistent with their initial statement, providing opportunities for defence to undermine the child's credibility. Problems caused by memory decay may be overcome by having the child watch their recorded interview prior to trial to refresh their memory. However, prosecutors have reported that children often do not pay adequate attention when watching the video and thus remain unprepared to answer questions in crossexamination (Bala et al. 2001). Once again, prosecutors' concerns about the State being disadvantaged by children being underprepared for crossexamination have persisted despite evidence that the mode of evidence presentation has little or no impact on conviction rates (e.g. Davies 1999; Taylor and Joudo 2005).

The perceived limitations, described above, of using recorded evidence rather than a live witness highlight the benefits of legislation that provides scope for supplementary questioning in court[2]. Where there is flexibility for the trial prosecutor to lead additional evidence in chief from the child, the prosecution has the opportunity to 'recover' from any poor persuasiveness of the interview, demeanour of the witness, or technical quality. Supplementary questioning could also provide the child with an opportunity to be better prepared for crossexamination.

Conclusion

Prosecutors prefer the system of recorded evidence compared to the taking of written statements of CSA; however, they perceive that considerable improvement is needed in order to improve the low rates of case prosecution and conviction. In this chapter, we have discussed the most prominent concerns of prosecutors, which reflect the need for interviewers to focus on the child's story rather than extensive questioning, cast the net narrower in terms of eliciting only the important evidential detail required for successful prosecution, and provide greater consideration to the presentation of the witness in the eyes of the jury. The consistency of the prosecutors' concerns over time and across jurisdictions reiterates the strong need for an overhaul of current training programmes (to ensure adherence to best practice) and better engagement with prosecutors in the protocol development process.

Given recent research trends (i.e. the majority of prosecutor studies have occurred in the past few years), we expect more research to focus upon the evidential usefulness of CSA interviews in the coming years. In addition to existing measures of interviewer performance (which record the type, number, and quality of various questions), future research should focus on addressing the impact of new procedures on actual trial outcomes as well as the establishment of reliable and valid measures of interview evidential quality. Understanding and accommodating the needs and perceptions of prosecutors will likely go a long way towards improving the persuasiveness and usefulness of CSA interviews on a global scale.

---

[2] Jurisdictions differ in the degree to which their legislation allows for supplementary questioning. For example, prosecutors in Australian jurisdictions have considerable flexibility in leading additional evidence from the child (e.g. a child may give evidence 'wholly or partly' via recorded interview, s 306S, *Criminal Procedure Act* 1986 [NSW]). Provisions in England and Wales are less flexible, and supplementary questioning can only be led on a matter which, in the opinion of the court, has not been dealt with adequately in the interview, or otherwise only with the permission of the court (s 27, *Youth Justice and Criminal Evidence Act* 1999).

References

Aldridge, J., & Cameron, S. (1999). Interviewing child witnesses: Questioning techniques and the role of training. *Applied Developmental Science, 3,* 136–147.

Bala, N., Lindsay, R. C. L., & McNamara, E. (2001). Testimonial aids for children: The Canadian experience with closed circuit television, screens and videotapes. *Criminal Law Quarterly, 44,* 461–486.

Bouffard, J. A. (2000). Predicting type of sexual assault case closure from victim, suspect, and case characteristics. *Journal of Criminal Justice, 28,* 527–542. doi:10.1016/S0047-2352(00)00068-4.

Burrows, K., & Powell, M. (2013). A prosecutor's guide to improving child witness interviews about alleged sexual abuse: A view from the Australian context. *Investigative Interviewing: Research and Practice, 5,* 12–22.

Burrows, K., & Powell, M. (in press a). Prosecutors' recommendations for improving child witness statements about sexual abuse. *Policing and Society.*

Burrows, K., & Powell, M. (in press b). Prosecutors' perspectives on using recorded child witness interviews about abuse as evidence in chief. *Australian and New Zealand Journal of Criminology.*

Burrows, K., & Powell, M. (under review a). Prosecutors' perspectives on clarifying sexual acts in child abuse interviews.

Burrows, K., & Powell, M. (under review b). Prosecutors' perspectives on clarifying terms for genitalia in child sexual abuse interviews.

Burton, M., Evans, R., & Sanders, A. (2006). Are special measures for vulnerable and intimidated witnesses working? Evidence from the criminal justice agencies. Home Office Online Report. http://collection.europarchive.org/tna/20080205132101/homeoffice.gov.uk/rds/pdfs06/rdsolr 0106.pdf. Accessed 10 Nov 2012.

Cashmore, J., & Trimboli, L. (2005). An evaluation of the NSW child sexual assault specialist jurisdiction pilot. Sydney: NSW Bureau of Crime Statistics and Research. http://www.lawlink.nsw.gov.au/lawlink/bocsar/ll_bocsar.nsf/vwFiles/r57.pdf/$file/r57.pdf. Accessed 10 Nov 2012.

Corns, C. (2001). Videotaped evidence of child complainants in criminal proceedings: A comparison of alternative models. *Criminal Law Journal, 25,* 75–89.

Criminal Justice Joint Inspection. (2012). Joint Inspection report on the experience of young victims and witnesses in the criminal justice system. http://www.hmcpsi.gov.uk/documents/reports/CJJI_THM/VWEX/CJJI_YVW_Jan12_rpt.pdf. Accessed 11 Nov 2012.

Criminal Procedure Act. (1986) (NSW) s. 306S (Austl.).

Cross, T. P., Whitcomb, D., & De Vos, E. (1995). Criminal justice outcomes of prosecution of child sexual abuse: A case flow analysis. *Child Abuse and Neglect, 19,* 1431–1442. doi:10.1016/0145-2134(95)00106-2.

Darwinkel, E., Powell, M., & Tidmarsh, P. (in press). Prosecutors' perceptions of the utility of 'relationship' evidence in sexual abuse trials. *Australian & New Zealand Journal of Criminology.*

Davies, G. (1999). The impact of television on the presentation and reception of children's testimony. *International Journal of Law and Psychiatry, 22,* 241–256.

Davies, G., Wilson, C., Mitchell, R., & Milsom, J. (1995). *Videotaping children's evidence: An evaluation.* London: Home Office.

Davis, G., Hoyano, L., Keenan, C., Maitland, L., & Morgan, R. (1999). *An assessment of the admissibility and sufficiency of evidence in child abuse prosecutions.* Bristol: Home Office.

Dent, H. R., & Stephenson, G. M. (1979). An experimental study of the effectiveness of different techniques of questioning child witnesses. *British Journal of Social and Clinical Psychology, 18,* 41–51.

Frazier, P., & Haney, B. (1996). Sexual assault cases in the legal system: Police, prosecutor, and victim perspectives. *Law & Human Behavior, 20,* 607–628.

Guadagno, B. L., & Hughes-Scholes, P. M. (in press). What themes trigger investigative interviewers to ask specific questions when interviewing children? *International Journal of Police Science and Management.*

Guadagno, B. L., Powell, M. B., & Wright, R. (2006). Police officers' and legal professionals' perceptions regarding how children are, and should be, questioned about repeated abuse. *Psychiatry, Psychology and Law, 13*, 251–260.

Hanna, H., Davies, E., Henderson, E., Crothers, C., & Rotherham, C. (2010). Child witnesses in the New Zealand criminal courts: A review of practice and implications for policy [online]. The Law Foundation: New Zealand. http://www.ipp.aut.ac.nz/__data/assets/pdf_file/0020/119702/Child-Witnesses-in-the-NZ-Criminal-Courts-full-report.pdf. Accessed 2 Oct 2012.

Home Office and Department of Health. (1992). The memorandum of good practice on video recorded interviews with child witnesses for criminal proceedings. London, HMSO.

Klettke, B., Graesser, A. C., & Powell, M. B. (2010). Expert testimony in child sexual abuse cases: The effects of evidence, coherence and credentials on juror decision making. *Applied Cognitive Psychology, 24*, 481–494. doi:10.1002/acp.1565.

Lamb, M. E., Sternberg, K. J., & Esplin, P. W. (2000). Effects of age and delay on the amount of information provided by alleged sex abuse victims in investigative interviews. *Child Development, 71*, 1586–1596.

McConachy, D. (2002). *Evaluation of the Electronic Recording of Children's Evidence: Final Report*. http://www.community.nsw.gov.au/docswr/_assets/main/documents/policy_evaluate_evid.pdf. Accessed 10 Nov 2012.

Mckenzie, D. (1993). Interviewing Children and Recording Evidence (ICARE) Pilot Program: Evaluation report to the ICARE Working Party. Policy & Programs Branch, NSW Police Service.

McLean, R., & Goodman-Delahunty, J. (2008). The influence of relationship and physical evidence on police decision-making in sexual assault cases. *Australian Journal of Forensic Sciences, 40*, 109–121.

Ministry of Justice. (2011). *Achieving Best Evidence in Criminal Proceedings: Guidance on Interviewing Victims and Witnesses, and Guidance on Using Special Measures*. London: Criminal Justice System.

Office of Director of Public Prosecutions (ACT) and Australian Federal Police. (2005). *Responding to sexual assault: The challenge of change*. Canberra: Authors.

Orbach, Y., & Lamb, M. E. (2007). Young children's references to temporal attributes of allegedly experienced events in the course of forensic interviews. *Child Development, 78*, 1100–1120. doi:10.1111/j.1467-8624.2007.01055.x.

Powell, M. (2008). Guide to designing effective training programs in the area of investigative interviewing of children. *Current Issues in Criminal Justice, 20*, 189–208.

Powell, M. (2012, May). Improving the quality of child investigative interviews about sexual abuse. Paper presented at the 'Truth, testimony, relevance: Improving the quality of evidence in sexual offence cases' (National symposium supported by Australian Institute of Criminology, Australian Institute of Family Studies and Victoria Police), Melbourne.

Powell, M., & Snow, P. C. (2007). Guide to questioning children during the free-narrative phase of an investigative interview. *Australian Psychologist, 42*, 57–65.

Powell, M., & Wright, R. (2009). Professionals' perceptions of electronically recorded interviews with vulnerable witnesses. *Current Issues in Criminal Justice, 21*, 205–218.

Powell, M., Fisher, R. P., & Wright, R. (2005). Investigative interviewing. In N. Brewer & K. Williams (Eds.), *Psychology and law: An empirical perspective* (pp. 11–42). New York: Guilford.

Powell, M., Garry, M., & Brewer, N. D. (2009). Eyewitness testimony. In I. Freckelton & H. Selby (Eds.), *Expert Evidence* (pp. 1–42). Sydney: Thompson Reuters.

Powell, M., Wright, R., & Hughes-Scholes, C. H. (2011). Contrasting the perceptions of child testimony experts, prosecutors and police officers regarding individual child abuse interviews. *Psychiatry, Psychology and Law, 18*, 1–11.

Price-Robertson, R., Bromfield, L., & Vassallo, S., (2010). Resource sheet: The prevalence of child abuse and neglect [online]. National Child Protection Clearinghouse, Australian Institute of Family Studies. www.aifs.gov.au/nch/pubs/sheets/rs21/rs21.html. Accessed 14 Oct 2011.

Richards, P., Morris, S., Richards, E., & Siddall, K. (2007). On the record: Evaluating the visual recording of joint investigative interviews with children [online]. Scottish Executive Social Research, Edinburgh. http://www.scotland.gov.uk/Resource/Doc/162579/0044250.pdf. Accessed 12 Nov 2012.

Stern, V. (2010). The Stern Review [online]. http://webarchive.nationalarchives.gov.uk/20110608160754, http:/www.equalities.gov.uk/PDF/Stern_Review_acc_FINAL.pdf. Accessed 10 Dec 2012.

Sternberg, K. J., Lamb, M. E., Hershkowitz, I., Esplin, P., Redlich, A., & Sunshine, N. (1996). The relation between investigative utterance types and the informativeness of child witnesses. *Journal of Applied Developmental Psychology, 17*, 439–451.

Suarez, E., & Gadalla, T. M. (2010). Stop blaming the victim: A meta-analysis on rape myths. *Journal of Interpersonal Violence, 25*, 2010–2035. doi:10.1177/0886260509354503.

Success Works (2011). *Sexual assault reform strategy: Final evaluation report.* Melbourne: Department of Justice (VIC).

S v. R. (1989). 266 CLR 168.

Taylor, N., & Joudo, J. (2005). *The impact of pre-recorded video and closed circuit television testimony by adult sexual assault complainants on jury decision-making: An experimental study.* Canberra: Australian Institute of Criminology. http://www.aic.gov.au/publications/current%20series/rpp/61-80/rpp68.html. Accessed 10 Nov 2012.

Ullman, S. E. (2010). *Talking about sexual assault: Society's response to survivors.* Washington, DC: American Psychological Association.

Washington Association of Prosecuting Attorneys. (2005). DVD recording the forensic child abuse victim interview: Washington state's pilot project 2003–2005 [online]. http://www.waprosecutors.org/docs/05finalDVD.pdf. Accessed 18 Jan 2013.

World Health Organisation. (1999). WHO recognises child abuse as a major public health problem [online]. www.who.int/inf-pr-1999/en/pr99-20.html. Accessed 10 Dec 2011.

Wright, R., & Powell, M. B. (2006). Investigative interviewers' perceptions of their difficulty in adhering to open-ended questions with child witnesses. *International Journal of Police Science and Management, 8*, 316–325.

Youth Justice and Criminal Evidence Act. (1999). (UK) s. 27.

Index

CPSIA information can be obtained at www.ICGtesting.com
Printed in the USA
LVOW10*2257180314

377997LV00008B/39/P